METAMODERNISM AND CONTEMPORARY BRITISH POETRY

This book discusses contemporary British poetry in the context of metamodernism. It argues that the concept of enigmatical poetics helps to recalibrate the opposition between mainstream and innovative poetry, and investigates whether a new generation of British poets can be accurately defined as metamodernist. Antony Rowland analyses the ways in which contemporary British poets such as Geoffrey Hill, J. H. Prynne, Geraldine Monk and Sandeep Parmar have responded to the work of modernist poets as diverse as Ezra Pound, James Joyce, T. S. Eliot, H. D. and Antonin Artaud since the 1950s. He shows how enigmatical poetry offers an alternative vision to that of the contemporary British novel.

PROFESSOR ANTONY ROWLAND is Chair in Modern and Contemporary Poetry at Manchester Metropolitan University. He is the author of seven books, including *Poetry as Testimony* (2014) and *Holocaust Poetry* (2005). He received an Eric Gregory award in 2000 from the Society of Authors, and the Manchester Poetry Prize in 2012. He is a member of the Higher Education Committee for the English Association.

CAMBRIDGE STUDIES IN TWENTY-FIRST-CENTURY
LITERATURE AND CULTURE
Editor

Peter Boxall, *University of Sussex*

As the cultural environment of the twenty-first century comes into clearer focus, Cambridge Studies in Twenty-First-Century Literature and Culture presents a series of monographs that undertakes the most penetrating and rigorous analysis of contemporary culture and thought.

The series is driven by the perception that critical thinking today is in a state of transition. The global forces that produce cultural forms are entering into powerful new alignments, which demand new analytical vocabularies in the wake of later twentieth-century theory. The series will demonstrate that theory is not simply a failed revolutionary gesture that we need to move beyond, but rather brings us to the threshold of a new episteme, which will require new theoretical energy to navigate.

In this spirit, the series will host work that explores the most important emerging critical contours of the twenty-first century, marrying inventive and imaginative criticism with theoretical and philosophical rigor. The aim of the series will be to produce an enduring account of the twenty-first-century intellectual landscape that will not only stand as a record of the critical nature of our time, but also forge new critical languages and vocabularies with which to navigate an unfolding age. In offering a historically rich and philosophically nuanced account of contemporary literature and culture, the series will stand as an enduring body of work that helps us to understand the cultural moment in which we live.

In This Series

Joel Evans
Conceptualising the Global in the Wake of the Postmodern: Literature, Culture, Theory

Adeline Johns-Putra
Climate Change and the Contemporary Novel

Caroline Edwards
Utopia and the Contemporary British Novel

Paul Crosthwaite
The Market Logics of Contemporary Fiction

Jennifer Cooke
Contemporary Feminist Life-Writing

Garrett Stewart
Book, Text, Medium: Cross-Sectional Reading for a Digital Age

Antony Rowland
Metamodernism and Contemporary British Poetry

Sherryl Vint
Biopolitical Futures in Twenty-First-Century Speculative Fiction

Joe Cleary
The Irish Expatriate Novel in Late Capitalist Globalization

Ankhi Mukherjee
Unseen City: The Psychic Lives of the Urban Poor

METAMODERNISM AND CONTEMPORARY BRITISH POETRY

ANTONY ROWLAND

Manchester Metropolitan University

CAMBRIDGE
UNIVERSITY PRESS

CAMBRIDGE
UNIVERSITY PRESS

Shaftesbury Road, Cambridge CB2 8EA, United Kingdom

One Liberty Plaza, 20th Floor, New York, NY 10006, USA

477 Williamstown Road, Port Melbourne, VIC 3207, Australia

314–321, 3rd Floor, Plot 3, Splendor Forum, Jasola District Centre, New Delhi – 110025, India

103 Penang Road, #05–06/07, Visioncrest Commercial, Singapore 238467

Cambridge University Press is part of Cambridge University Press & Assessment, a department of the University of Cambridge.

We share the University's mission to contribute to society through the pursuit of education, learning and research at the highest international levels of excellence.

www.cambridge.org
Information on this title: www.cambridge.org/9781108815338

DOI: 10.1017/9781108895286

First published 2022
First paperback edition 2023

A catalogue record for this publication is available from the British Library

ISBN   978-1-108-84197-9   Hardback
ISBN   978-1-108-81533-8   Paperback

In memory of Richard Jones (1972–2018)

Contents

Acknowledgements

When I first discussed the outline of this book with Dr Richard Jones in summer 2014, we were enjoying a bumper season of Red Admirals and outsized artichokes. Richard worked in the Geography department at the University of Exeter, and we had plans to create an app for Dartmoor that would explain physical aspects of the landscape, matched with excerpts of literature. I would like to think that we had an indefinite but important sense of the poetics of each other's subject. Mud was not just mud for Richard, but the beginnings of narratives of memory, adventure and trauma, from stories of caked showers when attempting to corral his samples to the uncovering of skulls when coring in China. My memories of learning physical geography at school included the savouring of new language ('cwm', 'arête', 'col') and the imaginative acts of trying to square the diagrams of glaciers with recollections of family hikes on Coniston Old Man and Helvellyn. Both of us were responding to the poetics of place in different but connected ways: bloom lines on Ordnance maps react to the landscape of Dartmoor in an imaginative way just as literature might respond expansively to its tors. I can see Richard smiling: 'Yes, but when you get lost in the fog near Ponsworthy, try getting home with a poem'.

*

Our children grew, and then there was COVID. I would like to thank all those colleagues and friends who have been so generous with their time in reading draft chapters during this difficult period, including James Byrne, Nikolai Duffy, Ben Harker, Marius Hentea, Peter Howarth, Tim Kendall, Angelica Michelis, David Miller and Sandeep Parmar. Especial thanks must go, as ever, to Emma Liggins, who had a major influence on the final shape of the book. A clumpy or overly complicated sentence is (Quorn) mincemeat in her eyes. An Arts and Humanities Research Council award in 2017 allowed me to explore the ideas surrounding metamodernism with a wonderfully diffuse and enthusiastic set of academics, students, writers and non-academics, including Jeroen Boon,

Katherine Burn, Linda Ceriello, Andrew Corsa, Greg Dember, Tom Drayton, Alison Gibbons, Robert Gould, Mika Hallila, Chantal Hassard, David James, Dennis Kersten, Janien Linde, Sarah Maclachlan, Divya Nadkarni, Alistair Noon, Kasimir Sandbacka, Will Self, Samuel Stuart-Booth, Robin van den Akker, Niels van Poecke, Tim Vermeulen, Usha Wilbers and Graham Young. I shall always be grateful for their papers, readings and conversations in European countries and towns that, during the COVID epidemic, have been very difficult to visit. As noted by some PhD students and early-career researchers, the conferences and symposia were remarkable for their supportive environments and a lack of academic 'edge'. Staff at Arendsnest in Amsterdam provided us with a perfect final venue: Bockbier on tap after the curtain closes; I am not sure we shall ever organise an event in a more salubrious abode. I would also like to thank the following colleagues, whose insights have improved this book, whether on the scale of Zoom support, discussions about theoretical contexts, copyright requests or a tweaked sentence: Robert Eaglestone, Martin Eve, Suzanne Fairless, Tony Frazer, Daniel Gavin, John Goodby, Angela Jarman, Germaine Loader, Gail Marshall, Edgar Mendez, Berthold Schoene, Portia Taylor, Scott Thurston, Dale Townshend, Jeffrey Wainwright, Tony Ward and Dinah Wood.

I am grateful to a number of staff at the Geoffrey Hill and Tony Harrison archives held in the Brotherton Library at the University of Leeds. Even with an electrical fault that took out the entire campus at one point, they still managed to accommodate me. Colin Taylor kindly allowed me to use a reproduction of his painting 'Mother Courage no. 3' for the cover of this book. The following publishers have granted copyright permission to reproduce extracts for Chapter 5, and lines of poetry from the authors discussed in this book: Arc, Bloodaxe Books, Faber and Faber, Graywolf Press, Knives Forks and Spoons, Oxford University Press, Salt and Shearsman Press. Some material for Chapter 5 is reproduced by permission from my chapter 'Modernism and the "Double Consciousness" of Myth in Tony Harrison's Poems and *Metamorpheus*', in *New Light on Tony Harrison*, ed. Edith Hall (London: Oxford University Press) © The British Academy 2019. The Don Paterson excerpt from 'The Sea at Brighton' from *Landing Light* is reprinted with the permission of The Permissions Company LLC on behalf of Graywolf Press, www.graywolfpress.org © Don Paterson 2005. The extracts from Geoffrey's poems are used by permission of the literary estate of Sir Geoffrey Hill. Jeremy Hill and Kenneth Haynes kindly allowed me to quote from his poems and the extensive Geoffrey Hill archives in the

Brotherton Library. Tony Harrison himself agreed that I could use material from his own archives in the Brotherton. In his characteristically direct way, Tony commented that 'I wouldn't have put the stuff in there if I didn't want people to use it'. If I have missed any copyright permissions, we would be happy to correct this in future editions of this book.

I would like to thank the series editor, Peter Boxall, for offering unwavering support and for responding patiently to my requests about submission details. I am indebted to Ray Ryan from Cambridge University Press for his initial faith in this project: we first exchanged emails about the book during that hot summer and autumn of 2014. My amazing family – Emma, Polly and Clara – has kept me going during some difficult years of changing jobs, COVID and family illness. They are indeed, as Polly once said, 'electric to glitter'. They even responded kindly to a flat in Newark when I worked in Lincoln. Last but not least, the late-night cheese boards in Tavistock with Richard and Sharon Gedye have kept me fuelled with ideas and striking dreams for many moons.

*

In 2016, Richard was diagnosed with terminal cancer. Despite increasing debility, he still walked with us to those tors and around the Devon and Cornwall coast: Cotehele, Bere Alston, Fowey. Just before he lost his eyesight, we wandered into an old railway cutting above Tavistock, exploring the tea-coloured water and sharp edges of dynamited stone. Chatting about mutual friends, he laughed in his characteristic way: 'There's been too many funerals this year!' Typical of Richard's humour, it is still the most astonishing thing I have ever heard anybody say. In April 2019, we visited his memorial stone at Urswick tarn in Cumbria. The village was peaceful and unseasonably warm, and our families milled around the stone's position at a jetty's edge. A plaque explains that 'Dr Jones was a physical geographer whose research at this tarn and elsewhere around the world added greatly to knowledge of the Holocene'. Given that this book completes the project that I had first discussed with Richard six years earlier, it would be suitable to end these acknowledgements with a poem:

Marl

Herons stumble the fetch: Urswick
holds its flash, setting the tarn
with our wake, appropriate
as our grief through laughter, where grass
spikes the meniscus and sun-motes blur
our digital snap. Hug

the embarrassment of this plaque:
mourning as clear as fish that roll
air and under the boardwalk. We
taste the edge of marram, faces
in all-shore directions; eyes
string the reed buntings jittering
their pad. Marl adds
to our knowledge of the Holocene:
your core sampler hods to pollen
where forests mould to a crick
and insects peat our memory. Grain
fires the cap to a dating spree.
Photos out-tilt the jetty's pitch, as
we walk out in our guilty retrieval.

Introduction

[A] great work of art [. . .] always has a secret that one can never quite grasp and which always reappears[1]

When Geoffrey Hill began his fourth lecture as Oxford Professor of Poetry in 2011, the audience members clearly expected a mischievous performance. They were not disappointed: nervous laughter greeted the semi-comic irascibility of his declaration that, as someone 'seven months short of eighty', he had a 'rule' to exasperate.[2] In his first lecture a year earlier, Hill had promised a future evaluation of contemporary British poetry, and in the subsequent oration he did not hold back, appraising creative writing as a neoliberal efflorescence of a doomed literary culture, with its 'plethora of literary prizes' and false evaluation of its own salubriousness. Anti-élitist 'accessibility' was the buzz word *du jour*, Hill argued in 2010, but 'accessible' should be reserved as an adjective for supermarkets or public lavatories, he added dryly, not as a value judgement in a discussion of poetry and poetics.[3] In contrast, Hill declared in 2011 that he was 'marooned' in the 1950s with the work of Ezra Pound and T. S. Eliot. Subsequent comments in the fourth lecture incurred media coverage: he accused Carol Ann Duffy of publishing poetry of the same quality as a Mills and Boon novel or the work of a creative writing student. Lemn Sissay offered a riposte in *The Guardian*, decrying the 'spat' between two esteemed contemporary poets as akin to opposite corners of a boxing ring.[4] Duffy's response was a dignified silence, and the media interest soon dissipated. Yet Hill's lecture posed a series of questions that have concerned me throughout the writing of this book. What would it mean if contemporary British poetry had a 'rule' to exasperate?[5] How might the critic account for this creative recalcitrance? If readers can never 'quite grasp' such challenging writing, how might critics account conceptually for that which we cannot understand?[6] It was also telling that Hill was silent in this lecture about 'exasperating' experimental writing. Would it be possible to conceptualise

1

the challenge of Hill's poems *and* 'innovative' writers in a way that would allow analysis of both kinds of poetry at the same time, despite their obvious formal differences? After all, Hill is clearly not the only twenty-first-century poet 'marooned' with the legacies of specific modernist writers.[7] Should Hill and other authors 'stuck' with these poets be regarded as late modernists, out of step with the current trend, as Hill regarded it in 2011, for accessibility conceived as 'democratic' writing? Or could their poetry be analysed in the context of metamodernism, a term that was beginning to gain critical traction in the same year that Hill delivered his fourth lecture as Oxford Professor of Poetry?

Poetry and Metamodernism

Four years earlier, Andre Furlani argued that metamodernism encompassed a 'departure as well as a perpetuation' from modernist concerns in relation to the work of the American writer Guy Davenport.[8] As well as deriving its impetus from modernist literature, metamodernism 'surpasses homage' for Furlani, and moves towards a 'reengagement with modernist methods to address subject matter beyond the range or interest of the modernists themselves' (p. 150). In this sense, the poetry I discuss in this book engages self-consciously with the formal innovations of early twentieth-century writing, valuing but also resisting tradition in order to produce transformations of the work of T. S. Eliot, H. D., Virginia Woolf, Antonin Artaud, Ezra Pound and Bertolt Brecht. Published in 2010, Tim Vermeulen and Robin van den Akker's 'Notes on Metamodernism' was the first manifesto to extend Furlani's concept to a new generation of artists and writers returning to issues of representation, reconstruction and myth, as theories of postmodernism appeared less able to engage with postmillennial developments in history and culture.[9] In the same year as Hill's fourth lecture, Luke Turner published a 'Metamodernist Manifesto', an impassioned plea to reembrace concepts such as truth, progress and grand narratives, as opposed to the 'cynical insincerity' of postmodernism.[10] In contrast, David James and Urmila Seshagiri emphasised the formal lessons of early twentieth-century literature in their 2014 article on metamodernism. These critics focussed on revolutionary narratives in contemporary fiction, and the latter's repudiation of rather than 'oscillation' with postmodernism.[11] They argued that their work was by no means 'the first investigation into the increasing breadth attributed to modernism', but what distinguished their approach was 'its defence of returning to the logic of periodisation' (p. 88). According to James and Seshagiri, contemporary novelists such as Will Self and Zadie Smith engage with a 'mythos' of early twentieth-century literature that places 'a conception of modernism as revolution at the heart of their fictions' (p. 87). This version of metamodernism 'regards modernism as an era, an aesthetic, and an archive that originated in the late nineteenth and early twentieth centuries' (p. 88), as opposed to 'new' modernism's geographical and transhistorical expansions across the globe, which results in modernism losing 'a degree of traction', and to critics dehistoricising it 'as a movement' (p. 90).[12]

There are various theoretical overlaps between these publications on metamodernism, but there have been two distinct approaches to the concept so far. Van den Akker, Vermeulen and Turner's critiques focus on the historicity of the present in relation to the arts more widely, whereas James and Seshagiri concentrate on the formal legacies of modernist writers in contemporary fiction. James, Seshagiri, Alison Gibbons, Nick Bentley, Dennis Kersten and Usha Wilbers have all engaged in wide-ranging critical debates about metamodernism in relation to the novel, yet critics of contemporary British poetry have not yet discussed the term extensively.[13] This abstention is curious, since, in contrast to the myriad ways in which twenty-first-century poetry continues to work through the lessons of modernist poetics, the term arguably proves less efficacious in relation to contemporary British fiction due to 'resurgent modes of realism' in the novel.[14] In one way, this refraining may simply be due to critical paucity: studies of fiction far outweigh equivalent accounts of poetry. Yet this is not, I propose, merely an argument about the extent of critical activity. The absence of an extended appraisal of contemporary poetry in the context of metamodernism needs to be understood in terms of the bifurcation I explore throughout this book between mainstream and 'innovative' poetry. Until recently, many 'innovative' poets from the London School embraced critical accounts that advocated an interweaving of poststructuralist and postmodernist theory with their poetics, particularly since the erudition of theory allowed for yet another divergence from mainstream poetry, that was content – in Peter Barry's characterisation of such writing – to scribble a few sonnets about Wimbledon common.[15] James, Seshagiri, van den Akker, Gibbons and Vermeulen would all agree, along with many poets from the London School, that postmodernism has lost its critical efficacy, and has been denuded of its radical connotations.[16] The absence of a subsequent debate about metamodernism may partly be because it might spotlight previous disparities between 'innovative' poetry and conceptions of postmodernism. However, the more likely cause is that metamodernism proposes a challenge to the very term 'innovative' itself with the former's emphasis on the dialectics of

literary tradition. Conversely, mainstream poets have not discussed the
emerging term due to a wider *a priori* suspicion towards theory that might
disturb 'the weekend pleasures to which art has been consigned as the
complement to bourgeois routine'.[17] To continue Alfred Alvarez's understanding of twentieth-century poetry as a series of dialectical negations in
The New Poetry (1961), the perceived iniquities of modernism such as
élitism still provide mainstream poetry with a counter-revolutionary vision
of literary democracy. It is this account of contemporary British poetry that
so incenses Hill in his fourth lecture as Oxford Professor of Poetry, and
which leads him to dismiss 'public' poetry that Duffy celebrates as '*the*'
literary form of the twenty-first century.[18]

Is there a certain belatedness in Hill's resistance to this current lauding of
'accessible' poetry, in which 'what I experience is real and final, and whatever
I say represents what I experience'?[19] Or, put another way, if we discuss Hill's
work in the context of debates about metamodernism, is this ostensibly the
same thing as labelling him a 'late' modernist? James and Seshagiri critique
the wider temporal expansions of modernism: transhistorical approaches
have rightly taken modernism to different corners of the globe, but at the
expense of a focus on what has made this period of early twentieth-century
literature so challenging to contemporary writers.[20] They argue that we
should avoid reference to 'early' and (implicitly) 'late' modernisms, and
emphasise instead the 'logic of periodization': 'Without a temporally
bounded and formally precise understanding of what modernism does and
means in any cultural moment, the ability to make other aesthetic and
historical claims about its contemporary reactivation suffers' (p. 88).
Modernism must be, if not a 'mythos' (p. 87), then an early twentieth-
century 'moment' (p. 88). This does not mean that contemporary literature
should be regarded as an adjunct to this period, as the term 'late modernism'
suggests. 'Late' is often a synonym for 'attenuated' in this phraseology, as
Fredric Jameson implies when he contrasts 'classical' or 'proper' modernism
with the 'modest [...] autonomies of the late modern'.[21] Going a step
further, Madelyn Detloff reimagines 'late' modernism in the form of cultural
productions that merely 'recirculate "patched" forms'.[22] Modernism for
Detloff can only be a form of cultural melancholia, a tempered modernism
that is 'recirculated' in reified patches of the original.[23] In contrast, James and
Seshagiri attack what they consider to be the 'reductive, presentist conception
of contemporary literature as a mere branch of modernist studies rather than
a domain whose aesthetic, historical, and political particulars merit their own
forms of intellectual inquiry' (p. 88). As I demonstrate later in this introduction, for example, Hill's antagonism towards and complex re-writing of

Eliot's *Four Quartets* (1943) in collections such as *Scenes from Comus* (2005) can hardly be read as the work of an epigone, and a belated 'patching' of the modernist antecedent. Quoting the sculptor Carl Andre in his seventh lecture as Oxford Professor of Poetry, Hill insists that poets should write work 'as strong as the art' they admire, but that they should not make it '*like* the art' they esteem.[24] *Scenes from Comus* engages rigorously with the poetics and pitch of *Four Quartets*, but it does not 'remint' the work of Eliot in an act of belated artistic pageantry.[25] Late modernism suggests attenuated endurance, whereas metamodernism connotes a self-conscious return to a formidable but also ephemeral phase in literature and culture.[26]

In contrast with Detloff's 'patching' of contemporary art, James's *The Legacies of Modernism* (2011) outlines his volume's effort to 'substantiate [this] basic speculation that the modernist project is unfinished' (p. 1).[27] The phrase 'modernist project' rather than 'modernism' allows for a modernist 'recrudescence' (p. 2) in 'models of continuity and adaptation (rather than demise)' in the post-war period (p. 3). For James, 'a more complex account of fiction's transitions from mid century to the present can only be achieved by an understanding not only of what modernism was but also what it might still become' (p. 3). Modernism here is paradoxically over, but not finished: the continuities expressed by the term 'metamodernism' suggest that 'fiction today partakes of an interaction between innovation and inheritance that is entirely consonant with what modernists themselves were doing more than a century ago' (p. 3). Yet this emphasis on fiction indicates the absence of a parallel critical debate about contemporary poetry that James and Seshagiri call attention to in the first footnote in their article: a discussion of the relationship between poetic innovation and the modernist tradition merits 'an account of its own' (p. 97). In *The Legacies of Modernism*, James emphasises that the novel proves to be an exemplar of metamodernism due to the voluminous script it can devote to working through the legacies of early twentieth-century literature and culture: 'it could be argued that narrative fiction (as distinct from poetry, drama, memoir or reportage) has in the postwar era offered the most capacious and dynamic medium for studying how writers have re-engaged with modernism's aesthetic and ideological challenges' (pp. 1–2). Yet many London School, Cambridge School, Language and mainstream poets too have engaged extensively with the formal propensities of modernist writers. Hill's statement in his fourth Oxford lecture that he is 'marooned' with Pound and Eliot in the 1950s forms merely one glaring instance of the importance of modernist authors to twentieth-first-century poetry.[28]

Rather than comply with Raymond Williams's conception of modernism as a monument to the end of an era, 'distant, solid, cold', I argue in this book that the 'modernist project' is revitalised in a specific kind of mainstream and 'innovative' poetry.[29] '[E]xasperating' poems display a dialectical approach to modernism in which the former – to deploy Theodor Adorno's term from *Minima Moralia* (1951) – 'hate' tradition 'properly'.[30] Despite Hill's indebtedness to Eliot's *Four Quartets*, for example, he reacts against what he perceives as the latter's false harmonies by creating an 'off-key' eloquence, an 'unlovely | body of Aesthetics', in his collections published from *The Triumph of Love* (1998) onwards.[31] This book outlines how contemporary British poets more widely have responded to the work of modernist writers as diverse as Pound, Eliot, H. D., Woolf and Artaud with such lyrical recalcitrance. I discuss how the legacies of modernism produce a specific variety of contemporary British poetry that thrives on 'a refractory relation between itself and dominant aesthetic values', and 'between itself and mass culture, between itself and society in general'.[32] However, whilst drawing on James and Seshagiri's account of metamodernism, I argue in this book that the qualities of 'exasperating' art are more important than any established intertextual links with modernist writers. To put it simply, poets' and novelists' attention to modernist antecedents does not necessarily mean that the resulting writing is deeply inflected by modernism. All the poets whose work I discuss extensively in this book – Geoffrey Hill, J. H. Prynne, Geraldine Monk, Sandeep Parmar, Ahren Warner, James Byrne and Tony Harrison – could be described as metamodernist in James and Seshagiri's sense of the term, in that they engage at length with the legacies of early twentieth-century literature, and absorb revolutions in form into divergent instances of contemporary poetry. However, my focus will be on both mainstream and 'innovative' poems that draw on modernist literature to produce an allusive and elusive writing that induces the curious reader to return time and again to the poetry. How, however, might we account conceptually for this 'exasperating' writing in both mainstream and 'innovative' poetry? To answer this question, I now turn to Adorno's account in *Aesthetic Theory* (1970) of such obduracy in modernist writing.

Adorno's Enigma

Returning to Hill's lecture in 2011, one of the questions it posed was how to account for poetry influenced by modernist writers that encourages the reader to keep coming back to the work, but without being able to 'solve' it. Adorno's account of 'enigmaticalness' allows for a conceptual under-standing of such 'exasperating' poetry.[33] In *Aesthetic Theory*, Adorno argues that works of art should not be treated solely as vessels for interpretation. Their enigmas also need to be appreciated: the artistic 'remainder' (*'der Rest'*) in modernist literature lies beyond the slipperiness of interpretation; it may defeat the critic's faculties, yet it remains central to understanding 'the discipline of the work' (p. 121).[34] Whereas Don Paterson argues in *New British Poetry* (2004) that poets must indulge their readers to a certain extent in order to be understood, Adorno warns against an '*intolerance to ambiguity*', and an antipathy towards that which is 'not strictly definable' (pp. 115–16).[35] If the poet ignores the complex process of creation, the 'consistency [. . .] of elaboration' that remains one of the lessons of mod-ernist literature, then the danger is that the quality of the poetry is attenuated in its ensuing 'husk of self-contentment' (pp. 129, 130). This does not mean that Adorno eulogises a supine version of autonomous art that resists the quotidian: as I explore further in Chapter 3, he outlines a dialectical conception of committed and autonomous literature, in which 'Art holds true' to the diurnal, 'but not by regression to it. Rather, art is its legacy' (p. 118).

This 'legacy' consists of a complex synthesis of form and content – the 'in-itself' of art – that risks the uninitiated's laughter (p. 125). Unlike Paterson's withdrawal from the lyric form when it appears to risk its own sublimity, Adorno argues that 'the more reasonable the work becomes in terms of its formal constitution, the more ridiculous it becomes according to the standard of empirical reason' (p. 119). A deliberate linguistic 'clown-ing' pervades the work of poets such as Hill and Monk: as Hill notes in his fourth Oxford lecture, it is the 'clown's rule' in particular to 'exasperate'.[36] As I explore further in Chapter 1, the effective 'ridiculousness' of collections such as Monk's *Ghost & Other Sonnets* (2008) configures an intense 'condemnation of empirical rationality' (p. 119). Hence art partly seeks solace in its enigmaticalness when it 'negates the world of things': it is *a priori* 'helpless when it is called on to legitimate itself to this world'. Whereas, for some critics, this undecodable art may seem merely unintel-ligible, for others, the enigmatic 'something' that artworks convey and then 'in the same breath conceal' encapsulates one of its most gratifying qual-ities. In contrast, those who are outraged by artworks' abstractions, and the fact that they are 'purposeful in themselves, without having any positive purpose beyond their own arrangement', unwittingly confirm 'art's truth' (p. 124). For such readers, 'the reality principle is such an obsession that it places a taboo on aesthetic comportment as a whole' (p. 120). Art's effacement of utility can be turned back on those who resist its allure: supposedly otiose artworks do not 'mean' something specific, just as the question 'What is the meaning of life?' has never been satisfactorily answered; the latter's immanent problem is usually 'forgotten as a result of its own overwhelming ossification' (p. 126). As Eleanor Cook emphasises in relation to Augustine's work, a rhetorical analysis of enigmaticalness can move from a conception of 'a small invented trope to enigma as the largest of tropes, a trope of the human condition'.[37]

This enigmatic 'comportment' of art, that appears to encapsulate 'what is enigmatical in existence', cannot be wholly explained, since 'Understanding is itself a problematic category in the face of art's enigmaticalness' (pp. 126, 121). As a form of imaginative imitation, hermeneutics can be perspicacious in terms of the 'objective experiential reenactment' of the work of art (p. 121); every 'authentic work' also invites rumination on 'the solution' to its unsolvable enigma (pp. 121, 127). After all, to shun interpretation, and allow artworks to 'simply exist' would be to 'erase the demarcation line between art and nonart' (p. 128): following that logic, Adorno argues, one might as well try to understand a carpet. In contrast, the philosopher likens criticism to enacting and simultaneously interpreting a musical score, at the same time as the latter's 'secret' remains elusive: even musicians who follow the score's most 'minute impulses' in a certain sense do not know what they are playing (p. 125). The more sagacious critics 'unpuzzle' any work of art, 'the more obscure [art's] constitutive enigmaticalness becomes': the latter remains, by definition, a 'vexation', and the enigma 'outlives' its attempted interpretation (pp. 121, 125). Music forms a prototypical example because it is 'at once completely enigmatic and totally evident' – a 'noninterpretative performance [would be] meaningless' – and yet it 'cannot be solved', and 'only its form can be deciphered' (pp. 125, 122). Various analogies aside from music in this passage from *Aesthetic Theory* then attempt to provide exemplars for this resistance to decoding, including natural phenomena, the Sphinx and picture puzzles. Adorno likens the enigma to a rainbow: 'If one seeks to get a closer look at a rainbow, it disappears' (p. 122); the reflection, refraction and dispersion of light, like the 'in-itself' of *Hamlet* (1609), does not have a 'message' (pp. 123, 128).[38] Adorno subsequently likens the experience of the enigma in *Aesthetic Theory* to that of an actor, who, like the musician, is playing something that they do not entirely understand: 'in the praxis of artistic performance' and 'the imitation of the dynamic curves of what is performed' lies the 'quintessence of understanding this side of the enigma' (p. 125). The 'gaze' of the Great Sphinx recurs throughout this passage in *Aesthetic Theory*: Egyptologists may have discovered that the mythical statue was constructed in approximately 2500 BC, and that it resembles the pharaoh Khafra, but they still do not understand its entire meaning: 'the enigma's gaze suddenly appears again; thus is preserved the artworks' seriousness, which stares out of archaic images' (p. 125). Every artwork is a 'picture puzzle', a conundrum to be 'solved', but art's enigmaticalness is constituted in such a fashion that it remains 'exasperating' (p. 121).

This book thus explores the ways in which the critical debates surrounding metamodernism might resonate in the context of this enigmatical poetry that challenges and enriches the reader's experience. Enigmatic poems are like the Sphinx: they are unsolvable puzzles, in which any infringements of critical understanding are tempered as the poetry's 'meaning' recedes into the distance.[39] Adorno's resistance towards hermeneutics in this context offers a methodological challenge not only to the study of contemporary poetry, but to the study of literature as a whole. Critical accounts of literature normally present the author as someone who can 'master' the literary text through close reading or the deft exposition of a theoretical response. Critics do not normally admit their failures to understand recalcitrant pockets of literary texts, and exorcise the 'remainder' that remains a threat to the certainty of their criticism (p. 121). In this context, Derek Attridge's *The Singularity of Literature* (2004) is openly in debt to Adorno's thinking: rather than seek to understand and thereby contain the work of art in an instrumentalist manner, the critic should be open to the methodological challenges of literature in subsequent readings of the text, which may involve subtly changing emphases.[40] Quoting from Walter Benjamin's 'The Task of the Translator', Attridge sums up a 'long history of critiques of the notion of literature as constative' with Benjamin's statement that 'the essential quality of the literary work "is not statement or the imparting of information"', and adds that 'surprisingly few of our readings acknowledge this in practice'.[41] Critics still discuss 'meaning', and 'ask what a work is "about"', in a manner that suggests a static object, transcending time, permanently available for our inspection' (p. 59). Attridge's focus on the performances of literature, 'events that can be repeated over and over again and yet never seem exactly the same', offers redress to any sense of literature's invariability (p. 2). However, whereas Attridge focuses on subsequent interpretations of literary texts in *The Singularity of Literature*, Adorno's concept of the enigmatical 'remainder' remains beyond the breadth of such readings.

Literary criticism has responded to the concept of the enigma as akin to that of the sphinx's riddle in Greek mythology, rather than in relation to this concept of the 'remainder' (p. 121).[42] Instead of exploring its methodological potential, critics have applied the term 'enigmatic' to a variety of individual texts whilst operating themselves as literary enimatographers. In contrast, this book provides the first extended study of the enigma in relation to a variety of 'exasperating' contemporary poems. In a rare example of a book that focuses on the enigma as a trope for wider concerns as well as a specific puzzle, Cook's *Enigmas and Riddles in Literature* (2006) explores, for example, a range of conundrums in the work of Dante, and Italian literature from 400 to 1399. The majority of literary-critical work on enigmas clusters around the medieval period when these 'obscure metaphors' were an integral part of literary expression, as Jeffrey Turco explores in *Piers Plowman and the Poetics of Enigma: Riddles, Rhetoric and Theology* (2017), and Shawn Normandin considers in relation to puzzles in Geoffrey Chaucer's *The Clerk's Tale* (1476).[43] In this version of enigmatology, these two critics adhere to the first definition of 'enigma' in English, dating from 1539, as 'a short composition in prose or verse, in which something is described by intentionally obscure metaphors, or in order to afford an exercise for the ingenuity of the reader or hearer in guessing what is meant; a riddle'.[44] As Cook argues, when the enigma is defined 'as a trope', such as in Aristotle's philosophy, it is often conceived rhetorically as a 'small conundrum, having nothing to do with broader concerns'.[45]

Rather than referring in general to an 'obscure or allusive' form of writing or 'a parable' – usages that *The Oxford English Dictionary* now lists as 'obscure' – in this book I explore the enigma in the specific manner that Adorno outlines in *Aesthetic Theory*, as inextricable with the legacies of modernist literature and supposedly 'hermetic' art more widely (p. 122).[46] Whereas Cook provides copious examples of the rhetorical figure as 'a closed simile where the likeness is concealed until an answer is provided', in *Aesthetic Theory*, art's riddles are never entirely solved.[47] The 'rage' that the philosopher surmises against such 'hermetic works' forms a symptom of the fallible 'comprehensibility' of 'traditional' works of art, a fulmination that betrays the potential enigmas surrounding the latter that, having been praised for aeons, appear to have lost their allure. Nevertheless, there is a clear intensification of enigmatic art in the modernist period: Adorno indicates this purling with references to Franz Kafka's 'damaged [fractured] parables' (p. 126) and Georg Trakl's Expressionist poetry (pp. 122–3).[48] Wary of the limited power of hermeneutics in relation to literature influenced by modernist writers, the chapters that follow do not present the critic as a masterful enigmatographer who can easily 'solve' recalcitrant poetry. Instead, this book engages with the intricate and elusive writing in collections such as Prynne's *Acrylic Tips* (2002) and Hill's *The Orchards of Syon* (2002) that offers potential elucidation, but my approach also registers aspects of the texts that 'await their interpretation' (p. 128).

My emphasis on enigmatical poetry thus draws on intertextual analyses in commentaries on metamodernism to focus on 'exasperating' rhetorical strategies: as Adorno outlines in *Aesthetic Theory*, the enigma of modern art is initiated through ambiguity, ambivalence and tricky *Rätsel* ('puzzles').[49] Hill, Prynne, Monk, Byrne, Warner and Parmar similarly 'revitalize perception' – a key consequence of modernist '"poetic" language' – by embracing challenging and often experimental forms.[50] Enigmatical poetry also complies with what Tony Pinkney, in his introduction to Raymond Williams's *The Politics of Modernism* (1989), terms the 'second modernist ideology' of a resistance to modernity in the guise of popular culture (p. 5). The latter ensures the 'greyly "standardizing" pressures of [the] contemporary environment'. Hill rails against such 'standardizing' in his fourth Oxford lecture, as in his irate response to Duffy comparing texting to poems in order to argue for poetry's continuing relevance.[51] Instead, Hill argues that poets should concentrate on creating 'an intensely crafted and parallel world'.[52] In *Aesthetic Theory*, Adorno maintains that critical responses that attempt to 'decode' this 'parallel world' are missing the point: critics who peruse art 'solely with comprehension make it into something straightforward, which is furthest from what it is' (p. 123). For Adorno, the 'remainder' that endures when the critic has temporarily exhausted their interpretative capabilities constitutes one of the defining aspects of modern art (p. 121). As in Irmin Schmidt's comment on 'great' art in the epigraph to this chapter, there is always something that eludes understanding in such music or writing, and which returns to delight, frustrate and engross the critic.

Such statements will be perceived by many champions of supposedly no-nonsense, 'straight from the heart' poetry as outdated and élitist nonsense. Yet, as Byrne argues through the satirical figure of the 'Chanel poet' in *Blood/Sugar* (2009), those who propose 'to market absolute clarity' usually inscribe 'nothing of minor importance'.[53] In *Aesthetic Theory*, outraged responses to enigmaticalness are symptomatic of an obsession with a 'reality principle' that actually despises 'aesthetic comportment', and has resulted in the 'contemporary deaestheticization of art' (p. 120). As I examine in Chapter 1, for example, an '*intolerance to ambiguity*' (p. 115) occurs in Paterson's poetry amidst a passage of arresting lyricism in

Landing Light (2003). In 'The Sea at Brighton', Paterson begins with an enigmatic stanza about memory and endurance, but the rest of the poem resists its lyrical profundity in a tactic that is symptomatic of a wider antipathy towards that which is 'not strictly definable' in modernist and metamodernist writing (pp. 115–16). In contrast, Prynne's work openly resists 'significative thinking' (p. 82), yet it is still the critic's paradoxical task to engage in 'interpretative reason' (p. 128) in order to try to understand collections such as *Acrylic Tips*. As I demonstrate in relation to Prynne's critique of market forces and consumerism in this collection, enigmatical poetry's resistance towards the 'reality principle' does not preclude an engagement with exigent political concerns (p. 120). Indeed, according to *Aesthetic Theory*, it is only in the autonomous *and* 'committed' art of writers such as Kafka, Samuel Beckett and Paul Celan that the barbarities of the twentieth century can be confronted and resisted in the 'fracturedness' of their work (p. 126). Hence in Chapter 3 I analyse how Hill's *The Orchards of Syon* draws on Celan's *Atemwende* (1967), but then – in Furlani's terms – 'surpasses' the antecedent with loquacious and sometimes irascible epiphanies.[54] In contrast, I illustrate the ways in which Harrison's deployment of Brechtian stagecraft in his verse plays is rooted in the limitations of 'committed' art, whereas Hill's deployment of 'off-key' eloquence to write about similarly appalling events in *The Orchards of Syon* has produced one of the most remarkable collections of poetry so far in the twenty-first century.[55]

This book explores diverse manifestations of such enigmatic writing, beginning with passages from Geoffrey Hill's *Scenes from Comus* that struggle to express 'ephemera's durance'.[56] The ending of this collection – 'What did you say?' (p. 66) – forms a challenge to complex writing from the perspective of a reader bemused with its magisterial language, 'gauged by the lost occasions of the sun': Hill offers a parting riposte to his ambitious attempt to wrestle with the mysteries of existence that deploys coterminous, obdurate poetics. In addition, the epiphanic moments in *The Orchards of Syon*, such as when a fell slowly releases its 'banded spectrum', are described in a linguistically intricate and condensed way precisely because such striking but bemusing moments cannot be pinned down with the 'reality principle' of a decoding and 'deaestheticized' poetics.[57] Similarly, Warner grapples with Artaud's attempts to comprehend his own intransigent states of anguish in 'Nervometer', and is sensitive to Artaud's impassioned rejection of logical reasoning and a ratiocinative style that would not do justice to the 'nebulous' mental states he seeks to elucidate but not explain away in *Les Pèse-Nerfs* (1925).[58]

In contrast, the enigma of Prynne's *Acrylic Tips* arises from a resistance to signification in every line, rather than Artaud's attempt to transform bewildering experiences into formal concretion. However, *Scenes from Comus*, *The Orchards of Syon*, *Acrylic Tips* and 'Nervometer' share a 'remainder' in the reader's confrontation with perplexing and stimulating language, conveying a sense that subsequent readings will uncover further meanings and appreciations of intricate form, even if the writing will never be 'solved'.[59] Monk's work thus revels in significative puzzles, such as the 'flambé | Shim' of the swift that might appear absurd to someone unfamiliar with poetry, or extravagant to a poet adhering to the 'reality principle', but actually courts the ridiculous in a way that is central to the formulation of modern art, as Adorno argues in *Aesthetic Theory*.[60] In contrast, I also analyse poetry that engages with modernist antecedents, but in which enigmatical poetics fail to arise, such as in Harrison's *Metamorpheus* (2000). This absence is due to the formal requirements, as Harrison perceives them, of the film-poem, and an incomplete reimagining of the raw material in the Orpheus workbook now held in the Brotherton Library. In addition, in Warner's 'Métro' a pastiche rather than transformation of Pound and Richard Aldington's work predominates in a neo-modernist diatribe against the supposedly vulgar.

These counterexamples of modernist-influenced writing that nevertheless reject modernism focalise the enigmatical poetics of the other authors discussed in this book. They also indicate a fault line between the theory and close readings: the summation above might suggest an unchallenged interweaving between *Aesthetic Theory* and my examples of elusive and allusive poetry, but the repercussions of Adorno expanding enigmatical poetics beyond modernist writing are fraught with potential contestation. 'All artworks', he argues, 'and art altogether—are enigmas' (p. 120). Adorno's initial examples – the works of Beckett and Kafka – obviously belong to 'high' modernism; the other listed instances of traditional enigmatic writing, Shakespeare's *Hamlet* (1603) and Goethe's poetry, point to the 'classic' texts of western literature. Adorno is critical of what he terms 'moderate' (p. 35) or 'temperate' (p. 34) modernism: for this philosopher, such palliating of experimentation implies formal conservatism. '[R]enaissances of temperate modernism' (p. 35) are 'promoted by a restorative consciousness and its interested parties' (p. 34); the mere idea of 'moderate' modernism is 'self-contradictory' because it restrains the 'innovative' impulses of modernist art (p. 35). In Adorno's example, Pablo Picasso's cubist works are therefore far more 'expressive' than 'those works that were inspired by cubism but feared to lose expression and became supplicant' (p. 44). These charges of losing formal potency through a belated appeal to tradition could be extended to enigmatical poetry such as Hill's that does not sit easily within either category of mainstream or 'innovative' writing. Pound's formal experimentation may be assimilated in Hill's work, but – following Adorno's argument – is also attenuated by Hill's frequent deployment of acatalectic metre. Similarly, Byrne's work may be rooted in the 'innovative' poetry of the London School, yet he is also attentive to rhythmical emphasis and metrical counterpointing in collections such as *The Caprices* (2019) that I discuss in Chapter 4. Yet, elsewhere in *Aesthetic Theory*, Adorno critiques experimental writing that constantly hankers after the 'new' as the aesthetic gold at the end of the formal rainbow (pp. 270–1). Adorno could not have foreseen a moment over fifty years later in which the 'temperate' modernism of *Scenes from Comus* and *The Orchards of Syon* would appear so radically out of step with the predominant voices in contemporary British poetry (p. 34). Thus the conception of enigmatical poetry is even more exigent today than it was when *Aesthetic Theory* was published in 1970. The philosopher could not have predicted a moment in which one of the most lauded poets of the day would compare poetry to texting, crystallising a moment in which the 'deaestheticized' writing he encountered in the 1960s has reached its apotheosis (p. 120).[61]

In this book, I indicate contrasting moments in poetry that slip beyond the critic's grasp and 'darken' when a provisional understanding of a singular text does not 'extinguish the enigmaticalness' of an artwork (p. 122). In Chapter 2, for example, I discuss how Hill strives for a new language to pinpoint 'Love's grief' in *Scenes from Comus* (p. 41), yet the similes of charabanc parties and rhododendrons remain as enigmatic as this amorphous psychological state. Rather than provide the reader with a narcissistic echo of their own idioculture, such poetry allows our critical understanding to be challenged, and sometimes to be defeated. The following close reading of *Scenes from Comus* is thus intended to convey what Attridge terms the 'power' of such writing, but this approach cannot entirely 'explain' the poetry.[62] This resistance to absolute semblance and the univocal also appertains to Prynne's collection *Acrylic Tips*, which I discuss further in Chapter 1. The elusive significations ultimately mean that the sequence remains difficult – but not impossible – to analyse. As Prynne wrote in a letter to the poet Steve McCaffery, to challenge the possibility of interpretation is in no way 'to extirpate it'.[63] Every line of *Acrylic Tips* resists signification, but does not negate it: the line 'soft sweet fury gums nodding milkwort in river-sway', for example, combines the traditional lyricism of the last four words with a more enigmatic beginning.[64] '[G]ums' may be read as mossy rocks or gum wrappers in the river, but this would be to 'normalize' the poetry in Robert Sheppard's phrase, to attempt to decipher the puzzle without opening the line up to alternative signification.[65] The first four words in this quotation from *Acrylic Tips* may be distinct from the second cluster: it is only the expectation of complete line sense in a poem rather than literary collage that insists that 'gums' must somehow connect with milkwort.

Poetry as Enigma: Geoffrey Hill's *Scenes from Comus*

If texts such as *Acrylic Tips* could be understood alongside the novels that James and Seshagiri cite in their article on metamodernism, it would be possible to discuss the 'remainder' across a variety of contemporary literature (p. 121). They discuss Tom McCarthy as an archetypal metamodernist novelist, yet, unlike Prynne's work, the overall form and language of novels such as *Remainder* (2005) and *C* (2010) do not resist conventional 'grammar, process, shape, syntax', as in Charles Bernstein and Bruce Andrews' conception of 'innovative' poetry.[66] If we compare this lack of formal resistance with the work of Geoffrey Hill, who has repeatedly engaged with the legacies of modernist writers such as Eliot, Pound, Kafka, Wyndham Lewis and W. B. Yeats throughout his *oeuvre*, the difference in the attentiveness to specific modernist antecedents is striking. In addition, Adorno's 'remainder' informs the following analysis of Hill's *Scenes from Comus* (p. 121): this allusive and elusive collection ultimately defeats comprehensive interpretation. Hill's enigmatic, but not 'innovative', poetics are crystallised in the final passage from *Scenes from Comus*:

> In shifting scapes eternity resumes.
> I cannot fault its nature, act by act,
> gauged by the lost occasions of the sun.
>
> Ephemera's durance, vast particulars
> and still momentum measures of the void.
> What did you say?[67]

Published in the same year as McCarthy's *Remainder*, these lines do not eschew conventional grammar, syntax or stanza shape. Yet they do form extensive evidence of what James terms modernism's capacity as 'a set of persisting resources, rather than as a collection of historical artefacts'.[68] In addition, they illustrate my argument that enigmatical poetics can be located in mainstream poetry as well as the London and Cambridge

Schools. In these stanzas, Hill's 'resource' consists of Eliot's *Four Quartets*, and the latter's Platonic vacillations between the particular and general. Past time is 'eternally present' in line four of Eliot's poem; in the first line of the passage above, shifting landscape in general is paradoxically proof of 'eternity' (p. 13). '[S]capes' contains its own ambiguity: it initially reads as a shortened version of 'landscapes', but can also refer to the particularly long stems of flowers that begin where the root ends.[69] Impermanent flowers and vast landscapes both evidence the stability of 'eternity', just as the 'transient beauty' of the 'Turning shadow' leads to Earth's 'slow rotation suggesting permanence' in part three of Eliot's 'Burnt Norton' (p. 17). This dialectical shuttling then crescendos in the final stanza of *Scenes from Comus* with the phrases 'Ephemera's durance', 'vast particulars' and 'still momentum' (p. 66). As well as being a shortened version of 'endurance' (as with land/scapes), 'durance' contains the archaic meaning of imprisonment: Hill's first oxymoron indicates that the transient endures in the seascape, but also that the poem captures and imprisons such ephemera. Poets are the 'artificers' in the previous stanza who are able to 'withhold' (as in 'restrain' and 'hold back') an enigmatic force that has 'long been destined to the dark'. In contrast to the 'immeasurable' dawns earlier in *Scenes from Comus* (no. 47), the poet-narrator's rumination on the sea and landscape's 'momentum' allows him a 'measure' of the unknowable void, rather than Eliot's more redemptive vision at the end of 'The Dry Salvages' of the 'life of significant soil' not 'too far from the yew-tree' (p. 45). Lyrical 'measure' refers directly to the lines that Hill quotes from 'Little Gidding' in his fourth lecture as Oxford Professor of Poetry, celebrating the poet's ability to 'move in measure, like a dancer'.[70]

In turn, the puzzling phrase '[S]till momentum' (p. 66) recalls the 'still point of the turning world' (p. 15) in 'Burnt Norton', and the Christian transition from the 'still and still moving' in 'East Coker' towards 'another intensity' and 'further union' (p. 32). However, Hill then attempts to 'surpass' Eliot in Furlani's terms by usurping what he refers to in his prose writing as the hectoring and complacent manner of the *Four Quartets*.[71] In *True Friendship* (2010), Ricks notes that, whereas Hill's poems 'make manifest a debt to Eliot which constitutes one of the highest forms of gratitude', Hill's criticism of Eliot's poetry 'mostly sounds anything but grateful'.[72] Hill declaims, for example, Eliot's decline 'over the years from acuity and the trenchant into a broad opinionatedness'; as a result, much of Eliot's later work is 'demonstrably bad', including the *Four Quartets*, that are 'half adequate [. . .] half articulate'.[73] For Hill, the poem encapsulates the 'ruminative, well-modulated voice of a man of letters, a tone which so weakens *Four Quartets*' (p. 579). Whilst I concur with Ricks's criticism that Hill undervalues the later Eliot, Hill is right that lines in 'The Dry Salvages' such as 'Pray for all those who are in ships, and | Whose business is to do with fish' are a travesty of the singularity of *The Waste Land* (1922) (p. 42).[74] Hill's conception of 'pitch' perplexes Ricks: 'I am unable to fathom just what Hill means by "pitch" and I am unable to imagine the grounds for judging "tone" to be not only inferior to "pitch" but inherently contaminated' (p. 32). Whereas Hill separates the terms, I would regard tone and pitch to be part of the same continuum. Hill draws attention to the hectoring tone, at times, of *Four Quartets*, which is at odds with the lyrical 'pitch' of Eliot's earlier work. Hill's conception of 'pitch' does not exclude the playful: in section seven of the 'Courtly Masquing Dances', Hill remarks that his stance 'contra tyrannos' (p. 3) does not encompass the 'lawful | lordship' of the Lord President in Cymru; the subsequent (and untranslated) phrase in Welsh, '*Diolch – diolch yn fawr!*' means 'Thank you, but I think you're having a laugh!' (p. 18).

So far, I have discussed the intense and intricate engagement with and subversion of a specific modernist antecedent in this enigmatic passage from *Scenes from Comus*. However, at the closure, Hill stresses the enigma of his entire collection with the intervention 'What did you say?', undermining the certitude of any critical understanding of the previous lines (p. 66). One reading of the interjection would be that it also 'surpasses' *Four Quartets* by allowing space, unlike Eliot's poem, for the voice of the dissenting reader; a voice that became more common in Hill's work after the publication of his collections *The Triumph of Love* and *Speech! Speech!* (2000).[75] The fulminating interlocutor may be akin to the uninitiated sampler of art in *Aesthetic Theory* who responds to such unashamedly abstract utterances as the ending to *Scenes from Comus* by denouncing them as ridiculous or incomprehensible (p. 119). This line itself remains beyond definitive signification: bemused, the interlocutor might be referring to the collection as a whole as well as this passage; aptly, in this jarring intervention, the dimeter undercuts the pentameter of this stanza and 'A Description of the Antimasque' in its entirety. Alternatively, the voice may be that of the critic responding quizzically to the sublimity of phrases such as 'the lost occasions of the sun' (p. 66). Rather than denoting incomprehension at what Hill would term the lyrical 'pitch' of the final stanzas of *Scenes from Comus*, the final line might also compound the less mysterious references to ageing throughout the collection. In the manuscripts for *Scenes from Comus* held in the Brotherton Library, a mirror 'shames' Hill and 'stares [him] down': these deleted lines are condensed into the melodrama in stanza forty-three in which he addresses a mirror and opines, '*spare me my own | rancour and ugliness*' (p. 36).[76] As opposed to Eliot's entrenchment in 'vast particulars' (p. 66), Hill's poem subverts itself with a line reminiscent of the alleged incident in 1797 in which the arrival of a postman curtailed the writing of Samuel Taylor Coleridge's 'Kubla Khan'. In *Scenes from Comus*, the poet may be drawn away from the 'pitch' of his stanza due to an outside voice; perhaps the expostulation arises from the poet's (figured) partial deafness. The absences in Coleridge's 'Kubla Khan' due to the infamous postman are then equivalent to the blank paper on page sixty-seven of *Scenes from Comus* that follows the closure. However, the difference is one of poetic intensity: compared to Coleridge's fragments, Hill is only disturbed after sixty-six pages of *Scenes from Comus*.

'What did you say?' thus calls attention to the enigma of the final stanzas of *Scenes from Comus* that is rooted in Hill's response to *Four Quartets*, and which cannot, despite my attempts above, be 'decoded' into definitive meanings. Impishly, the line also registers Hill's sense of alienation from the mainstream of contemporary British poetry that he explores more absorbedly in his fourth lecture as Oxford Professor of Poetry. In this context, Hill figures his tussles with modernist literature in an epigraph to *Scenes from Comus* as a seemingly anachronistic toil, and quotes from Kafka's *The Blue Octavo Notebooks* (1948): 'The good walk in step. Without knowing anything of them, the others dance around them, dancing the dances of the age'.[77] This quotation comes from Kafka's third notebook: 'walking' might appear to be an anachronism to the dancers, but 'in step' indicates a writer capable of Poundian 'reticence and of restraint' in the face of contemporaneous trivialities; Kafka's distaste towards the latter is registered in the repetition of '*tanzen, tanzen, tanzen*' and '*die Tänze*' in the original German.[78] To 'walk in step' forms a version of Eliot's appeal to poets to 'move in measure' in 'Little Gidding' (p. 55), in the sense of deploying artistic temperance as well as attentiveness towards the formal properties of poetry. Such stubbornness can be read as steadfastness and a resistance to accommodation, an invigorating legacy of modernist writers such as Kafka, rather than artistic conservatism. Indeed, Hill's second epigraph in *Scenes from Comus* – 'VERY WELL ACTED BY YOU AND ME' – originates in Wyndham Lewis's play *Enemy of the Stars* (1914), and presents walking (and acting) 'in step' as an enduring alternative to mainstream poetry. As Tyrus Miller argues, the 'Advertisement' for the Vorticist drama from which Hill excerpts his quotation 'was intended to assert and seal [Lewis's] leadership of the avant-garde circle around him'.[79]

In contrast, Hill has never been the figurehead for any anti-mainstream 'circle': instead, through the epigraphs from Kafka and Lewis's work, he asserts his intention to continue walking 'in step' with modernism, resisting the dance of 'poetasters' decried by John Milton and in the first section of *Scenes from Comus*.[80] Hill's appeal to the 'covenants' of language in the ninth line of the poem (p. 3) links with Milton's refusal in *The Reason of Church Government Urged Against Prelatry* (1642) to experience shame when in covenant 'with any knowing ['walking'] reader'.[81] For Milton and Hill, the paths of those who walk 'in step' are 'rugged and difficult' in contrast with the 'libidinous and ignorant poetasters': the former require 'industrious and select reading', and – in an early version of Poundian restraint – 'steady observation'. Pound's 'reticence' is evident in Hill's judicious editing of the manuscripts for *Scenes from Comus*: a stanza about a 'lovely Eurasian woman | on the Euston to Wolverhampton express' entertains a dullness of diction and awkward enjambment that can be found in many mainstream poems, but which he excises from the final version.[82] By associating covenants with aversions to 'tyrannos' in the first stanza (p. 3), Hill also draws on an influential Huguenot tract first published in 1579, as well as Milton's resistance to prelatry. Hill evokes *Vindiciae Contra Tyrannos* ('Defences Against Tyrants') as both a symbol of popular resistance against corrupt rulers, and a self-referential nod to his previous retort against mainstream accusations that his poetry is too difficult.[83] When asked to respond to his collection *The Orchards of Syon*, Hill retorted that 'Tyrants always want a language and literature that is easily understood'.[84] Whereas Paterson argues in *New British Poetry* that poets should provide the 'human courtesy' of providing a context in which they are to be interpreted (p. xxx), Hill and Milton prefer 'walking' readers who have 'insight into all seemly [. . .] arts and affairs', as the latter writes in *The Reason of Church Government Urged Against Prelatry*.[85] Rather than the 'dancing' reader that Paterson imagines in the introduction to *New British Poetry*, who remains in cahoots with the mainstream poet, the second poem in *Scenes from Comus* figures the ideal reader as momentarily waylaid: the writer's 'orbit' 'salutes' the attentive recipient, 'whenever we pass or cross' (p. 3).

Nevertheless, in a contemporaneous review of *Scenes from Comus*, Sean O'Brien dismisses the 'walking' reader, who may be attentive to the modernist allusions in the passage I analysed above, as seduced by 'interpreters' excited snobbery'.[86] In contrast, the reviewer Eric Ormsby is more open to conceiving the collection as an enigma, and questions the whole concept of 'interpreting' Hill's poem: 'I don't pretend to

"understand" it all, even after several [readings but] then, I don't "understand" Beethoven's Late Quartets or the paintings of Balthus; yet I love
them more each time I encounter them, as I do Mr. Hill's poetry'.[87] In
a similar appeal to literary tradition as in the epigraphs and opening
sections of *Scenes from Comus*, Hill's *Collected Critical Writings* (2008)
contains an epigraph from A. P. Rossiter's *Angel with Horns and other
Shakespeare Lectures* (1961): 'what is the appeal to tradition, when the
lords of the present never understand, but ideal self-commiseration in
the glasses of dead eyes' (n.p.n.). The Eliotian 'appeal' is couched with
an intriguing oxymoron ('ideal self-commiseration'), that suggests that,
if the contemporary poet engages in the intertextuality that O'Brien
decries, they will not be appreciated for the ensuing enrichment of
their poetry, but at least allusion remains a consolation that responds
to literary tradition. The 'glasses of dead eyes' in this quotation could be
those of the uncomprehending reader of recalcitrant poetry or the dead
poets themselves.[88]

Mainstream and 'Innovative' Poetry

In *Scenes from Comus*, this intensity of Hill's 'self-commiseration' in relation to the work of Eliot, Kafka and Lewis typifies the engagement of
enigmatical poetry with the legacies of early twentieth-century literature,
and its advocacy of refractory poems as recourse to merely 'dancing'
entertainment. This discussion of such challenging writing also opens
a specific breach in the poetry wars, as I demonstrate in the chapters that
argue for Hill and Prynne's poems as distinct examples of 'exasperating'
literature.[89] The elusiveness of Hill and Prynne's work contrasts with
a kind of mainstream poetry that Paterson advocates in his introduction
to *New British Poetry*, in which there is an over-anxious requirement to
placate the reader. Hill argues in his fourth lecture as Oxford Professor of
Poetry that it is not the poet's duty to mollify their readers: instead, they
must simply focus on being 'inventive'.[90] This book thus contains analyses
of poetry that sustain the enigmatic possibilities of contemporary writing,
rather than that of 'dancing' poems that desperately attempt to appease the
reader. Hill, Prynne, Monk, Parmar, Warner and Byrne offer an alternative vision of contemporary literature, in which art persists in its 'rule' to
delight, challenge and exasperate.

By focussing on a form of writing that crosses the divide between
mainstream and 'innovative' poetry, I am not calling for an abolition of
these categories. Even if they are fallible, they nevertheless sketch the formal

differences that perpetuate in contemporary poetry. For Sheppard, attempts to disavow these classifications with 'persistent claims to consensual inclusiveness' began around the publication of *The New Poetry* anthology in 1993.[91] For others, such as Barry, the dissolution began even earlier during the 1980s, after the mass resignation of 'innovative' poets from the Poetry Society after the 'Battle of Earls Court', and years of subsequent marginalisation that ultimately gave way to a 'new consensus'.[92] J. T. Welsh proposes that generational anthologies have projected 'an image of consensus' into the future, 'beyond historical divisions that appear antithetical to a shared vision and sense of community', and he outlines a recent collapse of the 'new consensus'.[93] I would concur with Sheppard that this 'peace process' (p. 82) actually never gained much traction: despite the temporary ententes and détentes, the categories of mainstream and 'innovative' endure, as became apparent in the visceral responses to the publication of Paterson and Charles Simic's *New British Poetry* in 2004. For some critics, the intervening years have brought about a less bifurcated response to contemporary poetics, in which poets such as Warner, Byrne and Parmar happily operate on the 'cusp' of these categories.[94] Yet, despite the formal efforts of the poets discussed in this book, 'deaestheticized' forms of writing still predominate in contemporary poetry that over-value the 'reality principle' in the clamour after a decreasing number of poetry readers.[95] As David Kennedy illustrates in his analysis of back-cover blurbs, mainstream poetry books today tend to be marketed through the author's personality rather than the 'truth content' of the writing.[96] In addition, as John Redmond, Marjorie Perloff and Hill have expressed, the augmentation of poetry awards and publications does not mean that twenty-first-century poetry luxuriates in an 'incredible renaissance' of formal salubriousness.[97] Hill's fourth Oxford lecture stresses the risks of comparing the supposed 'low vitality' of poetry in the 1950s to contemporary British poetry.[98] Redmond records a 'prize-giving culture, fuelled by favours and networking' in *Poetry and Privacy* (2013) (p. 10), and notes that, in reports on poetry competitions and public promotion, the emphasis is often on what poets do aside from being writers (p. 7). Such logic would be like assessing the quality of winemakers on their production of fetching hats. This bizarre demotion of the craft of writing relies 'too often on a thesis of public relevance' that 'arises out of a more general conviction: that the relationship between poetry and the public sphere is negatively woven' (p. 7). Redmond argues that universities have ended up in the odd position of 'nurturing a poetic class which is not merely anti-academic but, to an alarming degree, hostile to intelligent scrutiny' (p. 10).

This book thus attempts to recalibrate the overdetermined categories of the mainstream and 'innovative' not to pinpoint their absolute inefficacy, but to focalise on enigmatical poems that resist the 'dominant culture of contemporary poetry' that is 'promotional in outlook and anti-intellectual in spirit'.[99] Authors from both camps will contest this recalibration. Many 'innovative' poets will retort that writers usually categorised as mainstream, such as Hill and Warner, or 'cusp' writers, such as Byrne and Parmar, are encroaching on their established formal territory. Another response will be that the Cambridge School has been engaging with the possibilities of enigmatical poetics since the 1960s. The influence of *Aesthetic Theory* and *Negative Dialectics* (1966) may indeed be implicit in the writing of many examples of such poetry – as in the work of Drew Milne and Simon Jarvis – but there has never been an extended account of enigmatical poetry in the London and Cambridge Schools *and* mainstream poems equivalent to the scope of this book. On the other hand, many mainstream poets will disavow the 'exasperating' writing of poets such as Hill, Warner, Byrne and Parmar as misplaced within their category, and contend that it is actually symptomatic of late modernist writing that displays all the hallmarks of currently distrusted formal concerns such as intricacy, allusion and complexity. As Kennedy recounts in *New Relations*, one reviewer of *The New Poetry* opined that '"surely the myth of modernism, progressivism, and the perpetual avant-garde was laid to rest years ago?"' (p. 250). In the wake of such appraisals of contemporary poetry, the theory of enigmatical poetics becomes even more pressing. Unless accounts of contemporary poetics are attentive to instances of refractory poetry, then there is no guarantee that future generations will be able to understand works of art in a way that Adorno believed to be vouchsafed in 1969. For future generations, the 'secrets' of art that Schmidt has been drawn to throughout his career may be interpreted as merely formal intransigence.[100]

Compared to this focus on enigmatical poetry, critical discussion surrounding the metamodernist novel and artworks has centred around a perceived shift from postmodernism to a new historicity bound up with affect, the return of sentiment, post-irony and the impact of austerity. In 'Metamodernism Manifesto' and 'Metamodernism: A Brief Introduction', for example, Luke Turner registers the 'desires' of this new 'structure of feeling' in relation to 'the resurgence of sincerity, hope, romanticism, affect, and the potential for grand narratives and universal truths', rejecting the postmodernist irony and cynicism of the 1980s and 1990s, with its 'diet of *The Simpsons* and *South Park*'.[101] This narrative simply does not appertain in the context of contemporary British poetry:

there is no clear movement from the predominance of postmodernist poetry to the guarded sincerity of postmillennial poems. Indeed, any critic who claimed the prior existence of an uncontested postmodernist poetry that has now been superseded would be open to ridicule. Even though members of the London and Cambridge Schools have assimilated aspects of poststructuralism and theories of postmodernism, there has never been a definitive postmodernist poetry in an equivalent way to postmodernist metafiction. Moreover, mainstream poetry has marginalised 'innovative' poems since the 1960s, as critics such as Barry and Robert Hampson have tirelessly illustrated in books such as *New British Poetries* (1993) and *Poetry Wars* (2006), so the shift away from a predominant postmodernist form would be impossible to justify in the context of contemporary British poetry.[102] In contrast, I afford considerable space in this book to writing that that does not fit easily into the categories of postmodernist, mainstream or 'innovative' poetry. Hill's *Scenes from Comus*, Monk's *Ghost & Other Sonnets* (2008), Byrne's *White Coins* (2015) and Parmar's *Eidolon* (2015) share a formal recalcitrance that is out of kilter with much of mainstream British poetry, an 'off-key' eloquence that is not ashamed to present contemporary poetry as difficult and exasperating, yet – as I shall illustrate – these collections are not easily categorised as either mainstream or 'innovative'.[103] As Hill points out in relation to *The Orchards of Syon*, they are formally challenging precisely because the historicity that such poetry is intertwined with contains and resists its own wealth of obdurate complexities.[104] Anecdotal and positivist poetry may provide succour, but it does not create a parallel literary world capable of confronting and withstanding the vicissitudes of the present. The modernist critic R. P. Blackmur distinguished the 'art of poetry' from mere versifying through 'the animating presence of a fresh idiom': enigmatical poetry is similarly so 'twisted and posed' in its formal inclinations that it not only expresses 'the matter in hand', but 'adds to the stock of available reality'.[105]

CHAPTER I

Contemporary British Poetry and Enigmaticalness

As I outlined in the Introduction, the artistic 'remainder' (*'der Rest'*) that lies beyond the slipperiness of hermeneutics may defeat the critic's faculties, yet it remains central to understanding 'the discipline of the work'.[1] In *Aesthetic Theory* (1970), Theodor Adorno argues that modernist works of art should not be treated merely as 'objects' to be interpreted: instead, it is their overall incomprehensibility that needs to be understood.[2] Rather than functioning as texts akin to Roland Barthes' 'tissue of quotations' that can be unpicked and explicated, modernist artworks are resistant, to an extent, to rational interpretation.[3] These artworks seem 'to say just this and only this, and at the same time whatever it is slips away'.[4] In this chapter, I expand on this account of the enigma in *Aesthetic Theory* in order to scrutinise further the friction between the critical impulse and contemporary British poetry that does not 'extinguish [its] engimaticalness' (p. 122). I consider the implications of this tension in relation to J. H. Prynne's *Acrylic Tips* (2002), and subsequently analyse enigmatical poetics in examples of mainstream and 'innovative' writing from Don Paterson's *Landing Light* (2003) and Geraldine Monk's *Ghost & Other Sonnets* (2008). However, my argument is not that Prynne, Paterson and Monk's poems are all comparable examples of metamodernist poetry. I emphasise that Monk's collection, unlike Paterson's, does not flinch when engaging with the linguistic 'clowning' that will appear to some readers as merely ridiculous verbiage, as Adorno laments in relation to modernist art more generally in *Aesthetic Theory* (p. 119). Whereas Paterson flirts with but then draws back from enigmatical poetics, Prynne and Monk's 'exasperating' writing sustains the possibility of the enigma in strikingly different formal ways.[5]

T. S. Eliot argued that readers who are not flummoxed by writing that they do not understand may not be able to pinpoint what they like about a poem, but may yet have a 'deeper and more discriminating sensibility than some others who can talk glibly about it'.[6] Whereas Paterson contends instead in *New British Poetry* (2004) that poets must assuage their readers' apprehensions rather than pursue the latter's 'discriminating sensibility', Adorno warns in *Aesthetic Theory* against such critical narcissism.[7] The philosopher decries a 'restricted functional capacity' that establishes an '*intolerance to ambiguity*', and an antipathy towards that which is 'not strictly definable' (pp. 115–16) in diction reminiscent of Geoffrey Hill's attack on 'public' writing in his fourth lecture as Oxford Professor of Poetry. Eliot describes readers who are open to and relaxed about these 'darkening' propensities of literature (p. 122); for critics, however, professional reputations may be at stake as they grapple with allusive and elusive writing. Nevertheless, rather than attempting to assimilate artworks into established interpretative narratives, critics should appreciate that 'however consciousness seeks to safeguard itself from losing its way is fateful' (p. 121).[8] In this context, Derek Attridge's theory of singularity adheres to *Aesthetic Theory*, as the critic returns to literary texts with different critical and creative performances of the literary text on separate occasions. As Attridge acknowledges in the appendix to his influential book, Adorno's thinking permeates *The Singularity of Literature* (2004): 'there can be no doubt that his *Aesthetic Theory* is among the most significant twentieth-century contributions to debates about artistic practice and response. I have found my struggles with it immensely rewarding'.[9] Attridge's emphasis on the performance of literature in order to discern its singularity partly has its roots in the passage on enigmaticalness in *Aesthetic Theory*: Adorno writes that understanding individual artworks requires an 'objective experiential reenactment from within in the same sense in which the interpretation of a musical work means its faithful performance' (p. 121). Literary texts are thus 'performed' in the act of reading in a comparable way to musicians interpreting and performing a musical score. However, as I noted in the Introduction, whereas Attridge focuses on subsequent interpretations in *The Singularity of Literature*, Adorno's concept of enigmaticalness necessarily remains beyond the reach of such readings. Modernist and metamodernist art has to 'contain something permanently enigmatic' in order to remain 'uncapturable', and resistant to 'ready-made categories'.[10]

As Hill intimates in his fourth lecture, he is not willing to accommodate the reader with an 'openly servile' art; instead, he adheres to exasperating and 'uncapturable' poetics.[11] In contrast, Paterson argues in *New British Poetry* that mainstream poems should, in Adorno's disparaging phrase, 'narrow [their] distance' from the recipient.[12] If the enigmaticalness of metamodernist works such as *Scenes from Comus* (2005) was entirely decoded, they would, of course, immediately cease to be enigmatic. Hence Adorno's discussion of the enigma is itself inevitably enigmatic; otherwise, it would be yet another 'ready-made' category of reading. At the same time, Adorno paradoxically argues that the critic's impossible task is still to unpuzzle the enigma: each artwork turns 'toward interpretative reason' through the 'neediness implicit in its enigmaticalness' (p. 128). Whereas consciousness tends to 'safeguard itself from losing its way' (p. 121), the critic must nevertheless be prepared to admit failure when writing about literature influenced by modernist antecedents. Despite the sublimity of the enigmatic, Adorno is not arguing that critics should desist entirely from interpretation: critics should instead remain open to literature's unassimilable 'remainder', and modestly admit that 'one understands something of art, not that one understands art' (p. 122). The enigma is '*neutral zum Verhüllten*'; in other words, 'cloaked', so critics that attempt to colonise the artwork with their own thinking and interpretative procedures 'make it into something straightforward, which is furthest from what it is'.[13] As with Attridge's theory of singularity, the reader must not project their own concerns onto the artwork in order to be 'satisfied in it', but must instead 'relinquish' them in order 'to fulfil the work in its own terms' (p. 275). In contrast, the politics of assimilation are inevitably ideological: hence – to use Adorno's example – the alacrity with which the Nazis denounced artistic '*Rätsel*' ('puzzles') as decadent. When challenged about the difficulty of his poetry, Hill similarly turned to an example of heteronomy. Asked to comment on his collection *The Orchards of Syon* (2002), he replied that 'Tyrants always want a language and literature that is easily understood'.[14]

For Adorno, this resistance to heteronomy is inextricable with 'cloaked' modernist literature, and, more specifically for this section of *Aesthetic Theory*, with the literature of the absurd (p. 122). Yet it is in this passage that the possibility arises of applying the concept to mainstream writing as well as modernist and 'innovative' poetry. Adorno first mentions modern art's difficulty in relation to the cliché of the '*absurd*' that 'absorbs' and nullifies incomprehensibility rather than thinking through its 'truth' (p. 118). The theatre of the Parisian Left Bank in the 1950s then extends to all modern, hermetic art: for Adorno, it is only in the 'committed' *and* autonomous writing of Franz Kafka, Samuel Beckett and Paul Celan that the 'spirit of the epoch' (p. 180) can be confronted and resisted in the 'fracturedness' of their work (p. 126).[15] However, another dialectical turn then avoids establishing an opposition between modernist and pre-twentieth-century art. The derided 'incomprehensibility' of hermetic artworks amounts to the admission', Adorno argues, 'of the enigmaticalness of all art' (p. 122). Modernism can hardly be opposed to the absolute simplicity of pre-twentieth-century literature: re-workings of Shakespeare's plays, for example, partly respond to the enigmaticalness of the original texts. Since antiquity, the 'enigmas' of artworks have been 'an irritation to the theory of art' (p. 120): for Adorno, all artworks are '*Rätsel*'; he describes them as having 'always irritated conceptual responses to art' with their challenging '*Rätselcharakter*'.[16] Critics may think that they have understood a specific work of art, but the most profound artworks are still nevertheless able to return an 'empty gaze' of 'constitutive enigmaticalness', a 'constitutive darkening' that overwhelms interpretation 'for the second time with the question "What is it?"' in a 'preestablished routing of its observer' (pp. 120–2).

It is clear that Adorno does not mean every artistic output in this passage: he refers to complex works that submit, in his phrase, to their own discipline (p. 275), and in which 'enigmaticalness outlives the interpretation' (p. 125). Metamodernist artworks should thus be 'question marks' rather than unambiguous and 'univocal' (p. 124): in contrast, the mainstream poetics that Paterson outlines in his introduction to *New British Poetry* seek to accommodate, rather than exasperate with the 'twisted' language of 'innovative' poetry.[17] Adorno's reading of modernist art in *Aesthetic Theory* also has a different emphasis to David James and Urmila Seshagiri's focus on revolution, dissent, defamiliarisation and experiment: metamodernist novels that draw on this 'myth' of modernism but 'unfold to contemplation' without the enigmatical 'remainder' are simply – according to *Aesthetic Theory* – 'not artworks' (p. 121).[18] The original German I am referring to here in *Ästhetische Theorie* is as follows: '*Kunstwerke, die der Betrachtung und dem Gedanken ohne Rest aufgeben, sind keine*' ('Artworks that give rise to contemplation and thought without any remainder are not artworks') (p. 184).[19] These failed works of literature are open to instrumental projections of various kinds, Adorno argues, but they do not function as '*Rätsel*', and avoid the complexities of modernist 'vexation'. In contrast, writers and critics, such as Paterson, who are irritated by 'the enigmaticalness of art' provide, via a 'defective attitude', 'a confirmation of art's truth' (p. 120). Many examples of mainstream poetry can be assessed in terms of Adorno's derision towards the 'reality principle', an 'obsession' that 'places a taboo on aesthetic comportment', and that has resulted in the 'contemporary deaestheticization of art' (p. 120).[20] Compared to mainstream poetics that do not challenge the reader's idioculture, enigmatical artworks of the 'highest dignity' 'await their interpretation' (p. 128).[21] The critic should be humbled in that 'the task of a rendering that will do justice to [such works] is in principle infinite' (p. 186).

Prynne and Enigmaticalness

J. H. Prynne's work might seem to encapsulate the theory of enigmaticalness in *Aesthetic Theory*. If the enigma lies beyond hermeneutics, then Prynne's poetry confronts the reader with the 'empty gaze' of a literary Sphinx (p. 120). Yet this difficulty of interpretation is not coterminous with incomprehensibility: true to his dialectical thinking, Adorno argues that 'incomprehensible works that emphasize their enigmaticalness are potentially the most comprehensible' (p. 122). Eliot's readers would no doubt be surprised to learn that Prynne's *Acrylic Tips* is more 'comprehensible' than Paterson's *Landing Light*. Instead, it is the 'fracturedness' of Prynne's writing that reveals pockets of meaning, at the same time as these fragments point to the overall enigma of his *oeuvre* (p. 126).[22] To paraphrase Adorno on the 'remainder' in *Aesthetic Theory*, the critic can only admit that one understands something of Prynne's work, not that one understands his poetry (p. 122). As in Adorno's account of modernist literature, a poem such as *Acrylic Tips* resists 'significative thinking' (p. 82), at the same time as art – as Jacques Rancière argues in *The Politics of Literature* (2011) – cannot help but be 'significative'.[23] Adorno returns to this problem of mimesis throughout *Aesthetic Theory*, and concludes that art cannot avoid being a form of semblance in that, 'in the midst of meaninglessness, it is unable to escape the suggestion of meaning' (p. 154). As Prynne writes in the letter to Steve McCaffery, that I discuss further in Chapter 2, to challenge the possibility of interpretation is in no way 'to extirpate it' (p. 44).[24] Every line of *Acrylic Tips* resists signification, but does not negate it: for example, as I argued in the Introduction, 'soft sweet fury gums nodding milkwort in river-sway' intertwines the significations of individual words with enigmatical poetics.[25] As with the potentially distinct images of the crowd and petals in the two lines of Ezra Pound's 'In a Station of the Metro' (1913), the first four words in this quotation from *Acrylic Tips* may be distinct from the second cluster: it is only a critical supposition of complete line sense that coerces the reader into thinking that 'gums' must somehow interact with the milkwort. Similarly, 'Ever calling at cirrus credit flapjack' suggests that the final three words might be connected (p. 538), and yet the reader may be pursuing errant hermeneutics if they attempt to connect clouds' precipitating fall streaks with tray-baked oat bars. These words may function as three separate responses to 'Ever calling'; so, atmospheric clouds, money 'on tick' and oats combined with syrup may particularly enamour the poet-narrator. However, 'cirrus' is not so stable in its signification as might initially be imagined: it could refer to clouds commonly known as 'mares' tails', but also, in biological terms, thin, threadlike structures on the body of an animal, a tendril, or, in astronomy, filamentary structures seen in infrared light.[26] Even 'krook' in the first stanza forms a single-word puzzle (p. 537): it may indicate the dialect word 'crook' ('ill'); or it may denote a specific building, the Waalse Krook Public Library in Gent, that is 'stepped' like the rising pathways in the same line; or, less likely, it might appertain to a rotund pimp in urban slang.

Hence these lines and images from *Acrylic Tips* are enigmatic not because of any deduced meaning, but because, as Adorno writes of Beckett's plays, they put 'meaning on trial' (p. 153). Trying to understand a Prynne poem is not akin to participating in a conversation: as readers, we witness a lexical performance in which different discourses, registers and references jostle in complex euphony. Yet, even in modernist music hostile to repetition, Adorno argues, 'similarities are involved', and 'many parts correspond with others in terms of shared, distinguishing characteristics [. . .] without sameness of any sort, chaos would prevail as something ever-same' (p. 141). Reading Prynne's work is often akin to the performance of an enigmatic musical score that Adorno deploys as a metaphor for all art in *Aesthetic Theory*. Readers of lines such as 'Careen through what fortune | caps with a swollen wave, the deck is cluttered with snap' in *Acrylic Tips* may be attentive to its 'minute impulses', the combination and clash of [k], [u], [o] and [æ] sounds, but such readers still do 'not know what he plays'.[27] Colin Winborn argues that Prynne's work – as in these lines – 'insists on cacophony and discordance', but, at the same time, the sequences contain motifs that do not eschew rational interpretation.[28]

In *Aesthetic Theory*, '[H]ermetic and committed art converge' in such discordant refusals 'of the status quo' (p. 248). The satirical elements in *Acrylic Tips* begin with the epigraph 'The murderous head made from a motor car number-plate' (p. 535). This unsettling personification establishes the vision of the head through the image of a number-plate as a mouth and recalls Aldous Huxley's contrasting merriment in *The Doors of Perception* (1954), when, under the influence of mescalin, the novelist encounters an automobile: 'what an absurd self-satisfaction [. . .] Man had created the thing in his own image [. . .] I laughed til the tears ran down my cheeks'.[29] Unlike this hubris, and without J. G. Ballard's simultaneous fascination with destructive technology, Prynne's car joins the litany of sinister technologies throughout *Acrylic Tips*, as in this gothic depiction of workers:

> Split-screen seepage tills. Miracle cheap shots, entitled
>   of the morning bulletin all savage and reckonable,
> raise a clamour to sober digits, true bone mounted
>   like beasts sucking their fill of the cooler morning light (p. 537).

A necessarily provisional reading of this passage would suggest that the tone and diction appear to be satirical: rather than raising a toast to successful business, the raised clamour becomes a din as workers mount their 'sober digits' onto keyboards.[30] This uproar is akin to beasts sucking 'morning light': 'cooler' evokes perhaps both the office 'watering hole' and the 'cooling' of market trading after a frenetic night. Reversing an image of milking cows, the bovine workers may be 'sucking' the teats of the financial market. Prynne returns to similarly abject images of consumer dependence in a stanza where 'Profit', cash and rank (rather than risk) assessment result in the deathly image of 'milk | at a lip trickle' (p. 538). In contrast with the fluidity of capital registered on the computer screens, the motif of the clogged human body runs throughout *Acrylic Tips*: Prynne introduces 'infarct', a region of dead tissue caused by the lack of blood circulation, to contrast with 'heparin', a substance extracted from animal livers to prevent blood clotting.[31] These images of congestion contrast with the misguided vision of a glorious, unfettered capitalism in the two lines I quoted earlier, in which punters 'Careen' through fortune with 'a swollen wave' (p. 538).

This clash of medical and financial discourses points to Prynne's lament for what, as Jacques Derrida commented, 'used to be now and then called humanity', undermining Paterson's charge against apolitical, postmodernist bogeymen in *New British Poetry*.[32] However, as Adorno outlines in relation to Bertolt Brecht's plays in *Aesthetic Theory*, such 'committed' anti-capitalist politics are neither 'dew-fresh' nor surprising (p. 123). As opposed to these writers' innovative uses of form, the authors' politics are the least challenging aspect of Brecht and Prynne's work. In such passages, Prynne's commitment has more in common with Brecht's didacticism than the 'committed' and autonomous art of Beckett and Celan, in which critiques of capitalism appear 'only distantly', yet 'more faithfully and powerfully than do any novels about corrupt industrial trusts' (p. 230). Moreover, the anti-capitalism in *Acrylic Tips* verges on self-parody when Prynne encompasses 'engrish' in the phrases 'Get plenty get quick' (p. 537).[33] Prynne's politics appear more 'distantly' elsewhere, as in the enigmatic ending to

Acrylic Tips: 'pipes to ground glass to unslaked level fields' (p. 546). Initially, the 'ground glass' appears anti-pastoral, compounding the image of human activity in the flooded fields. This reading would equate with Adorno's sense in *Aesthetic Theory* that 'To survive reality at its most extreme and grim, artworks that do not want to sell themselves as consolation must equate themselves with that reality' (p. 39). This semblance results in the anti-pastoral images of a 'sundered' nature throughout *Acrylic Tips*: the motif of cavities recurs in the 'riven grove' (p. 537), 'Ruck flutter at the mouth' (p. 541), 'Cavity grill' (p. 544) and 'open breech' (p. 545).[34] Moreover, the anti-pastoral title of the collection connotes mountains of manufactured fibre, as well as maintaining the possibility that the term 'tips' refers to the ends of acrylic cloth or false nails. Yet 'ground glass' could also signify a more traditional image of a lake bathed in sunlight and a final flourish of lyricism in a poem that has paradoxically grated against a relapse into such unguarded signification. However, the danger of reading the line as redemptive is that it presents the poem as culminating in a lyrical epiphany that belies the scathing politics elsewhere in *Acrylic Tips*. Moreover, such a critical move might pander to Paterson's sense, that in Prynne's work, 'one halfway comprehensible line will stand out, and is often hailed as, an epiphany, a wisdom, or a great literary bravery'.[35] Moreover, the line's ambiguity, and its resistance to absolute semblance and the univocal, ultimately means that its politics and images remain enigmatic, unlike the bovine image in the passage quoted earlier that openly satirises economic machinations.

However, it would be an example of David Caplan's derided 'simple oppositions' to deduce from this reading of *Acrylic Tips* that 'innovative' poetry contains an inherent enigmaticalness at the expense of all other literary forms.[36] In the 'Paralipomena' section of *Aesthetic Theory*, Adorno is suspicious of 'the concept of the new' (p. 270): as with his formulation of 'hating tradition properly' in *Minima Moralia* (1951), any advent of the 'new' must, for Adorno, be dialectical in spirit.[37] Innovation for innovation's sake risks aligning assumed subversion with the simplistic politics of constantly attempting to *épater les bourgeois* (p. 271). Pound's famous dictum to 'make it new', as with any such declaration, 'radiates the allure of freedom', yet also remains in peril of producing a literature of 'putative contingency and arbitrariness' (p. 271).[38] Adorno likens the 'new' to a child at a piano searching for a new chord: whatever new combinations are found, they were always implicit in the finite possibilities of the keyboard. Hence the 'new is the longing for the new, not the new itself' (p. 32). The 'innovative' must be embedded in tradition at the same time as it negates it, and must not mistake itself for pure innovation: as early as 1969, Adorno announced that 'the concept of the avant-garde, reserved for many decades for whatever movement declared itself the most advanced, now has some of the comic quality of aged youth' (p. 25).[39] Hence *Aesthetic Theory* might be seen to chime with, but also grate against, the poetics of *Acrylic Tips*.

However, as I pointed out in the Introduction, the term 'innovative' is necessarily problematic when it is applied to the differing poetics of the London and Cambridge Schools, and remnants of Language poetry. Prynne's work would be better described as metamodernist rather than 'innovative' or 'late modernist', and as forming an exigent resistance to heteronomy rather than a symptom of cultural ossification that the latter phrase implies. Yet, following on from this critique of the 'innovative', the possibility remains that Adorno's theory of enigmaticalness nevertheless accommodates Prynne's poetics too easily. The enigmatic may be a particular concern of literature influenced by modernism, but, as Adorno indicates in his application of the term to pre-twentieth-century literature, it cannot remain absolutely specific to such texts. In the following section, I aim to show that Paterson's theory of mainstream poetics in *New British Poetry* sits uneasily, at times, with his own practice, and the potential enigmaticalness of the more lyrical writing comes to the fore in poems such as 'The Sea at Brighton' from *Landing Light* when he eschews the intermittent tone of demotic chumminess.[40] This discussion indicates that mainstream poets as well as writers from the London and Cambridge Schools can potentially achieve the enigmatical 'remainder', at the same time as an adherence to the 'reality principle' reappears much more frequently in mainstream poetry.[41]

Paterson's Enigma

Unlike *Acrylic Tips*, 'The Sea at Brighton' opens with a stanza that does not resist the referential, but is nevertheless still enigmatic in its combination of abstraction and lyrical ambiguity:

> To move through your half-million furnished hours
> as that gull sails through the derelict tearooms
> of the West Pier; to know their shadowed realm
> as a blink, a second's darkening of the course . . .[42]

In 'A Talking Book' from *Landing Light*, Paterson harangues critics who enjoy 'that sudden quickening of the pulse | when something looks a bit like something else' (p. 26), but the main literary antecedent is clear in the opening lines of 'The Sea at Brighton'. Paterson reimagines Saint Bede's famous metaphor for life as the flight of a sparrow through a mead-hall into darkness: a gull replaces Bede's passerine as it sails through the derelict tearooms of Brighton's West Pier.[43] Closed in 1975, the pier now embodies transience rather than pleasure: the 'million-petalled flower' of being in Philip Larkin's 'The Old Fools' becomes the 'half-million furnished hours' that the bird glides through.[44] Even though the rooms' 'shadowed realm' has something of what Hill terms the 'poetry kit' in his fourth Oxford lecture, the precursors of Bede and Larkin are subsumed into the striking lyricism of the darkness as a 'blink' in life's hours, a 'second's darkening of the course'.[45] Paterson reverses Bede's image, so that the light and life in the hall transform into the dark tearooms, that partly signify the 'death' of decaying memory. Whose memory remains ambiguous: the opening infinitive results in an ambiguous addressee; does the subsequent 'your' refer to the poet, reader or an unnamed other (p. 70)? If addressed to someone else, the poem declares an impossible desire to experience the interlocutor's opaque memory in a mere instant. Aside from the difficulty of rationalising memory as a 'blink', the lines contain further ambiguities that add to their elusiveness. For example, the gull and poet encounter the 'furnished' hours in the contrasting image of the unfurnished ('derelict') tearooms. '[T]heir shadowed realm' is deliberately ambiguous in that it could refer to the tearooms, or memory (the half-million hours), or both simultaneously.

However, these enigmatic subtleties then cease with the ellipsis at the end of the stanza, that signals the incurrence of the 'reality principle'.[46] The subsequent shift in tone constitutes a self-confessed decision not to sustain the lyrical, as if the latter can only persist parenthetically in twenty-first-century British poetry. Rather than a switch between the lyrical and what Peter Robinson refers to as Paterson's demotic 'bloke-speaking-to-you-guys strategy', a parallel adjustment occurs here between lyricism and the empirical that is signalled by the ellipsis.[47] A more prosaic description follows as the bird aims for the Palace (the Royal Pavilions): this image forms an example of Paterson 'giving' the reader a more accessible passage after an enigmatic, and – following his defence of mainstream readers in *New British Poetry* – potentially alienating first quatrain.[48] The only potential lyrical moment in stanza two lies in the movement between the banal personification of the gull 'heading' towards the Pavilions, and the self-consciously poetic verb 'skites':

> The bird heads for the Palace, then skites over
> its blank flags, whitewashed domes and campaniles,
> vanishes. Today, the shies and stalls
> are locked, the gypsies off to bank the silver (p. 70)

The simplicity of 'The bird heads [. . .]' is subverted when the gull 'skites' over flags: akin to the precision that Hill discusses in his fourth Oxford lecture in relation to 'treasured' in Carol Ann Duffy's *The Christmas Truce* (2011), the word indicates that the bird glides as if it were slipping on ice, and changes direction as if smitten with an oblique blow.[49] In contrast, 'heads', 'vanishes' and 'bank' are relatively unsurprising verbs, as Paterson moves away from the enigmatic abstractions of the first stanza (p. 70). These lines do not remain – to deploy Peter Howarth's phrase – 'uncapturable', and implicitly comply with an '*intolerance to ambiguity*' that is resisted in the first stanza.[50] It is as if the potential embarrassment of the lyricism in the previous lines is eschewed in order to 'narrow [the poem's] distance' from the reader, as when Paterson interjects with '*I can't keep this bullshit up*' in the last part of 'Phantom', his extraordinary elegy for Michael Donaghy in *Rain* (2009).[51] As Adorno remarks in *Aesthetic Theory* in relation to the cultural critic, Paterson's poetics are safeguarding from 'losing [their] way' after the enigmaticalness of stanza one (p. 121). The mainstream 'obsession' with the 'reality principle' here 'places a taboo' on Paterson's own 'aesthetic comportment' (p. 120).

Despite this momentary turn from its opening enigma, the lyricism returns in the final stanza:

> *back home from the country of no songs,*
> *between the blue swell and the stony silence*
> *right down where the one thing meets the millions*
> *at the line of speech, the white assuaging tongues.* (p. 70)

These pentameters with conventional metrical leeway might not adhere to the 'fracturedness' of modernist art, but there is no '*intolerance to ambiguity*' at the end of the poem.[52] 'The Sea at Brighton' may appear to be a mainstream poem in terms of its conventional deployment of metre, but this is not conciliatory poetry in that it explains away its evocative images in the first and last stanzas: the narcissistic and 'standardized echo' of the demanding reader cannot solve the *Rätsel* in these final lines (p. 17). Paterson's subversive persona is initially evident in the cheeky redress to a Hindu god when the poet-narrator offers the day to old 'sky-face, pachyderm' in the penultimate stanza, but this is followed by the elusive image of the poet walking along deserted roads above Ganesha's listening. The poet then reminisces about his earlier ruminations over memory: he has returned to the 'blue swell' (the sea) and the 'stony silence'; the latter may represent the truculence of a class since the setting is explicated as '*the first morning of term*' (p. 70).[53] More exactly, the poet-narrator is '*between*' these entities, as if held at a liminal point akin to the 'hinge' of the November forenoon and its shadows earlier in the poem. This 'hinge' is superbly poised with a line break: the 'long | instant' elongates the final word of the twelfth line; the rhythm of the thirteenth then immediately quickens with the word 'instant'. In the final stanza, these liminal points are compounded when the poet announces that they are '*right down where the one thing meets the millions | at the line of speech, the white assuaging tongues*' (p. 70). In a more positive version of the classroom, the lines may mean that instances of thinking, speech or writing conjoin with a multitude of previous thoughts, vocalisations and texts, and also potential future connections. Whereas the first stanza worries about the vicissitudes of memory – fifty-eight years (half a million hours) as merely a 'blink' – the last stanza focuses more positively on connectivity, and the inscription of memories. '*[W]hite assuaging tongues*' refers back to the waves, so that the 'blue swell' transforms into an image of creativity; aptly, since the sea and pier inspired the Brighton lines at the beginning of the poem. Hence the '*millions*' here hearkens back to the 'half-million furnished hours' in the first stanza. The interrupted lyricism of the initial stanza connects with and leads to the allusive and elusive images in the final stanza's italics.[54]

Geraldine Monk's 'Clowning'

Eschewing ellipsis, the closure of 'The Sea at Brighton' nevertheless registers a self-conscious unease with its lyricism through the deployment of italics.[55] However, even if the first and last stanzas of Paterson's poem are – in Adorno's terms – enigmatic, 'The Sea at Brighton' does not, overall, return the 'empty gaze' of 'constitutive enigmaticalness', and is therefore not a metamodernist poem in the sense I explore throughout this book. For a 'constitutive darkening' unhampered by suspicion towards the lyrical (p. 122), we need to turn to a poet such as Geraldine Monk, whose work forms a bridge between Prynne's resistance to signification and Paterson's awkward response to his own lyricism.[56] Monk's collection *Ghost & Other Sonnets* opens with a poem that grates against the 'reality principle' (p. 120), at the same time as the sonnet forefronts an ambiguous response to adolescence:

It started with a tryst and twist of
Lupine lovely arms along a rural railroad
Bank. Winter rose up summer's rise.
Throes of profound bafflement.
Vague was the impression of fossil
Teeth across the false breast
Yearning for a straight line in
Nature digging the *what* that lies
Oblong and lewd in the tube of
Afterlife lingerings.
Unsourced scent so strong it
Overpowered sense and narrative.

Disturbed earth grew stripes.
A stalk broke too far.[57]

Starting with 'It started', the first four lines register the more accommodating diction that the reader experiences elsewhere in the sequence. As in
Basil Bunting's *Briggflatts* (1966), Monk's deployment of alliteration in the
first two lines – with its emphasis on voiceless stops and resonants – cannot
distinguish the poetry at this point from mainstream writing.[58] At the same
time, the 'ghost' of a sonnet introduces the conventional metaphor of the
adolescent as a werewolf with the image of the 'Lupine lovely arms': these
two lines would not be out of place in a Carol Ann Duffy poem.[59]
However, they are brought to an abrupt halt with the awkward caesura
at the beginning of the third line, as adolescent bafflement begins to screen
out adult nostalgia. Longing for a 'straight line in' to adulthood (and sex),
this depicted confusion results in a series of enigmatic images that resist the
'poetry kit': the Eliotian image of winter encroaching on 'summer's rise'
gives way to a sense of disgust in the 'impression of fossil | Teeth across the
false breast'.[60] As indicated with the diction of 'Petrifaction' and the
'megalithic' in the sixth sonnet in the sequence (p. 8), desire here encompasses ancient, mysterious scripts that are nevertheless bound up with the
abject in the 'fossil' teeth that scrape across the 'false', underdeveloped or
male breast (p. 3). Throughout this gothic sequence, Monk associates
abjection with orifices in particular, as with the 'Shady plankton mouth'
that drags with a 'Leery-long' and 'slow green | Face' in the next sonnet
(p. 4). The unsettling and elusive images then continue with the metaphorical switch to sexual desire as akin to nuclear contamination or a time
capsule: the 'megalithic' script of desire (p. 8) should lead to the obscure
'*what*' of fulfilment, but stubbornly remains instead in the 'Oblong and
lewd [. . .] tube of | Afterlife lingerings' (p. 3). An unidentified (but clearly

sexual) 'scent' overpowers 'sense and narrative' both in the depicted adolescent scene and the poetry itself: the 'remainder' here is inextricable from the powerful but elusive experiences of the young couple.[61] Finally, the pastiche of the Shakespearian couplet results in enigmatic personification that avoids the 'poetry kit': the lovers' confusion and frustration opens out into 'Disturbed earth' that 'grew stripes', and a stalk that 'broke too far'.[62] In relation to sonnet 39 that ends with the surreal and disturbing evocation of 'Neglected screams in a field of unwashed forks' (p. 43), Robert Sheppard argues correctly that the poem is 'more powerful for not revealing its content in a narrative unfolding, but through an excess of compressed and detailed violent imagery'.[63] With simple diction, the closure of the first sonnet similarly ensures a 'remainder' with its 'uncapturable' images that respond powerfully to adolescence, but do not accommodate the reader with the 'reality principle' of an ending that could be easily paraphrased or understood.[64]

In relation to Monk's collection *Interregnum* (1994), Christine Kennedy and David Kennedy argue that this elusive 'textual [...] exuberance' is inextricable from the perceived difficulty of Monk's poetry; not, as one might imagine, due to its 'mixing of voices, registers and poetic forms', but as a result of 'its emotional pitch'.[65] This 'pitch' is explicated as inextricable with the 'emotional content of the testimonies of the captured, interrogated and tortured characters of *Interregnum*' that is 'difficult for the reader' to comprehend (p. 24). The Kennedys expand this close reading to comment on 'innovative' poetry as a whole: if the latter is 'difficult this is to do with the type of experience it explores and the intensity with which it does so' (p. 11). Their close analysis of *Interregnum* is cogent throughout their chapter, but I demur from this assumption that the subject matter and reader-response defines the difficulty of 'innovative' poetry, as opposed to its formal elements. For Adorno in *Aesthetic Theory*, the enigma lies beyond mimesis and semblance as the product of formal synthesis – the 'truth content' that I discussed in the Introduction – rather than readerly imbrication in the text (p. 129). In relation to sonnet 29 in *Ghost & Other Sonnets*, for example, what is 'difficult' in writing about a swift and a hot drink? Instead, the original, sinuous and powerful deployment of language – particularly collocation – marks out Monk's enigmatical work as challenging for readers, but not inexplicable:

> A second glance and then another
> Swift. Was it me or? Were my
> Eyes in the back of my beyond-head
> Reeling a bird-riff? I can't rightly
> Remember never having called

Quits with beak. It did a flambé
Shim. Joy within the saucer flipped its
Own volition over. A rare day. So
This was spirit. Dunk away! Tasty
Dregs leave me wanting.
Tell me it's true what I saw in the
Doodle behind the drab.

Burnt toast. Spectaculars undreamt at
Breakfast. Blinds I drew. Ruffle-down riot. (p. 33)

Sonnet 29 reverses the structure of Paterson's 'The Sea at Brighton', as it moves from the more clearly significative beginning to the enigmatic language surrounding the beverage, rather than initiating an unrestricted lyricism that is then self-consciously resisted. Yet the beginning of Monk's poem cannot be extricated from the 'reality principle' that governs mainstream poetry: even the stream-of-consciousness fragment 'Was it me or?' clearly refers back to the opening line's potential glimpse of the elusive swift.[66] However, the sonnet has already triggered its formal resistance. Catalexis avoids the potential iambic pentameter of the first line, which would have been completed with the stressed 'Swift' that – as with the caesura on 'Bank' in the first sonnet – jars at the beginning of the next line: 'A second **glance** and **then** another | **Swift**'. By the third line, the 'reality principle' is complicated when lexical association rather than referentiality takes over the poem's narrative: 'back' might logically be followed with 'of the beyond' or 'of my head'; Monk simultaneously subverts and confirms these expectations with the coinage of 'beyond-head', that encapsulates the potential reality of the bird at the same time as its imaginative rendering.[67]

After the relatively unsurprising [r] alliteration in the fourth and fifth line, the joy of original collocation signals the enigmatic centre of the poem as the real swift or imagined 'bird-riff' 'did a flambé | Shim' (p. 33). The 'reality principle' would insist that the combination of these words – that emphasises their nasal bilabial resonants – somehow reflects the movements of the actual swift as it suddenly changes direction.[68] Yet this 'interpretative reason' is foxed by the conventional meanings of the words: 'flambé' is a cooking procedure in which alcohol is added to a pan in order to create a burst of flames; 'shim' usually means a wedged or tapered piece of material or object that plugs gaps in order to provide a level surface.[69] 'Shim' connotes 'shimmy', which might seem to be the more accurate word, as it denotes the graceful movement of a dance or an effortless and swaying motion. Yet 'shimmy' would still not 'normalize' (in

Sheppard's phrase) the meaning of the 'flambé' swift, to connote, perhaps, its accelerated and yet elegant movements; nor would it provide a linguistic 'shim' for the ambiguity of 'It', which could refer to the 'beak' as well as the swift or 'bird-riff'.[70] However, amongst this sustained enigmaticalness, it would also be wrong to argue that all these words are emptied out of reference, becoming the 'material otherness' that Ron Silliman refers to in his cover blurb for *Ghost & Other Sonnets*. Silliman's comment draws on Archibald MacLeish's comment that poetry 'should not mean | But be'; whilst this may be true of sonnet 29, there is also a 'neediness' in this enigmatic passage that draws the critic back towards interpretative reason.[71] 'Joy' here is partly the joy of language in the previous two lines, with the memorable combination of [k], [ɛi], [m] and [ʃ] sounds, but the subsequent referential linkages of 'tasty', 'dunk' and 'saucer' anchor the sonnet in a significative arena that is mostly absent from Prynne's *Acrylic Tips*. Then again, it would be a critical banality to conclude that the poem is clearly 'about' the Platonic 'spirit' revealed in the vision of a swift, or the transience denoted in an encounter with an empty drink. As soon as the referential 'Dregs' enter the poem, the puzzling language recurs with the lines: 'Tell me it's true what I saw in the | Doodle behind the drab.' The latter word might refer to the 'Dregs', as 'drab' normally refers to fabric of a light-brown colour. Or it might signify the colour of the swifts, in which case the 'Doodle' could be the imagined design behind the birds' seemingly erratic flight.[72] However, given that Monk is attuned in her work to the silencing of women – most memorably, in the accounts of the 'witches' in *Interregnum* – it is unlikely that she is unaware that 'drab' can also archaically mean a 'slattern' or 'prostitute'.[73] There may be a link established here between the female fortune teller who interprets the 'Dregs', the linguistic violence of the 'drab' and the 'Smocked-ones throwing turnips at a witch' in sonnet 48 (p. 54).

However, such interpretative gestures cannot contain the enigmatical writing in the middle of the sonnet that is 'not strictly definable'.[74] As Adorno writes primarily of modernist literature in *Aesthetic Theory*, 'enigmaticalness outlives the interpretation' (p. 125), and this is true even of a poem such as sonnet 29 that lies between the 'deaestheticized' middle section of Paterson's 'The Sea at Brighton' and the anti-significative poetics of *Acrylic Tips* (p. 120). As in Prynne's work, there is an inherent 'clowning' to Monk's poetry that distinguishes it from the 'reality principle' of Paterson's middle stanzas (p. 120). In the 'divergence of the constructive and the mimetic' there is – according to Adorno – an 'element of the ridiculous and clownish that even the most significant works bear and that,

unconcealed, is inextricable from their significance' (p. 119). '[F]lambé |
Shim' has something of this 'clownishness' about it, and the collocation
stands as a synecdoche for the deployment of 'clownish' language in
enigmatical poetry as a whole. As Hill illustrates in his fourth lecture as
Oxford Professor of Poetry, artistic clowning, as opposed to mere buffoon-
ery, is a serious as well as comic matter, as when he introduces himself as
a 'sinister old harlequin bellowing for pittance some gibberish about the
shirt of Nessus', who does not share the mainstream's 'generous and
egalitarian literary-missionary zeal'.[75] Adorno notes that the 'inadequacy
of classicism of any persuasion originates in the repression' of this clowning, 'a repression that art must mistrust' (p. 119): hence the enigma is bound
up with Hill's refusal to 'repress' language. Paterson attempts instead to
separate the lyrical and empirical in 'The Sea at Brighton', which illustrates
perfectly this lexical 'repression' alongside Paterson's adherence to the
harmony and restraint of metrical form. In contrast to 'The Sea at
Brighton', 'Flambé | Shim' risks a 'ridiculousness' that is 'part of
a condemnation of empirical rationality' (p. 119). This ridiculous aspect
of art is one that 'philistines recognize better than do those who are naïvely
at home in art' (p. 119).

For Adorno, this absurdity must be 'shaped' in order to attain the level
of enigmaticalness: in contrast, any clowning that 'remains on the level of
the childish [...] merges with the calculated *fun* of the culture industry'
(p. 119). Serious clowning, the 'constellation of animal/fool/clown', is 'a
fundamental layer of art', and is central to the formation of metamodernist
poetry in the twenty-first century.[76] However, as with Adorno's account of
pre-modernist literature, 'innovative' poetry does not solely engage with
elements of the ridiculous and enigmatic at the expense of all other kinds of
writing, as my analysis of 'The Sea at Brighton' indicates. Yet, despite the
evidence of *Rätsel* in such mainstream writing, the *intensity* of the 'remainder' is clearly more evident in the poetry of Prynne, Monk and Hill, even
if – as Ken Edwards illustrates – the first two poets draw on different
aesthetic traditions to Hill.[77] Whereas Hill's emphasis on what Edwards
terms the lyric voice nevertheless engages with the juxtaposition of registers
and usurpation of metre in a way familiar to readers of *The Waste Land*
(1922) and Pound's Cantos, Prynne's work is far more interested in further
resistances to – but not eschewals of – signification. Indeed, Paterson's
blurring of postmodernist and 'innovative' writing in *New British Poetry*
that I discuss in the next chapter indicates something distinctive about the
development of twenty-first-century British poetry as opposed to other art
forms (p. xxiii). Whereas Daniel Libeskind's 'Building with no Exit' forms

a specific postmodernist response to the utilitarian forms of modernist architecture, the chimera of postmodernist poetry does not demarcate itself from modernist poems with the convenience of a historical epoch or movement.[78] The legacies of modernism are still relevant to complex forms of art that, as in Prynne, Monk and Hill's poems, oppose 'the standardized life'.[79]

Peter Howarth amply demonstrates that claims such as Paterson's for postmodernist characteristics in contemporary poetry can usually be traced back to modernism. Charles Olson, for example, avowed that open field, Projective poetry went beyond modernism in its resistance to individualistic poetics, yet, as Howarth argues, 'getting rid of the controlling "ego" was a basic move within modernism – not just in Eliot's "impersonal" poetry, but in Yeatsian séances and Objectivist procedures'.[80] As I discuss in the next chapter, the 'poetry wars' since the 1970s have produced writing that engages with the enigma in ways that have retained and reimagined the vitality of modernism, rather than angling for its mere reprisal. Paterson's attack on supposed postmodernists in *New British Poetry* and Hill's critique of poetic 'democracy' in his fourth Oxford lecture are just two instances of very different responses to the legacies of modernism in twenty-first-century British poetry. Nevertheless, Ian Gregson wonders if 'there could be a *rapprochement*' between the mainstream and 'parallel tradition', arguing that it could 'produce poetry of immense interest and power'.[81] In Chapter 4, I examine how a younger generation of what Roddy Lumsden terms 'cusp' poets has attempted to engage with this possibility.[82] Due to the divergent traditions informing 'innovative' and mainstream writing, Gregson's vision is distinctly utopian, but it does link with the overlap I have analysed in this chapter between these opposed camps in relation to the enigmatical poetics of Prynne, Paterson and Monk. To put it another way, metamodernist writing is not the preserve of Prynne and other poets in the Cambridge School. At least Gregson's idealist sense of a potential rapprochement between mainstream and 'innovative' literature offers the possibility of sustaining the enigmaticalness of poetry in forms that reject these different traditions as absolute, and as perpetuating a 'knife fight in a phone booth'.[83]

CHAPTER 2

Continuing 'Poetry Wars' in Twenty-First-Century British Poetry

Having analysed the links and tensions in the last chapter between mainstream and 'innovative' poems that wrestle with the concept of enigmatical writing, I now turn to explore the repercussions of the 'poetry wars'. Any engagement with contemporary poetry in relation to David James's sense of a 'recrudescence' of modernism needs to confront the legacies of these arguments over form and literary tradition.[1] In an attempt to consign these conflicts between mainstream and 'innovative' poets to history, David Caplan and Peter Barry argue that we need to 'move discussion beyond the simple oppositions' that impede expositions of contemporary poetry.[2] My account in Chapter 4 of the vacillations between the enigmatic and insouciant in Ahren Warner's poetry indicate this book's wariness towards these 'simple oppositions'. At the same time, I register the latter's endurance, and their critical efficacy in distinguishing – as I illustrated in Chapter 1 – between the elusive 'clowning' in Geraldine Monk's poetry, and Don Paterson's refutation of what he apprehends as lyrical indulgence. For Caplan, the split between mainstream poets and the London and Cambridge Schools cannot adequately differentiate between 'Establishment' poems and the 'innovative', 'experimental' or 'avant-garde'. Similarly, Derek Attridge contends that these critical labels are more distracting than incisive, and that only 'good' and 'bad' poetry is worth noting in each camp.[3] These categories can indeed obscure stylistic differences contained within each binary, but, rather than vying to register the obsoleteness of these terms, I argue that the persistence of enigmatical poetics in mainstream and 'innovative' writing signals that the poetry wars are still continuing today in a modulated form. As I argued in the Introduction, metamodernist poetry by vastly different writers such as Geoffrey Hill and J. H. Prynne is contained within these opposed camps. Nevertheless, when a reader commented that the poetry scene in the UK was 'like a knife fight in a phone booth', this fantasy scenario of violent containment emphasised the tenacity of these 'simple oppositions'.[4]

As one of the few 'Establishment' poets to affirm the existence of the mainstream, Paterson's introduction to *New British Poetry* (2004) ironically proved that the London and Cambridge Schools had not been struggling against a poetic chimera since the early 1970s, at the same time as his embittered writing provided a convenient focus for embattled redress.[5] In a modulated version of these categories, the distinctions between mainstream and metamodernist writing were evident when, seven years after Paterson's polemic, Hill challenged Carol Ann Duffy's conception of democratic art in his fourth lecture as Oxford Professor of Poetry.[6] Yet the gleeful portrayal in 2011 of a 'spat' between two high-profile poets in *The Guardian* omitted the elements in Hill's speech in which he professed to be uncomfortable with his critique of mainstream writing. *The Guardian* also failed to elucidate Hill's ambivalent position in relation to the poetry wars: he has avoided reference to the Cambridge School, at the same time as his modernist antecedents have more in common with the precursors of Prynne's *Acrylic Tips* (2002) than those of Duffy's collections. In Chapter 1, I demonstrated how Theodor Adorno's theory of enigmatical literature and the 'remainder' helps to account for Prynne's resistance to signification.[7] Subsequently, I illustrated through a reading of Paterson's 'The Sea at Brighton' that the possibility of enigmatical poetics in mainstream poetry cannot be accounted for with the absolute purity of Paterson's 'simple oppositions'.[8] In this chapter, I discuss Paterson's controversial anthology in more detail to contextualise these formal 'battles' in relation to Hill's invective against Duffy's account of poetry as equivalent to texting, and to critique the poets' work in relation to their contested ideas of democratic poetry. For Hill, the term 'democratic' is not coterminous with 'accessible': his 'exasperating' poetry encompasses the enigmatical remainder that I consider further in relation to passages from *Scenes from Comus* (2005).[9] In contrast, Paterson's defence of 'accessible' writing is by proxy an attack on the version of metamodernist writing that I outline throughout this book.

New British Poetry and Paterson's Mainstream

Natalie Pollard deploys understatement when she refers to Paterson's 'rather incendiary commentaries on the so-called contemporary divide between mainstream and postmodern poetics' (p. 7).[10] The qualifier 'so-called' indicates a wariness towards this supposed rift, whereas for Paterson the definitive schism of the poetry wars endures: in his introduction to the *New British Poetry*, '"Mainstream" practise [*sic*]' requires defending against the contradiction of a 'general ubiquity' of '"Postmoderns"'.[11] In his poem 'A Talking Book', Paterson warns readers against cursory engagements with texts, yet he himself is guilty of a 'one-day travel pass' into literary and cultural theory when he attempts to tar the London and Cambridge Schools with the erroneous slight of postmodernism.[12] During his T. S. Eliot lecture in 2004, Paterson dismissed postmodernist poetry in a way that actually shaped an unintended attack on metamodernist writing, and, ironically, the modernist poet giving his name to the lecture series.[13] Rather than a specific attack on the playfulness, irony, pastiche and preponderance of non-referentiality in the work of a postmodernist poet such as John Ashbery, Paterson condemns the 'Postmodern' foregrounding of form, the juxtaposition of archaic and contemporary registers and self-conscious artifice, yet the first two aspects are more characteristic of 'high' modernist texts such as *The Waste Land* (1922) and Ezra Pound's *Cantos* (1925) than Ashbery's *oeuvre*. Paterson's more specific complaint that readers may as well pore over the 'Norwich phone book or a set of log tables' as consider Prynne's work indicates that, for Paterson, Prynne – or, more accurately, Paterson's caricature of Prynne – represents archetypal postmodernist poetry, rather than, for example, the pastiche poems of Kenneth Goldsmith.[14] In *New British Poetry*, Paterson awkwardly fuses Language poets with the London and Cambridge Schools into a distinct tribe of postmodernists: there is no critical reflection on the formal (or personal) rifts between the writers within each group, as with Prynne's diatribe against the 'innovative' approach to readership and consumerism in 'A Letter to Steve McCaffery'.[15] Instead, homogenous 'Postmodernists' are accused of a 'joyless wordplay that somehow passes, in their country, for wit'.[16] Paterson laments that the herculean efforts of readers engaging with postmodernist writing should be an embarrassment to the guilty poets, who refuse to provide the 'human courtesy' of providing the context in which they are to be understood (p. xxx).

This description of internecine 'warfare' is hard to countenance in the context of the contemporary novel: it is difficult to imagine a recent novelist berating the postmodernist novels of, say, Thomas Pynchon or John Fowles as 'joyless wordplay'.[17] In contrast with Paterson's diatribe, Adorno writes of those critics who (like Paterson) ignore the enigmatical possibilities of art, and 'embarrass themselves by blathering that art must not forget humanity', and demand meaning 'in the face of bewildering works'.[18] As Tristan Tzara argued in his Dada manifesto of 1918, an entirely comprehensible work 'is the product of a journalist'.[19] In contrast, Paterson disavows the perceived incomprehensibility of postmodernist poetry with his contention in the T. S. Eliot lecture that he seeks only simplicity and precision in his own writing. The latter could equally apply to early modernist writing such as that of the Imagists, but it cannot help but feature in the context of this lecture as a retort not only to his chimera of postmodernist poets, but also to Eliot himself, who argued that modern poetry must be 'difficult' if it is to respond to the complexities of modern life.[20] Contradicting his more positive reference to modernism as 'invigorating' in *New British Poetry*, Paterson argues that the introduction of further complexity beyond his own striving for clarity would be deceitful and inept. In fact, Paterson lauds what Adorno terms 'conciliatory forms', and capitulates to 'the philistine demand that the artwork give [the reader] something'.[21] In contradistinction to the self-interest that Paterson applies to the supposed 'postmoderns', Adorno argues that this 'something' is usually the narcissistic and 'standardized echo' of the demanding reader (p. 17).

Deploying the same terms with which Hill dismissed Philip Larkin's infamous attack on Charlie Parker, Pound and Picasso, the introduction to *New British Poetry* could be said to contain the erudition of the postprandial.[22] In an article that reads akin to a review of Paterson's introduction sixteen years before it was published, Alan Golding argues that such attacks on the avant-garde are symptomatic of a 'scapegoat-hungry literary culture' in which the 'Language group' is 'superficially dismissed with "a few cracks about tedium, fragmentation, a desiccated esthetic [*sic*], and dehumanisation".'[23] Attridge advises that Paterson's 'bad-tempered' piece of writing is best left ignored: it would be tempting simply to follow this advice, were it not for the fact that, as Natalie Pollard points out, Paterson has 'many important allies and supporters' in the contemporary poetry world, and is soliciting 'a steadily increasing academic readership'.[24] Paterson's cultural influence in the field of contemporary poetry can also be measured through his status as chief editor of one of the most extensive poetry lists in the UK; as he has admitted in interview, the poetry that appears on the Picador list owes more to an informal network of mainstream contacts – a 'jungle' vine of connections, as he puts it – than the overall quality of submitted manuscripts.[25] John Redmond, alongside 'innovative' writers and critics such as Robert Hampson, argues that such machinations are symptomatic of a nepotistic 'prize-giving culture, fuelled by favours and networking' rather than intrinsic value.[26] Pollard also notes that Paterson's position could be considered to exemplify an insidious aggression 'common in commercial literary poetics: the corporate publisher's promotion of work that possesses recognisable and accessible formal and linguistic features goes hand in hand with a rejection of alternative formal strategies, and vigorous dismissal of their literary value' (p. 10).[27] In response to Andrea Brady's accusation in the *Chicago Review* that he was acting like a neo-conservative general protecting the establishment, Paterson replied that he regretted his comments in *New British Poetry*, continuing: 'I don't regard them [the 'Postmoderns'] as *they* any more [. . .] the division we created between us [was] entirely false'.[28] After sifting through the invective that the anthology inspired, one can only puzzle over that adverb 'entirely'. In another interview in 2013, Paterson opined that he has 'Far more time for JHP these days, as his language actually honours his project'.[29] He contrasts Prynne's poems with Hill's work: Paterson regards the latter as unethical in that it presents a moral point in language 'likely to confound the reader'. The propositions that Hill has a simple proposal to make in his work – or that Prynne might have an overall 'project' – are unsubstantiated. Despite his disavowal, ten years later, of his introduction to *New British Poetry*, Paterson's more recent attack on Hill's work fuels a sense that he still revels in 'negotiating and perpetuating factions in the contemporary poetry industry' rather than 'entirely' dispelling false distinctions between mainstream and 'innovative' poetry.[30]

In the ensuing furore over Paterson's diatribe, it was easy to forget that an 'innovative' critic had written a comparable essay only four years earlier. Ken Edwards' 'The Two Poetries' examines the similarities and differences between mainstream and 'innovative' writers in an avowal of different aesthetic traditions that might still invigorate twenty-first-century poetry. Edwards describes the 'energetic complexity' of Allen Fisher's antagonistic response to mainstream writing through what he labels as the 'parallel tradition': his article thus forms the equivalent of Paterson's introduction, but from the opposite perspective.[31] Subsequent descriptions of 'The Two Poetries' do not form a prescriptive taxonomy, but Edwards notes that mainstream writing is generally interested in clarity of expression, coherent narratives and a single point of view, whereas the 'parallel tradition' tends to foreground non-normative language use, multiple voices and open form (p. 34). Of course, it is not surprising that an essay published in *Angelaki* – an academic journal focussing on philosophy and literary theory – did not achieve the notoriety of a 'bad-tempered' piece of journalism by a Faber poet. Yet Edwards' article is more measured in its laudable attempt to distinguish between two types of writing; even if alternatives could be provided to his version of mainstream writing in terms of its supposed emphasis on the single viewpoint and lyric voice – Hill's later poetry forms an obvious counterexample – and its disavowal of the politics of form. Edwards' shuttling between mainstream and 'innovative' poetry ultimately indicates that these different kinds of writing may overlap, as in the conception of enigmatical writing I outline throughout this book, but they are not interchangeable. Unlike Paterson, he is also careful not to homogenise 'modernist-derived' poetry (p. 28). Edwards is critical, for example, of Fisher's defence of open signification, arguing – akin to Paterson – that 'the strategy runs the risk of failing entirely to engage the uncommitted reader' (p. 28). On the other hand, he is also critical of Peter Riley's suggestion that 'innovative' poets conspired to marginalise their own work during the 1970s and 80s by resigning *en masse* from The Poetry Society, an event that Barry recounts so compellingly in *Poetry Wars* (pp. 26–7). Instead, Edwards defends Eric Mottram's conception of the 'establishment' as 'a consortium of public funding bodies [and] main-stream commercial publishers' (p. 26), who are 'inhospitable' to art that might derive its impetus from an enigmatical 'remainder' (p. 27).[32] Nevertheless, even if he remains committed to 'modernist-derived' poetry, Edwards does not dismiss the poets on the opposite side to the 'parallel tradition', unlike Paterson in 2004: he praises, for example, a mainstream poem by Matthew Sweeney for its 'economy of means', and its rejection of 'flash' intellectualism (p. 30). However, 'parallel' poetry for Edwards consists purely of 'innovative' writers such as Fisher, Riley and Mottram: Hill's grappling with the legacies of Pound and Eliot in his 'exasperating' and autonomous art is, for example, ignored.[33]

Despite the critical rigour of 'The Two Poetries', then, Edwards' article complies overall with Paterson's construction of a division between 'post-modernist' poetry (the 'parallel tradition') and the mainstream, a rigid opposition that this book challenges with its discussion, for example, of Hill's work, and a new generation of 'cusp' poets such as Warner, Sandeep Parmar and James Byrne.[34] Where can Hill's work be located within this binary? The following passage from Hill's *Scenes from Comus* is not, in Adorno's terms, 'conciliatory', but neither is it bewildering, or excessively playful:

> While the height-challenged sun fades, clouds become
> as black-barren as lava, wholly motionless,
> not an ashen wisp out of place, while the sun fades.
> While the sun fades its fields glow with dark poppies.
> Some plenary hand spreads out, to flaunt an end,

> old gold imperial colours. Look back a shade –
> *Guþriþur Þorbjarnardottir* – over your
> left shoulder or mine | absolute night comes
> high-stalking after us.[35]

This passage both resists and embraces empirical reality: the clouds, sun, poppies and night are comprehensible, yet we also encounter the enigmas of the 'plenary hand' and 'high-stalking' night, and the puzzling Icelandic interjection. Nevertheless, the latter are not conveyed with the mannerist techniques that Paterson associates with 'postmodernist' poets: indeed, metrical dexterity – usually associated with mainstream rather than 'innovative' writing – is more evident in this passage. When Hill writes that there is not 'an ashen wisp out of place', the metre is ironically 'out of place': the metrical break on 'out' allows him to stress, delicately, the imagined perfection of the clouds.[36] Yet the passage is also self-consciously resistant to its own form: after six lines of the epiphanic lyricism that Edwards associates with mainstream writing, awkward poetics enter the poem with the reference to Gudrid Thorbjarnardottir, the 'true central character of the [Icelandic] sagas'.[37] Gudrid does not feature in the early manuscript versions of this poem held in the Brotherton Library, yet the 'off-key' intervention here in the lyrical passage is perfectly apt: the intervention introduces a different linguistic, historical and literary context into a passage about Iceland in order to avoid the lyrical thrust settling into a self-centred rumination on death.[38]

As Edwards puts it in relation to 'innovative' poetry, there is a concern here with non-normative language use, extended vocabulary and a foregrounding of register. As throughout Hill's work, the manipulation of form, and intrusion of awkward poetics, indicates that the lyrical must be hard earned if it is to become anything more than a 'brief gasp between one cliché and another'.[39] This struggle is enacted in the metrical tension throughout the passage: the metrical regularity of the second line (an Alexandrine) contrasts, for example, with the bunches stresses of 'the height-challenged sun fades' in line one. Rather than vying to coerce the reader, the enigmatic passage seems – as Hill remarks of the Duffy poem that I discuss later in this chapter – to 'hover over itself', indicating a concern with precision rather than, as Paterson puts it, the 'human courtesy' of creating a context in which the poem might be understood.[40] A reference that sends the reader to *The Sagas of Icelanders* (1997) in order to discover more about Thorbjarnardottir is hardly 'conciliatory', nor is the evocation of Eurydice and Lot in the final two lines.[41] Yet Paterson would find it impossible to argue, as he does with Prynne's work in 2004, that signifieds and referents are entirely arbitrary in this passage. The extract has more in common with mainstream poetry in its classical engagement with death, and what Robert Sheppard disparagingly terms the 'normalization' of a scene: 'high-stalking' and 'absolute night' echo the 'height-challenged sun', and 'high-stepping' ruin earlier in the sequence (p. 29), but unlike Orpheus and Lot's wife, the poet has no control over his fate.[42] Even if he resists looking over his shoulder at death – as he does not, metaphorically, in this passage – the 'night' remains, like the Furies, implacably persistent.

Carol Ann Duffy's Texting

At the same time, this hermeneutical approach to elusive writing cannot account for the entire meaning of the passage. Whose is the 'plenary hand', for example, that 'flaunts an end': God's, the poet's or both? How can the poppies be dark when the fields are glowing in the disappearing sun? Is it because the flowers are located in the shadows of the sunset? These enigmatic lines eschew such questions that rely on a straightforward relationship between the text and empirical reality, as the stanza engages in lyrical brooding on future death. This passage from *Scenes from Comus* exemplifies Hill's 'twisted' language that 'not only expresses the matter in hand but adds to the stock of available reality'.[43] His work thus offers resistance alongside 'innovative' writing to Paterson's opposition between mainstream and 'postmodernist' poetry. However, Hill's silence on the London and Cambridge Schools does not result in an immunity to the continuing poetry wars.[44] Characterising himself as 'marooned' with his readings of Eliot and Pound in the 1950s, Hill has refrained from commenting on the 'innovative' poets that Paterson dismisses.[45] Nevertheless, in 2011 Hill became more openly antagonistic towards the 'conciliatory forms' that Paterson endorses.[46] The continuing poetry wars emerged in unfamiliar territory when, during his fourth lecture as Oxford Professor of Poetry, Hill criticised Duffy's poetry as simplistic, and proposed an alternative and distinctly metamodernist conception of democratic writing.

Initially, Hill directs his ire at the (then) Poet Laureate's attempt to equate texting with poetic language. Duffy's comments first appeared two months earlier in an interview published in *The Guardian*:

> The poem is a form of texting ... it's the original text [. . .] it's a way of saying more with less, just as texting is [. . .] it allows feelings and ideas to travel big distances in a very condensed form [. . .] The poem is *the* literary form of the 21st century. It's able to connect young people in a deep way to language ... it's language as play.[47]

Duffy's vindication of 'text-speak' is analogous to some linguists' attempts to resist the clamour around texting's supposed debasement of language, such as David Crystal's monograph entitled *Txtng: The Gr8 Db8* (2009).[48] Hill's counterargument is that texting forms truncated instances of language that, unlike poetry, are not condensed into an 'intensely crafted and parallel world'.[49] Jeffrey T. Nealon takes a different stance to Duffy and Hill on such compressed language: if advertising and the greeting card industry 'have completely territorialised short, pithy expressions of "authentic" sentiment', he opines, 'showing us how to reenchant even the most mundane corners of everyday life [. . .] then what's left for poetry to do in a post-postmodern world?'[50] Hill's response would be that this textual brevity does not 'reenchant'; only the intensely imagined, parallel world of enigmatical poetry can succeed in this process. For Duffy, 'pithy expressions of "authentic" sentiment' allow contemporary poetry to operate alongside such commodified language. Duffy, he argues, is 'policing' her remit as the Poet Laureate with over-statements such as poetry is the most efficacious literary form of the twenty-first century in a laudable attempt to make poetry more attractive to schoolchildren.[51] In contrast, Hill depicts himself in the fourth Oxford lecture as a 'sinister old harlequin bellowing for pittance some gibberish about the shirt of Nessus', who does not share Duffy's 'generous and egalitarian literary-missionary zeal'.[52]

Despite such 'generous' comments, Hill argues that Duffy's anti-élitist vision of democratic poetry hinders the quality of her own writing. He quotes the middle section of Duffy's poem 'Death of a Teacher' from the article in *The Guardian*:

> You sat on your desk
> swinging your legs, reading a poem by Yeats
> [. . .] and I [. . .] heard the bird
> in the oak outside scribble itself on the air.[53]

Hill then asserts that these are 'cast-off bits of oligarchical commodity English, such as is employed by writers for Mills and Boon and celebrity critics appearing on *A Good Read* or *The Andrew Marr Show*'.[54] For Charles Bernstein, lines such as 'You sat on your desk | swinging your legs, reading a poem by Yeats' would be symptomatic of mainstream 'craft', that eschews the enigma, and 'denotes not the modernist aesthetic of difficulty and technical complexity, but the apparent simplicity and seemingly straightforward use of the direct personal voice'.[55] Those poets, such as Lemn Sissay, who crowded to defend the Laureate's 'voice' in the aftermath of the lecture were particularly incensed at Hill's further accusation that the poem 'could easily be mistaken for a first effort by one of the young people she wishes to encourage'.[56] Sissay was certainly right in that many teachers of creative writing would be delighted if a first-year student composed a line equivalent to one in which a bird 'scribble[s] itself on the air', but for Hill such an image is symptomatic of poetry that is lazily composed, and then celebrated as inclusive.[57]

Hill's criticisms share 'innovative' writers and critics' distrust towards the unreflective championing of supposedly democratic poetry.[58] For Hill, these reservations extend to a simplistic lauding of democracy itself. Often attacked as a conservative writer, it may come as a surprise to his detractors that in this Oxford lecture Hill displays a suspicion towards democracy similar to that of Che Guevara, who thought that the concept must mean more than elections that are 'managed by rich landowners and professional politicians'.[59] Rather than 'a system of government in which *all* people [. . .] are involved in making decisions about its affairs', Hill depicts western democracy as a disguised plutocracy; in other words, a state in which we are ruled by a small and extremely wealthy group of people.[60] Democracy constitutes a paradox in that it can never satisfy 'all people': the political scientists Martin Gilens and Benjamin Page point out, for example, that the majority of American voters have little influence over policies adopted by the US government.[61] Rather than endorsing John Carey's attack on modernism as an élitist attempt to stem the 'triumph of "hyperdemocracy"', Hill would have agreed with Herbert Read that any ideal of democracy – such as sortition – had been replaced by the mid-twentieth-century with 'the ascendant oligarchy of monopoly capitalism'.[62] Published just two months before Hill's lecture, Jeffrey A. Winters' article on oligarchy and democracy suggests that the two terms are, as Hill proposes, not mutually exclusive in the contemporary, unlike the example of the Athenians attempting to reduce the power of a professional ruling class via elections in the fourth century BC.[63] For Winters, the terms now operate 'within a single system, and American politics is a daily display of their interplay'. Composing his lecture at the start of the Eurozone crisis, Hill argues that we participate not in European democracies, but in 'finance oligarchies with aristocratic and democratic trimmings'.[64] His response to Greek debt resonates with that of the radical finance minister Yanis Varoufakis when Hill complains that elected European governments have been dissolved 'by fiat of an international finance rating agency'. Alison Gibbons, Robin van den Akker and Timotheus Vermeulen argue that such concerns are key to the historicity surrounding their version of metamodernism. They point out that the

International Monetary Fund conceded that the austerity measures imposed on Greece were 'an unnecessarily cruel and highly unproductive act [. . .] as the plight of the many unemployed young people in, especially, Greece and Spain underlines'.[65]

It is not clear how seriously Hill took these views on oligarchy, and he may well be guilty of accepting a 'one-day travel pass' into the field of political theory.[66] Nevertheless, it is important to consider how this Readian thinking interweaves his account of supposedly democratic poetry. Like Christopher Beach in *Poetic Culture* (1999), Hill attacks the mainstream's 'complicity in reified systems of discourse' (p. 80), not from the perspective of the 'avant-garde', but from the viewpoint of a writer of enigmatical poetry who has ignored the 'parallel tradition'. For Hill, Duffy's accessible 'Death of a Teacher' is actually symptomatic of a culture in which complexity is denigrated in order to perpetuate literature that is 'familiar' and 're-assuring' for Hampson and Barry's 'general poetry reader'.[67] Similarly, Tim Kendall argues that the analogy between the popular and democratic is 'entirely false', and bemoans proponents of what he terms 'pop poetry', who are 'fixated with [the] market, with giving the people what they think they want'.[68] Moreover, the popular does not necessarily equate with copious sales: as Paterson admits, many of the poets included in *New British Poetry* enjoy only a limited readership, whereas, as Kendall points out, Hill, the 'bugbear of those who advocate a people's poetry, manages to sell far more books, worldwide, than [. . .] the so-called popular poets' (p. 26).[69] Indeed, Hill's 'bellowing' – as he himself terms it in his Oxford lecture – is encapsulated in Kendall's contention that 'serious poetry, being élitist, is the greater servant of democracy than its pop cousin' (p. 26).

In contrast, Paterson's vision of mainstream writing pretends, falsely, to be democratic: for Hill, this 'oligarchical creative style' actually represents a debased English that is as 'frenetic and passive' as excited participants at a winter sale.[70] Hill thus aligns himself – without comment – with 'innovative' writers who also believe that popular tirades against 'difficult' poetry are a form of cultural tyranny. As Mottram bemoans in *New British Poetries* (1993), 'if Eliot, Pound, David Jones, MacDiarmid, Bunting or Dylan Thomas turned up today with their unknown works', the chances of publication with a large UK publisher 'would be nil' (p. 49). A quarter of a century after the publication of Mottram's chapter, his admonition can still be applied to contemporary poetry, despite the tokenistic efforts of publishers such as Picador and Carcanet to feature the work of 'innovative' writers such as Tom Raworth and Denise Riley; after, of course, their reputations have been established by the labour and risks of smaller presses.[71] In accord with Hill's attack on simplistic reviews of poetry in what 'used to be broadsheets but are now tabloids', Hampson also argues that reviews of mainstream poetry are always reassuring, and eulogise poems that 'contain some kind of utilitarian reference' that has 'an easily paraphrasable meaning'.[72] For Hampson and Hill, 'accessible' poems, like propaganda – and unlike enigmatical poetry – are easily understood: Hill underlines this connection with a reference to Joseph Goebbels who 'managed [. . .] the tricks' of oligarchical culture in the form of the media perpetuation of Nazi myths, and his rejection of modernist art as decadent.[73] In his defence of modernist literature, Peter Howarth argues that 'Plain speaking or "easy" poetry [. . .] will not be real communication, but a complicated culture's fantasy of plain speaking, which actually reinforces sentimental ideas about being in touch with the real or the democratic'.[74] Against the 'oligarchical strut' of career politicians who pretend to be 'in touch' with the people, Hill recommends in his fourth Oxford lecture that writers engage instead in constructive, Swiftian obscenity.

Whereas some 'innovative' poets dismiss the 'bargain basement offerings of the Centre's noisy trash', however, Hill demurs from such attacks on the mainstream with his coterminous if uneasy defence of Duffy's version of democratic writing.[75] In the interest of 'simple oppositions', these comments were elided in the report on his controversial lecture in *The Guardian*.[76] Hill's additional, and, he admits, 'incompatible' reaction to 'Death of a Teacher' is that this is actually democratic language 'pared to the barest bean', and he would not have the 'moral courage' to write in such a manner.[77] It is unlikely that many 'innovative' poets would ever engage with Duffy's poetry written for children, yet Hill goes on to praise the word 'treasured' in *The Christmas Truce* (2011):

> But it was Christmas Eve; *believe*; belief
> thrilled the night air,
> where glittering rime on unburied sons
> treasured their stiff hair.[78]

Whereas 'thrilled' and 'glittering' are part of a 'standard poetry kit', Hill argues – despite the latter's fleeting appearance, in a modulated form, in Eliot's *Four Quartets* (1943) – 'treasured' is 'magically' placed, so that the poem seems to 'hover over itself' in metapoetics that utilitarian texting would find impossible to achieve.[79] The same phenomenon occurs in Michael Symmons Roberts's poem 'My Father's Death' from *Mancunia*

(2017). At the beginning of the poem, a wedding bowl is smashed, predictably, into 'smithereens', but four stanzas later the 'poetry kit' is certainly not in evidence when an apple is 'pursed with mould' in a 'magical' moment of poetic condensation.[80] Hill's extolling of Duffy's 'treasured' as a 'well-struck thing resonating' – without a subsequent explanation of exactly why the word is 'beautifully chosen and placed' – links to my discussion in the last chapter of the enigmatical poetics in Paterson's 'The Sea at Brighton'.[81] '[T]reasured' works 'magically' partly because it connects back to the precious medal, moon and soldiers' aspirations introduced nineteen lines earlier: the bereaved mothers become the 'rime' that then 'treasures' the corpses. (It may be significant that Hill also deploys a pun on rime/rhyme in *Scenes from Comus* [p. 29], and is remembering this line seven years after the publication of that collection.[82]) However, this rational explanation of echoing diction and repeated imagery in Duffy's poetry still does not quite account for the 'magical' and resonant singularity of 'treasured'.[83] The enigmatical precision of the 'treasured' hair is central to Hill's sense of 'well-struck' poems: even though the concept of the enigma arises out of Adorno's account of modernist art, it provides an opportunity to create poetic resonance in both mainstream and 'innovative' poetry.

Nevertheless, Hill's account of one word in Duffy's poem as resonating beautifully should not occlude the glaring differences between this meta-modernist poet 'marooned' with Eliot and Pound, and Duffy's 'democratic' writing, in which language is pared to its 'barest bean'. Duffy's 2012 collection *The Bees* commences, for example, with the 'poetry kit' of repetitive alliteration: in the first poem, 'Bees', the bilabials afford both a pun on the subject matter, and establish connections between the insects, diction and poetry with 'my bees, | brazen, blurs on paper, | besotted; buzzwords'.[84] The 'accommodated' reader is carried along with the alliteration, that then changes to 'golden', 'glide', 'gilded', 'glad' and (again) the 'poetry kit' of 'golden' (p. 3).[85] Duffy's poet-bees have 'Been deep' in flowers, searching for pollen, but this does not result in enigmatical poetry that, following Hill's description of 'treasured' in *The Christmas Truce*, 'hovers' above itself. The opening line ('Here are my bees') introduces the subject matter and medium of the collection in a way that becomes self-confident (the bees are 'flawless' and 'wise'), but which the quality of the poem itself undercuts (p. 3). A predictable ending that consummates the overriding metaphor ('honey is art') takes place within an unpredictable form that consists of iambic trimeter, but with eight regular lines and seven diversions. Within the collection's dominating metaphor and subject matter there is a sense of 'democratic' language and poetry that belongs, like the bees, to everyone: from this (and Paterson's) perspective, to alienate the reader in the first poem through intricate form and language would be an artistic betrayal. However, according to Hill's Oxford lecture, such writing becomes indistinguishable from that of a first-year creative writing student in its eagerness to accommodate the reader.[86]

Such barbed criticisms in Hill's 2011 lecture are also implicit critiques of the role of Poet Laureate. The 'gilded' and 'golden' cover of *The Bees* announces that Duffy was the 'Winner of the Costa Prize for Poetry 2011', and that the collection is the property of the Poet Laureate. However, the latter role encompasses an ambiguous heritage, one that includes William Wordsworth as well as Thomas Shadwell; John Dryden in addition to Colley Cibber. In 1671, the tradition of lampooning the Laureate was initiated when the Duke of Buckingham ridiculed Dryden's work: the Duke also caricatured him as 'Bayes', a name that was subsequently applied 'to several future Laureates'.[87] Colley Cibber has become the apotheosis of 'Bayes': after his first 'New Year Ode' was performed in 1730, the 'wits were at once in full cry and parodies, lampoons, epigrams and the like crowded all the papers'.[88] Even the more recent example of Ted Hughes, who was the Poet Laureate between 1984 and 1998, forms a problematic antecedent: the relative success of his first Laureate piece 'Rain-charm for the Duchy' – with 'Cranmere's cracked heath-tinder', and the 'ulcer craters [...] of river pools' – gives way to the formal failures of 'Two Poems for Her Majesty Queen Elizabeth the Queen Mother' and 'A Birthday Masque', with their ponderous mythic accounts, respectively, of the 'Land of the Lion' and the 'Angel of Water'.[89] As Kenneth Hopkins bluntly puts it in *The Poets Laureate* (1973), the role has 'led to the composition of a huge body of the worst poetry in the world': he adds that 'to this appointment we owe the greatest political satires in English poetry, satires which are perennially fresh long after the dust of their occasion has settled'.[90] Thomas Shadwell introduced the custom of writing poems for specific occasions, for the delectation of the monarchy and hoi polloi, such as the start of a new year, and the monarch's birthday: a tacit accommodation to a wide readership who would not be familiar with the latest trends in contemporary poetry is contained within the Laureate's expected public duties, alongside the undeniable perk (revived by John Betjeman) of a barrel of sherry.[91] Duffy – to the chagrin of the *Daily Mail* – refused to write poems to mark royal occasions during her laureateship, apart from odd pieces such as 'Rings', that was penned for Prince William and Kate

Middleton's royal wedding in 2011. However, she has turned to occasional poems in a different sense, to mark, for example, the decline of the analogue gas meter, an injured David Beckham and the bric-a-brac sold in Oxfam. In 2009, Duffy became 'one of 12 famous Britons' helping to launch a charity campaign, Oxfam's 'Give a Helping Hand'.[92] Following Hill's assessment of the laureateship in his Oxford lecture, perhaps he would have condoned such generous community work as beyond his 'moral courage', but he certainly would not have approved of the ensuing poem in *The Bees*, 'Oxfam', that lists items sold in the shop, including a tie, bowl and boots, along with their prices, such as '50p' for the tie and '£9000' for 'Rare 1st ed. Harry Potter and the Philosopher's Stone' (p. 19).[93]

Democratic Poetry and *Scenes from Comus*

Whereas Paterson argues that democratic poetry should not embrace complexity, and prefers 'conciliatory forms' – such as this list of items – that 'give [the reader] something', Hill's poems evince a different form of literary democracy, in which enigmatical writing encourages the reader to engage intensively with the work, as meaning is only gradually and never totally revealed over multiple performances.[94] As I argued in the Introduction, a critical appraisal of such writing often approaches poems as if the critic were a 'plenary' figure who hovers over the language, understanding perfectly every denotation and nuance. Yet I would argue that this hardly reflects the process and challenge of reading metamodernist poetry. Sometimes, Hill's language does not 'give' the reader much poetic information in Paterson's terms, yet the 'event' of subsequent readings can lead to further interpretations, as with the following passage from *Scenes from Comus*:

> Heady September heat with shadows thrown
> across white walls. Sun – fetching us this instant!
> Where áre we sans our lovers, yoú name the place?
> The place itself is common; I have been here
> many times and enough.
> Love's grief is full, always popular,
> like ghosted memories or the old
> fashioned chara-tours,
> like the Welsh hills covered in rhododendrons (p. 41)

Hill concedes in relation to *Speech! Speech!* (2000) that some readers may find his work just difficult – rather than enigmatic – but retorts that he merely aims to fulfil Milton's description of poetry as 'more simple, sensuous, and passionate' than other arts.[95] Section 53 begins with what Paterson could not dispute as the 'simple' and 'sensuous' clarity of an epiphanic image in which the sun, rather than being dismissed by the amorous couple at the start of John Donne's 'The Sunne Rising', immediately obeys the implied lovers by 'fetching' them 'this instant' (p. 41). Hill then undercuts the sun's metaphysical duress with an elegiac lament for an unnamed place, 'sans' lovers. '[S]ans' may appear affected on a first reading, but subsequently it can be recognised as deliberately echoing D. H. Lawrence's *Sons and Lovers* (1913). Reasons for this intertextual link remain unclear, however: a comparison between the Welsh landscape and the Nottinghamshire and Derbyshire vistas of the novel remain possible but indeterminate; an echo of Paul Morel's angst towards his lovers Miriam and Clara (and mother Gertrude) in the novel is also a potential but unspecified connection. The place 'sans our lovers' is unidentifiable, yet is paradoxically 'full' and 'common [. . .] enough': the latter phrase certainly puns on 'common' as in collectively owned land.

Scenes from Comus ruminates on love, ageing and sex throughout, from the 'Titagrams' that still 'work' as 'balls-ache at the threshold' of death in section 3 of 'The Argument of the Masque' (p. 4), to the mask 'not of perversion' in 'Courtly Masquing Dances', but of 'contrived' sleep (p. 36).[96] Rather than dwell on enduring desire (as in section 3 of 'The Argument of the Masque'), 'enough' here functions as a call for the cessation of 'Love's grief'. Evoking a sense of the democratic by describing the latter as 'common' and 'popular' – but with the possible connotation of 'vulgar' too – Hill then eludes the conciliatory with an enigmatic succession of four similes to encapsulate this popularity. 'Love's grief' is 'like a ghosted memoir', as if mourning were somehow scripted by a third party, with unsatisfactory results; the comparison retains the sense in the previous line of this psychological state as akin to a sensationalist confession. By deploying a line break to separate 'old' from 'fashioned', Hill is then able to pun momentarily on this grief as being 'like' the elderly, but also akin to the elusive efficacy of the image of 'old | fashioned chara-tours'. Mourning for love may be akin to a charabanc tour in the sense that it appears almost comically distant, but its meaning remains far from clear and conciliatory. Finally, this enigmatic image is compounded with the simile of grief 'like the Welsh hills covered in rhododendrons'. Rather than a straightforward lyrical moment of personification, the image may be returning to and transforming the idea of 'Love's grief' as 'common'. After all, *Rhododendron ponticum* is threatening to overwhelm the natural habitat in the United Kingdom and Ireland with its hardy roots. Alternatively, the 'like' in the stanza's final line may switch to indicate a specific instance of 'Love's grief' that is briefly referred to, but then withheld.

Yet again, clearer understandings of this enigmatic passage must be left for future readings of *Scenes from Comus*, at the same time as the reader can still appreciate fragmented meanings and intertexts, and the sonority of the 'simple, sensuous, and passionate' lines of section 53.[97] It may be retorted that I began my analysis of Hill's stanza with an appeal against a pretended critical 'mastery' of the passage, but subsequently attempt to perform just that kind of reading. In reply, I would return to Adorno's paradox in *Aesthetic Theory* that enigmatical works of art withhold their meaning, at the same time as the critic's task is precisely to understand them. In the close reading above, I have also indicated the moments that slip beyond the critic's grasp and – to deploy Adorno's term – 'darken' when a provisional understanding of a singular passage does not 'extinguish the enigmatical-ness' of an artwork.[98] Beyond the potential fatuousness of the ghosted memoir, Hill is maybe striving for a new language to pinpoint 'Love's grief', yet the final similes remain as elusive as this 'common' yet amorphous psychological state.[99] As I argued in the Introduction, Hill's reading of Eliot's *Four Quartets* in particular is central to the allusive and enigmatic ending of *Scenes from Comus*, when the book concludes with 'Ephemera's durance, vast particulars | and still momentum measures of the void' (p. 66). Eliot's oscillations between the general and particular are replicated in this closure, but with the additional impishness of an interjecting voice in Hill's work ('What did you say?') that challenges his potentially grandiose evocation of a sublime landscape (p. 66). In contrast, Duffy's later poetry is full of such impishness, as in *The Bees* when she anticipates the full rhyme for 'My beautiful daughter' with 'Orta St Giulio' (p. 69). However, *The Bees* does not entertain the counterpoint of poetry that responds to the concept of democratic writing as a formal challenge. Whether in the guise of Hill's *Scenes from Comus* or the 'innovative' poetics of Geraldine Monk that I analysed in Chapter 1, metamodernist poems' resistance to accommodation cannot help but perpetuate the poetry wars in a modulated fashion. Rather than adhere to Paterson's default position of aesthetic conciliation, and provide the reader with the narcissistic and 'standardized echo' of their own idioculture, such poetry allows our critical acumen to be challenged, and, sometimes, to be defeated.[100]

CHAPTER 3

Committed and Autonomous Art

In *The Orchards of Syon* (2002), Geoffrey Hill is delighted or awe-struck by enigmatic yet quotidian aspects of nature, as when 'prinking' butterflies delicately fuss 'this instant', and a fell changes colour as sunlight moves its 'banded spectrum'.[1] For this poet, such epiphanies are often coterminous with grace: these 'small' metaphors are indicators of the whole puzzle of existence that Eleanor Cook acknowledges to be the 'largest of tropes'.[2] In Chapter 1, I examined Theodor Adorno's conception of the enigma in relation to J. H. Prynne's *Acrylic Tips* (2002) and Geraldine Monk's *Ghost & Other Sonnets* (2008), and argued that Don Paterson's 'The Sea at Brighton' vacillates over but ultimately rejects 'exasperating' writing that surpasses the reader's idioculture.[3] In the last chapter, I discussed the modulation of the poetry wars in relation to Hill's dismissal of 'public' writing in his fourth lecture as Oxford Professor of Poetry, and subsequently examined the 'remainder' in passages from *Scenes from Comus* (2005).[4] I now proceed to explore the concept of enigmatical poetry in the wider context of Adorno's discussion of autonomous and 'committed' art.[5] Literary enigmas are not coterminous with autonomous writing, but they are certainly integral aspects of such work: in *Aesthetic Theory* (1970), the 'remainder' arises out of art that affirms its recalcitrance as 'the social antithesis of society' (p. 8), at the same times as it is 'related to its other as is a magnet to a field of iron filings' (p. 7). In 'Commitment', an essay written seven years before *Aesthetic Theory*, Adorno contrasts 'committed' literature that perceives art in an 'extra-aesthetic' fashion with 'drossless works' (p. 6) that resist the 'spell' of 'empirical reality' (p. 5). I therefore engage first in this chapter with two 'committed' works of literature – Tony Harrison's *The Kaisers of Carnuntum* (1996) and *The Labourers of Herakles* (1996) – in order to focalise Hill's ruminations over elusive moments of awe and grace. At the same time, I begin to develop an account of enigmatical poetry that forges '*der Rest*' out of engagements with specific modernist antecedents, a form of analysis that I shall return to in

Chapters 4 and 5: in this instance, Hill responds to Paul Celan's *Atemwende* (1967) with a loquacious departure from Celan's later minimalism.[6] In contrast, Harrison's verse underlines that wrestling with modernist lineage concurs with understandings of metamodernism that are bound up with intertextuality, but does not fulfil the definition of metamodernist poetry as enigmatic that I outline throughout this book.[7]

Harrison's verse plays react to political modernism in that they are an endorsement of as well as a 'departure' from Bertolt Brecht's theatre.[8] Developed in collaboration with the stage designer Jocelyn Herbert, *The Kaisers of Carnuntum* and *The Labourers of Herakles* – the latter of which was performed at the University of Leeds in 2017 – draw on Brecht's minimalist props, interjected narration, audience participation and interspersed songs or music, in order to create what Raymond Williams referred to as 'the consciously participating, critical audience' in epic theatre.[9] Yet the links between Brecht and Harrison have never been studied in detail: perhaps this anomaly is due to a common misperception in which Harrison revokes modernist writing, despite his ruminations on Joseph Conrad, Arthur Rimbaud, Ezra Pound and the modernist Bulgarian poet Geo Milev in, respectively, *The Loiners* (1970), *V* (1985), *The Gaze of the Gorgon* (1992) and *Metamorpheus* (2000).[10] Nevertheless, in these texts and the verse plays, Harrison's impassioned narration and didacticism sometimes cohere at the expense of formal achievement. In 'Commitment', Adorno argues that the politics of Brecht's plays are less radical than the formal experimentation of his theatre, whereas autonomous art that aspires to the enigma engages with a 'deluge' of historical and political calamities, but rarely signifies them directly.[11] As with Adorno's critique of Brecht's plays, it is the more 'singular' aspects of Harrison's verse plays rather than their politics that are the most arresting aspects of the poet's work, such as Marcus Aurelius' opening speeches in *The Kaisers of Carnuntum*, and those of the workers in *The Labourers of Herakles*, that are entirely conducted in ancient Greek, recalling Ezra Pound's use of untranslated Greek, Latin and Chinese in the Cantos.[12]

Harrison and Hill are usually labelled as mainstream poets, but their 'committed' poetics differ vastly: in contrast with these verse plays, Hill addresses a 'deluge' of atrocious twentieth-century events in *The Orchards of Syon*, but through Adorno's dialectical conception of committed *and* autonomous art.[13] As Hill's notebooks for *The Orchards of Syon* exemplify, lyrical moments are under constant pressure in this collection, as when the 'kempt fields | basking' outside York open out into subsequent references to Ivor Gurney and Wilfred Owen (p. 17), or when the Normandy *bocage* is interlaced with the 'sloughed odours of death' from obliterated tanks (p. 44). The title's Orchards of Syon are like the *purpurnem Gewühle* ('purple turbulence') in Eduard Mörike's poetry that Adorno discusses in 'On Lyric Poetry and Society': as with the impending industrial revolution in relation to Mörike's sky, the presence of the 'deluge' in Hill's collection is intertwined with passages of exquisite lyricism.[14] These ensuing awkward poetics contrast with the composition of the similarly committed and autonomous art in Celan's *Atemwende*. This collection comprises the most extensive modernist influence on *The Orchards of Syon*: the title is referenced six times in Hill's book, as he considers different translations for the title, such as 'breath-hitch' (p. 28), 'catch-breath', 'breath-ply' (p. 31) and 'breath-fetch' (p. 32). Compared to Celan's minimalist lyric 'breaths' in *Atemwende*, however, Hill has produced seventy-two extensive stanzas in one of the most extraordinary poetry collections of the twenty-first century. Harrison and Hill are both metamodernist writers in an intertextual sense of the term in that they draw on specific modernist authors in order to create the verse plays about Herakles and *The Orchards of Syon*. However, only the latter constitutes a truly enigmatical text in the definition I have outlined so far in this book: the attentive reader is drawn back to *The Orchards of Syon* time and again in order to re-read the puzzles of the lyrical epiphanies, but without being able to 'solve' the collection.

Autonomous and Committed Art: Theodor Adorno's 'Commitment'

In *What is Literature?* (1948), Jean-Paul Sartre contends that autonomous literature in the mid-twentieth century has become separated from history and politics: he adheres to Brecht's theory of 'culinary' art that, as 'spiritual dope traffic', is merely a 'home of illusions'.[15] In contrast, Adorno argues that this perceived ahistoricism leads to a misreading of modernist literature.[16] Sartre reacts against this supposed 'idle pastime' of art with his treatise on commitment in *What is Literature?*, whereas Adorno emphasises a potential fusion of autonomous and committed art.[17] Superficially, the enigmaticalness of Samuel Beckett's work may appear less 'committed' than Harrison's verse plays or Brecht's political theatre. Yet for Adorno, autonomous art such as Beckett's work – and Hill's poetry – engages more intensely with history and politics, at the same time as avoiding 'popularization and adaptation to the market' (p. 190). Beckett's plays and novels 'deal with a highly concrete historical reality: the abdication of the subject'; his work – and Franz Kafka's prose – 'have an effect by comparison with which officially committed works look like pantomimes' (p. 191).[18] Such examples of committed and autonomous literature are 'necessarily detached as art from reality', whereas 'art for art's sake' is a flawed version of autonomous art that pretends it has nothing to do with politics via its evasive, 'absolute claims' (p. 178). In contrast, Adorno's concept of committed and autonomous art 'dissolves' the 'tension' between these 'two poles'. Sartre focuses instead on a positivistic notion of committed literature in which a transparent relationship exists between the signifier and referent, rather than arguing, as Adorno does, that the formal properties of art transform the signified. In Chapter 1, I explored Prynne's resistance towards signification in *Acrylic Tips*: rather than comply with Sartre's version of literature that attempts to convey a 'message', Adorno argues that readers should instead 'listen patiently' to texts such as Prynne's, whose language 'challenges signification and by its very distance from meaning revolts in advance against positivistic subordination' (p. 179).

In enigmatical works of art such as *Acrylic Tips*, hermeneutics are not – as they are for Sartre – the most important aspect of such literature: after all, 'meanings' are 'the irreducibly non-artistic elements in art' (p. 178). It is not the 'office of art to spotlight alternatives' to reality, as in Sartre's vision of 'committed' art, but to 'resist by its form alone the course of the world' (p. 180).[19] Hence Adorno admires Brecht's recourse to modernist and avant-garde 'aesthetic forms', but is less enamoured with the political commitment that threatens to undermine his plays (p. 180). For example, Brecht's understanding of Nazism primarily in terms of capitalism results in a false allegory in *The Resistible Rise of Arturo Ui* (1958):

> Instead of a conspiracy of the wealthy and powerful, we are given a trivial gangster organization, the cabbage trust. The true horror of fascism is conjured away: it is no longer a slow end-product of the concentration of social power, but mere hazard like an accident or a crime [. . .] for the sake of political commitment, political reality is trivialized.[20]

Aside from the first clause, this analysis constitutes Adorno's most perceptive critique of a Brecht play, and Sartre's notion of commitment: as Eugene Lunn argues, Brecht's fascination with an analogy between 'business machinations and anarchic crime made him dangerously trivialize the Nazi juggernaut as a ring of petty gangsters' (p. 138).[21] In this chapter, I analyse the potential distortions of committed literature in relation to Harrison's allegory of culture and barbarism in *The Kaisers of Carnuntum*, as well as the threat of prurient representation when he redeploys Brecht's alienation effects in order to taunt the audience of the verse play with re-enacted Roman atrocities.[22]

In contrast with the limitations of Brecht's 'committed' plays, Adorno defends enigmatic art as a committed response to heteronomy. As the editors of *Aesthetics and Politics* (1977) point out, Adorno's political stance here expresses 'a distinctively modernist Marxism' (p. 149). Autonomous art cannot be completely autonomous: works that 'react against empirical reality [still] obey the forces of that reality' (p. 190). Rather than representing atrocity, as Harrison's verse plays do, Beckett's plays make audiences 'shudder' because they are 'about what everyone knows but no one will admit' (p. 190): as opposed to Sartre's idealist notion of choice, they are about the '*Abdankung* ('abdication') *des Subjekts*'.[23] Beckett's 'moribund grotesques' indicate the 'truth' about 'the idea that human beings are in control and decide, not anonymous machinery'.[24] Instances of realism in Brecht's theatre contrast with the abstract, 'polemical alienation' in Beckett's work; similarly, the 'inescapability' of Kafka's prose 'compels the change of attitude which committed works merely demand' (p. 190). Unlike these 'monstrous' examples of autonomous art – Adorno singles out Beckett's novel *The Unnameable* (1953) – Hill's work is less obviously disconcerting. However, to borrow from Adorno's critique of Brecht, *The Orchards of Syon* still contains an 'uncompromising radicalism' (p. 188) in its passages of epiphanic lyricism that strain against, and encompass, the constrictions of recent history. As I argue later in this chapter, the collection's enigmaticalness – the 'very feature' of autonomous art 'defamed' by Sartre as mere 'formalism' – gives the collection a 'power, absent from helpless poems to the victims of our time' (p. 188), as in Harrison's speeches in the verse plays that lament atrocities in Srebrenica. In the following section, I analyse such shortcomings of Harrison's 'committed' writing as a way of underscoring the enigmas of *The Orchards of Syon*. At the same time, I emphasise the more intricate metamodernist reworkings of Brechtian theatre in Harrison's work in an intertextual understanding of the term. These revitalisations of Brecht's work provide recourse to Adorno's diatribe against Sartre's conception of 'committed' art.

Commitment and the Herakles Verse Plays

Harrison's collaboration with Jocelyn Herbert forms one of the unremarked connections between Brecht and the Leeds poet. In 1956, Herbert produced the set at the Royal Court Theatre for the first UK performance of *The Good Woman of Setzuan*, and subsequently designed the stages for the world première of *Baal* (1963), the production of *Mother Courage and Her Children* at The Old Vic (1965), and *The Life of Galileo* (1980). Like Brecht's favoured set designer, Caspar Neher, Herbert preferred the minimalist stage props and designs of modernist theatre, typified by the productions of Beckett's plays that Herbert contributed to, such as *Endgame* (1958), the first performance of *Krapp's Last Tape* (1958), *Happy Days* (1962) and *Not I* (1973). In a postcard from Harrison held in Herbert's archive, the poet notes that the first play he attended in London was one of Herbert's early productions: in 1957, she produced the sparse (single) set of walls and doors for Eugène Ionesco's *The Chairs* at The Royal Court. Harrison records that 'my destiny was sealed' when he attended this play, in terms of 'such an important [future] collaboration' with Herbert.[25] The notebooks held in the Herbert archive indicate that their work together nearly forty years later on *The Kaisers of Carnuntum* and *Labourers of Herakles* should be treated as integral parts of the same project: Herbert switches between discussions about the two sets for the verse plays in her notebooks, such as when she records her long discussions with Harrison 'over lunch after Stephen Spender's funeral'.[26] Harrison's workbooks also intersect between the two verse plays: he includes, for example, a picture of Herakles on a cement sack with a handwritten note 'Cement mixers [Delphi] chorus' in the middle of the second Carnuntum workbook.[27] Indeed, as Frederick Baker's review of *The Kaisers of Carnuntum* indicates, the plays were originally intended to be 'part of a trilogy with a Herculean theme'.[28] However, given that *The Labourers of Herakles* is a much shorter (and slighter) play, my focus in the analysis below will be on *The Kaisers of Carnuntum*.[29]

Links between Brecht's epic theatre and the verse plays are evident in the political commitment of Harrison and Herbert's *Verfremdungseffekte*. Firstly, the production of *The Kaisers of Carnuntum* was 'epic' theatre in a more literal sense than Brecht's in that hundreds of supporting staff and technicians were employed: as Michael Kustow's review stresses, the producer Piero Bordin 'made Ben Hur-size demands, calling on the local fire brigade and army, hunting-horn bands, safari-park animals and choirs drawn not only from Austria but from Hungary and Slovakia'.[30] More specifically, Brecht's plays sometimes discomfort the audience through the violence depicted on stage, such as when clowns saw off the limbs of the giant Mr Smith in *The Baden-Baden Lesson on Agreement* (1929): Hans Eisler observed at its première that 'one critic fainted in his seat and [the author] Gerhart Hauptman walked out in disgust'.[31] Harrison builds on such alienation effects by directing the threat of atrocities directly at the audience in the verse play. As the theatregoers assemble on 'four tribunes of modern seating', they can see '"border towers"' reminiscent of Nazi architecture flanking the arena; moreover, the *assembled soldiers in their riot gear* that *surround the whole arena* threaten the action and audience throughout the play.[32] The 'Sound Cue List' held in the Herbert archive demonstrates the attempt to unsettle the audience at the beginning of the verse play through the amplified sounds of 'Animals, starting soft, then crescendo', 'Orpheus's lyre, calming the animals', and then 'Boosted animals, especially lions'.[33] Such acoustic discombobulations adhere to Brecht and Harrison's 'committed' distaste towards the 'culinary', which has a tendency to 'intoxicate' a bourgeois audience, and act – as the second notebook phrases it – akin to a 'perfume' that disguises a 'smell so shocking when a creature dies' (p. 382). In contrast to the 'culinary', the audiences for *The Kaisers of Carnuntum* never have an opportunity to settle into an unreflective appreciation of the classical: the third notebook begins with Marcus Aurelius on his tower, representative of high culture, with a 'Women chorus' and 'celli', as though a '"concert" is about to happen', but then the 'Song' is 'broken by sirens' (p. 607).

Other 'committed' alienation effects reimagined by Harrison and Herbert include the frequent deployment of signs – akin to the intertitles in *The Baden-Baden Lesson on Agreement* – and the poet's own particular incitement to audience participation. Even though Brecht's *Lehrstücke* ('teaching-plays') were meant to be performed by workers and other nonprofessional actors, Brecht's anti-naturalistic theatre does not otherwise tend to draw actors from the audience, or audience members, into the main action onstage. In contrast, Commodus' first violent act is to entice the 'Sign-designer' from the audience into the 'orchestra' and then 'crown' him by breaking his 'brain-box' (pp. 73–4). Although one of the notebooks includes an article that questions its historical veracity, Commodus then opines that everyone in the arena has the power to kill, 'imperium, | residing in the way you show your thumb' (p. 544).[34] A whole sequence in the central section of the play then details the 'THUMBS ROUTINE' (p. 545), in a version of democracy that emphasises the audience's potential complicity: 'You see how democratic dealing death can be. | You decide, the people, not the emperor, me!' (p. 87). Akin to the signs that Brecht deploys in his plays, such as 'No man helps another' in *The Baden-Baden Lesson on Agreement*, Herbert's photograph album of the rehearsals includes an image of Julius Bollux with a 'JUBELN LAUTER' ('cheer louder') sign, as he attempts to steer the audience's reaction to Commodus' behaviour.[35] The difference between the two playwrights' version of this particular alienation effect lies in Harrison's emphasis on the didactic properties of Bollux's forced intervention on behalf of Commodus, in contrast with Brecht's emphasis on political commentary and theatrical innovation, which, Lunn argues, Adorno undervalues in his critique of Brecht.[36] Proposed audience participation as a *Verfremdungseffekt* then 'departs' from the antecedent – in Furlani's sense of metamodernism in *Guy Davenport: Postmodern and After* (2007) – with an instance of alienation that 'surpasses' the structural innovations of Brecht's theatre (p. 150). Harrison's third notebook contains a passage that invites two members of the audience to a sex show in order to re-enact Commodus' promiscuity:

> I'll need someone to administer a muscle rub
> some volunteer masseuse, or volunteer masseur.
> You'll do, madam, and you'll do, sir.
> then I could shaft you, and then after
> you could have a turn at being shafter (p. 536)

Subsequently, Harrison considers including circus acts in this 'show' like the clowns in *The Baden-Baden Lesson on Agreement*, with a 'knife throwing act' and 'Juggler'; the poet then wonders 'Any more circus from Jaro? Use whatever there is' (p. 609). These ruminations on Jaro Frank's circus team recall Brecht's indebtedness to Vsevelod Meyerhold's deployment of 'court jesters, circus acrobats and clowns' in order to 'assault the conservative traditions of high art'.[37]

Harrison's development of Brecht's alienation effects into the prowling marines, celli and threat of a sex show focalises the particular 'commitment' in this verse play, that centres around Harrison's exposition of a dialectic between culture and barbarism.[38] This conceptual shuttling that dominates the structure of *The Kaisers of Carnuntum* has its origins in the conflicted figure of Hercules. In a section pasted into the 'Carnuntum 2' workbook on Commodus' bust in the Conservatori Museum at Rome, Harrison underlines the section about Hercules being worshipped by Romans at Ara Maxima in the Forum as 'the creator of order and destroyer of barbarism'.[39] In this Benjaminian version of culture, civilisation requires colonial violence in order to preserve itself: hence Hercules was the particular hero of the western Greek colonies that were more frequently threatened by other tribes.[40] Thomas Wiedemann's article in workbook one records that, 'Whatever the truth behind such tales' about Commodus, several emperors 'liked to see themselves as performing the services for humanity that Hercules had once performed: ridding the world of wild beasts, and establishing civilisation' (p. 35). Indeed, the article in workbook two notes that the link between the emperor and Hercules was a common association between political leaders and fighters, such as Mark Antony and Antonius Pius. Compared to the revulsion most contemporary readers would experience in encountering descriptions of leopards attacking chained prisoners in the amphitheatres, the workbook emphasises that, for Romans, the arena symbolised 'the place where the civilised world confronted lawless nature'.[41] Harrison deploys the tension between the amphitheatre and Roman state as an allegory of late twentieth-century Europe: workbook two includes a picture of the violinist Vedran Smailovic – pencilled in as a possible actor for Orpheus – playing 'amid the ruins of the Skenderija Concert Hall' near the centre of Sarajevo (p. 370).[42] The bloodying of Marcus Aurelius' white suit when he embraces Commodus in the verse play encapsulates this structural dialectic: in a typescript in workbook two, Harrison commentates that the former 'first agrees with the rumour that COMMODUS was the son of a gladiator, then admits that he is the father. How can the philosopher and the brute share the same blood [?] They do in Europe' (p. 431). Hence the third notebook includes lines in the typescript in which Aurelius and Commodus as a 'pair' are 'as difficult to accept as | Beethoven and Belsen', and – in a handwritten note underneath – 'like Hitler and [Václav] Havel' (p. 655).[43]

The alienation effect of animal cages underneath the audience forms the most spectacular example of this commitment to explore the tensions between culture and the 'barbaric' Roman arena. One of Herbert's note-books reveals that the cages formed an integral part of the stage design from the outset: Herbert has sketched the audience stands with their watch-towers, and notes: 'Cage for animals | running underneath or behind | seat stands'.[44] As Baker's review of *The Kaisers of Carnuntum* reveals, 'Not everyone in the audience was happy' when Commodus 'ripped down tapestries flanking the arena to reveal real lions and tigers pacing in cages directly below the audience'. However, Baker considers this Brechtian subversion of 'illusion' to be 'a masterstroke':

> When the cages rattled as the animals lunged against the bars in response to Commodus dumping huge chunks of meat on the floor of the arena, so we in the audience were rattled into the awareness that only a few centimetres of steel separated the animals' role in today's performance from the barbarous spectacle of the Roman era. Indeed, the difference diminished further when a bear accidentally came on stage without

a muzzle, and [Barry Rutter] showed not only that he can act, but also that he has strong nerves.[45]

In the workbooks, Harrison considers further options for the endangering of Rutter: at one point, he writes: 'LIONS grab [the actor's] robe. Sew steak in lining???' (p. 335). This alienation effect certainly banishes 'the illusion that the stage action is taking place in reality and without an audience': in the second workbook, a draft typescript that includes the fragments 'I'll make sure those cages get unbarred [. . .] you'll see stage | blood [turn] real when they're out of the cage' contains the handwritten couplet underneath: 'you look [a] tasty meal to a beast | madam, and you sir, you're such a feast' (p. 359).[46] In the final version, these 'few centimetres' of cage bars – holding apart, through artifice, the poles of culture and barbarism – are then united in Harrison's soliloquy at the end of the play, in which he 'stands above the sump the Romans built to drain all the blood shed in the arena into the Danube, making the claim that this Roman Red Danube is as much a part of Europe's cultural heritage as Strauss's Blue Danube'.[47]

The 'Barbarism' of Committed Art

The examples I have outlined above of Harrison metamodernist deployment of alienation effects – in an intertextual understanding of the term – need to be considered in the context of Adorno's criticisms of 'committed' art, that lead to the latter's defence of autonomous and enigmatical art. Harrison's third workbook for *The Kaisers of Carnuntum* contains excerpts from an article entitled 'The Entertainment Industry', in which K. M. Coleman critiques the Romans' increasing desire to replace the artifice of Greek theatre with spectacles that enact rather than represent violence and death. Whereas the violent acts take place off-stage in Greek theatre, Coleman observes that 'in the *damnationes* performed in the amphitheatre, dramatic scenes that had hitherto been acted out in the theatre as mere make-believe could now be actually reenacted and played out "for real"'.[48] In an extract from *Animals for Show and Pleasure in Ancient Rome* (1937) pasted into the first handbook, for example, George Jennison refers to 'Orpheus [on a stage] among birds and beasts; but Orpheus was a criminal and the scene ended with a bear killing him' (p. 144). Harrison's satirical play clearly denounces such *ad bestias* obscenities, yet there is still a potential prurience in the director's threat to embody such violent acts on stage, and turn 'suffering into images'

(p. 189), as Adorno puts it in 'Commitment'. '[L]et's slaughter lions and butcher a few bruins', promises Commodus in workbook three, 'Brace yourself you'll see them hacked | before your very eyes. Not fiction, fact' (p. 543). Coleman's article on Roman executions begins with such a 'demand for brutal public entertainment' that 'will be seen to act as a "market force" in the selection of punishment at Rome' (p. 299). Yet this 'brutal' entertainment – in a different form – has hardly disappeared entirely from contemporary culture. Harrison emphasises that his play takes place in the context of contemporaneous cinematic violence when Commodus threatens that 'We're going to butcher beasts. We'll have a butcher beano | bloodier and realler than Quentin Tarantino'.[49] After the Sign-designer is murdered, the audience confronts the sound of '*the butcher's block and cleaver noises of a body being chopped into pieces*'; ironically, given Commodus' desire to replace Greek theatre with Roman enaction, this figured obscenity takes place after the body is '*dragged off* the stage (p. 80). Harrison's off-stage atrocity here is meant to satirise contemporary cinema; however, the 'committed' satire cannot escape the repercussions of its own violent spectacle. As Carol Rutter remarked on the first performance of *The Labourers of Herakles*, it 'turned out to celebrate, not to critique male violence. The audience did not just "sit and stare". They gave the rage of Herakles a round of applause'.[50] In the Carnuntum verse play, the danger is that the audience receives the 'suffering [turned] into images' in the same way as enthusiastic (or passive) viewers of the gangster murders in Tarantino's *Pulp Fiction* (1994).[51]

In addition, Harrison's deployment of captive and dead animals in the play offers a potentially 'barbaric' enactment of the culture/barbarism dialectic that underlines the verse play's entrenchment in 'committed' art rather than the enigmas of autonomous literature. One of the typescript production notes for *The Kaisers of Carnuntum* in the Herbert archive records that the stage carpet 'Must be washable because of the blood from meat carcases', in a modern re-enactment of the Romans' draining of the amphitheatre's blood into the Danube sump.[52] A later version of the typescript in notebook three imagines Commodus stirring a 'mess of meat' with the signpost used earlier to murder the 'Sign-designer' (p. 620), akin to the various lumps of flesh deposited on the map of the Roman empire. Ironically, the first notebook also contains an article on the maltreatment of animals ('Last grim waltz for the dancing bears'), and a 'bear swoop' to remove 'as many as 50 bears from Istanbul's tourist sites' (p. 137). Despite Harrison's dramatic ingenuity, the audience might still remain uncomfortable with the raw meat and exploitation of bears in order to add dramatic spice to the undoubtedly spectacular performance: William Shakespeare's famous stage direction from *The Winter's Tale* (1611) – 'Exit, pursued by a bear' – becomes 'exit emperor pushed by a bear' in the final version of the play (p. 129).[53] In a replication of the Romans' culture/barbarism dialectic, the bears also function as part of the 'barbaric' pole in the play that threatens the cultured poet with their 'savagery': the beasts 'will tear apart' Orpheus on behalf of 'people who no longer want the poet's art' (p. 177). Animals marauding under a cultured audience representative of Orpheus may constitute, for Baker, a 'masterstroke', but this alienation effect also risks a 'barbaric' taunting that capitulates to rather than resists the structural dialectic of the verse play.[54]

Hence the anti-barbarity of committed art can become a kind of cultural barbarism itself when there is an attempt to engage with or 'represent' atrocity, rather than responding to violence with the 'monstrous' abstractions of autonomous art.[55] The second workbook contains various passages in which Commodus delights in his threats surrounding the beasts: a lion 'mauls | some poor Mauretanian and rips off his balls', and opines 'Shall I let [the animals] out to roam around here [. . .] They're safe behind steel bars until | I give the signal to let them out for the kill' (p. 379). In a subsequent reworking of this passage, the emperor proposes to 'let a few out of the crate | and instead of bloody talking, | demonstrate [. . .] Plenty of time, they'll be hungrier later' (p. 383). A fake bar in the cage then 'COMES AWAY IN HIS HAND', and Commodus mocks that the audience is only 'comparatively speaking safe' (p. 379). Soon afterwards, a stage direction proposes that the emperor 'cuts off [the] head' of an ostrich (p. 381): 'they'd collide || but go on | till they died || Their plumes were ruffled and the'd [*sic*] prance || in [a] sort of Totentanz' (p. 383).[56] 'One to swing', the playwright notes in the third notebook, as 'Austria doesn't allow killing' (!) (p. 523). Hence Harrison's critique of realism in *The Kaisers of Carnuntum* does not encompass the 'barbarism' of the 'stink of blood' on stage in the final version of the play (p. 384). Commodus cajoles that the audience prefers 'a bit of blood and guts to poetry' (p. 409), but at moments such as these in *The Kaisers of Karnuntum* the 'blood and guts' constitutes an integral part of Harrison and Herbert's stagecraft.

As Adorno's essay proposes, 'committed' literature, unlike autonomous art, also risks distortion in order to convey a consumable political message. In the second 'Carnuntum' workbook, Harrison includes an excerpt on the design of the Column of Trajan (c.110 AD) during Commodus' reign: the artist 'seemed to be more concerned with expressing the horror and suffering of war than with giving a factual record of events, and to do this they were prepared to distort the features, exaggerate gestures, and pay less attention to modeling [*sic*] and proportion'.[57] As Adorno demonstrates in his critique of Brecht's commitment, the playwright distorts the reality of 1930s Germany in *The Resistible Rise of Arturo Ui* when he represents leading Nazis as bumbling criminals. Similarly, Harrison exaggerates the historical record when he underplays Marcus Aurelias' role in imperial warfare in order to provide more dramatic tension between the 'cultured' Aurelias, author of philosophical meditations, and 'barbaric' Commodus – a 'gangster ghost' – who allegedly introduced faeces into his own and courtiers' food for his own deprived pleasure.[58] In contemporaneous accounts, some but by no means all of Commodus' transgressions are expressed in terms of his homosexuality: in Rome, for example, he led a triumphal procession with Saotems, 'his partner in depravity, seated in his chariot, and from time to time he would turn around and kiss him openly' (p. 257). The homophobic sources are hardly trustworthy, as is corroborated by the conflicting accounts of Aurelias' wife Faustina, who allegedly had an affair with a gladiator. One commentator in workbook two contends that Faustina (played by Siân Thomas in *The Kaisers of Carnuntum*) used to 'choose out lovers from among the sailors and gladiators' while at Caieta (p. 419), whereas another source in the first workbook insists that 'the slanders and libels of [Commodus'] later years accordingly declared that he was no son of Marcus at all; and that Faustina, in fact, had loved a gladiator [. . .] There is no reliable evidence to support the monstrous charge' (p. 218).

In the context of Harrison's dismissal of this slander around Faustina, it is ironic that rumours and disputed facts – such as the 'thumbs routine' – are presented elsewhere in the play as historical truth for the sake of 'committed' dramatic entertainment. Thomas Wiedemann's article in workbook one notes that 'Commodus in particular *was rumoured* to have been keen on decapitating ostriches by shooting sickle-head arrows at them' (p. 35).[59] By page sixty-nine of the same workbook, this supposition has become the more assertive 'Commodus decapitated ostriches' (p. 69). Commodus himself is also a more complex dramatic figure than Harrison's attack on his transgressive behaviour might suggest. Extracts from *Historia Augusta* in the second workbook emphasise that Commodus was 'adept in certain arts which are not becoming in an emperor for he could mould goblets and dance and sing and whistle, and he could play the buffoon and the gladiator to perfection' (p. 253).[60] There are traces of this more artistic version of Commodus in that the character partly functions as an anarchic satyr figure; understandably, given that Rutter had returned to Carnuntum where, six years earlier, he played the leading satyr Silenus in Harrison's play *The Trackers of Oxyrhynchus* (1988).[61] Thus, despite the remarkable alienation effects in this verse play, Commodus courts empathy as the 'barbaric' figure familiar to Harrison's readers in the form of, for example, the skinhead in *V*, who displays traces of artistic sensibility, but remains too marginalised by high culture to attain a sustained artistic voice. Sensitive to such cultural erasures, Harrison is alert to a footnote in *Historia Augusta* that describes how 'Many inscriptions found throughout the empire show Commodus' name carefully erased' (p. 253); this brief comment transforms into a major conceit in *The Kaisers of Carnuntum*, in which the emperor discovers his absence on the 'Dreikaiserwein' bottle, rails at the audience and then kills the Sign-designer. Baker's review indicates that Harrison 'saw this as a sanitisation of history, like Stalin's excision of Trotsky from official photographs'.[62] The comma makes it unclear whether Harrison or Baker is establishing this connection: Trotsky's dismissal from the Communist Party and subsequent deportation from the Soviet Union hardly encourages historical comparison with a violent Roman emperor. Yet Harrison's determination to subvert these diverse historical erasures nevertheless betrays a degree of attraction to the 'barbaric' figure of Commodus.[63]

Despite Harrison's steadfast response to these gaps in the historical record, he nevertheless shares Adorno and Sartre's pessimism over autonomous art and 'committed' literature's power to intervene directly in the social and political sphere. In one of Herbert's notebooks, the designer ruminates over the final scene of *The Labourers of Herakles*: 'Bosnian refugees' (cut from the final version) enter with old men and 'women in wheelbarrows'; like the labourers, 'they too get stuck' in the concrete, and then, for the soliloquy, 'Tony appears—somehow—perhaps a Forklift Truck and Speaks of [the] powerlessness of Art to have any influence on man's violence and inhumanity'.[64] Harrison's depiction of the workers who, like Commodus, find nothing efficacious in the theatre allows him to engage with invisible histories of labour, as well as the ineffectuality of art. The metadramatic moment in *The Labourers of Herakles* when Labourer 1 proclaims 'I'm a labourer of Herakles, and a labourer lays | fucking concrete. He doesn't act in plays' forms a paradoxical rejection of Adorno's (rather pious) admonishment in 'Commitment' that 'all roles may be played, except that of the worker' (p. 187). Furthermore, the Brechtian allegory of war and the workers during the Persian conflict in *The Labourers of Herakles* is more subtle than the Nazis portrayed as gangsters in *The Resistible Rise of Arturo Ui*.[65] Just as Brecht focuses on the exploitation of labour in *Mother Courage and Her Children*, Harrison transforms the five labourers into hypermasculine killers, complicit workers, or victims in the form of the Women of Miletos. As for Brecht in *Mother Courage and Her Children*, Harrison's implication is that these roles of perpetrator, bystander and victim are easily interchangeable for the workers during the wars. In Harrison's 'Herakles (Delphi)' notebook, the powerful alienation effect in which the workers get stuck in concrete and then harangue the audience for abandoning them strives for connections between the invisibility of the working class in the context of historical architectural delights, and the limitations of art in terms of averting atrocity:

> In the set orchestra stuck fast
> We see the horrors of the past
> With these new brewing
> We see Srbrenica fall
> Some lined up against the wall
> And what are we doing? (p. 282)

In the final version of the play, Harrison attacks 'culinary' theatre, in which the spectators are present only in order to be entertained, rather than – as in epic theatre – instructed at the same time: the audience is made to ruminate on their potential complicity when Labourer 2 complains 'All they're allowed to do is sit and stare. | However deep the sorrow, or severe the pain, | they think we're only here to entertain'.[66] The labourers' depicted invisibility has its origin in Harrison's *School of Eloquence* sequence (1978): 'The Earthen Lot' begins with an epigraph from William Morris's *The Art of the People* (1879) – 'From Ispahan [in Iran] to Northumberland, there is no building that does not show the influence of that oppressed and neglected herd of men' – and the next poem, 'Remains', records the words of a forgotten paperhanger in William Wordsworth's cottage, whose pentameter is discovered during restoration work (*'our heads will be happen cold when this is found'*).[67] Similarly, in 'Questions From a Worker who Reads', Brecht wonders about the voices of those who built 'Thebes of the 7 gates', Babylon, the Great Wall of China and Rome.[68] These class invisibilities intertwine awkwardly in the 'Herakles (Delphi)' workbook with the recounting of atrocities in the war in the former Yugoslavia: the line 'young woman hanged herself in a tree' (p. 286) refers to a newspaper photograph pasted into the workbook six pages later. Using exactly the same phrase as in Herbert's notebook, a poetic fragment then refers to 'the powerlessness of art' after two articles about Serbian and Croatian violence (p. 340). In the final version of Harrison's monologue in *Plays Three* (1996), the 'Spirit of Phrynichos' reveals a paradoxical approach to committed literature: at first, Phrynichos 'gave theatre a start | in redeeming destruction through the power of art', but then five lines later 'art cannot redeem | the cry from Krajina or the Srbrenica scream' (p. 143). Elsewhere, Harrison has spoken of the 'whole fatuity of the belief that writing poetry will *do* anything'.[69] Unlike Brecht's plays, a more pessimistic allegory of the limitations of 'committed' art is built into the structure of *The Labourers of Herakles*.

The Orchards of Syon: Committed and Autonomous Art

As opposed to the allegorical failure of commitment in Harrison's verse play, *The Orchards of Syon* forms an example of committed and autonomous art that confronts similarly atrocious historical events, but responds with enigmatic poetry to provide a '*sad and angry consolation*'.[70] A compromised euphony engages with twentieth-century history tangentially to create poems of considerable 'semantic energy'.[71] Before I turn to Hill's references to the Allied invasion of Normandy and the Manchester Blitz, I wish to outline his initial deployment of enigmatical poetry in *The Orchards of Syon*, that – as in *Scenes from Comus* – is instigated with recourse to T. S. Eliot's work. Alongside these concerns with Adorno's 'monstrous' aspects of modern history, Hill frequently returns to the prospect of his own demise, as in the elusive opening: 'Now there is no due season. Do not | mourn unduly'.[72] Adorno's lament for 'damaged' post-war life in the subtitle to *Minima Moralia* (1951) merges here with Hill's sense of *The Orchards of Syon* as a 'late' collection. The enigma of *The Orchards of Syon* is, from the beginning, inextricable from lexical ambiguities bound up with 'damaged' existence: does 'due' mean that the poet is writing mid-season, that the seasons have blended into one, or – as in *Minima Moralia* – that all post-war existence appears somehow posthumous? This line also echoes and repudiates the beginning of *The Waste Land*, in which April breeds 'Lilacs out of the dead land'.[73] There may be no 'due season' due to the poet's own imagined demise, rather than Eliot's attenuated spring: 'unduly' wryly hints that the author's passing should indeed be 'duly', as in appropriately, mourned. Hill's conflicted and ambiguous responses to a potential last collection are evident in the very first drafts for *The Orchards of Syon*: 'Good. Good', begins one version, there is 'Time for amendment', but then immediately 'No time', that has a pencil emendation above it ('still time').[74] 'No time' then undergoes a qualification through the enjambment that appends 'like the present' to 'still time'. Subsequently, 'my last | performance' becomes a 'final' collection; but the 'performance' is not 'final' because it refers to Hill's previous book, *Speech! Speech!* (2000), which may have seemed to be a 'dance of retirement', but – with another pencil emendation – is actually only a gesture towards 'retiring'.

In the subsequent lines of the first section, Hill undercuts these elusive and allusive ambiguities when he switches to the dissenting voice that he has encompassed in his work since the publication of *The Triumph of Love* (1998): 'You have sometimes said | that I project a show more | stressful than delightful' (p. 1). In the notebook drafts for *The Orchards of Syon*, Hill emphasises his readers' potential dissent towards his enigmatic poetics even further: 'As you have *always* said | we can put on a show, sometimes more sombre'; 'sombre' later becomes the more self-critical 'convoluted', 'deadlier' and 'mendacious'.[75] The reference to Plato's allegory of the cave is clearer in these drafts, in which Hill implores the bemused reader to 'watch my hands gesturing | shadows against the light', like the cave dwellers entranced by the fire shadows on the wall. Hill then likens his 'stressful', autonomous art to that of the local 'Hippo' (the Hippodrome), and concedes that it is 'not as funny'.[76] Echoing the lilacs' mixture of 'Memory and desire' in *The Waste Land* (p. 51), this linkage accedes that the plumbing of memories in *The Orchards of Syon* may well lead to extended passages of 'sombre' and 'stressful' art. '[S]tressful' also alludes here to the heavy stresses in the declarative opening lines of this collection: '**Now there** is **no due** sea**son. Do not** | **mourn** un**duly**' (p. 1). Eliot's 'intolerable wrestle with words' in 'East Coker' manifests itself here in off-key 'Eloquence', as Hill conceives of such 'stressful' rhetoric in his notebook, which is 'cogent', 'succinct', 'hard-won' and 'hard-fought'.[77]

As I discussed in Chapter 1 in relation to Prynne's *Acrylic Tips*, the enigmas of such 'off-key' lines can be stressful for the critic if the latter insists on attempting to decode autonomous art systematically.[78] In the passage discussed above, the 'due' (dew) season remains 'due' in Adorno's sense of the artistic 'remainder', that can never be entirely comprehended.[79] A resistance to hermeneutics appertains to individual lines and images in *The Orchards of Syon* – rather than every section of *Acrylic Tips* – such as when the 'time-struck Minster doles greed by the clock' in section XVII (p. 17). Hill clearly alludes to York Minster among 'the broad Ouse levels', yet the enigmaticalness of the previous line is inextricable from its ambiguity: do the minster and clock

distribute greed in that they somehow register the covetous parish
outside the cathedral, or does 'by' indicate that this avarice is 'doled'
alongside the clock? Or is the clock more abstract, in which case the
minster is guilty of greed 'by the clock'; in other words, constantly?
A more positivistic account of the line might argue that 'greed' refers to
an admission charge, as well as the subsequent appeals for charity:
notebook fifty-two evokes the 'coin-slot improved | Minster' (p. 88).
'[T]he clock' may signify the minster's astronomical clock in particular,
which was installed in 1955 as a memorial to the airmen killed during
World War Two who worked at local bases in Yorkshire, County
Durham and Northumberland. Drafts of section XVII in notebook
fifty-two indicate that Hill was also toying with a connection between
upper-class privilege and English heritage: Hill writes of a 'Lord' who
ropes off the clock, and asserts that the 'coin-slot Minster' belongs to
him; this aristocrat is named 'Ebor', after the Roman name for York
('Eboracum') (p. 88).[80] This Ebor is certainly a sign of avarice,
'untouched on his side of the ropes'. '[G]reed' may also have something
to do with the 'snarled' 'coast-traffic' earlier in section XVII (p. 17),
since the packed roads merge in the notebook with York's tourist
crowds: the town is 'too crammed even for organ congas', and is 'a
medieval hell-mouth' (p. 93). In the final version, Hill reimagines the
'chorus' as the 'lines of road-rage' that 'shunt to yet more delay' (p. 17):
not 'entirely at peace', the greed may be an unexplained symptom of the
tourists, 'Hawks over the dual carriageways' and a 'snarled, snarling'
traffic jam. Despite these clues in the notebooks, the line in which the
minster 'doles greed by the clock' nevertheless remains elusive, and
beyond definitive interpretation: its 'power' – as Derek Attridge might
term it – lies precisely in its resistance to positivistic decoding and
critical attempts to 'solve' its ambiguity.[81]

A similarly enigmatic and impervious passage occurs towards the end of
notebook fifty-four during a 'committed' portrayal of urban rubble. In this
instance, the 'remainder' arises out of Hill's elusive engagement with Blitz
imagery.[82] The poet depicts

> this narrow
> scorched earth pomarium [sic] between Salford
> and Manchester not the Orchards
> of Syon but near enough (p. 68)

In the final version in section LXI, these lines become:

Initiative – that
New Age *pomerium* between Salford
and Manchester: not só far the Orchards
of Syon grown to be ours (p. 61)

In notebook fifty-four, Hill records his arrival in Manchester for a reading: 'Manchester Piccadilly you could | have watched it | burn well enough' (p. 63). Recalling images of the Coventry Blitz that Hill witnessed from afar as an eight-year-old child, the poet is absorbed in the Manchester Blitz, which severely damaged the city's main train stations in December 1940. A military strategy of destroying anything that might be useful to enemy forces ('scorched earth') is referred to in the initial draft for this passage (p. 68), but the emphasis in the final version is on the '*pomerium*', a religious boundary around the ancient city of Rome, as well as the cities controlled by the capital (p. 61). Derived from the Latin phrase '*post moerium*', meaning 'beyond the wall', the *pomerium* denoted an often deserted area of land just inside and also outside of the city walls. In fact, Hill merges images of the Blitz, 'scorched earth' and *pomerium* in an attempt to describe the swathes of rubble visible between 'Salford | and Manchester' when he witnessed them on 1 July 2000: Hill began work on a second version of this passage eleven days later.[83]

The 'scorched earth' that Hill ponders here as a 'committed' image of military devastation was actually caused by the demolition of factories on the border between the cities (p. 68): initially, a dry ski-slope was intended to cover part of this area, but the plan was abandoned, and the space remained covered in rubble until the construction of high-rise flats. Hill transforms this landscape into an area that denotes a religiose space 'ploughed by, or for, the priests', and also a '<u>cordon sanitaire</u>' between deliberating 'civic officers' and 'city-planners' (p. 86). '[P]*omerium*' even becomes a sign for 'word-painting', a 'wash of | language': the rubble appears like '<u>impasto</u>', in which paint is applied in thick layers (p. 86). Contexts of historical engagement then proliferate even further in the notebook: 'Mine-pickled', the landscape also becomes 'prison | ground', the 'Berlin Wall' and even Carthage during the main engagement of the Third Punic War (p. 89); these images are subsequently deployed in section LXX (p. 70). Hill wrestles with aligning these visions of devastation with the collection's oft-mentioned utopia of the Orchards of Syon: the rubble is first 'not the Orchards', but 'near enough' (p. 89), then emphatically 'nót orchard' (p. 89), but ultimately not 'só far' from the Edenic; by section LXX the *pomerium* will definitely 'not | pass muster as *orchard*' (p. 70).

Even more grandly, the *pomerium* hovers on the edge of functioning as a sign of Hill's entire career: 'To draw up my account', he writes, 'Í could have tóld you | pomerium is nót orchard' (p. 89); this statement echoes a line in notebook fifty-three in which he demands that he 'list all | [his] achievements previous to dying' (p. 34). In notebook fifty-five, these poetic 'achievements' are transformed into an image reminiscent of Beckett's *Endgame* (1957), in which he is 'chest deep in rubble | of my own making' (p. 13).

In Hill's version of committed and autonomous art, references to devastating events such as the Blitz and Punic War fuse here with the 'monstrous' figures that Adorno admires in Beckett's work, alongside the 'rubble' of Hill's *oeuvre*.[84] Hence *pomerium* initiates a personal 'Valediction' (p. 69), but this becomes the more prosaic 'Initiative' in the final version (p. 61), which may refer to a scorned council strategy. However, what does the rubble have to do with 1970s mysticism as a 'New Age' track of land between two cities in the final version, a phrase that jars like the 'new-fangled light' in section XIII (p. 13) that I discuss later in this chapter? Ultimately, the meaning of this frequently altered passage in the notebooks remains undecodable; a veritable 'impasto' of images and attendant contextual information that cannot 'solve' its enigma. However, this enigmaticalness does not signal a failure of poesis: only a positivistic notion of language akin to Sartre's in *What is Literature?* would insist that Hill fails to communicate something transparent in a sharply defined manner. As in many of Hill's twenty-first-century collections, he weaves together collages of poetic threads – the Blitz, atrocity, urban clearance and renewal, religious segregation – without synthesising them into a 'committed' sequence that might depict a specific object. As Hill retorts to Ezra Pound's 'I cannot | make it cohere' in notebook fifty-five, 'Already it coheres', as the images fuse in an ordered incoherence that, as in *Acrylic Tips*, grates against, but does not eschew, signification (p. 22).[85] However, there is no overarching theme in *The Orchards of Syon* that Hill wishes to convey, unlike Harrison's emphasis on the culture/barbarism dialectic in his verse plays. Hill's metamodernist 'word-painting', as he phrases it in notebook fifty-four, resolutely resists settling into a definitive subject or Sartre's exported 'message' (p. 86).

In notebook fifty-three, Hill turns to a more specific commitment to depict the suffering of Allied forces during the invasion of Normandy:

> Treasured things, lose things—loosed things, orchards
> of the Bocage June to October, the sloughed

> flesh of the dead, wrenched-apart carriers
> of multiflame their bursting carcasses (p. 85).

'[B]ocage' in the final version denotes an area of woodland and pasture in Normandy (p. 44): such farmland is now inextricable from the devastation caused during the Allied advance; as Jeffrey Wainwright notes, the apt placement of this section on page forty-four of *The Orchards of Syon* gestures towards the date of the invasion in June 1944.[86] 'Umbelliferae', aromatic flowering plants (p. 44), are inseparable from memories of parachutes that 'umbrella'd the hedgerows' (p. 85), images of destroyed barns and 'splintered crofts' (p. 44). Hill crosses out 'round St Lô' next to this passage in the notebook (p. 85): this example of the 'treasured' Orchards of Syon is 'shadowed' by the intense fighting on the Cotentin peninsula around the town, in which sunken lanes with high hedgerows provided the Germans with enduring defensive positions. '[F]lesh of the dead' and 'bursting carcasses' risk committed art's potentially prurient representation (p. 85): in the final version, these phrases have been replaced with the more abstract 'odours of death from tracked armour | gone multiflame' (p. 44). Hill's concern over the potentially lurid aspects of committed art are ingrained in the final version of section XLIV: emphasised with a metrical inversion, a body 'splays' for the camera, and, by proxy, the poem, as if the corpse is actively inviting the audience's prurient gaze (p. 44). In a line break that links the visual to the destructive, the phrase 'Hand-held or swivel' at the end of line ten appertains not, as expected, to the camera in line eight, but to the subsequent firearm, the 'carbine', in line eleven. As in the movement towards abstraction in the notebook version of section XLIV, lines nine and ten move from the corpse to the more general human 'midden', a northern dialect for a refuse or dung heap. In a poetic montage, the specificity of the 'machine-carbine' at the crossroads 'of Hauts-Vents' then shifts into a discussion of Stanley Edgar Hyman's *The Armed Vision: a Study in the Methods of Modern Literary Criticism* (1948). Hill wonders if Hyman similarly did not 'go to the wars': the American critic actually graduated from Syracuse in 1940, and then worked for *The New Yorker* magazine.[87] Hill equates their non-combatant status with the potential problems of commitment in relation to the involved yet also distancing camera: 'not going' recalls the camera 'staying put' in line nine; in contrast, the 'veterans are dying', and the poet 'cannot say | what they care to remember' (p. 44).

Hill's advocacy of such fraught yet committed autonomous art is evident in the 'shadowed rhetoric' of the very first stanza in *The Orchards of Syon* (p. 1). Bound up with Plato's illusive shadows in the cave allegory, and María Casares' 'tragic shadow' of Death in the film *Orphée* (1950) (p. 4), the phrase also connotes the 'shadows' of twentieth-century history. In *The Orchards of Syon*, pastoral images frequently admit their 'shadowed rhetoric', as in 'blooded scrub maples' that 'torch themselves in the swamp', and which should be read in the context of the 'death-songs' mentioned two lines earlier (p. 3).[88] These sections of committed rhetoric are nevertheless counterbalanced with moments that draw on the modernist conception of epiphany and the Christian notion of grace. Whereas the swamp and 'death-songs' are inextricable in section III, these metamodernist epiphanies are part of but also grate against the committed and autonomous art in the Blitz and Normandy sections that I have analysed above. One of the first drafts for the opening lines in notebook fifty-two begins: 'Good. None of this is past | redemption', and then refers to an abstract 'thrashing convulsive', which is 'under notice of grace' (p. 7). Grace, a '"chance occasion" that suggests the eternal', remains by definition enigmatic as a sign of God's absent presence.[89] As Robert Macfarlane argues, these moments are beyond knowledge and intellect, recalling Eliot's remark that 'genuine poetry can communicate before it is understood': language's 'elisions and indeterminacies accept and act the obliquity of this [. . .] elided experience of grace'.[90] Yet in notebook fifty-two, Hill intervenes after a memorable passage about the liminality of 'Distant flocks' merging 'into the limestone's half-light' (p. 14) with the emphatic 'Awe is *not grace*' (pp. 52, 74).[91] Here, the more secular phenomenon of modernist epiphany is bound up with the sublime, the 'insubstantial substance' of nature (p. 13), as the enthralled poet witnesses the fell metamorphose from grey to coral, then 'rare Libyan sand colour or banded spectrum' (p. 14).

The possibility that these enigmatic images might be representative of a 'spirit consciousness' is exorcised from the final version in notebook fifty-two (p. 75). These are not simply 'Signs [. . .] taken for wonders', as in Eliot's 'Gerontion'.[92] Elusive phenomena are not symptomatic of 'peace' either in the final qualification of awe (p. 14): in an 'off-key' moment during the drafting of this passage in the notebook, Hill emphasises in a highlighted line that 'Nothing earthy is perfect now forget it' (p. 74). Does 'now' denote the specific moment of composition, or does an absent mark of punctuation lie before (rather than after) 'now'; in which case, 'nothing earthy' is ever untarnished, so the poet should never attempt to mediate the sublime? Hill's agitated intervention occurs after a passage that transforms Matthew Arnold's 'darkling plain' where 'ignorant armies clash

by night' into a more positive image of 'constant life', in which 'the
wheeling | of grand armies' is nevertheless 'overtaken by darkness'.[93]
Whereas the lyrical images of the fell are gently qualified with 'Awe is
not peace' (p. 14), a more irascible voice from *The Triumph of Love* and
Speech! Speech! enters the drafts with 'Nothing earthy is perfect now forget
it', but is then exorcised from the final version in notebook fifty-two
(p. 74).[94] 'Nothing earthy' can be perfect due to the present absence of
Adorno's 'deluge' of atrocious events in the twentieth century, but such
epiphanic passages in *The Orchards of Syon* stubbornly persist in the
committed and autonomous visions of an awe-struck poet.[95]

Hill inserts a comment on Shakespeare's verse into notebook fifty-four
that exactly describes these enigmatic instances of linguistic power as 'a
heave and swell, from depths beyond verbal definition [...] a gathering
power, a ninth wave of passion, an increase in tempo and vitality' (p. 56).
Critics such as Wainwright have been drawn to the 'gathering power' of
a particularly striking passage in section XIII (p. 119). Hill declares in
notebook fifty-two that

> These are starts of memory, a strange
> blessing out of confusion. Await
> the sharpened light, the slate roofs
> caught in scale-nets of silver, then
> blurred with thin oils. These and like tokens
> I now associate with apprehension (p. 69).

'[S]tarts' recalls the Proustian concept of involuntary memory: these 'starts'
are both the beginnings of poetry and abrupt interruptions. '[B]lessing out'
becomes a blessing 'slid' from confusion in the final version (p. 13), stressing the involuntary nature of this epiphany. The notebook and collection
then contain the parallel enigmatical images of, respectively, the 'sharp-
ened light' (p. 69) – reminiscent of 'Blade-light' from Ted Hughes's
'Wind' – and 'new-fangled' light (p. 13).[96] '[S]harpened' suggests an
intensification of luminosity, whereas 'new-fangled' – a word that critics
have avoided in their discussion of this passage – indicates a change in
brightness that remains more awkward due to its potentially comic connotation of novelty, and its resistance to exact signification, like the 'New Age
pomerium' in section LXI (p. 61). These 'starts' are more assuredly 'apprehension' in the subsequent and final versions – 'I now associate' soon
converts to 'I now establish' – but the meaning of these 'fleeting' moments
and 'signals' remains necessarily enigmatic in the secular epiphany or
religious experience of grace (pp. 69, 70). Poetic 'truth' is here the

intrinsically mystified and lyrical response to nature's 'insubstantial substance' later in this section (XIII): Hill transfers the 'blurred' oils in the manuscript version to the 'blurred and refocused' rain at the end of the stanza (p. 13). As well as 'abrupt', these 'starts' of memory are 'strange' in the notebook (p. 69). The epiphany is, by definition, a passive *and* active experience as the poet responds to the 'signals', in the final version, of 'the slate roofs briefly | caught in scale-nets of silver' (p. 13).

Autonomous Art and Paul Celan's *Atemwende*

These epiphanic passages of lyrical autonomy are inseparable from Hill's engagement with the poetry of Paul Celan. Whereas Harrison's assimilation of Brechtian theatre remains hampered by the problems with 'committed' art that I outlined earlier in this chapter, Hill strives to make *The Orchards of Syon* 'as strong as the art' he admires – in this instance, Celan's later poetry – but the collection is not '*like*' Celan's work.[97] As I noted in the introduction to this chapter, the phrase 'Atemwende' recurs throughout the collection: Hill is drawn to the title of Celan's book due to the enigma of the phrase which resists, but does not defy, translation, as well as its denotations of a change in poesis towards more autonomous lyrics in the context of personal survival. The first reference to *Atemwende* occurs in the second notebook for *The Orchards of Syon*, in which Hill refers to 'Atemwende or CELAN or breath-hitch' (p. 16). '[B]reath-hitch' immediately situates Hill's response to Celan's collection beyond the literal translation of the title: '*die Wende*' usually refers to a turn, lock, turning point or circle, but not a hitch ('*die Störung*'). Drafts following this variation on 'breath-turn' indicate that Hill associates *Atemwende* with the theme of survival that runs throughout *The Orchards of Syon*: '[A]re you a survivor', he asks in one of the very first drafts in notebook fifty-two, 'awaiting | delivery from the furnace or den?' (p. 12). This image returns to the Daniel reference in *The Triumph of Love*, that connotes more widely Jewish victims of the Holocaust.[98] However, in notebook fifty-three, the notion of survivorship conjoins with a more personal struggle: Hill jots down 'breath-ply' and 'breath-plight', and then asks 'How long | must one survive in this survival'? (p. 43). An extraordinary passage then follows in which Hill plays with various deliberate mistranslations and creative responses to the phrase '*Atemwende*':

> breath-pulse, breath-take and return
> tack-breath, breath-lease, breath-purchase

breath-find, breath-fend, breath-fund
breath-mark, breath-sign, breath-splice
breath-loop, breath-stroke, breath-tap
breath-twitch, breath-snag(ged), breath-tip
breath-frond, breath-filament, breath-grace
touch-breath, breath-touch, breath-turn and re-take
breath-hover, hover-breath, breath-transfer
breath-mute, breath-mate, breath-kin
breath-kind, breath-scope, breath-fits
breath-snatch, breath-catch, breath-will
breath-hilt, breath-twin, breath-thrill (p. 48)

This repetition is comparable to but also extends beyond Celan's ruminations over alternative titles for his 1967 collection, such as '*Atemkristall*'
('Breathcrystal') and '*Atemgänge*' ('Breathpassages').[99] Next to this passage
in notebook fifty-three, Hill underlines 'breath-fetch', the only phrase out
of this extensive list that survives into section XXXII (p. 32). As Hill states
in this section, *Atemwende* 'beggars translation': the reader encounters
poetics in which Hill wrestles with the elusive phrase in order to engage
with but never 'confess' his own compromised health (p. 32). '<u>Atem</u>' might
'become <u>stem</u>', Hill writes before the memorable list of mistranslations,
'the eye | undeceived': this line gestures towards his interest in the devel-
opment of stem cell technology in order to combat macular degener-
ation (p. 46).

In addition to these deflected glimpses of autobiography, the '*Wende*' in
Atemwende refers to a poetical 'turn' in the poets' work; for Celan, the shift
forms an integral part of his poetic autonomy. In *Breathturn into Timestead*
(2014), Pierre Joris summarises the change in Celan's poetics as follows:

> In the early sixties, that is, midway through Paul Celan's writing career,
> a radical change, a poetic *Wende*, or turn occurred, later inscribed in the title
> of the volume *Atemwende/Breathturn*, heralding the poetics he was to
> explore for the rest of his life. His poems, which had always been highly
> complex but rather lush, with an abundance of near-surrealistic imagery and
> sometimes labyrinthine metaphoricity—though he vehemently denied the
> critics' suggestion that his was a 'hermetic' poetry—were pared down, the
> syntax grew tighter and more spiny [. . .] while the overall composition of
> the work became much more serial in nature [. . .] he moved towards
> a method of composition by cycles and volumes (p. xl)

'[L]ush' does not quite account for the 'cold heat' of Celan's most well-
known early poem, 'Todesfugue', but Joris correctly accounts for the poet's
artistic *Wende*: the critic notes that the phrase '*Atemwende*' does not refer to

a specific poem in Celan's collection, and is thereby a metapoetical statement about his creativity rather than 'evocative of a specific poetic content' (p. xlii).[100] Similar charges have been made against both poets that focus on their supposedly hermetic autonomous art, as Hill registers at the beginning of *The Orchards of Syon* with his concerns over his supposedly 'stressful' and sombre rather than 'delightful' poetry (p. 11). Joris's comments about 'cycles and volumes' also indicate that '*Atemwende*' suggests a 'turn' in Hill's publishing strategy: after *Canaan* (1996), Hill wrote the trilogy encompassing *The Triumph of Love, Speech! Speech!* and *The Orchards of Syon*; Hill's evocation of Celan thus involves metapoetics that comment on the trajectory of these collections. However, Celan's 'turn' from expansive 'metaphoricity' to 'pared down' and 'spiny' poems hardly represents the extensive sequences in these collections, the breathless pace of *Speech! Speech!*, the 'louder' voice, and what Wainwright refers to as the 'comparative loquacity, even garrulity, of the style'.[101] Hill's clipped and agonised poetics in 'Tenebrae' and *Tenebrae* (1978) – published twenty-four years earlier – are more 'pared' than *The Orchards of Syon*, whose diurnal concerns in stanzas of twenty-four lines are more akin to Louis MacNeice's *Autumn Journal* (1939) than Celan's later minimalism. Indeed, the workbooks reveal that Hill first intended to structure the long poem as a series of canzone – he writes in his first notebook of 'the heart | of substance, the cánzone' (p. 75) – yet the prospect of hendecasyllabic lines with end-rhyme soon gives way to the twenty-four lines of each stanza, and the collection as a 'Book of Days'.[102] Another initial possibility presents the poem as an extended diptych (p. 13), with the first section entitled 'The Orchards of Syon' and the second 'The House of the Forest of Lebanon', that refers to a building in Solomon's palace mentioned in Kings 7 (pp. 2–5).

Rather than an embracing of autonomous art in the form of skeletal poetics, the 'radical change' in Hill's work denotes instead a 'turn' to serial form – like Celan after *Atemwende* – but with a 'departure' from the modernist antecedent in the form of critical voices that Hill interspaces throughout his poetry from *The Triumph of Love* onwards.[103] The poem beginning 'Eroded by . . .' in *Atemwende* attacks the '*bunte Gerede*' ('gaudy chatter') of Celan's earlier work, leading into a 'bare northern landscape of snow and ice': *The Orchards of Syon* is not 'gaudy', but it is certainly loquacious poetic 'chatter' compared to the sparse 'Tenebrae'.[104] Furthermore, in contrast with the Eliotian 'ghost' of the pentameter in Hill's collection, Celan 'breaks away from the traditional metrics and rhymes still present in the early work toward a line based on different units (breath, syllable, word)' (p. lxxvi), as in the poem starting 'Before your late face | a loner | wandering between | nights' (p. 5). *The Orchards of Syon* thus represents a distancing from Celan's late poetics, unlike the influence of Celan's stylistics on Hill's 'Two Chorale-Preludes' in *Tenebrae*, that I have analysed elsewhere.[105] However, the tension that Hill perceives between Celan's later working practices and his own poetic garrulity after *Canaan* is actually a misconception: as Joris emphasises, rather than *Atemwende* symbolising a gradual lapse into silence, between 1948 and 1963 'Celan published five collections of poems [...] With "Breathturn", this pattern changes drastically [...] To talk of *Verstummen* in the case of such high, not to say hectic, productivity is simply nonsense [...] Rather than falling silent, Celan became truly voluble in those, the last years of his life' (p. lxii).

Nevertheless, there are more specific metamodernist links between Celan's *Atemwende* and *The Orchards of Syon* in the context of Adorno's 'Commitment': both poets are striving in different ways to forge enigmatical poetry in their later work. As Joris indicates, the phrase '*Atemwende*' occurs in Celan's 'Meridian' speech on 22 October 1960, his 'most important and extended statement on poetics' (p. xlii), which took place seven years before the publication of the eponymous collection. In this lecture, Celan endorses Arthur Rimbaud's '*je est un autre*' as allowing for a 'single short moment', a 'breathturn', in which the 'estranged' is 'set free'. As well as a revised and elusive poetics, 'Atemwende' thus signals the importance of the epiphanic moments I have analysed above in *The Orchards of Syon*, as when Hill 'sets free' 'an Other' in the form of a bemusing heron: through the poet's encounter with this 'strangeness', the poem 'breaks open new reality'.[106] Yet, as I have demonstrated in relation to the passages about Normandy and the Manchester bombings, these enigmatic epiphanies always occur in the wider context of an engagement with modern history. The 'snow' for Celan in the poem beginning 'You may confidently ...' represents a post-war landscape that arises from but does not allude directly to recent historical atrocities (p. 3), just as the *pomerium* I explored above gestures towards the Blitz and Berlin Wall (another '*Wende*'), but focalises a 'marginal borderland' akin to Celan's *Grenzegelände*, 'into which, and from which language has to move for the poem to occur' (p. li). 'You may confidently ...' appears like a poetical antecedent to Adorno's aphorism in *Minima Moralia* that even 'the blossoming tree lies the moment its bloom is seen without the shadow of terror': Celan recounts that even the youngest leaf of the mulberry tree 'shrieked' when he 'strode through summer' (p. 3).[107] In 'Bad Time for

Poetry' Brecht writes of encroaching historicity in similar terms, but less aphoristically, when his 'Delight at the apple tree in blossom' is marred by 'the house-painter's speeches'.[108] Henri Lefebvre reads Celan's 'terror' in a positivistic sense: 'snow' here is 'the meteor of 20 January, of the Wannsee conference, of Auschwitz' (p. 462), whereas within committed *and* autonomous art the snow is representative of but also separate from such phenomena. Hill and Celan's work grapples with the 'scream [that] never falls silent' – as the latter's translated ending to the film *Night and Fog* (1956) puts it – but also strives to find this autonomous *Grenzegelände* in which, in Celan's poem 'Before your late face . . .', there is something '*un-* | *berührt von Gedänken*' ('un- | touched by thoughts') (pp. 4–5).[109] This closure recalls that of *The Orchards of Syon*, in which Hill imagines the eponymous orchards shorn of all human interaction, 'neither wisdom | nor illusion of wisdom, not | compensation, nor recompense' (p. 72). Of course, Celan's enjambment indicates that this imagined space may just be an 'illusion': after all, that autonomous 'something' ('*etwas*') is inevitably 'touched' (p. 5); similarly, the 'harvests we bring' to the Orchards of Syon may just be the compensations of human thought (p. 72).

April Warman argues that these orchards 'become a figure for grace untainted by the processes of history', but Hill's closure accedes that, in simultaneously committed and autonomous art, the paradisal can never be entirely unblemished by the 'deluge'.[110] Nevertheless, as early as section VIII, Hill hopes that he can conclude the book 'in some shape other | than vexed bafflement' (p. 8). *The Orchards of Syon* does not form a metamodernist text in terms of a baffling puzzle, but because Hill works through Celan's poetics in *Atemwende* in order to strive to understand epiphanic and enigmatic moments such as the encounters with the 'prinking' butterflies (p. 65) and 'banded spectrum' (p. 14) that I alluded to at the beginning of this chapter. Hill's collection adheres to Adorno's suggestion in *Aesthetic Theory* that the primary function of art should be 'a negation of a completely instrumentalised world', unlike Harrison's representation of Roman barbarities in *The Kaisers of Carnuntum*.[111] In contrast with Hill's work, Brecht champions the requirement for what Walter Benjamin termed '*plumpes Denken*' ('crude thinking'), 'that need for thought to simplify itself, crystallize out into essentials before it [can] be made practice', a conception that Adorno 'deplored'.[112] Benjamin's metaphor of crystallisation implies a process of purification, whereas Adorno argues in 'Commitment' that, in fact, the opposite is the case: the simplification of Nazism through gangster characters in *The Resistible Rise of Arturo Ui* is comparable to the creative approach to historical sources in

Harrison's verse plays, and the 'pornographic' threat of violence in *The Kaisers of Carnuntum*. A Brechtian retort to this formulation of autonomous art would be that the metamodernist 'perpetuation' of, and 'departure from', Celan's poetics in *The Orchards of Syon* results in hermeticism rather than productive enigmas: as Brecht commented on Expressionism and Dadaism, 'to write in such a way that as few people as possible dare to claim they understand you is no great art'.[113] According to this particular Marxist interpretation of modern art, Harrison's reimagining of Brecht's political and avant-garde theatre in the Herakles verse plays would be superior to Hill's revitalisation of Celan's understanding of committed and autonomous poetry. Yet Hill's enigmatical poetics, grappling with 'the largest of tropes', the enigma 'of the human condition', hardly constitutes the 'pretty pictures and aromatic words' in literature that Brecht despised.[114] Hill's wrestling with and against the 'deluge' of history in *The Orchards of Syon* situates it as one of the most important works of literature in the twenty-first century, compared to the 'compromised radicalism' of Harrison's work.[115]

CHAPTER 4

Iconoclasm and Enigmatical Commitment

In the previous chapter, I outlined the commitments of autonomous art when Geoffrey Hill engages with historical atrocities and 'enigma as the largest of tropes, a trope of the human condition'.[1] I now proceed to explore how the concept of enigmaticalness might be relevant to a younger generation of writers who, unlike Hill and Tony Harrison, draw on the formal predilections of both mainstream and 'innovative' poets. In response to a question about the supposed obduracy of his poetry, Ahren Warner asserted that 'a reader for whom a certain level of erudition is a problem is not a potential reader for my work'.[2] Warner demands the 'walking' readership that I discussed in the Introduction to this book: Hill admires patient, curious and attentive readers who are open to autonomous art, and who avoid writing that attempts simply to 'give' them something.[3] Moreover, Warner's engagement with the poetry of T. S. Eliot, Antonin Artaud and Ezra Pound suggests that his work might thrive on a 'recrudescence' of a 'refractory relation' between contemporary literature and 'dominant aesthetic values', 'mass culture' and 'society in general'.[4] For example, the 'Nervometer' sequence from *Pretty* (2013) is a 'collage and liberal translation' of Artaud's combative *Le Pèse-Nerfs* (1925), 'Métro' rewrites Pound's 'In a Station of the Metro' (1913) as a diatribe against human 'types', and 'Near St Mary Woolnoth' resituates *The Waste Land* (1922) amongst satirised 'Windsor-knotted ties' carousing near to the eponymous church.[5] David James's understanding of metamodernism as 'continuity and adaptation' in relation to early twentieth-century texts also chimes with Warner's interlacing of various languages, registers and discourses in the long sequence '*Lutèce, Te Amo*' from *Pretty*, in which twenty sections creatively 'map' the respective Parisian arrondissements against the city of Guillaume Apollinaire, Ernest Hemingway and Pablo Picasso.[6] As with Pound's Cantos, many of Warner's lines remain untranslated, including an entire section from '*Lutèce, Te Amo*' (XVI): Warner's uncompromising engagement with European languages has irked many poets and critics, who accuse him of an anachronistic and (implicitly) modernist élitism. Tony Williams berates the Lincolnshire poet for including 'untransliterated Greek in a poem' as a form of 'bad manners'; 'Ahren Warner's poems', Michael Woods laments, will be 'considered obscure by some readers'.[7] For a reader unfamiliar with Warner's poems, these criticisms might indicate an author rooted firmly in the 'innovative' tradition, or a poet aspiring to the enigmatical poetry that I have discussed throughout this book. Yet these suppositions would be inaccurate: allusions to modernist writers and a 'certain level of erudition' are not coterminous with the enigma.[8] Warner's poems are grounded in the modernist tradition, and often resist categorisation as either mainstream or 'innovative'. Yet his work is certainly not 'marooned' alongside Hill's with Pound and Eliot in the 1950s: as I shall illustrate in this chapter, Warner also shares with Don Paterson and Philip Larkin an innate suspicion towards enigmatical poetry.[9]

Nevertheless, critical responses to Warner's immersion in languages other than English reflect the tendency of mainstream poems to accommodate the reader, as Paterson recommends in his introduction to *New British Poetry* (2004), rather than to challenge 'complaisant aesthetics' with allusive and elusive poems.[10] In this context, the publication of Warner's work by Bloodaxe, a purported champion of accessible poetry, might appear surprising.[11] However, his recourse to the demotic introduces a register into his poetry familiar not only from the work of modernist writers such as Pound and Artaud, but also, with added insouciance, of Paterson and Larkin. Paterson's tendency to subvert his own poetics – as in the reference to his own '*bullshit*' in *Rain* (2009) – is mirrored in Warner's lines such as those from 'Pictogramme' in *Confer* (2011) in which the poet-narrator opines that television is 'shite really' (p. 25).[12] Warner's vacillation between modernist and anti-modernist forebears thus situates his work on the 'cusp', as Roddy Lumsden terms it, between mainstream and 'innovative' writing.[13] In contrast, James Byrne's poetry initially appears to have more in common with writers from the London and Cambridge Schools: 'Inclub Satires' from *Blood/Sugar* (2009) begins with an epigraph addressed to Pound, and proceeds to satirise a poetry reading in which the 'Chanel poet [. . .] cares to market absolute clarity' (p. 71).[14] This sequence draws on a long history of 'innovative' antipathy to the commodification of contemporary poetry, as in Basil Bunting's dismissal of poetry prizes as the symptom of 'a philistine establishment encouraging mediocre poets to write for an indifferent public'.[15] As with Bunting's appraisal of Ford Madox Ford's poetry, Byrne's tentative poetic explorations 'never end in discovery, only in willingness to rest content with an unsure glimpse'; as the latter phrases it in 'Apprentice Work' from *Blood/Sugar*, '*everything is invitation*' (p. 11).[16] Yet Byrne's work is also 'cusp' in that he draws on the formal propensities of both mainstream and 'innovative' poetry.[17] Whereas 'Historia' from *White Coins* (2015) starts Byrne's collection with the 'open form' that Peter Howarth has noted is indebted to modernist poetry, in the subsequent sequence, 'Economies of the Living', the abstractions, imperatives and metre have more in common with Hill's collection *Scenes from Comus* (2005) than the work of George Oppen.[18] Byrne's work, like Hill's, forms an instance of the 'temperate' or 'moderate' modernism that I discussed in the Introduction, which is open to the formal capacities of the enigma.[19]

This chapter thus explores whether debates surrounding metamodernism should be attuned to formal engagement rather than the frequency of allusion to modernist writers. In the context of Warner's poetry, Andre Furlani's sense of metamodernism as 'a perpetuation' as well as a 'departure' – akin to James's 'continuity and adaptation' in *The Legacies of Modernism* (2011) – is most keenly felt in 'Nervometer', the Lincolnshire poet's creative translation of Artaud's *Le Pèse-Nerfs*.[20] Artaud's narrator attracts Warner as one version of the iconoclastic outsider in literary modernism, such as the protagonist Ferdinand Bardamu in Louis-Ferdinand Céline's novel *Journey to the End of the Night* (1932).[21] Drawn to the immodesty and singularity of *Le Pèse-Nerfs*, Warner nevertheless 'departs' from Artaud's misogyny, anti-intellectualism and sometimes overly florid rhetoric to produce a sequence that develops the enigmatical poetics of the French poet's original text. This particular 'recrudescence' of modernism is anticipated in Warner's first collection, *Confer*, in which he reimagines Pound's 'In a Station of the Metro' in his ruminations on the Parisian underground.[22] As I discuss later in this chapter, rather than resulting in the lyrical puzzles of 'Nervometer', 'Métro' forms a neo-modernist pastiche of its predecessor: Warner's poem does not 'depart' from its modernist antecedents – that also include Richard Aldington's 'In the Tube' (1915) – in its élitism and antipathy towards the human form. In contrast, the '*Lutèce, Te Amo*' sequence from *Pretty* revitalises a modernist Paris of intellectuals, iconoclasts and eccentrics, and reimagines Charles Baudelaire's insalubrious city of poverty, and 'women of "pleasure"'.[23] In *Hello. Your Promise has been Extracted* (2017), the exuberant *flâneur* of '*Lutèce, Te Amo*' metamorphoses into a more disillusioned narrator who considers the 'implicated subject' during his European excursions.[24] However, this extended engagement with the individual's entanglement in histories of oppression halts when the poet-narrator comments – after an exposition of various trauma victims – that there is 'nothing to be done'.[25] In contrast, Byrne's knowledge of colonial implication in recent atrocities in Syria, Iraq, Libya and Burma results in a different kind of commitment in his collection *Places You Leave* (2021). Rather than considering inertia, in 'Cox's Bazar' Byrne recounts his workshops in a Bangladeshi camp in which traumatised survivors of the Myanmar massacres recall 'some of the worst human rights abuses committed this century' by the Burmese army.[26] Rather than capitulate to the formal restrictions of committed writing that I discussed in the last chapter, Byrne has produced a haunting poem that draws on the tradition of 'innovative' writing, and engages with survivor testimony by including lines into the texture of the poem that originated in the poetry workshops that he conducted in the camp. After an exposition of enigmatical commitment in relation to *Places You Leave* and *The Caprices* (2019), the final section of this chapter then discusses a selection of Byrne's open form poems: 'Historia' from *White Coins* and the sixth poem in *Withdrawals* (2019). These poems illustrate that writing considered in the context of debates about metamodernism should be understood in terms of formal achievement, the 'in-itself' of an artwork, rather than primarily in relation to a wrestling with modernist antecedents.[27]

The Enigmas of Le Pèse-Nerfs and 'Nervometer'

In this section, I discuss Warner's engagement with Artaud's work in terms of a 'continuity' with and 'adaptation' of modernist predecessors, but also, more importantly, in the context of the literary enigmas at the heart of *Le Pèse-Nerfs* and 'Nervometer'.[28] Warner is attracted to Artaud's iconoclastic acts in their various – and sometimes contradictory – forms, from his diatribes against canonical literary figures such as Samuel Taylor Coleridge and Franz Kafka, to his discussions with and subsequent rejection of André Breton's group of Surrealist artists.[29] In turn, Artaud was clearly drawn to the artistic insurrections of the Surrealists, and their dedication to 'the strongest possible attack on literature and art'.[30] The enigmatical-ness of *Le Pèse-Nerfs* forms an inextricable aspect of this iconoclasm, as Artaud attempts to describe the 'unnamed states, these superior positions of the soul [. . .] these periods in the mind, these tiny failures' that he argues are ignored by psychologists; the poet might not 'appear to advance much' in this matter, but he claims that he is nevertheless 'advancing more' than his literary peers, who are dismissed as 'bearded asses'.[31] In

'Nervometer', these 'shadows of men' cannot understand Artaud's distinctive conception of reality, which consists of a fragmented and amorphous
state, 'in a corner of one's self', and an anguished condition 'of extreme
shock, enlightened by unreality'.[32] Artaud describes *Le Pèse-Nerfs* as 'a kind
of constant waste of the normal level of reality' (*'Une espèce de déperdition
constante du niveau normal de la réalité'*).[33] These 'low voiced' words are
a deliberate travesty of the 'reality principle', since the French poet can 'no
longer touch life'.[34] Artaud rails against the 'shadows of men', including
psychologists and artists, who refuse to share this 'puzzle' of his alternative
vision of reality.[35] In the second section of 'Nervometer', Warner delays the
predicate ('[. . .] are lost in the shadows of men') for eleven lines as Artaud
augments his description of acquaintances who chose to pathologise him
with the less radical 'angst' rather than a more amorphous mental state of
'luminous pestling' (p. 64). The 'darkness' of men, in Jack Hirschman's
translation of *Le Pèse-Nerfs* (p. 34), cannot understand Artaud's experience
of the physicality of his angst. Moreover, there is 'a point, phosphorescent,
where reality | finds itself [. . .] metamorphosed': Artaud's descriptions of
his disrupted thought processes, a 'decanting at my core', are actually
a productive 'waste', an enigmatic and creative morass that – in
R. P. Blackmur's words – change and add to the 'stock' of reality, rather
than merely trying to replicate it.[36]

   This railing against 'shadows' of professionals who cannot understand
Artaud's mental distress encompasses the anti-intellectualism that Artaud
endorses throughout the enigmatic form of *Le Pèse-Nerfs*, and that Warner
wrestles with in his creative translation.[37] The rejection of 'bearded asses' in
Le Pèse-Nerfs obviously contrasts with the intellectual propensities of other
modernist writers – such as Eliot's absorption of Henri Bergson's lectures
at the Collège de France in 1910–11 – even if Artaud's anti-literary statements can partly be understood in the context of his flirtation with
Surrealism between 1924 and 1926.[38] However, Artaud's denigration of
the arts does not accord with Warner's allusions to philosophy, literature
and art elsewhere in his *oeuvre*, as I shall demonstrate in relation to the
latter's excisions from *Le Pèse-Nerfs*. Nevertheless, at the start of
'Nervometer', Warner emphasises the first instance of Artaud's provocative
statements in *Le Pèse-Nerfs*, *'Il ne faut pas trop laisser passer la littérature'*
('You must not admit too much literature'), by relocating it as the final line
in part one: this sentence anticipates the anti-literary bravura of the
extended 'All writing is pigshit' section later in *Le Pèse-Nerfs* that constitutes part ten of 'Nervometer'.[39] Warner's poet-narrator relishes the provocation, just as Larkin delighted in Wilfred Owen's declaration that his war

poems were not concerned with poetry: 'Isn't that a marvellous thing to say', the Hull poet eulogised in a letter to Monica Jones.[40] The artistic piquancy here lies in the purported rejection of the art form that these writers utilise, but which, for Larkin and Artaud, is dominated by coteries of 'bearded asses'.[41] However, Warner is attentive to the fact that the translation of '*Il ne faut pas trop laisser passer la littérature*' is not as simple as Jack Hirschman's version suggests, in which 'You have to do away [. . .] with literature'.[42] In Artaud's *Collected Works* (1968), Victor Corti translates the sentence instead as 'Literature must not show too much' (p. 70). '[S]how' introduces an ambiguity into Artaud's ostensibly anti-literary statement: allusions to literature may be present in the writing, but they should be implicit or at least avoid ostentation. Warner's translation, 'You must not admit too much literature', permits a similar, but different, ambivalence towards the literary. '[A]dmit' may mean 'disclose' various literary derivations, or it may indicate that the poet-narrator should debar examples of literature in a Surrealist resistance towards artistic tradition. In this instance, Warner's tracking of Artaud's iconoclasm in *Le Pèse-Nerfs* errs on the side of caution when addressing the ostensibly anti-literary. However, if the Surrealist diatribe against the canon appears partly checked in Warner's translation of this early line in *Le Pèse-Nerfs*, the 'all writing is pigshit' sequence is less equivocal.[43]

To paraphrase this section of *Le Pèse-Nerfs*, any writing that seeks to control experience, adheres to the 'reality principle', or thinks it can eschew ambiguity, the enigmatic and the slipperiness of language is 'pigshit'.[44] Yet Warner translates '*Toute l'écriture est de la cochonnerie*' as 'All writing is dishonest', rather than Hirschman's 'all writing is pigshit' and Corti's 'Writing is all trash'.[45] Rather than the more dismissive 'trash', Warner's 'departure' from *Le Pèse-Nerfs* introduces, it seems, either a structuralist sense of 'dishonest' writing, in that the signifier splits from the referent, or a poststructuralist approach to language in which meaning is constantly deferred.[46] However, the following clause makes it clear that 'dishonest' appertains specifically to '*Les gens qui sortent du vague*', 'Folks that shun the nebulous'.[47] Later on in this passage from *Oeuvres Complètes* (1956), Artaud's 'folks' are not 'all' writers, as in the initial, provocative statement, but rather '*cochons pertinents, maîtres du faux verbe, trousseurs de portrait, feuilletonnistes, rez-de-chaussée, herbagistes, entomologistes*' (p. 96). Corti translates this astonishing diatribe as aimed at 'pertinent pigs, masters of the false word, despatchers of portraits, gutter writers, graziers, entomologists' (p. 75); Hirschman prefers the more florid 'confectioners of portraits, pamphleteers, ground-floor lace-curtain herb collectors, entomologists' (p. 39). Rather than 'gutter writers' or 'pamphleteers', Warner chooses 'serial novelists' for *feuil-letonnistes* (p. 73); a more literal translation would simply be 'serialists'. Warner's phrase recalls Adorno's critique of Sartre's conception of the 'committed' novelist that I discussed in Chapter 2, as someone who can convey historical truth through prose. Entomologists – and probably 'ground-floor lace curtain herb collectors' too (p. 39) – wish to classify nature: Artaud compares this process to a circumscribing of words, the dully empiricist version of language that Adorno rejects in his defence of autono-mous art in 'Commitment'. In a passage that Warner excises from his version of *Le Pèse-Nerfs* a few sentences later, Artaud explains further his commit-ment to 'nebulous', anti-scientific writing: 'Do not expect me to tell you what all this is called or into how many sections it is divided, or to tell you its value [. . .] Or clarify it, or bring it to life, to adorn it with a host of words, polished meaning'.[48]

This passage provides an apt description of the enigma of *Le Pèse-Nerfs* as a whole, and Artaud's conception of 'nebulous' poetry that Warner pits against 'serial novelists' (p. 73). Yet the French writer's conception of elusive writing is directed against intellectuals and 'bearded' poets as much as popular culture. In addition, Artaud's defence of the obscure in this section from *Le Pèse-Nerfs* is ironic in the context of Warner's restructuring of 'Nervometer' that indicates another divagation from the modernist ante-cedent. Warner sometimes deliberately eschews Artaud's more 'nebulous' writing so as to produce a more fluid and cogent sequence (p. 72). In his striving to 'detail the events of thought' elsewhere in *Pretty* – as in his extended ruminations on somatic minutiae in 'Metousiosis' – and his wish to produce a concise version of *Le Pèse-Nerfs*, toiling 'for precision' with the 'unoiled movements' of translation, he cannot help but become one of the 'contemporary bastards' of exactitude that Artaud dismisses. This tactic leads to a refinement of the following clause, '*Tout la gent littéraire est cochonne*' (p. 95), that Hirschman and Corti translate, respectively, as 'the whole literary scene is a pigpen' (p. 38), and 'the whole pack of literati are trash' (p. 75).[49] '[S]cene' is suitably vague, and 'literati' refers to the learned and those who read widely: this description certainly appertains to Warner's labours. Yet Warner's 'men of letters' draws attention away momentarily from 'contemporary bastards' such as the translator himself, and focuses instead on clubbable and usually aged connoisseurs of literature (p. 72). Artaud's iconoclasm then veers away from these 'bastards' to target scientific writing, and inferior novelists in Warner's translation. In the next sentence, Artaud adumbrates those who '*ont des points de repère sans l'esprit*' (p. 95), who have Hirschman's 'vantage points in their spirit' (p. 38), Corti's 'landmarks in their mind' (p. 75); or, in Warner's version, those 'who would map the mind' (p. 72). In the midst of this anti-literary and anti-scientific diatribe, Warner's version of *Le Pèse-Nerfs* then prudently exorcises a passage that recalls Eliot's women who 'come and go | Talking of Michelangelo' in 'The Love Song of J. Alfred Prufrock'.[50] Artaud similarly indulges in misogyny in the 'pigshit' passage when, in Hirschman's translation, there are 'those [authors] about whom women talk so well, and also those women who talk so well, who talk of the contemporary currents of thought; those who [. . .] drop names, who fill books with screaming headlines [. . .] are pigs' (p. 38). As I discuss later in relation to *Hello. Your Promise has been Extracted*, Warner has been accused of misogynistic portrayals of female characters, but here he is careful to disassociate women from '*la cochonnerie*' (p. 95).

From my analysis of 'Nervometer' so far, it can be deduced that Warner adheres to the intertextual sense of metamodernism as a complex working through of modernist antecedents, including sensitive interpretations of the 'nebulous' *Le Pèse-Nerfs*. But how does Warner inscribe Artaud's enigmatical poetics into the *form* of the creative translation? Having outlined Warner's adherence to and divergence from the iconoclasm of *Le Pèse-Nerfs*, it is important to consider the way in which he deals with 'stylistic tenor and texture' and 'idioms of diction' in 'Nervometer', as well as 'the overarching organization' of the narrative.[51] In his notes to *Pretty*, Warner describes 'Nervometer' as lurking 'somewhere between a version, collage and liberal translation of Antonin Artaud's *Le Pèse-Nerfs*' (p. 79). However, some critics have interpreted the '*After*' at the beginning of the sequence (p. 61) to indicate an entirely creative response to rather than translation of Artaud's work: Paul McDonald refers to a 'beautiful suite of poems *inspired* by Antonin Artaud'.[52] Despite some divergences, 'Nervometer' is in fact best understood as a close and often ingenious translation of *Le Pèse-Nerfs*, which sometimes improves on the original in its compression of the sequence, and its excision of superfluous or offensive material. Translation thus forms a way to get as close as possible to a modernist antecedent in another language, without denying the possibility of contemporary refinement. Unlike Artaud, Warner toils for concision in 'Nervometer', and a requirement to avoid what Pound termed the emotive 'slither' of poetry.[53] It is commendable that Warner manages to evade this pitfall in a sequence that is steeped in heightened rhetoric: indeed, Artaud referred to his cerebral ruminations as 'imperceptible slitherings', a phrase that recalls Pound's admonishment.[54] Warner achieves Poundian exactitude in his translation of *Le Pèse-Nerfs* through creative extemporisation on the original, and judicious editing. 'After' in epigraphs to translations functions as a temporal adverb denoting continuity as well as rupture: after all, the contemporary piece is usually 'in imitation of' or 'in the style of' the previous artist.[55] Continuation here designates a creative rendition of Artaud's *Le Pèse-Nerfs* that is still entuned to the Surrealist sequence, but also willing to take creative risks in order to enhance Warner's version. Part two of 'Nervometer' contains an example of this creative approach to translation. Corti and Hirschman translate the enigmatic phrase *'une trituration effervescente'* as, respectively, 'an excited manipulation of powers' (p. 33), and 'an excited grinding of powers' (p. 70), whereas Warner conceives the phrase as 'a luminous pestling' (p. 64), a more concise, rhythmical and aptly poetic version than the alternative translations.

At the same time, this succinct rendition chimes with Artaud's depiction of angst in this passage as an enigmatic but nevertheless physical manifestation. Similarly, Warner's compact phrase 'myoclonic belief' (p. 65) provides a sharper alternative to Corti's translation of *'Le sommeil venait d'un déplacement de croyance'* (p. 88) as 'Sleep came from the shifting of belief' (p. 70). However, Warner also veers from the original French here in order to create a tauter alternative, since 'myoclonic' links to the previous clause, that replaces Hirschman's 'nerves taut the leg's whole length' (p. 34) with a more effective verb: 'nerves tense the legs' whole length' (p. 65). Warner's divergences from the literal result in a more elegant translation: in the same section, Hirschman and Corti translate *'ce brusque renversement des parties'* (p. 88) as, respectively, 'this brusque reversal of parts' (p. 34), and 'this brusque reversing of roles' (p. 71), whereas Warner chooses a less awkward phrase, 'the sudden inverse of opposites' (p. 65). Similarly, Warner plumps for the terser 'Desiccated minds' to translate *'tous les esprits se dessécher'* (p. 74), rather than Hirschman's 'all minds parched' (p. 39) or Corti's 'all minds dry up' (p. 76). Through this concision, Warner is able to reject the unnecessarily verbose, as in Hirschman's translation of *'les ratiocenations d'une nature imbécilement pointilleuse, ou habitée d'un levain d'inquiétudes dans le sens de sa hauteur'* (p. 89) as 'the ratiocinations of an imbecilically fastidious nature, or inhabited by a leaven of worries in the sense of height' (p. 35). In contrast, Warner opts for the succinct phrase 'dim finickiness', and 'the inhabiting of angst rising to its height' (p. 67). Three lines later, Warner then avoids rhetorical rather than emotional 'slither' when he exorcises the hifalutin lines *'Un impouvoir à cristalliser inconsciemment, le point rompu de l'automatisme à quelque degré que ce soit'* (p. 90), that Hirschman translates as the impotence 'to crystallize unconsciously the broken point of automatism to any degree whatsoever' (p. 35), and Corti – equally awkwardly – as 'A powerlessness to fix unconsciously the point of rupture of automatism at any level whatsoever' (p. 72).

In adhering to Pound's warning about 'slither', Warner thus simultaneously condenses Artaud's enigmatic writing about his amorphous states of mind. This process is also evident in the manipulation of narrative structure: Warner compresses the first four paragraphs of *Le Pèse-Nerfs* into four lines that allow for a more dramatic opening to the sequence. Rather than begin with Corti's 'I really felt you break down the environment around me, I felt you create a void to allow me to progress' (p. 69), Warner hones in on Artaud's lines that are translated in Corti's third paragraph: 'I have always been struck by the obduracy | of mind – by how it must always want to think | in dimensions' (p. 63). Warner is thus able to focus immediately on disrupted mental processes – the main theme of *Le Pèse-Nerfs* – and emphasise Artaud's desire for the impossibility of being able to think outside of thinking. Subsequently, whereas Hirschman's grandiose translation refers to the 'glacial blooms of my inner soul' that dribble 'all over me' (p. 26), Warner's version is much crisper: 'I admit of an intricately wrought soul – | brimstone, phosphoric' (p. 63). In part four of 'Nervometer', Warner writes of 'A word – precise, subtle' (p. 66): he aims for this lexical neatness throughout his version of *Le Pèse-Nerfs*, as at the end of this section, when '*la portée*' (literally the 'range' of a word) is translated as 'import', rather than Corti and Hirschman's 'scope' (pp. 72, 35). Indeed, the English title itself forms a key example of this process: the latter translate '*Pèse-Nerfs*' (p. 96) as 'Nerve Scales' (p. 75) and 'Brain-Storm', whereas Warner coins the more precise 'Nervometer'. Moreover, in part five, Corti and Hirschman render '*le tout es dans une certaine floculation du choses*' (p. 90) as, respectively, 'the whole thing lies in a certain flocculation of objects' (p. 72), and 'Everything lies in a certain flocculation of things' (p. 35), whereas Warner compresses these sentences into four words: 'All this is flux' (p. 67). Translation itself is a form of Poundian 'cleansing' here, as a choice word or phrase renders the original French in a more singular fashion than the other translators.

'Métro', '*Lutèce, Te Amo*' and Neo-Modernism

The fulmination in *Le Pèse-Nerfs* against precise 'bastards' encompasses Artaud's sense of his work's enigmatic irreducibility.[56] As I have outlined, the objects of his ire in this sequence include artists, scientists and, by proxy, his translators. However, in relation to the rest of his *oeuvre*, these 'shadows' of men who misunderstand him include the working class as well as the cultural élite.[57] Artaud renounced, for example, 'as a coward every being who does not agree that life is given to him only to separate himself from the masses'.[58] Such disdain forms a key attribute of the first reference to Artaud in *Pretty*: Warner ruminates on the photograph in *Portraits d'écrivains* (2010) of a youthful Artaud in '*Lutèce, Te Amo*', and emphasises the sneer of the youthful, attractive iconoclast, rather than the dishevelled and drug-ravaged poet in 1947, whose rants included an anti-Semitic diatribe against Kafka.[59] Warner's poet-narrators in *Confer* and *Pretty* often share with Artaud his sense of élitism as a prerequisite for the artist's distinctiveness. In '*Legare*' from *Confer*, the narrator rewrites a sentence from *The Great Gatsby* (1925), in which Nick Carraway ponders that 'Every one suspects himself of at least one of the cardinal virtues, and this is mine: I am one of the few honest people that I have ever known'; in Warner's poem, élitism 'in Fitzgerald's vein' is considered instead 'a cardinal virtue' (p. 52).[60]

In this section, I examine how Warner's *flâneurs* in 'Métro' and '*Lutèce, Te Amo*' similarly separate themselves from the alleged vulgarity of the crowd, which Pound typifies as '*un visage stupide*' ('a stupid face') in '*Dans un Omnibus de Londres*' (1916).[61] Andrew Thacker considers underground travel as 'the central symbol of *urban* modernity in the twentieth century', because it 'produces the perilous necessity of trying to individualise one's identity and thus distance oneself from the lumpen mass': 'Métro' functions as a neo-modernist rather than metamodernist examination of disdain, in which Warner reimagines Pound's 'In a Station of the Metro' in a contemporaneous Paris of rejected clones.[62] Albert Bermel argues that Artaud intended to 'strip sexuality of its sentimental disguises', and the same claim could be made for the poet-narrator's depiction of a blonde woman on the underground in 'Métro', who enables him to 'distance' himself from the 'mass'.[63] She initially attracts his attention through what he further considers to be superficial physicality: this rejection results in an apocalyptic ending that replicates Richard Aldington's attack on his fellow passengers in his 1915 poem 'In the Tube', which ends with the accusation 'What right have you to live?'[64] Thacker analyses the contractions in time and space afforded by the underground of the modernist city, but these are not Warner's concerns in 'Métro': instead, the poet-narrator argues that such conforming objects of desire as the anonymous woman are 'asking' to be 'cut down'.[65]

Artaud's sense of the iconoclastic writer who dismisses cowards who do not agree 'that life is given to him only to separate himself from the masses' is clearly important to Warner's mordant poet-narrator.[66] However, rather than a metamodernist continuation and adaptation of the modernist antecedent in 'Nervometer' or an enigmatic exposition of Thacker's sense of compressed time and space, in 'Métro' a neo-modernist élitism predominates that replicates rather than transforms its predecessor. In Pound's 'In a Station of the Metro', the 'apparition' of plural faces immediately takes the reader away from any specificities of the crowd: this movement eases the shift in the second line to the even more abstract petals and bough.[67] In contrast, Warner's 'Métro' initially moves in the opposite direction, from the amorphous huddle to '*that*' blonde's décolletage (p. 30). During the *outré* exposure of 'unsentimental' desire, the first two stanzas invite the reader to register her distinctiveness: this process is reflected in the stanzas' metrical tension, as her arresting image instigates metrical breaks or inversion on 'Take', 'take', '*that*', 'scrape', 'seeps', 'cheeks' and 'roughed high'.[68] In the third stanza, the poet-narrator dispels this illusion with the assertion that she is not 'special': his distaste is registered in the repetition of her 'seeping' features, akin to the 'Antagonism [. . .] Disgust [. . .] antipathy' in Aldington's poem: she is only 'of a certain kind', one of '*those* faces', like the collective eyes that interweave 'In the Tube'.[69] The tone here is that of Artaud's élitist whose 'life is given to him only to separate himself' from the 'wet dogs' that he refers to in his essay on Van Gogh: the poet-narrator appropriates the 'bough' in Pound's poem to refer to the 'branch' of humankind, on which various 'kinds' or 'scions' eclipse individuality.[70] A 'scion', from the old French '*ciun*', denotes a young root, but also a descendant of a noble family: 'Métro' replicates Pound's sense in 'Hugh Selwyn Mauberley' that our diminished and 'botched' civilisation is old and corrupted, a 'bitch gone in the teeth'.[71] Of course, the disposable 'types' that the neo-modernist poet-narrator abhors in 'Métro' do not appertain to his own persona, just as Aldington distinguishes himself from the depicted 'Eyes of greed, of pitiful blankness, of plethoric complacency'.[72] As with a female prostitute in Baudelaire's *Les Fleurs du Mal* (1857), the poet-narrator in 'Métro' may primarily be concerned with the ruminations of a *flâneur*, but he thereby inevitably 'denies her the power of observation, entirely objectifying her'.[73] Indeed, it may be possible that the depicted woman may herself be a *flâneuse*: as Deborah Parsons argues, 'in the modern city of multiplicity, reflection, and indistinction, *la femme passante* is herself a *flâneuse*, just as the "man of the crowd" is also a *flâneur*' (p. 6).

Rather than reworking the modernist antecedent to hone enigmatical poetry, therefore, as in Hill's response to Eliot's *Four Quartets* (1941), Warner's 'Métro' is 'marooned' in 1915 with Aldington's 'In the Tube'.[74] In this pastiche of the modernist outsider, who becomes 'increasingly detached from his asphalt experience', the implication remains that the poet-narrator is in some way distinctive as opposed to his object of desire, and the travellers described as a 'growth of soft flesh, rattling minds, | just asking to be cut down'.[75] '[S]oft flesh' functions here as the amorphous and anonymous 'meat' in Céline's *Journey to the End of the Night*, akin to a 'seepage' of cancerous growth that underpins the supposedly vacuous brains of the masses, with their 'rattling minds'.[76] The murderous impulse in response to Aldington's question, 'What right have you to live?', transforms the comic violence contained in 'Take [...] that' in the first stanza into the unpleasant similarities between the closure of 'asking to be cut down' and the colloquial phrase 'asking for it', a misogynist response to the voluptuousness described in the first stanza. In the space of eighteen lines, desire has quickly metamorphosed into violence: there is more than a hint of pseudo-modernist fascism in the poet-narrator's reaction that she, and, by extension, humankind, deserve to be 'cut down' for their lack of distinction. Thacker argues that John Carey's inditement of modernist élitism in *The Intellectuals and the Masses* (1992) can be read in the context of literary responses to the underground as an 'anxious rejection of one's travelling companions [...] another spatial phobia, where what produces panic is [...] the crowded density of other people'.[77] Such a generous reading is hard to glean from the closure of 'Métro': far from panicking, the controlled diction suggests a suave and cynical poet-narrator, who is perfectly relaxed in his summation that the 'soft flesh' of humanity should be obliterated.[78]

Compared with 'Nervometer', and its considered engagement with the enigmas of Artaud's *Le Pèse-Nerfs*, 'Métro' therefore functions as a pastiche of modernist tropes and sensibilities, regurgitating them in a form of poetic melancholia. It may be that the poem is deliberately 'marooned' in 1915, and is intended to be a satire of early twentieth-century élitism. Indeed, due to the lack of contemporaneous detail – unlike Aldington's 'slates on the floor' and 'woodwork pitted with brass nails' (p. 74) – 'Métro' could as easily be set in the modernist as the contemporary period: the possibility remains that Warner could be depicting a response to the underground from the early twentieth century, rather than replicating the abhorrence in the present. In contrast, '*Lutèce, Te Amo*' returns to Paris as the archetypal modernist city in order to revitalise its depiction in early twentieth-century writing as a centre for intellectuals, iconoclastic artists and eccentric individuals. As Thacker outlines, Paris is a 'thoroughly overdetermined cultural space: the city of light, the capital of modernity, the home of the "lost generation", or a magnet for avant-garde writers and artists across Europe and far beyond – these are just a few of the epithets and

descriptions used to capture the cultural standing of the French capital'
(p. 24). In the twenty sections of '*Lutèce, Te Amo*', Warner utilises his
characteristically macaronic diction to engage with a litany of modernist
writers, artists and ex-pats, including Apollinaire, Artaud, Picasso,
Hemingway, Jean-Paul Sartre, Egon Schiele, Fernand Léger and Chaïm
Soutine.[79] Paris here is a city intertwined with its modernist antecedents:
Warner puns, for example, on 'grenadine' and 'grenade' when Hemingway
offers Picasso a carton of explosives after the liberation of Paris (p. 19).[80] In
addition, the reader encounters reimagined 'outsider' figures from
Baudelaire's *Les Fleurs du Mal*, such as prostitutes and beggars. Warner
adheres to Baudelaire's conception of the *flâneur*: he is 'open to the stimuli
and walks the streets of the city at a slow and leisurely pace, an observer and
recorder [. . .] the archetypal modern subject, passive and open, restrained
and appreciative'.[81] Moreover, as in Walter Benjamin's *Arcades Project*
(1927–40), '*Lutèce, Te Amo*' maps 'the relationship between things, the
thresholds and invisible boundaries of Paris', and functions similarly as
a 'vascular network of imagination' (p. 52). However, Warner does not
merely perpetuate a 'structure of feeling' surrounding Benjamin's Paris in
the 1930s, but 'departs', in Furlani's terms, from modernism by depicting
a contemporaneous Paris concerned with issues such as homelessness,
racism, the European Union and the legacies of collaboration during
World War Two.[82] There is no attempt in '*Lutèce, Te Amo*' to transform
the destitute into Baudelaire's symbols of transcendence in *Les Fleurs du
Mal*, as when the poet-narrator exclaims, in 'The Seven Old Men', '*Ces sept
monstres hideux avaient l'air éternel*' ('These seven hideous freaks had a look
of eternity about them!).[83] Nor does Warner replicate Baudelaire's departure from 'loathsome things' into phantasmagoria in *Les Fleurs du Mal*:
'everything', the poet-narrator contends in 'The Little Old Woman', 'even
horror, turns to magic' ('*Où tout même l'horreur, tourne aux enchantements*')
(p. 179). Indeed, the utopian spirit of Benjamin's project – or, indeed, Le
Corbusier's modernist architecture – is entirely absent from '*Lutèce, Te
Amo*'. There is no prospect that the 'fractures and joins of the everyday' will
reveal exciting Surrealist possibilities '*of what might be*', as in Benjamin's
city.[84] Instead, in the epigraph to '*Lutèce, Te Amo*' from Durs Grünbein's
'Europe After The Last Rains', Europe flounders as an unsettling 'dream'
of late capitalism (p. 11).

This intensive assimilation of and then 'departure' from modernist
forebears does not mean that Warner then strives for the enigmatic
sublimity of 'Nervometer', as the first section of '*Lutèce, Te Amo*'
demonstrates.[85] In 'Here', pigeons represent the masses, and are associated

with tourist sites in the first arrondissement. Deploying one version of the three words that Warner repeats throughout this sequence in *Pretty* ('*désinvolte*', '*envolver*' and '*in-vólvere*'), the birds are also '*désinvoltes*' (p. 13), parading an 'excessive liberty' (p. 11) as they defecate on the statues of Molière, Voltaire and Joachim Murat.[86] Warner then links these Columbiformes to less 'libertine' outsiders, the peripatetic workers in 'the old slum shacks of the Carrousel': the latter recall Baudelaire's labourers in 'The Swan', who toil in the Carousel's 'makeshift booths, those piles of rough-hewn capitals and pillars' (p. 175); in '*Lutèce, Te Amo*', the stalls are no sooner 'unwrapped' than 'packed off' north beyond the palace wall (p. 13). Like Benjamin's arcades, the fairground in '*Lutèce, Te Amo*' symbolises a Paris that is about to vanish: similarly, Baudelaire notes the ephemera of the 'makeshift' and 'rough-hewn' in 'The Swan', lamenting that 'The Paris of old is there no more – a city's pattern changes, alas, more swiftly than a human heart' (p. 174); Baudelaire's '*Tableaux parisiens*' track this 'pattern' of disappearing lifeforms and objects. However, Warner's emphasis is on a celebration of liberty in the dissolute form of these 'flying rats', and their iconoclastic defecations. Pigeons let 'piss-shit combos' fall on a representative of revolutionary history (p. 13): Murat was an admiral and Marshal of the Empire during Napoleon's reign. It is no coincidence that the final two statues are themselves iconoclasts: the birds' actions underline Molière's satire of church pieties, and Voltaire's critiques of religious dogma. This demotic of 'piss-shit combos' can be aligned with a desire to *épater les bourgeois* (p. 13), as in Artaud's dismissal of all writing as 'pigshit'.[87] In this section, the repetition of 'I guess' suggests a less revolutionary intertextual link to Larkin's poetry. The second instance of 'I guess' indicates a necessary failure of memory, and act of imagination, as the poet-narrator envisages but cannot vouch for the historical authorities corralling the fairground vendors. In contrast, at the exact moment in which Warner introduces a simile for the first time in the poem and entire collection ('like [. . .] the old slum shacks'), he simultaneously undermines this metaphorical gesture with poetic insouciance ('I guess'). Warner's phrase recalls Larkin's similar ending to 'Mr Bleaney' ('I don't know') that undercuts the suppositions about the factory worker that Larkin has outlined in the preceding twenty-seven lines.[88] Similarly, the first 'I guess' subverts the putative connection between the libertine pigeons and the slum shacks, just as Larkin betrays his concern that Mr Bleaney may be entirely unlike the vulgar figure he has imagined, who prefers working-class sauce bottles to the more ubiquitous gravy. 'I guess' ('*je suppose*') is not a phrase that one can imagine Artaud deploying, whose emphasis instead is on iconoclastic overstatement rather than the vacillations over the poetic encountered in the work of Larkin, Paterson and Warner.

In other words, mainstream poetry's suspicion towards the artistic form it purports to celebrate remains an undercurrent in Warner's *oeuvre*. In contrast, part four of '*Lutèce, Te Amo*' returns to an implicit veneration of modernist antecedents peppering the sequence, that is opposed to the perceived vulgarity of 'Continental Culture' (p. 18). In the last chapter, I outlined Brecht's rejection of 'culinary' art, which exists merely for the audience's pleasure rather than mindful engagement: Warner's poet-narrator is trapped between the incessant bells of Notre Dame, and what he perceives as a vulgar repetition of Bach's Toccata. The 'culinary' is then associated with prostitution, as the 'phantasm' ambles to rue Blondel and a young '*putain*': the phrase ('whore' rather than 'prostitute') is reminiscent of Baudelaire's use of '*catin*' in '*Au Lecteur*' to describe an 'old whore' in the first poem of *Les Fleur du Mal*.[89] Warner then associates her with the cheese wrappers of Tommes des Pyrénées and Saint-Marcellins, similarly 'pimped and pressed against the glass' (p. 16), in an implicit attack on commodification that encompasses the 'culinary'. Artaud makes the same link between culture and prostitution when he comments that 'There are those who go to the theatre as they would go to a brothel. Furtive pleasure. For them the theatre is only momentary excitement'.[90] Warner and Artaud focus on the perils of commodification, rather than Baudelaire's moralising about prostitutes in *Les Fleur du Mal*.[91] In part six, Artaud and Brecht's sense that the classics are often merely 'pimped' to an audience desperate for a thrill reaches its apotheosis in Warner's diatribe against 'Continental Culture' that is sustained for thirty-one lines (p. 18).[92] Here, the poet-narrator disdains classical musicians who strive to make their music more palatable to tourists, as well as philistine celebrations of Left Bank establishments such as Les Deux Magots or Café de Flore. Even when 'possessed with a rabid sense of vulgarity', as Buse *et al* put it in *Benjamin's Arcades* (2005), the 'flâneur haunts the streets in search of material' (p. 11): the poet-narrator joins the 'coterie' from Romford, Phoenix and Denver, and winces at the 'culinary' appreciation of the violinists' 'jazz hands', as musicians 'add a little theatre' to 'demanding' music (p. 18). Recalling the tempting cheese wrappers 'pimped' in windows in part four (p. 16), the dangers of accommodating culture are likened to the glass panes of Mulberry, Vuitton and Christian Dior that flank the medieval square where the concert takes place. Subsequently, the 'tainted' music funnels into Left Bank cafes, where trinkets harbour allegedly tempting smears of 'intellectual spunk' that Sartre discharged around the time he wrote the articles on ethics finally published as *Cahiers pour une morale* (1983) (p. 18).[93] Part six of '*Lutèce, Te Amo*' thus presents élitism, as in '*Legare*', as a necessary virtue in its dismissal of what the neo-modernist poet-narrator, an 'autocratic Le Corbusian *flâneur*', perceives as egregious vulgarity and errant philistinism.[94]

Enigmatical Commitment in 'Cox's Bazar' and *The Caprices*

In *Hello. Your Promise has been Extracted*, Warner quotes – one assumes with approval – Adorno's statement in *Aesthetic Theory* that by 'crystallising itself as something unique to itself, rather than complying with existing social norms and qualifying as "socially useful," [art] criticises society by merely existing'.[95] Throughout this book, I return to Adorno's conception of enigmaticalness as a form in which art can register its resistance to the 'reality principle' (p. 120) and the '"socially useful"' (p. 226). Poems such as '*Lutèce, Te Amo*' could be argued to oppose 'existing social norms' through their endorsement of modernist-influenced writing and their dismissal of 'Continental Culture'.[96] However, as I noted in Chapter 1, Adorno's understanding of art in *Aesthetic Theory* does not encompass all instances of literature: despite its underpinning modernist ex-pats, '*Lutèce, Te Amo*' does not comply with the philosopher's sense that modern art embodies an 'abstractness' and 'irritating indeterminacy' than distinguishes it from 'older aesthetic norms' (pp. 21–2). Moreover, the irony of Adorno's quotation embedded in *Hello. Your Promise has been Extracted* is that the collection does not resist 'existing social norms' or predominant aesthetic expectations in the form of the passages that engage with the implicated subject (p. 226). These sections are the most prosaic in the entire book, as when the poet-narrator refers to the explosion in Tianjin on 12 August 2015: 'I know you care. I know the effort it takes to forget the river running between Tianjin and Beijing, the corruption of which is utterly complete' (p. 76).[97] As Adorno stresses in *Aesthetic Theory*, 'Art holds true to the shudder, but not by regression to it': literature may 'merely exist', but only books that respond adequately to atrocities through their 'truth content' can truly, in Adorno's definition, be referred to as art (p. 118).

In contrast with these passages in *Hello. Your Promise has been Extracted*, the form of the poetry as well as the words' import in Byrne's *Places You Leave* offers recourse to the poet-narrator's provocation in Warner's collection that there's 'nothing you can do – there's nothing to be done' (p. 76). As Rothberg notes in *The Implicated Subject*, the temptation is often towards despair and inaction that 'prop up the structures of inequality that mar the present' (p. 1). On the one hand, the prosaic sentence in *Hello. Your Promise has been Extracted* replicates a platitude about social inertia; but it only does so ironically, as the previous phrase, 'Just a note to softly lull', intimates (p. 76). The implication is that there *is* something to be done, but what this 'is' demands remains unexplored in the matrix of 'indirect, structural, and collective forms of agency that enable injury, exploitation, and domination'.[98] In contrast, Byrne and Shehzar Doja delivered poetry workshops in April 2019 on the work of Eliot, Pound, H. D. and Mina Loy in Cox's Bazar, the world's largest refugee camp.[99] Many of the inhabitants had escaped from the Tatmadaw, the armed forces of Myanmar, and had no formal education. Yet together they produced the poetry anthology *I am a Rohingya: Poetry from the Camps and Beyond* (2019), that was submitted to the evidence at the International Court of Human Rights in The Hague surrounding Aung San Suu Kyi's actions during the atrocities.[100] Nevertheless, the opening poem in *Places You Leave* begins with fragmented ruminations on the failures of 'committed' poetry to respond to the atrocities recounted in *I am a Rohingya*. In 'Cox's Bazar', trauma 'is missing' on the 'blank page', and a mother's letter to a guard about a 'non-trial' is a merely a 'windbreak'.[101]

Enigmatic lines proliferate during this lament for poetry's inefficacy, such as 'Without "art", it's just "he", meaning brother. Come here, brother, but he isn't listening'. These lines do not work in terms of the 'reality principle': even if we appreciate that the first clause links back to 'putting the art back into heart' in a previous line, we do not know exactly what they signify; but this in no way attenuates the affective field of traumatic dissonance.[102] Rather than conceive of his response to the Myanmar massacres in terms of the neo-modernist outsider, Byrne's engagement combines personal recollections of the camp with these allusive and elusive examples of Rohingya testimony: a second-person narrative encapsulates the different perspectives, at the same time as Byrne stresses his 'comfortable seat of western privilege'.[103] Testimony's fractured narratives form the 'Scars of damage and disruption' that are the 'modern's seal of authenticity' in *Aesthetic Theory* (p. 23). However, rather than representing the 'scarred' western subject of post-Holocaust philosophy, the 'fracturedness' of this testimony refers to human rights abuses in Myanmar, and the poet's struggle to assimilate aspects of the survivors' grief into his work (p. 126). Whereas the 'you' in *Hello. Your Promise has been Extracted* wishes to implicate the reader in the poet-narrator's ironic response to implication ('there's nothing you can do' [p. 76]), the second-person narration in 'Cox's Bazar' implores the reader instead to listen carefully to the testimony, such as the recounting of a brother who 'ran towards the Tatmadaw, crying "Jayzu, Jayzu"', and whose subsequent fate is unclear. Thereafter in the poem, the brother's narrative is compressed into the enigmatic phrase 'Jahaj of air': 'Jahaj' means 'ship' in Bangla; the phrase may refer to the traumatic capture of the brother, his internment in the 'Jail' recounted in the next sentence, the anguish of the addressee or the 'jail of fresh air' in a poem from *I am a Rohingya* that describes Pacifist Farooq as lost in a 'dark cosmos'.[104] Such instances of suffering conveyed through this prose poetry are considered at the end of the first page to be 'bare as a pulse, a knife' (p. 7). If this simile continues into the next clause, then this writing establishes a vulnerable attempt to engage with the workshop attendees' mourning, as the next sentence, 'Siblings in graves', indicates. However, Byrne then reverses the elusive simile in the next line, so that poem is, subsequently, 'bare as a knife, a pulse'. This, more redemptive, reading of the testimony and overall poem offers 'Cox's Bazar' as a more potent response to the atrocities, a 'pulse' in itself that underscores the Rohingyas' survival and the possibility of future redress, as with the presentation of the anthology amongst the evidence surrounding Aung San Suu Kyi's implication in the atrocities.

Yet how are these ambiguities of consolation contested in the enigmatic lines of fractured testimony, and the puzzle of the poem as a knife or 'pulse'? In the tradition of the elegy, reparations of form are always implicated in an economy of suffering. The beginning of 'Cox's Bazar' alludes to one of Pound's Cantos (CXVI) when the poet-narrator complains that 'you', rather than the modernist poet's work, 'would like to cohere' (p. 7): the elegiac irony here is that the traumatised writer or anguished interlocutor may not 'cohere', but the poem as a whole certainly does with its terse yet elusive sentences.[105] Attentive to the long history of compromised solace in the elegy, James notes that modernist forms are especially potent and fraught in their engagement with the iterations of trauma: 'Consolation for modernism [...] is often legible—and controversial—in works whose ruptured forms draw energy and articulacy from traumatic, sorrowful, or foreboding situations that seem beyond the textual representation, let alone recovery'.[106] Indeed, there has been a critical 'turn' against the seeming inextricability of modernist legacies and trauma fiction since the publication of Roger Luckhurst's *The Trauma Question* (2008): other literary forms, such as realism, are clearly efficacious in dealing with traumatic experiences. Yet this critical development risks occluding Adorno's conception of the 'truth content' of a work of art to make a (true) point about the capaciousness of literary form.[107] In *Discrepant Solace*, James stresses that the heightened 'expressive vigour' of modernist – and, by extension, metamodernist – works of literature risks 'giving the appearance of form parrying the traumas they dramatize—turning the pathetic consolations of precarious continuity into the aesthetically thrilling consolations of linguistic redress' (p. 27). An 'expressive vigour', the 'in-itself' of poetry, or what Eliot terms 'concentration', certainly predominates in 'Cox's Bazar', as opposed to the prosaic passages about implication in *Hello. Your Promise has been Extracted*.[108]

However, maybe Warner wishes precisely to circumvent 'aesthetically thrilling consolation' through the 'deaestheticization' of poetry.[109] This might be the case, were it not for an 'expressive vigour' straining underneath the prose, as when the poet-narrator in *Hello. Your Promise has been Extracted* characterises the world as 'a writhing slaughterhouse of blood and garbage' (p. 76), an image akin to that of the globe 'flapping its bandages' in 'Cox's Bazar'. In contrast, the puzzle of the lines about the poem as a knife or pulse in Byrne's poem resist the 'thrilling consolation' of form by endorsing elegiac redress and fallibility at the same time: the poem is a 'weapon' against trauma – like the '100 poets in English' that the poet-narrator 'reloads' for the workshops – but also a useless 'windbreak' (p. 7).[110] Subsequently, such ruminations on the testimonial qualities and drawbacks of the poetry develop into the conflicted ending to the first part of the poem, with its re-writing of the Orpheus myth in 'Cox's Bazar'. Wary of his adjudication on this fractured testimony, the poet-narrator rejects any concept of himself as an orphic, 'eternal traveller'; a 'centre' that 'does not hold', in a gesture towards W. B. Yeats's 'The Second Coming'.[111] If the Yeats reference still appertains to the next sentence, 'To think of poetry as orphic' also 'does not hold': testimonial poetry such as 'Cox's Bazar' may not be mellifluous, entrancing or mystic in this understanding of 'orphic', but there is nevertheless a productive awkwardness in the dissonant fragments and macaronic style that arise out of traumatic events (p. 7).

These cautious, ambivalent and enigmatic poetics in 'Cox's Bazar' continue, to an extent, in Byrne's engagement with the repercussions of austerity and maximalist politics in *The Caprices*. However, although the collection contains enigmatical lines such as the 'hissing face, chained | to sleep in a star's coda' in '*The sleep of reason produces monsters*', and 'treasures buried under numerals' in '*Why hide them?*', the emphasis in *The Caprices* is often on 'committed' responses to contemporary crises in the context of Goya's perplexing images.[112] In *Hello. Your Promise has been Extracted*, the passage in which Warner engages with the implicated subject and declares 'there's nothing to be done' (p. 76) is followed by a section (IIII) that recounts the impact of austerity in Greece during the Eurozone crisis: Athens comprises a city of riots, police brutality, random shootings and insalubrious neighbourhoods. This section contains the quotation from *Aesthetic Theory*: as with my critique above of Warner's passages about implication, the segment does not 'crystallise' into '*something unique to itself*' (p. 92) due to its prosaic form in which he recalls a café owner's expletive, inebriated anarchists and a girl asking for directions: 'From behind the girl's trousers flaunt four tiny stitches of white thread below the waistband, announcing their four-figure price tag' (p. 88). For Adorno, the 'in-itself' of a work of art, the dialectic between form and content, is much more important – as in his critique of 'commitment' – than the artwork's 'message' (p. 125). Rather than asking 'What is it all about?', the critic's main question should be 'Is it true?' (p. 127); the 'facture' of the artwork (p. 129), the quality of its artistic execution, should be the author's priority. In contrast with the prosaic passages in *Hello. Your Promise has been Extracted* that present a litany of traumatic experiences, from the explosion in Tianjin to the impact of austerity in Greece, the 'facture' of *The Caprices* consists of terse and sometimes ambivalent responses to structural violence in Goya's images from *Los Caprichos* (1799). '*Why hide them?*', for example, presents alternative readings of Goya's apparent diatribe against greed:

> To avarice pocketing a pouch sack.
> To treasures buried under numerals.
> Money disappears into haircracks
> like a lizard scuttling into a wall.
> Old man, face wracked by the sea,
> buried under this Great Depression.
> Living alack, what's owed is illusory.
> The banker smirks like a sovereign. (p. 51)

Initially, the poem follows the interlocution indicated by the title: four figures at the back of the image, identified as bankers, laugh at the monk in the foreground, who forlornly attempts to hoard his money. The ironical toast suggested in Byrne's first preposition ('Here's to . . .') clearly denounces the avaricious figure '**po**cketing a **pouch sack**'. Emphasised by the metrical breaks in the first line, the poet notes that Goya's careful positioning of the money bags in relation to the main figure's body indicate that, for the monk, the relinquishment of the money amounts to castration.

The enigmatic line that follows appears to relate to the monk's greed, as 'treasures' are 'buried under numerals': his money may be concealed in that it forms an integral part of the 'numerals', but it may also be 'hidden' from the figures in the sense of stashed away, in an action akin to those of unscrupulous financial advisors. At the same time, Byrne begins to draw attention to the ambiguous process of identification in Goya's print.[113] The banker-figures could be accused of greed as much as the monk: in lines that appertain to the financial crisis of 2008 and subsequent austerity, the poet-narrator notes that money begins to disappear into 'haircracks | like a lizard scuttling into a wall'; skilled financiers are also those who can squirrel away money 'under numerals' (p. 51). Unusually for the satirical *Los Caprichos* sequence, the viewer's sympathy is directed away from, as well as towards, the 'victim', whose bowed head is positioned in the centre of the frame. In a sense, the real casualties, the destitute who suffer from the avarice of the religious hoarders and bankers, are absent from the frame. Attentive to these visual ambiguities, Byrne then directs the reader's empathy in the rest of the poem towards the monk, the 'Old man', whose face is 'wracked by the sea', and the anguish in divulging his savings.[114] The repetition of 'buried' in line six stresses that the monk – and, by extension, the reader – is a victim of wider financial pressures. In the last line, Byrne refers to the most prominent banker on the right-hand side of Goya's frame, who 'smirks like a sovereign' (a coin or ruler). The reversal of identification is complete in the poem, as the closure suggests that 'sovereign debt' is, in some senses, 'illusory', since the reader, like the monk, is implicated in a financial system of ubiquitous credit, 'buried under numerals' (p. 51).

Byrne and Warner are thus responding to similar historical events in *Hello. Your Promise has been Extracted* and *The Caprices* – in this instance, the financial crisis and subsequent austerity – but with vastly different artistic 'factures'.[115] Similarly, in *'The sleep of reason produces monsters'* from *The Caprices* we are presented with an enraged response to the European Union. Akin to the Greek café owner in Warner's book who suddenly rages against the Eurozone (*'Fuck the Germans'*) (p. 82), a man is 'hissing' into a mirror in *The Caprices* (p. 64) in a markedly different cultural context:

> Now that the state legitimates hate,
> a wakeful trump of doom thunders
> valley deep (where are the Blakes
> and Miltons now?) Crisis of mirrors
> where my neighbour reasons only
> with himself: a hissing face, chained
> to sleep in a star's coda. A fantasy
> that whatever is pure is ENGLAND (p. 64).[116]

As Byrne recounts in the introduction to his collection, *The Caprices* 'was written during times of increased polarisation in Europe, when political events like BREXIT were painfully debated': this poem from *The Caprices* 'was written on the day of Britain's EU referendum' (p. 18). The opening line is prescient in that it anticipates President Trump's response to the 'Unite the Right' rally in August 2017: despite the presence of white supremacists at the event, and the murder of Heather Heyer, he commented that 'very fine people on both sides' were involved.[117] Goya's title for the most well-known image in *Los Caprichos* contains an enigma that impacts on any potential response to Trump's infelicities. If reason metaphorically 'sleeps', does it produce monsters by neglecting to pay heed to, in this instance, the rise of alt-right politics? Or does 'real' sleep in Goya's title engender fantastical creatures that have somehow – as a counterpoint to reason – transferred fantasy into the political arena? With a pun on John Milton's line 'A wakeful trump of doom must thunder through the deep' from 'On the Morning of Christ's Nativity', the poet-narrator indicates that both possibilities appertain in Trump's assemblage of alt-right desires and fantasies into political concretion.[118] Byrne's 'sleep' also echoes P. B. Shelley's response to Peterloo in 'The Masque of Anarchy', that citizens must 'Rise like Lions after slumber' in the wake of such governmental atrocities.[119] The elusive image of the 'crisis of mirrors' denotes, perhaps, a calamity of entrenched and bifurcated politics in which a neighbour 'reasons only | with himself', akin to the 'no-name couple' in *Withdrawals* who hoist the national flag 'as if [their house] were a consulate' (p. 64).[120] This serpent-like character is 'hissing' and 'chained | to sleep in a star's coda', that recalls Satan 'Chained on the burning Lake' in *Paradise Lost*.[121] In Byrne's enigmatic image, the 'star' is likely to appertain to the 'star' of popular culture in this poem, Donald Trump: the president's irrational politics – as the poet-narrator regards them – have hypnotised the neighbour, who needs to be 'awakened' by reason, but remains stubbornly 'chained' to the constant reprisal ('coda') of Trump's maximalist politics (p. 64). In an angry retort to the 'hate' that begins the poem, the poet-narrator alludes to the politics of race that are, for him, 'chained' to Brexit: the last line emphasises the fantasy of a 'pure' England denuded of immigrants.

The Enigmas of Open Form: 'Historia' and '6'

The simmering resentment at bifurcated politics in '*The sleep of reason produces monsters*' thus strives to create something 'unique to itself' in poetry that is attentive to the enigma of Goya's original image.[122] In 'Historia' from *White Coins*, the allusive and elusive responses to atrocity, austerity and polarised politics outlined in 'Cox's Bazar' and *The Caprices* switch to the more personal context of the poet's childhood, and a 'fracturedness' in which the poet-narrator recalls being 'bombarded' with an 'impulse | of survival'.[123] 'Historia' can refer to an 'investigation, inquiry, research, account, description, written account of past events, writing of history, historical narrative', but the stable signification indicated in this diction is undercut by the poem's fragmented narrative.[124] The trajectories specified in the epigraph, 'moving on or going back to where you came from' (p. 11), are evident throughout the poem: 'Historia' portrays a return to (for the reader) puzzling events, and – as in 'Cox's Bazar' – a potentially redemptive transition away from this traumatic past. Akin to the 'dialysis of rain | inside a garden well' (p. 14), the imaginative return to childhood suggests a form of purging, as unnerving images as 'toxins' are pored over and expunged. This process, as with the rain and dialysis, is repeated: the disconcerting images reprove any possibility of the 'aesthetically thrilling consolations of linguistic redress', as in the isolated and unexplained line 'merely to show up'.[125] Discomfiture is registered in the first line of the poem, as 'sharp toys' give way to a 'field zesty with fire' (p. 11). In one sense, the latter image registers 'expressive vigour' through poetic synaesthesia that combines the sunset with its supposed 'taste'.[126] On the other hand, the 'field zesty with fire' links with the more unsettling image later in the poem of the 'naphtha mirage | over the wheatfield' (p. 13). This depiction of a shimmering sunset as flammable oil connects with the unsettling domestic scene on the same page in which the poet-narrator is 'cupping at the curtain frame | fearful of fire | on the domestic zodiac'; moreover, the mother figure is 'admonished' at the 'fire-grate' with a passive verb that suggests understatement (p. 14).

These fractured images form the 'hieroglyphs' that Adorno discusses in *Aesthetic Theory* (p. 124), a 'remainder' of enigmatic and unexplained images that explore, in 'Historia', a sense of constant edginess (p. 121). In a singular description of the poet's 'lightly strung' nerves and aesthetic sensibilities, the poet-narrator becomes a six-year-old child 'made of violins' who is 'stumped' by the 'metronomic light': the reader encounters a striking yet also puzzling image that hints at the signified (intermittent or diurnal light beams) but which is not, in Adorno's phrase, strictly 'decodable' (p. 12). Associated with liminal objects in the house such as window frames, the poet-narrator is 'on the edge', with 'blackish fingernails | from

window-mould' (p. 13). Violence is intimated but never directly repre-
sented in 'Historia': the child is 'left alone | in the dry season'; this
connotation of alcohol abuse links to the image of history as 'cool as
a shot to the mouth' at the start of the poem (p. 11). Suddenly, the air in
the house may be 'divided', 'like cutting a loaf' (p. 13): in an unsettling
collocation, the kitchen is also 'gazebladed' (p. 13). This tangential response
to suffering is summed up in the image of the 'foxfur grinning on
a spiderweb': violent acts may be alluded to in the spaces between the
clauses in the open form of the poem's lines, but the perpetrator remains
absent, 'grinning' like the fox fur, and never 'caught' in formal representation (p. 13). These lexical spaces as perturbing absences also suggest that
there is always something 'beyond' the poem that the reader is not party to,
as if the 'lopped off' fragments are akin – in Adorno's memorable description of enigmatic art – to those 'allegories in graveyards, the broken-off
stelae' (p. 126).

The 'remainder' of these enigmatic 'stelae' are clear evidence of metamodernist poetics in the sense I have explored throughout this book.[127]
These 'stelae' continue in the sixth poem from the collection
Withdrawals, in which the poet describes an unspecified family member
in terms of the fractured images of a 'swaddled cradle. A dipper's
thirst' (p. 12):

> I write to you like an unarmed gunsler in plain sight.
> Go back to yourself. Runaway convict with a cashier's head for business –
>   your last letter like someone divided at birth.
> What kind of meat have you cooked into now?
> As if you never asked what consciousness is made from
>   and might absolve yourself under the sun.
>   A swaddled cradle. A dipper's thirst.
>   You speak, you haggle, it is the same.
> Consistent as a coin
> in the rust of empire –
>   you would bid for the wind
>   if you knew where it lived.

Byrne's positioning of the seemingly disparate images of the cradle and
dipper on the same line suggests a connection, yet the allegory remains
elusive. The period indicates continuity as well as dissonance: *Cinclus
cinclus* remains close to streams and rivers, unique amongst passerines in
its ability to move underwater; there may be a hint of the Moses basket in
the previous 'cradle', but the images remain 'unsolved'. In other 'stelae' in
the poem there is an 'off-key' eloquence: in the first line, for example, the

simile of the poet-narrator writing 'like an unarmed gunsler in plain sight' appears to jar, but only if the expectation is a rational account of elusive art.[128] The collocation 'gunsler' fuses 'gunsel' – a criminal carrying a gun – and 'gunslinger': the poet-narrator's writing of the letter and the poem are potentially incendiary but also hopelessly exposed acts (p. 12). After all, it is impossible to be a 'gunsel' without a gun: the intimation perhaps is that narrator's anger remains unassuaged apart from in the context of the enigmatic poem. Any redress to the relative's last letter, 'like someone divided at birth', occurs through metaphor: the latter is a 'convict', with a 'cashier's head for business'. Subsequently, in the most memorable image in the poem, the poet-narrator asks, 'What kind of meat have you cooked into now?' Byrne deploys a Célinian metaphor of humans as decaying carcasses that we have already encountered in Warner's 'Métro', and adds the tropological piquancy of 'cooked' to suggest, in another example of 'off-key' eloquence, that the family member has somehow hardened into a well-done 'meathead'.[129] A neo-modernist distancing from the subject, as in 'Métro', potentially enters the poem when the poet-narrator retorts 'As if you never asked what consciousness is made from', but the subjunctive suggests that they may well once have engaged in such philosophical rumination, and the accusation is dispelled in the sibling's attempt to 'absolve' himself 'under the sun'. The last five lines then conclude with an inditement of the character's inability to distinguish conversation from the discourse of business: he remains 'Consistent as a coin | in the rust of empire' (p. 12); this perplexing simile suggests indefatigability despite economic and historical restrictions, as in the money 'scuttling into cracks' during financial crises in '*Why hide them?*' from *The Caprices* (p. 51). In a final, irrational statement that incorporates the irrationality of constant haggling, the poet-narrator announces that the family member would 'bid for the wind | if [they] knew where it lived' (p. 12).

The 'Chanel' Poet versus the 'Innovative'

My analysis of these elusive allegories in *White Coins* and *Withdrawals* might suggest that Byrne's metamodernist poems should be considered solely within the remit of 'innovative' poetry. 'Inclub Satires' from *Blood/Sugar* complements this association: the sequence forms a riotous admonishment of the mainstream poetry scene, depicting gratuitous posturing, artistic self-congratulation and indulgence in insubstantial glitz. In his review of the collection, Paul Stubbs concurs with the 'necessary, devastating and much needed wake-up call for those still deluding themselves that British poetry is in a healthy state. Byrne hurls his pen like a spanner into the clunking machinery of this lie'.[130] 'Inclub Satires' certainly undercuts writerly fatuities, such as tired assertions during 'Q&A' sessions ('*It just came to me*'); the 'Egg Head' in Ted Hughes's 'Famous Poet' becomes '*The Combover*', the 'hard-boiled top-per' who considers his artistic legacy more than his poetry, that consists of 'familiar orchestral gesturings'.[131] Addressed to Pound, the first poem in the sequence begins with a mainstream poet depicted as a sexual predator, a more dangerous version of Hughes's ageing rhymester, who abuses his fame to molest 'like a young rooster'; he is transformed into a grotesque combination of a Tiny-Tears doll and a louche swaggerer in his 'gastric-sagging suit' (p. 70). The prize-winning ceremony of the Jeffrey Deamer Prize is satirised as 'The Dreamer Prize', a 'vernal farce': Byrne transfers Pound's admonition of his supposed friend's '*malignant buncomb*' in a review of his Cavalcanti translations to the prize-winner.[132] In a costume of useless ornamentation, the 'porcelain apple' of the 'Chanel poet' then 'cares to market absolute clarity | and so, says nothing of minor importance' (p. 71). In adhering to the discursive, the 'Chanel poet' 'de-aestheticises' poetry in a way that means that the Dreamer Prize rewards literature that is, ironically, not actually a work of art in the context of *Aesthetic Theory*, but the attenuated legacy, according to the narrator, of 'Larkin' and his 'limpet-clinging proxy-squad' (p. 78). In part two of the sequence, Byrne proceeds to contrast 'Q&A' clichés with more elusive poetics that chafe against the underlying banalities, with lines such as 'Spoilbank of domesticity, inspiration a spiderplot | *It leapt up and said WRITE ME! A complete ambush*' (p. 72).

However, despite this diatribe against mainstream poetry in 'Inclub Satires', the form of Byrne's writing often indicates poetics shifting between the categories of mainstream and 'innovative' writing. In *The Caprices*, for example, Byrne deploys the basic structure of iambic pentameter in order to emphasise numerous subtle divergences, such as the '**pouch sack**' in '*Why hide them?*' that stresses the impotence of the avaricious monk (p. 51): such metrical intricacy is comparable to the deft switches in rhythm and emphasis that I analysed in the last chapter in relation to Hill's *Scenes from Comus*. In contrast, Warner's main-stream poetics consists of his iconoclastic deployment of Paterson's demotic and Larkinesque insouciance, rather than Byrne's assimilation of rhythmical dexterity. Yet Bloodaxe's championing of Warner's sup-posedly 'public' poetry is not straightforward: the editor Neil Astley has stated in a documentary that he wishes to publish 'poets who've been around for some time, but haven't had the readership which their work deserves', as the camera pans across collections by Peter Didsbury and B. S. Johnson's *House Mother Normal* (1971).[133] There is an inevitable tension between a desire to publish neglected poetry influenced by modernism alongside 'accessible' poets. With its intricate collage and creative translation of Artaud's enigmatical *Le Pèse-Nerfs*, Warner's 'Nervometer' can hardly be considered to be 'public' poetry in the sense Paterson outlines in *New British Poetry*, that has an '*intolerance to ambiguity*' and an antipathy towards that which is 'not strictly definable'.[134] Yet Warner and Byrne are 'cusp' poets in markedly different ways. Byrne's metamodernist writing is primarily concerned with elusive poetics that aspire to a 'zone of indeterminacy' where poetry 'await[s] its interpretation' (p. 128). In contrast, despite his engagement with modernist antecedents in a more explicit way than Byrne – as in 'Métro' – Warner's writing often draws back from the enigmatic: as Adorno argues in *Aesthetic Theory*, it is exactly the responses of those who flinch from art that emphasise the potential of an artwork's enigma (p. 119).

Apart from the notable exception of 'Nervometer', Warner's abstaining from enigmatical poetics thus indicates the limitations of any version of metamodernism that relies solely on 'the importance of the relation of the poem to other poems by other authors'.[135] This capacious model of metamodernism focuses on the authorial manipulation of prior ingredients rather than the formal qualities of the resultant texts. Julian Barnes's *A Sense of an Ending* (2011), Zadie Smith's *NW* (2012) and Tom McCarthy's *C* (2010) have been utilised as examples of metamodernist fiction: the first two novels are examples of 'experimental fiction shaped by an aesthetics of discontinuity, nonlinearity, interiority and chronological play'.[136] Yet all these novels draw primarily on the legacies of nineteenth-century realism rather than the revolutions in form of early twentieth-century modernism. Mirroring the conservative nature of the form of Barnes's novel, the protagonist Tony Webster compares himself on several occasions to Larkin, the *enfant terrible* of mainstream poetry for the narrator of 'Inclub Satires'.[137] Smith's concrete poem about an apple tree ('Apple tree, apple tree | Thing that has apples on it. Apple blossom') and stream-of-consciousness narrative at the beginning of *NW* is striking in its brevity compared to the overall neo-realist narrative, and cannot help come across as a tokenistic engagement with the legacies of modernism compared to the work of poets such as Hill and Prynne.[138] In contrast, throughout this book I have outlined a form of writing in which authors engage with modernist antecedents but also, as with Warner's 'Nervometer' and Byrne's open form writing, produce enigmatic poetry that remains a 'question mark', a 'constitutive darkening' that is not undercut by insouciance, or embarrassment that art remains a vexation.[139]

CHAPTER 5

The Double Consciousness of Modernism

In the last chapter, I explored enigmatical poetics in Ahren Warner's 'Nervometer' and James Byrne's poems that are situated on the 'cusp' between mainstream and 'innovative' writing.[1] I now turn to explore the legacies of modernism in relation to two poets who have been categorised differently in the bifurcation of the 'poetry wars'. Despite his indebtedness to Brechtian poetics that I analysed in Chapter 3, Tony Harrison's work has never been confused with experimental writing, whereas Sandeep Parmar's poetry is clearly influenced by exponents of the London School: she has 'reviled' the 'Movement tones' of Philip Larkin and 'the small, digestible, miserable [artefacts] of everyday British life'.[2] Yet Harrison and Parmar have both responded to modernist writers' conceptions of myth: James Joyce and T. S. Eliot advanced a 'double consciousness' in their approach to mythic narratives that pervades Harrison's *Metamorpheus* (2000) and Sandeep Parmar's *Eidolon* (2015). Michael Bell argues that this process of counterpointing forms an integral part of modernists' engagement with myth:

> The story of Odysseus, in so far as it is a cultural myth, suggests a timeless structure of experience given to the writer, but Joyce's spatialising holds the archaic structure in *counterpoint* to its modern re-enactment. As the modern *construction* of a world enfolds the older sense of a *given* form, neither has complete meaning by itself.[3]

This double consciousness is not unique to modernism: in the ballad opera *Penelope* from 1728, for example, John Mottley and Thomas Cook set the *Odyssey* in a working-class tavern in London.[4] Nearly a century later, Mary Shelley's *Frankenstein* (1818) formed a version of the Prometheus myth rewritten in the light of scientific discoveries. However, an intensification of double consciousness permeates early twentieth-century literature that inscribes a desire to explore 'the problematics of history under the sign of myth'.[5] Similarly, in Harrison's film-poem *Metamorpheus* there are structural counterpoints between the Orpheus myth, homosexuality, the modernist poet Geo Milev and the author himself. This mythic 'counter-pointing' that underpins Harrison's work indicates that his modernist influences have been neglected – as I argued in Chapter 3 – by critics eager to position his writing as eschewing unnecessary complexity. In *Eidolon*, Parmar similarly interweaves mythic narratives about Helen of Troy with contemporary narratives about a disillusioned model, a duplicitous wife and racism in an American supermarket. Akin to the work of Byrne and Warner, Parmar has produced work that could be labelled as mainstream or 'innovative' poetry, depending on its formal propensities. Section two of *Eidolon*, for example, blends parataxis with the euphonious iambs of 'Helen, dispirited | camera-bound', and juxtaposes these opening lines with the more prosaic 'Helen | fetching the paper from the front lawn in her dressing gown a lot of the time' (p. 10). Indeed, *Metamorpheus* and *Eidolon* would both be symptomatic of metamodernist literature in Andre Furlani, David James and Urmila Seshagiri's under-standing of the term, since both poets draw on specific modernist antecedents.[6] However, it is only in Parmar's *Eidolon* that the legacies of 'fractured' writing allow for an enigmatical account of one of the most enigmatic figures in Greek myth.[7]

Modernism and 'Double Consciousness'

As Edith Hall notes, Joyce was not the first author to locate a mythic narrative in 'a contemporary context', but 'it was *Ulysses* that prompted the flood of updated *Odyssey* plots in the fiction and cinema of the twentieth and twenty-first centuries'.[8] In contrast, during the Romantic period myth operates as frozen symbols locked in time that are suitable for incorpor-ation into poetry as solidified emblems. This process is vital to John Keats's 'Ode to a Grecian Urn' and 'Lamia': myth becomes available for intertext-ual manipulation within literature, but it is not fully 'textualised', as in early twentieth-century literature.[9] In Alfred Tennyson's 'The Lotus-Eaters', the mariners, 'consumed with sharp distress', do not root their conflict in the contemporaneous, unlike Joyce's account of Bloom's ablu-tions in *Ulysses* (1922).[10] Furthermore, Tennyson's 'Ulysses' is – in the poet's own words – about the struggles of life in general: its structure, akin to the 'companion' poem 'Tithonus', does not depend on a counterpointing between myth and the particularities of Tennyson's suffering after the death of Arthur Hallam. In contrast, one of Eliot's notes to *The Waste Land* (1922) argues that Tiresias unifies the narrative's personages.[11] Put another way, in Tennyson's poetry we are closer to classical myth than the contemporaneous, whereas, in *The Waste Land*, Tiresias' underworld is re-enacted with the deadened commuters wandering through their daily katabasis. To redeploy Michael McKeon on allegory, there is a fictionalisation of myth in modernist literature that is quantitively different to previous literary ages.[12]

Of course, modernist engagements with myth are not identical: as opposed to *Ulysses*, in which, for example, the rogue drinker is both the imbiber and the Cyclops, Bell criticises the deployment of myth as mere 'scaffolding' in Ezra Pound's work and 'ordering' in Eliot's poetry (p. 122). Yet Tiresias' centrality to part three of *The Waste Land* is surely more than 'ordering': as in *Ulysses*, the personages are both mythical and literal; the typist and suitor are locked into the contemporaneity of gramophones as well as imaginative reconstructions of Tiresias' mythic unity of the sexes. Nevertheless, Bell asks if myth is 'merely a method of enabling the artist to *express* the futility and anarchy' of modern life in Eliot and Pound's work, comparable to the moments when Tennyson expresses stalwartness in the face of suffering in 'Ulysses' (p. 122)? Pound's translation of lines from Book II of the *Odyssey*, for example, locates contiguity with myth in the very first word ('And'), as well as signalling – as Harrison does – the rootedness of his poetry in what Theodor Adorno and Max Horkheimer referred to as 'the basic text of European civilisation'.[13] Pound's use of myth in the *Cantos* (1925) thus seeks to 'find the proper human viewpoint overall' that Bell finds central to modernist literature, the 'Archimedian point from which the whole culture can be judged and improved' (p. 131). However, at the beginning of the *Cantos*, Pound does not establish a double consciousness between myth and the everyday, unlike Joyce in *Ulysses* with the activities of Bloom and Dedalus. Tennyson's 'Ulysses', Percy Shelley's *Prometheus Unbound* (1820) and the initial sections of the *Cantos* have 'complete meaning' in and of themselves without the '*counterpoint* to [myth's] modern enactment' in Tennyson's grief, Shelley's polemics or Pound's lauding of 'the basic text'.[14] In contrast, the legacies of modernist double consciousness are evident throughout Parmar's *Eidolon* and in Harrison's plays such as *The Common Chorus* (1992), which sets Aristophanes' *Lysistrata* (441 BCE) in Greenham Common.[15]

In *Eidolon*, Helen of Troy appears as various figures from classical texts that present alternative views of her elusive character, such as Euripides' *The Trojan Women* (415 BCE) and *Helen* (412 BCE), and Stesichorus' *Palinode* (C7th BCE), as well as Helen in the guise of an office worker, a guest on a television show and a downtrodden wife. In Harrison's film-poem *Prometheus* (1998), the mythic theft of fire enters comparable 'chains' of meaning that encompass Auschwitz crematoria, Pontefract coal and the firebombing of Dresden.[16] Since the publication of Michael Rothberg's influential monograph in 2009, this double consciousness would now be deemed inextricable with unfolding multidirectional and transnational memories.[17] Some of these 'chains' link to egregious ideology: as in Thomas Mann's *Dr Faustus* (1947), Harrison is required to wrestle myth from its fascistic misappropriation. Harrison sets myth against myth – as Bell puts it in relation to *Dr Faustus* – accepting that the rejection of 'regressive political ideologies is to be overcome by a recognition of the mythopoeic basis of [Mann's] own humanism' (p. 2).[18] Although Parmar's collection is less self-conscious than Harrison's work about its engagement with humanism, *Eidolon* also draws approvingly on Virginia Woolf's sense that the Greeks celebrated every moment of existence, at the same time as Parmar critiques Woolf's conception of classical impersonality in relation to traumatised survivors in Euripides' *The Trojan Women*.[19] Parmar argues that Woolf's endorsement of the cold objectivity of the classics is a replication of formal violence: the enslaved women at the end of *The Trojan Women* become the 'blackest coals of mourning' in *Eidolon*, 'hard' in their infinite wailing (p. 51).

Both *Metamorpheus* and *Eidolon* thus draw on Joyce and Eliot's sense of the contemporaneity of myth, but Parmar's collection is more attuned than Harrison's work to Adorno's conception of enigmatical poetry. Parmar reimagines H. D.'s *Helen in Egypt* (1961) within a complex series of fragmented sections and experimental vignettes that also engage with the diverse versions of Helen throughout literary history. In contrast, the framing of Harrison's work in terms of double consciousness and modernist antecedents requires a recalibration of his critical reception: as I indicated in Chapter 3, Harrison's work has been characterised as the product of an anti-modernist by the author himself, critics and fellow poets. Simon Armitage, for example, recalls the revelation of first encountering Harrison's sonnets whilst reading

> the more impenetrable outer regions of Ezra Pound at the time, so the contrast couldn't have been greater [...] the classical references were just as thick on the ground, though far more assimilated and accommodated in Harrison, as opposed to being set up like snares and trip wires in Pound.[20]

Armitage's references to 'assimilated' and 'accommodated' mythic narratives implicitly respond to the double consciousness that I engage with throughout this chapter. This criticism of Pound's work also shares Bell's concern that the deployment of myth may be mere 'scaffolding' in the *Cantos* (p. 122). Yet it glosses over the variety of modernist and proto-modernist influences on Harrison's work, including Pound himself, Basil Bunting, Arthur Rimbaud and Charles Baudelaire, in its caricature of Harrison's poetry as anti-modernist. From Armitage's perspective, Harrison is the poet of 'openness and approachability', rather than the writer who quotes Rimbaud when he wishes to distinguish himself from a local skinhead in *V* (1985).[21] As I illustrated in Chapter 3, Harrison includes long, uninterrupted passages of untranslated Greek in his play *The Labourers of Herakles* (1996): he also deploys Pound's 'Hugh Selwyn Mauberley' to corroborate a distinctly modernist vision of democracy and popular culture in the poem 'Summoned by Bells' from *The Gaze of the Gorgon* (1992).[22] Harrison's work thus adheres to James's sense of a 'recrudescence' of modernism in contemporary literature: his poetry engages with a variety of modernist influences, deploying 'models of continuity and adaptation (rather than demise)'.[23] However, whereas Parmar and Harrison both allude to modernist antecedents, *Eidolon* develops allusive and elusive poetics that, like Pound's Cantos, challenge the reader's idioculture and adherence to the 'reality principle'.[24] In a counterargument to Armitage's conception of 'assimilated and accommodated' classical references, it is possible that Harrison's re-workings of Greek myth are enervated through formal conservatism, and – unlike *Eidolon* – are univocal, rather than entertaining the productive and ambiguous 'constitutive darkening' of enigmatical poetry (p. 124).

Metamorpheus and Double Consciousness

Nevertheless, in *Metamorpheus* there is certainly a 'self-conscious reconstruction of the already given' in its rigorous investigation of the Orpheus myth.[25] Workbooks held in the Brotherton Library reveal Harrison's extensive research on transformations of the Orpheus myth, including a picture from the sixth century BCE of a 'sculptured metope' in which Orpheus was depicted as a musician for the 'first time in history', records of how he was punished by the gods for accusing them of theft, adultery 'and many other kinds of outrageous conduct', and ruminations on how he was 'generally reckoned a Thracian, like other legendary poets of the Pierian group – Linos, Pamphos, Thamyris, Philammon, Musaeus, Eumolpus'.[26] Screened in December 2000, a Poundian fascination with myth as source runs throughout *Metamorpheus*, as the film-poem persists in returning to the classical preoccupation with Orpheus as the first suffering poet and homosexual. This deployment of myth as Poundian 'scaffolding' is mirrored in the deployment of Harrison's 'Orpheus' workbook within the film-poem itself in an early scene; indeed, the workbook contains notes on Pound's discovery of the Sappho fragments that inspired the poem 'Papyrus' in 1916.[27] Rather than transforming the workbook into a final creative piece, Harrison's 'work in progress' features in a section of the film-poem in which the poet discusses his recce in Bulgaria with the academic Oliver Taplin. A postmodernist delight in tracking the legacies of myth in eclectic popular culture endures in Harrison's film-poems, and *Metamorpheus* is no exception: the workbook contains pasted-in photographs and reproductions of Orpheus chocolates, café and restaurant signs, T-shirts, nuts and even a football team calendar. However, as with Pound's work, Harrison's interest does not lie in a fascination with popular culture itself. In Harrison's film-poems as a whole, myth is figured dialectically as both an ancient source and powerful imaginative material that metamorphoses as it engages with exigent concerns. *Metamorpheus* thus provides the opportunity for Joycean double consciousness in its account of Orpheus' homosexuality and his status as a persecuted poet. Harrison re-imagines the myth of Orpheus in terms of contemporaneous homosexuality when images of a Bulgarian boy's head are juxtaposed with an image of Orpheus and shots of Lesbian bathers at Skala Eressos.[28]

An extension of such montage into an allusive and elusive artwork could have encompassed a critique of the suppressions inherent in the classical world that are inextricable with Greek myth. Indeed, an article pasted into Harrison's workbook recounts that 'Contrary to popular opinion, [ancient Greece] was not a paradise for homosexuals [...] There were laws that forbade homosexuals from entering the agora [marketplace] or participating in rights and rituals that involved the state, like the Dionysian festivals in Athens'.[29] This workbook also illustrates Harrison's interest in the medieval artist Albrecht Dürer's use of the word *'puseran'* ('bugger') in relation to Orpheus.[30] Jonathan West, who worked in the Early Modern German Text archive at Newcastle University, replies to Harrison's request for further information on *'puseran'*:

> English *bugger* is also derived from *bulgarus* 'Bulgarian' (see Onions, *Dictionary of English Etymology*), although whether this practice was associated with the Bulgarians via popular etymology, the name word having a different source (e.g. Lat *bulga* 'bag'), or whether it developed out of their being heretical Eastern Orthodox (i.e. Greek) Christians, I'm afraid I haven't had time to consider properly.[31]

In the final film-poem, traces of this research remain in the opening word ('Bugger!') as the impious engagement with myth registers Orpheus' homosexuality. Intriguingly, the workbooks for *Metamorpheus* also trace an early desire to parallel Orpheus' suffering with the plight of the modernist Bulgarian poet Geo Milev, scourge of the police authorities in Sofia, who was brought to trial for the publication of a new magazine, *Plamak* ('Flame') in 1924, and then murdered the following year in 'massive repressions which followed a terrorist bomb explosion in Sofia'.[32] Another article included in the workbook that was written by his daughter Leda recalls how he left with a policeman for questioning about the terrorist incident and never returned. After sustaining horrific injuries to his head during the First World War, Milev described his skull as a '"blood-stained lantern with shattered windows"' (pp. 7–8): the double consciousness of myth in *Metamorpheus* thus counterpoints Orpheus' head with Milev's skull, that was 'found in a pit near Sofia, together with the bones of hundreds of other victims'.

These mythopoeic possibilities that are never fully developed in *Metamorpheus* contrast with the informative documentary narrated by Taplin in the second half of the film-poem. Taplin's main concern is not to impart new narratives in old bottles, as Angela Carter conceived her approach to fairy tales, but a Poundian desire to explore the rootedness of myth: 'I'm going right back', he states at one point, 'to [the myth's] source'.[33] The most powerful sequence of *Metamorpheus* arises at the end of the film-poem, in which Harrison ruminates further on 'the problematics of history under the sign of myth' in relation to Orpheus' severed head in Lesbos.[34] Joycean counterpointing entreats the viewer to consider Orpheus' visage alongside a modernist vision of the poet as rooted in history, suffering in an attempt to forge 'barbaric' poetry out of atrocious history, like Milev in his poem on the brutal suppression of the uprising in Bulgaria:

> Sun and sea in gerbera hues
> salute this servant of the Muse.
> Gerbera, orange, yellow, red
> flow in the sunset round his head.
> Though his head is dead and cold
> the voice still turns shed blood to gold.
> The voice, that heals and seeks to mend
> men's broken souls that men's deeds rend.
> When men are maimed and torn apart
> they call on Orpheus and his art [. . .]

I think it needs that ancient scream
to pierce the skulls of Academe
to remind them that all our poems start
in the scream of Orpheus torn apart.[35]

As I discussed in Chapter 3 in relation to 'Commitment', Adorno questions the aesthetic purchase gained when writers turn atrocious events into potentially redemptive art that 'seeks to mend'. Whilst acknowledging that poetry arises from the 'deluge' of atrocious events, Harrison's emphasis is different here. As the original poet, Orpheus passes on his lyre to future writers who must grapple with its legacy in terms of its rootedness in the Thracian's individual suffering, as well as modern events such as the Bulgarian uprising when 'men are maimed and torn apart'.[36]

Such artistic commitment relies here on the opposition between the poet and scholar sustained throughout the film-poem, in a Brechtian rejection of conceptual intricacy that simultaneously precludes any engagement with enigmatical poetics. Any camaraderie established between the 'pontificating poet' and 'my friend Taplin' (p. 381) in the workbook scene is eroded throughout the film-poem in order to perpetuate a suspicion towards the intellectual in *Metamorpheus*. The latter extends to the form of the poetry: rather than the 'remainder' in enigmatical poetry, Harrison strives for accessibility with the simple diction, couplets and iambic tetrameter that he favours in his film-poems.[37] However, any charge in this passage against academic activity is belied by Harrison's extensive research on Orpheus within the workbook, which contains extracts and notes on, for example, Ivan Mortimer Linforth's *The Arts of Orpheus* (1941), Z. H. Archibald's *The Odrysian Kingdom of Thrace: Orpheus Unmasked* (1998) and Giuseppe Scavizzi's 'The Myth of Orpheus in Italian Renaissance Art 1400–1600' in *Orpheus: the Metamorphoses of a Myth* (1982).[38] The film-poem's caricature of academic complexity attempts to evoke dramatic tension: as opposed to Harrison's attempt to endorse an ancient genealogy of poets wrestling with suffering, 'Codgers' in the workbook are 'cloistered in calm Academe', and relish their summers touring around Europe.[39] Yet the work of both Taplin and the author-poet is intimately bound up with research into historical violence: as Taplin himself writes in an article on the classics in contemporary poetry, Harrison has always been an 'avid scholar'.[40]

The Orpheus workbook indicates that this dramatic tension between poetics and the intellectual arose early in the drafts for the film-poem: Harrison first introduces Taplin as a 'complacent academic cunt' (p. 234).

Such expressions – which do not make the final cut – become part of the film's syntax: an extreme close-up on Taplin's mouth during the workbook scene establishes the supposed gluttony of this character, who will later gorge on chocolates and be witnessed lecherously gazing at a can-can in a hotel basement. Poetry then literally interrupts the scholarly, first when Taplin discusses Orpheus by a bridge in Svilengrad, and then when the severed head induces him to drop his sheet of translation in the final scene. The poet's need to 'pierce the skulls of Academe' at the end of the poem draws on the leisured complacency of the Taplin character throughout the film-poem, and the supposedly parasitic scholar who 'Scoffs his fill | then leaves the poet to pay the bill'.[41] Yet Harrison sidesteps Adorno's charge that *any* writing that arises out of atrocity is inevitably tainted by association: poetry as well as criticism would ultimately, to rephrase a section from *Negative Dialectics* (1966), be parasitic 'garbage' in this context.[42] Moreover, the dismissal of 'Academe' at the end of the poem is ironic in the sense that an academic and Harrison's scholarship have created the entire film-poem. This anti-intellectual ending simultaneously records Harrison's artistic failure to transform his workbook into a more extended piece of mythic double consciousness about Orpheus in the present, rather than Taplin's documentary about sources of the myth that predominates in the second half of the film-poem.

The Enigma of Myth in Sandeep Parmar's *Eidolon*

As I argued in relation to Warner's 'Métro' and '*Lutèce, Te Amo*' in the last chapter, then, the assimilation of modernist antecedents in Harrison's *Metamorpheus* does not lead to enigmatical poetics. As I have argued throughout this book, modernist influences do not necessarily result in metamodernist poetry. Similarly to *Metamorpheus*, the double consciousness of *Eidolon* relocates myth within the politics of recent history, but Parmar's collection does so with a more successful integration of narrative counterpointing. Unlike Harrison's work, the 'fracturedness' of a specific modernist intertext impacts on the allusive and elusive narrative in *Eidolon*.[43] The parataxis in H. D.'s *Helen in Egypt* guides the form of *Eidolon*: in a review of Parmar's collection, Nabina Das emphasises its 'staccato sentences, jaunty phrases [and] abrupt transitions'.[44] These three characteristics predominate in the fragmented sections of *Eidolon*, as when the felicitations of a call centre operator are juxtaposed with the lamentations of the enslaved women at the closure of Euripides' *The Trojan Women*: 'Good morning | blight | Good morning |

blackest coals of mourning' (p. 51). Harrison's engagement with Joyce and Eliot's work involves a perpetuation of their double consciousness at the same time as he formally repudiates their 'fracturedness', and their creation of enigmatical poetics through the elusive 'remainder'.[45] In contrast, Parmar quotes approvingly from Robert Sheppard's *The Poetry of Saying* (2005) in her article 'Not a British Subject: Race and Poetry in the UK': Sheppard criticises mainstream poems that consist of 'empirical lyricism', and laud 'discrete moments of experience'.[46] Yet despite their stylistic differences, Harrison and Parmar's work similarly draw on the narrative counterpointing of myth: in *Eidolon*, Parmar fictionalises various classical and post-classical reworkings of the story of Helen of Troy in, for example, Homer's *Odyssey* and *Iliad*, Euripides' *The Trojan Women* and *Helen*, Stesichorus' *Palinode*, Virgil's *Aeneid* (19 BCE) and Christopher Marlowe's *Doctor Faustus* (1592). As with Harrison's comparison between Orpheus and the modernist poetry of Milev, Parmar also draws on more recent artistic iterations of the Helen myth, such as Gustave Moreau's painting *Hélène à la Porte Scée* (1880–2) and Lawrence Durrell's 'Troy' (1966). However, unlike the protestations of the anti-academic narrator in *Metamorpheus*, Parmar is forthright about the scholarly apparatus that underpins these creative reclamations and interpretations of classical myth. As she outlines in an afterword to *Eidolon*, entitled 'Under Helen's Breath', Parmar's research includes work on Gorgias' *Encomium of Helen* (144 BCE), Virginia Woolf's 'On Not Knowing Greek' (1925) and Bettany Hughes's *Helen of Troy* (2005). Rather than espousing a modernist 'belief' akin to Harrison's Nietzschean sense of an aesthetic life, Parmar analyses the 'ancient scream' of classical poetry in terms of its suppression of specific issues of gender and race: she interprets, for example, Woolf's commentary on the impersonality of classical literature as a form of textual violence when women cry 'on the banks of Scamander | Where the troops drew lots for them' in Euripides' *The Trojan Women* (p. 7).[47]

Throughout the fifty allusive and elusive sections of *Eidolon*, Parmar is absorbed in confronting the sheer variety of available narratives that Hughes terms 'a promiscuous range of "Helens"'.[48] H. D.'s *Helen of Troy* alone draws on the treacherous Helen depicted in the *Odyssey*, an alternative version in which the Greeks and Trojans 'fought for an illusion' on Troy's ramparts, and a lesser-known myth in which Helen returns to Sparta and is hanged on Rhodes, where 'the cord turned to a rainbow'.[49] Parmar refers to the enigma of Helen in the afterword to *Eidolon*:

there are several versions of Helen's fate and several differing views of the cause of her elopement [with] Paris, starting of course with the apple of discord and culminating in a ship chase to Asia Minor sometime in the 11th century B.C.E. What Hilda Doolittle, the modernist poet, clings to is the Helen/eidolon best celebrated by Euripides' 5th-century tragedy simply entitled *Helen*. (p. 66)

Before the action of Euripides' play begins – following Herodotus and Stesichorus' versions of the mythic events – Paris and Helen depart from Sparta for Troy, but their ship is blown off course; washed up in Egypt, King Proteus is so disgusted by Paris' behaviour that he dismisses him. An eidolon or 'shadow' of Helen then appears on Troy's ramparts, whereas the 'real' Helen spends ten years in Egypt.⁵⁰ After Proteus' death, she consistently rebuffs the advances of his successor, Theoclymenus: Parmar writes that in Euripides' *Helen*, the queen 'is redeemed by the simple replacement of the real flesh-and-blood Helen for the image/ghost who vanishes into thin air at the war's end' (p. 66). In *Eidolon*, Parmar primarily follows the narratives of Euripides and H. D.'s reclamations of Helen, but – as in Harrison's *Metamorpheus* – she is attuned to the disparity of mythic narratives; hence in section xlv Parmar refers to the Helen in both of Euripides' plays, *The Trojan Women* and *Helen*, who is 'dragged by her golden hair | onto Argive ships to be judged by the widows of those who fell | or blown off course with Paris | to be subsumed by middle age' (p. 56). Euripides and H. D.'s versions thus allow for Parmar's counterpointing in the guise of Helen as a bored office worker, 'camera-bound' model (p. 10) or trophy wife trapped thematically and formally in the chiasmus of 'mindless purposeless walking' and 'hands waving mindless purpose' (p. 14). In this section of Parmar's *Eidolon* (vi), Helen's office is 'a place of palor where | silk shrinks around her throat': mythic double consciousness here encompasses Euripides' Helen patiently waiting for the return of her husband Menelaus from Troy in the form of a 'denuded' Helen, a 'Demi-goddess – not woman, not god' (p. 10), whose clothing indicates her lost status and sense of constriction (p. 14).

'[S]ilk' also deftly indicates Parmar's contemporary construction of Helen as a postcolonial subject: the word links three sections later with the Silk Road (p. 17), the territorial and maritime routes that connected ancient Asia and Europe. Even Stesichorus features in this section in a moment of counterpointing: the Sicilian poet was allegedly blinded for an initial negative treatment of Helen in his verses (hence his atonement with the later *Palinode*); in *Eidolon*, he loses his sight just 'for watching her | cross the street' (p. 14). In this section (vi), the contemporary Helen

features as an extraordinarily beautiful office worker who enraptures
Stesichorus, but her identity then multiplies in section xvi, that draws on
the older myths of Helen as culpable in her elopement with Paris. The
leitmotif of anxious phone calls pervades the collection, as with the
Plathian 'plugging numbers into the godhead' (p. 20), and in this passage
it registers the potential adultery of Helen in her plea to her partner that she
'*went to the Fair*', and '*tried to call | but it rang and rang*' (p. 25). However,
even in this scenario the enigmatical poetry is able to hold the disparate
narratives about Helen in balance. Identities often shift or merge in the
'fracturedness' of *Eidolon*: it is ambiguous in this section's counterpointing
whether the 'peck on the cheek' that 'does not stir him' refers to the
husband representative of Menelaus or the potential lover in the guise of
Paris (p. 25).[51] The evening's 'warm air' then sticks to Helen 'like
a poisoned memory' as the spouse or paramour 'blinks and sips'.
Similarly, in section xvi it remains unclear whether Helen imbibes
a 'gauntlet of gin', or whether the cuckolded husband consoles himself
with alcohol whilst she gallivants at the fair (p. 25). In these elusive
vignettes, the 'peck on the cheek' may be for the lover as she returns to
her spouse, or the desultory husband as he challenges her plans when she
departs the conjugal home.

Attuned throughout the sequence to Helen's enigma, Parmar frames her
response to the mythical figure in the context of Walt Whitman's poem
'Eidolon'. Whitman's eidolon endures as a puzzle throughout the poem,
which begins by describing it as an apparition gleaned from but also
surpassing art, philosophy and concretion, and concludes that it remains
an elusive 'entity of entities'.[52] The latter phrase might suggest that it
embodies the soul, but Whitman denies this possibility at the closure:
the 'round, full-orb'd eidolon' only forms one of the 'mates' of the
Christian conception of an immortal element. Whitman's eidolon perse-
veres as a wider puzzle about existence: as in Eleanor Cook's discussion of
the enigma in relation to Aristotle, the concept of the eidolon embodies the
'largest of tropes, a trope of the human condition'.[53] In 'Under Helen's
Breath', Parmar similarly figures this conundrum as 'the enduring shadow
into which life is subsumed *and* the force from which life springs
eternal' (p. 65). The eidolon endures in Whitman's poem through diverse
embodiments – as a ghost, for example, a troublesome portent or exquisite
product of an artistic community – and remains elusive at the end of the
narrative. Perhaps its most striking figuration is as this spiritual embodi-
ment of artistic perfection that Whitman argues is strived for in ateliers.
For Parmar, this spectral figure or essence resonates instead in the ghostly

versions of Helen haunting Troy's ramparts, and luring the Greek and Trojan heroes to their deaths, only to vanish when the battle and epic narrative concludes. In Parmar's reading of Whitman's poem in 'Under Helen's Breath', the apparition is not symptomatic of a puzzle that Whitman refuses to solve, and is summarised more specifically as 'an image, a ghost, a spectre, a scapegoat'; 'the idea of an eidolon is something beauteous' (p. 65). The gaps in Parmar's open form vignettes thus indicate that Helen as eidolon is present in the scene, but also elusive, shifting identities as swift as a break in the diction. These lexical absences also indicate the 'remainder' in Helen's mythical narrative that can never be solved: frustrated by the aporetic aspects of her legend that remain beyond interpretation, Parmar regrets Helen's silence, her lack of excuses and absence of narratological redress in 'Under Helen's Breath'. In addition, the double consciousness of *Eidolon* allows for a more contemporary concretion of Whitman's apparition in Parmar's collection. '[F]actories' remain 'divine' artistic communities in Whitman's poem, but in Parmar's sequence Helen's 'beauteous' idea transforms the elusive spectre into a commodity: new 'eidolons of false value' haunt the book, from the supermarket shelves to the model's diurnal activities.[54]

As with the form of *Aesthetic Theory* itself, enigmatical poetry can be Delphic, and 'inimical to exposition'.[55] This is not the case in *Eidolon*, which shifts between these accounts of Helen as an allusive ghost, and less elusive embodiments of her figure as, for example, the maligned plaything of a daytime talk show. *Eidolon* contains enigmatic sections, such as the vignette above set in 'warm air' (p. 25), but it is not Delphic in the sense of wilfully inscrutable: hence Parmar criticises Whitman's poem as beguiling but also 'too grand. It is too vague' (p. 65). Indeed, in these sections about Helen's amorous behaviour, *Eidolon* takes the form of a specific feminist project – akin to H. D.'s – to save Helen from her fate as the archetypal 'Whore' (p. 66). In section xvii, Helen blots her lipstick and indulges in small talk in a hotel room (p. 26): the potentially adulterous scene is then interrupted with a quotation from the first book of H. D.'s *Helen in Egypt*: '"I am a woman of pleasure"' (p. 12).[56] H. D. adheres to a version of the Helen myth in which she endures the afterlife with Achilles: 'I am a woman of pleasure' is spoken 'ironically into the night' in *Helen in Egypt*, since Achilles has simply 'built [her] a fire' (p. 12) in an empty landscape. This irony encompasses Achilles' temporary forgetfulness in H. D.'s collection: addled with traumatic flashbacks of the ten-year war, he 'knew not Helen of Troy, | knew not Helena, hated of Greece' (p. 14). Whereas Helen worries that Achilles will soon remember the liturgy of 'Goddess, Princess,

Whore', the double consciousness of Parmar's collection engages with a less impressive hotel lover who has 'no *"sea-enchantment in his eyes"*'.[57] The latter quotation also originates in *Helen in Egypt*; the phrase recurs three times in H. D.'s book. Achilles has lost the '*accoutrements of valour*' in his afterlife, and is left only with '*"the sea-enchantment in his eyes"* (p. 7): Helen then notes 'the sea-enchantment in his eyes | of Thetis, his sea-mother' (p. 7), and prays to '*love him, as Thetis, his mother* [. . .] I saw in his eyes | the sea-enchantment' (p. 14). In contrast with Helen's maternal response to Achilles' traumatic behaviour in *Helen in Egypt*, Parmar's Achilles courts bathos in a Conrad Hilton hotel, and Helen is, significantly, 'misplaced' in the adulterous scene, 'blotting her lipstick | on industrial-quality tissue' (p. 26). Section xvii of *Eidolon* effectively reverses the Tiresias and typist scene in *The Waste Land*: instead of the post-coital woman Eliot imagines marooned among her supposedly tawdry possessions, Parmar presents an absent male lover denuded of any mythic pretensions.

Lawrence Durrell: Helen as 'Fig'

Rather than ruminate on the eidolon or enigma of the mythical Helen, Lawrence Durrell portrays her instead as a tiresome seducer in 'Troy'. Published five years after H. D.'s *Helen in Egypt*, Lawrence Durrell's poem is particularly culpable in *Eidolon* of endorsing the 'whore' myth, alongside Euripides' *The Trojan Women*. Helen is attacked by the second word of Durrell's sonnet: she is 'maunding', a seventeenth-century coinage meaning a counterfeiting demand or trick.[58] Durrell alludes to Helen's lasciviousness before the infamous beauty that launched a thousand ships in *Doctor Faustus*: in line two, she is figured as an 'Eater of the white fig', the 'candy-striped' or Adriatic fig that comprises an extra sweet version of the fruit – as opposed to, for example, the Calimyrna or Kadota varieties – and one that has obvious sexual connotations (p. 273). Parmar quotes the third and fourth lines of the Durrell poem at the beginning of section xlv in *Eidolon*: in Durrell's misogynist vision of Helen, she has '*Some beauty, yes, but no more than her tribe | Lathe-made for stock embraces on a bed.*'[59] It is not clear whether the 'tribe' refers to Spartans or women in general, and the metrical leeway at the beginning of the fourth line allows for the heavy stresses on 'Lathe-made' that emphasise the poet-narrator's contempt (p. 273). He registers astonishment that the monotonous whining of this 'drone' should have been such a 'test for cultures'; in his final references to Helen in this sonnet, she is merely a 'doll', and then just a synecdoche, a 'sarcastic cheek' (p. 273). Significantly, the mythic female figure in Durrell's companion poem 'Io' does not fare much better: modernist counterpointing transforms Zeus' lover into a Greek prostitute, a 'contemporary street-walker'; she contains 'repulsion' and 'joy in one' body, and an 'inward whiteness' which 'harms not | with dark keeping' in an unsettling and potentially racist ending to the poem (pp. 273–74). In *Eidolon*, Parmar quotes the lines from 'Troy' that include the 'sarcastic cheek' and 'astonished' poet (p. 273), and then attempts to exculpate Helen from his unnecessarily scurrilous charges through interjections between the quoted Durrell lines. 'Valves of lips' in Durrell's poem 'Strip-Tease' become the *Hello!* magazine face in Parmar's collection as an 'eidolon' counterpoint to Parmar's 'flesh-and-blood' Helen (p. 66). Mythic beauty is figured in Parmar's collection as the counterpart of 'immortal' selfies in what Anna Reading has termed our 'memobile' age: Parmar's point is that both are equally insubstantial as distracting eidolons.[60] Unlike the reversal of the typist scene in *The Waste Land* in section xvii of *Eidolon*, Helen is reminiscent of Eliot's postcoital typist in this passage, 'a little dumb, a little worn down by the machinery of love' (p. 56). Compared to Helen's 'maunding' account of her actions in Euripides' *The Trojan Women*, her 'defence' is promised in the middle section of xlv, but is then never actually 'offered' (p. 56). In a retort to Durrell's 'sarcastic cheek' (p. 273), Parmar reverts to Helen's aristocratic and haughty tone in *The Trojan Women*: the tear for Menelaus is 'for you to keep | commemorative souvenir | of the royal bedchamber' (p. 56).

Parmar's rebuttal of misogynistic visions of Helen that attempt to reduce the enigma of the mythical character to univocal misogyny is much more surefooted in her critique of Euripides' play. In *The Trojan Women*, Hecuba follows the usual condemnation of Helen when she introduces the infamous Queen of Laconia as 'the whore of Sparta, | Menelaus's loathsome wife, | Who caused the death of Priam | And all his fifty sons' (p. 11). As opposed to Durrell's anti-mythic vision of Helen as a commonplace, 'Lathe-made' 'drone' (p. 273), Andromache in *The Trojan Women* abhors the hyperbole of 'Evil', 'Murder', 'Death' and a 'monster' that begat 'the infernal butchery of her eyes!' (p. 31).[61] Menelaus initially complies with Andromache and Cassandra's indictments, but then assures them (unconvincingly) that 'It was not so much for her that I came to Troy, | As men seem to think. No, it was for him: | To meet that honoured guest of mine [Paris]' (p. 35). As an appendage in this purported erotic triangle, Helen's voice is silenced until the end of the play: she then excuses herself due to the immortal powers that intervened in the action. Euripides concurs with the version of mythic events that discloses Aphrodite's present of Helen to Paris after he announced that Aphrodite was the most beautiful goddess as opposed to Hera or Athena. In the afterword to *Eidolon*, Parmar takes issue with the impersonality that Woolf detects in Euripides' descriptions of the 'enslavement of women by the noble Greeks': Parmar asks whether we can 'model a civilisation on one that exploits, ensnares and silences women, the more "advanced" it becomes?' (p. 68). As she underlines, the 'real' Trojan war was more likely to have been initiated due to disputes over trade routes and strategic geographical dominance than the serendipity of a 'Lathe-made' beauty.[62] Through Parmar's double consciousness of myth, Helen becomes a woman simply shopping for 'donut peaches' in a supermarket, 'Lathe-made' not in terms of her provocative sexuality but a diurnal performance in 'the cash only express line', trying, on this occasion, to conjure a suitable response to a racist rebuke addressed by 'The blonde man' to a Mexican attendant.[63] In section xxxi, she confronts the textual violence of the 'narratological failure' of the account of the enslaved women in *The Trojan Women* by countering with the image of war as the 'pitiless circle' of a crop duster: instead of the space filling with children's 'laughter', the 'outriggers of war' dominate the field as they 'pitch and move in | a merciless circle' (p. 41). Unsurprisingly, Parmar endorses Euripides' second version of the Helen myth when – following Stesichorus and Herodotus' narratives – she remains in Egypt and maintains herself as 'a virtuous lady of great wit and charm' (p. 55). In Euripides' *Helen*, the steady wife of Menelaus opines that 'if only my face were like some picture | That could be wiped clean and done again' (p. 64). Gustave Moreau's painting of a ghostly Helen adorns the cover of *Eidolon*: as Hughes argues, in this image 'She is white and insubstantial, an *eidolon*, more akin to the wisps of smoke rising from Troy than to a real woman'.[64] Elsewhere in *Helen of Troy*, Hughes notes that 'the wonderful irony about the most beautiful woman in the world is that she is faceless' (p. 3): Helen's enigma encompasses the fact that she is representative of no particular woman, and all women, at the same time. In a sense, Parmar's mythic counterpointing does 'wipe' Helen's face and replace it with a woman queueing for fruit in a riposte to the version of the myth in Durrell's poem and Euripides' *The Trojan Women* in which Helen is a composite of an unambiguous and misogynist version of 'many women' (p. 42).

Despite her strictures against Woolf's version of Greek impersonality in 'Under Helen's Breath' and *Eidolon* as a whole, Parmar nevertheless quotes approvingly Woolf's comment on the ancient Greeks' attentiveness to 'every tremor and gleam of existence' (p. 65). Woolf, Parmar and

Harrison all share this humanist insistence on what Adorno disapprovingly termed 'limiting situations': in contrast, for all three poets such 'tremors' form antidotes to what Woolf derided as the 'confusion' of Christianity 'and its consolations' (p. 65).[65] Harrison's dialectical humanism allows him to enjoy swimming in Lesbos whilst lamenting Orpheus' demise in *Metamorpheus*, or to celebrate with a glass of wine under the shadow of Vesuvius and twentieth-century atrocities in the poem 'The Grilling' from *Under the Clock* (2005). Das's review of *Eidolon* points to an equivalent 'sparkle' in Parmar's language that eulogises Imagist moments in which, for example, Helen rolls down the 'cool glass' of a cab's window, 'quiet as water' (p. 23).[66] The legacies of modernist double consciousness thus allow these two poets to achieve moments of aesthetic and ideological salvation amongst the chaos of the more bigoted ideologies of racism and misogyny that are condemned outright in *Eidolon*. Harrison and Parmar also both draw on the modernist legacy of mythic counterpointing in order to target the banalities of popular culture: Parmar even imagines Clytemnestra on daytime television, debating the tag line: 'So your husband sacrificed your only daughter [Iphigeneia] that he might win the war' for his brother Menelaus' wife? (p. 44). However, despite their shared suspicion towards the 'fearful eidolons of false value and worthless commodity' (p. 67), the gender politics of the two poets differ vastly. Whereas Harrison's 'The Grilling' ends with the satyrs and their defiant 'cock tips high', Parmar remains excoriating of any 'buffed-up version of [Greek] heroism' that elides women and occludes the machinations of ancient masculinities with the chimera of a woman who can destroy cities merely with 'her sighs'.[67] Stylistically, too, the texts diverge in terms of the enigmatical poetics that I have discussed throughout this book. Harrison's work could be described as metamodernist in terms of its early twentieth-century antecedents, and indebtedness to the development of double consciousness in Joyce and Eliot's work, but this would preclude any discussion of formal achievement. Partly due to the structural inducements of the film-poem, *Metamorpheus* relies on 'accommodating' the reader, denies its underpinning research in order to dramatise a clash between an academic and the poet as a modern-day Orpheus, and neglects to give full expression to the counterpointing between the modernist poet Milev and classical myth.[68] In contrast, with the fractured vignettes, narratorial aporia and paratactic sections in *Eidolon*, Parmar deploys enigmatical poetry to engage with the most elusive character in classical myth.

Conclusion

I began this book with a discussion of Geoffrey Hill's fourth lecture as Oxford Professor of Poetry, in which he railed against the misconstruction of democratic writing as merely 'accessible', and conceded that he felt 'marooned' in the 1950s with the work of T. S. Eliot and Ezra Pound.[1] Hill returned to these themes throughout his tenure: in his eleventh lecture (11 March 2014), he warned that 'it is public knowledge that the newest generation of poets is encouraged to think of poems as Facebook or Twitter texts [...] the poem as selfie is the aesthetic criterion of contemporary verse'.[2] What might it mean, I asked at the beginning of the book, if contemporary poetry had a 'rule' instead to exasperate rather than to assuage?[3] As I argued in the second and third chapters, Hill's poems form exemplary examples of metamodernist poetry in their assimilation of modernist antecedents in order to create the enigmatical poetics of *The Orchards of Syon* (2002) and *Scenes from Comus* (2005). The questions that his fourth lecture posed have concerned me throughout the writing of this book, and the close link between Theodor Adorno's conception of enigmatical art and these two collections might suggest that Hill's evaluation of contemporary poetry should also be received as exemplary. Yet the allusive and elusive poems I have discussed in the last two chapters by Sandeep Parmar, Ahren Warner and James Byrne clearly contradict Hill's statements about the insalubriousness of twenty-first-century poetics in his lectures as Oxford Professor of Poetry. Indeed, Hill's comments on contemporary poetry in these orations are often as provocative, generalised and untrustworthy as those in Don Paterson's maligned introduction to *New British Poetry* (2004). Moreover, the twenty-first-century authors that Hill does mention in his Oxford lectures have been brought to his attention by the very processes of commodification that he attacks in his fifteen orations. He has demonstrated critical pertinacity in ignoring two generations of poets from the London and Cambridge Schools – most notably, J. H. Prynne – who write with the 'semantic energy' that Hill claims is absent in contemporary poetry, and who are equally committed as Hill to responding to the formal legacies of modernism.[4]

In contrast to the claim in these allocutions that there is no one writing like Geoffrey Hill anymore, so that he endures as a 'freak survivor' and 'holy fool', other critics have argued for a 'recrudescence' of modernism in contemporary literature.[5] David James and Urmila Seshagiri's account of the contemporary novel's engagement with revolutions in form in early twentieth-century literature has provided an important critical context for this book on enigmatical poetics.[6] Their research has also been indicative in its resistance to any sense that contemporary literature is merely an adjunct to modernism, a poor relation that continues under its spell in an attenuated form. Hill characterises himself instead as a 'high modernist' in his eighth lecture, and they would argue that he does so erroneously.[7] Modernism is a discrete cultural 'moment' or 'mythos' in James and Seshagiri's work, whereas Hill's comment suggests it endures, and that he persists as an anachronistic disciple of its definitive tenor.[8] Alternatively, if Hill were to deploy the term 'late modernism' instead, how late, we might enquire, can 'late' become? A century after the publication of *Ulysses* (1922) and *The Waste Land* (1922), it might be more persuasive to emphasise that modernism is paradoxically over, but not finished.

Rather than apply James and Seshagiri's account of metamodernism and the novel to a different literary form, I have drawn on their critical framework in order to formulate a narrative about the formal recalcitrance of contemporary poetry from both the mainstream and 'innovative' traditions. These poems form the missing context in Hill's rudimentary account of contemporary poetry in his lectures as Oxford Professor of Poetry. When considering arguments about metamodernism and contemporary fiction in relation to poems, distinctive technical issues and conceptions of literary history have clearly been at stake. The numerous debates surrounding the term analysed by critics such as James, Seshagiri, van den Akker, Alison Gibbons, Timotheus Vermeulen, Andre Furlani, Luke Turner, Nick Bentley, Usha Wilbers and Dennis Kersten have provided an important critical context for this book, but I have not simply applied them to the poetry in instances of critical determinism.[9] Rather, these insightful critical interventions have allowed me to focalise the primary concern of this book, that the concept of enigmatical poetics should be central to any discussion of 'innovative' and mainstream poetry influenced by modernist antecedents. Close readings in this book have engaged with poems by Hill, Prynne, Geraldine Monk, Ahren Warner, Sandeep Parmar and James Byrne which still allow for a 'remainder' – aspects of the texts that, for the present, remain beyond interpretation – in poetry conventionally located in either of these categories.[10] As in Harrison's *Metamorpheus* (2000) and Warner's 'Métro', I have also discussed the moments in which a 'convergence of modernist forms and modernist histories' occurs, but a 'remainder' fails to arise.[11] In focussing on enigmatical poetics, and critics' attempts to breach the 'secret' of artworks 'that one can never quite grasp', I have argued for a kind of writing that resists the enduring bifurcation of contemporary British poetry into mainstream and 'innovative' writing.[12] Nevertheless, these distinctions continue to be valuable: whereas many mainstream poets have resisted the 'remainder' in order to court the 'general reader' of poetry, there is undoubtedly an intensification of modernist legacies in the Cambridge and London Schools with writers such as Prynne and Monk, who – with all the incumbent internecine warfare – have been aligned with the 'innovative' scene. However, the formal achievements of supposedly mainstream contemporary poets such as Hill who have embraced the concept of enigmatical poetics have been misconceived within the categories of the mainstream and 'innovative'. In addition, a younger generation of writers – including Warner, Byrne and Parmar – have attempted to renegotiate the strictures of this binary. These poets draw on aspects of both traditions to create enigmatical works such as 'Nervometer', *White Coins* (2015) and *Eidolon* (2015), rather than exploiting the 'innovative' in acts of short-term aesthetic piracy.

In *Post-Postmodernism or, the Cultural Logic of Just-in-Time Capitalism* (2012), Jeffrey Nealon responds to the legacies of modernist art in a very different way to these writers and this book. Nealon would concur with Hill's statement in his eighth lecture as Oxford Professor of Poetry that artists have to respond to 'the habit of thought' that insists that 'in order to survive an age of commodity, the art of poetry must itself become a form of commodity'.[13] However, whereas Hill argues in this lecture that commodified poems become 'a vehicle of entertainment, somewhere between someone's idea of a stand-up comedian in a scout hut and a sex hang-up agony column', Nealon discusses 'innovative' writers' responses to this conundrum. Nealon argues that the capitulation of art to the prevailing market needs to be contested from within the economy's own terms now that creative resistance appears as a distant efflorescence of an outdated modernism. However, Nealon's book forms one example of how the relationship between experimental and mainstream poetry can be misunderstood, and how an account of enigmatical poetry can aid in recalibrating the distinctions between modernist, mainstream and 'innovative' writing. He contends that poetics of resistance – akin to enigmatical poetry's challenge to accommodation that I have focussed on in this book – are simply a '"modernist" mistake', since Fredric Jameson contends that 'Everything does in fact exist on the same flat surface of culture' (p. 153).¹⁴ Yet Nealon and Jameson ignore, for example, the alternative publishing strategies of independent presses, and social networks that allow for experimental reading series, such as the Other Room (2008–18): instead, they insist that 'we're all inexorably forced to work through the omnivorous levelling logic of "the market"' (p. 154). In a misreading of *Aesthetic Theory* (1970), Nealon argues against Adorno's concept of literature as a 'noncommodity par excellence', with its 'contentlessness' and 'aesthetic self-autonomy' (p. 154). In fact, Nealon reduces literature to one side of Adorno's paradox in *Aesthetic Theory*, that literature cannot be understood, whereas Adorno also emphasises that, in addition, art *must* be understood. Adorno does not argue that literature is 'contentless', but that the artwork is a 'congealed process' between 'impulse' and 'form' in the section of *Aesthetic Theory* precisely on 'truth content' (p. 129). The 'truth content' consists of how well this synthesis is achieved, rather than a hermeneutic insistence on what the artwork simply means.

Nevertheless, Nealon continues his anti-Adornoian proposition that art's 'semi-autonomy' should be negated in the form of a post-postmodernist literature whose force lies in 'its *imbrication* with contemporary economic forces [. . .] a positive (maybe even joyful) form of critical engagement with bio-political and economic life', otherwise 'all you have left is a kind of saddened nostalgia', with 'a "tiny minority" upholding and venerating tradition [. . .] in a world where most people don't have time or inclination to care about preserving the past' (p. 154). Given Adorno's dialectical approach to tradition, Nealon's thinking can only appear as a capitulation to the commodifying processes that he and Jameson criticise. Nealon advocates Kenneth Goldsmith's marshalling of pre-existing language, and Bruce Andrews' 'relentless provocation' in poems 'where there's no attempt to "mean" something', as an 'effective arsenal against the present and its ubiquitous post-postmodernism of speed and production' (p. 169). Yet Andrews' 'provocation' in books such as *I Don't Have Any Paper so Shut Up* (1992) is indistinguishable from the 'aesthetic self-autonomy' that Nealon dismisses as an aspect of outdated modernism; a modernist 'mistake' of 'contentlessness' as he terms it earlier in his book (pp. 153–4). In contrast, Goldsmith's amalgamation of pre-existing material presents a different formal (and postmodernist) approach to Andrews' work, one which exists alongside, and arguably complicit with, commodifying processes rather than – as Nealon argues – presenting a Foucauldian '"strong" power of the false' that is resistant to modern practices of power (p. 162).[15] In contrast, enigmatical poetry initiates a powerful critique of commodification, even if this criticism resides in the 'essentially powerless power of poetry'.[16]

Metamodernist poems that assimilate early twentieth-century antecedents in order to resist the 'reality principle' should not be dismissed in Nealon's terms as symptomatic of anachronistic nostalgia.[17] Enigmatical poetry fills in the gaps in Hill's account of contemporary poetry in his Oxford lectures, and forms a potential rejoinder to his claim that the 'general prospect' for contemporary poetry 'is bleak'.[18] If the recalibration of mainstream and 'innovative' poetry in the context of enigmatical poetics were accepted, it would not be necessary to conceive of poems today as entirely in thrall to a desiccated market, desperate to become a 'vehicle of entertainment, somewhere between someone's idea of a stand-up comedian' and an 'agony aunt' column.[19] Prynne, Monk, Warner, Parmar and Byrne have all published poems that display the qualities that Hill claims are lacking in contemporary poetry, such as an understanding of the 'electrical tremor' between words.[20] It would be foolhardy to attempt to prove, for example, that Prynne's poems do not display a sensitivity towards 'semantic strata'.[21]

In order to further this research on the 'semantic energy' of twenty-first-century poetry, the relationship between metamodernism, enigmaticalness and recent poems could be considered further in the following ways:

1. To think through the legacies of modernist writing, but in relation to specific conceptual or formal devices, such as my analysis of enigmatical poetry in this book. How might further critical discussions about contemporary poems develop around, for example, lyrical epiphany, minimalism, multivocal writing, defamiliarization, parataxis, implicitness, polyphonic subjectivity, mixed registers, discontinuity, indeterminacy, 'flick imagery' or collage?[22]

2. To consider a postcolonial 'turn' in studies of metamodernism. Does postcolonial poetry beyond the UK respond to enigmaticalness? Given that metamodernism more widely has responded to the configuration of Western capitalist societies, is there a danger of homogenizing disparate postcolonial experiences through the term? If metamodernism is indicative of these Western societies, then must it be resisted, even if the term itself inherently contains the notion of critique?

3. To deliberate further the overlaps, bifurcations and fault-lines between the mainstream, and the London and Cambridge Schools. Are there

other formal or conceptual categories that might account differently for this schism? Whilst stressing the dangers of critical simplification in relation to these terms, what other narratives might wish to sustain them? Is a new skirmish originating in the poetry wars imminent, such as that of the indignant response to Paterson's introduction to *New British Poetry* (2004), that would revitalise these categories? Or will they persist as formal immanence in twenty-first-century poetry?

4. Would an account of a metamodernist poetry be possible in terms of the version of the concept outlined by van den Akker, Gibbons and Vermeulen? How might the distinctive formal traditions of contemporary poetry account differently for affect, post-irony and sincerity? I have indicated above that there are specific formal and conceptual problems in discussing the latter's manifestation in relation to contemporary poetry, as opposed to the contemporary novel. However, their overall project suggests a critical mapping that extends beyond metamodernism itself, that constantly puzzles over the development of contemporary art and literature. How will future 'structures of feeling' manifest themselves in relation to contemporary poetry?

5. After considering Adorno's ruminations on modern artistic endeavours in *Aesthetic Theory*, and Geoffrey Hill's irritable and impish response to contemporary poems in his fourth lecture as Oxford Professor of Poetry, how might critics respond to an accusation that the poetry scene exults in an increase of publishers and laurels, yet the most lauded contemporary poetry still does not qualify as art?

A 'Structure of Feeling' and 'Recrudescence': Two Metamodernisms

In the following section, I shall begin to respond to some of the ruminations in the fourth set of questions above. The work of Furlani, James, Seshagiri, van den Akker, Gibbons and Vermeulen has been invaluable to this monograph as a critical background to centre my discussion of contemporary poetry around the notion of the enigma. However, my account of enigmatical poetry in this book could be paralleled by a completely different narrative about metamodernist poems. This section illustrates how further research on poetry and metamodernism could develop in the context of van den Akker, Gibbons and Vermeulen's specific sense of how the concept might respond to the waning of postmodernism. Whereas Furlani, James, Seshagiri and this book stress the perpetuation of modernist legacies in recent literature, Gibbons, van den Akker and Vermeulen have formulated an influential narrative of post-postmodernism. In the following discussion, I suggest ways in which studies of contemporary poetry might learn from the capaciousness of the term, emphasise divergences from current narratives about contemporary fiction and art, and resist metamodernism's temptations of over-determinism.

In this book, I have analysed the work of poets who respond to modernist authors as diverse as Ezra Pound, T. S. Eliot, H. D., Antonin Artaud and Bertolt Brecht.[23] In contrast, Vermeulen and van den Akker argue that metamodernism primarily attempts to account for the emergence of a wider 'structure of feeling' in the twenty-first century that responds to our historicity, bound up with the aftermaths of 9/11, the financial crash and austerity.[24] Vermeulen and van den Akker's specific framing of metamodernism continues in their book with Alison Gibbons, *Metamodernism: Historicity, Affect and Depth after Postmodernism* (2017), in which the term engages with a 'structure of feeling' in contemporary western societies that 'emerges from, and reacts to, the postmodern as much as it is a cultural logic that corresponds to today's stage of global capitalism' (pp. 5–6). Vermeulen and van den Akker quote a review of an 'Altermodern' exhibition – an alternative term for metamodernism – at Tate Britain in 2009 (p. 3): Adrian Searle asserts that 'postmodernism is dead, but something altogether weirder has taken its place'.[25] Within this 'weirdness' – that Gibbons characterises in *Metamodernism* as enacting an 'affective turn' (p. 84) – Vermeulen and van den Akker contend that 'what is needed is a new language to put into words this altogether weirder reality and its still stronger cultural landscape' (p. 3). Postmodernism is not repudiated, but considered in a dialectical relationship to modernism, in which contemporary artists 'attempt to incorporate postmodern stylistics and formal conventions while moving beyond them' (p. 2).[26] Importantly, for these two critics such artistic endeavours are also coupled with an underlying postmodernist doubt about the efficacy of such concepts. Such polemical assertions attest to the admirable scope of van den Akker, Gibbons and Vermeulen's version of metamodernism, as it attempts to define the machinations of the contemporary. Conversely, these critics are also aware that their broadly historicist approach to metamodernism risks ridicule, since the contours of the present only become clear belatedly; they openly concede that 'the hubris of delineating a historical moment and describing a social situation in terms of yet another " – ism" opens us up for Homeric laughter at best and fierce scorn at worst' (p. 3). Indeed, whereas metamodernism could be regarded as one of many 'structures of feeling' in wider contemporary culture, these critics sometimes discuss it interchangeably with post-postmodernism, as a telling comment in the acknowledgements section of *Metamodernism* indicates. As in their influential online journal *Notes on Metamodernism*, van den Akker and Vermeulen have sought since 2010 to 'document and conceptualise developments in the arts, aesthetics and culture that are symptomatic *of the post-postmodern or, rather, metamodern condition*' (p. xi, my italics). Metamodernism is 'today's *dominant* structure of feeling among a host of subordinate structures of feeling that [Raymond] Williams dubbed residuals and emergents' (p. 8, my italics). In contrast, James MacDowell, one of the contributors to *Metamodernism*, admits that this particular 'structure of feeling will only be one of many such localised "structures" at work in a particular time and place'.[27]

Inauthenticity and the 'Implicated Subject' in 'Near St Mary Woolnoth' and *Hello. Your Promise has been Extracted*

Despite MacDowell's judicious response, van den Akker, Gibbons and Vermeulen's attempts to pinpoint a 'structure of feeling' in contemporary culture could provide fruitful ways to engage with poetry in a very different way to the account of enigmatical poetics in this book. An alternative approach to Warner's poetry provides an example of how this critical trajectory might flourish. As opposed to his grappling with the 'nebulous' mental states of Artaud's *Le Pèse-Nerfs* (1925) in 'Nervometer', and the neo-modernist extrapolations of 'Métro' and '*Lutèce, Te Amo*', Warner flirts with, and then rejects, a postmodernist approach to contemporary culture in 'Near St Mary Woolnoth' from *Confer* (2011), that resonates in the context of van den Akker, Gibbons and Vermeulen's version of metamodernism.[28] The title alludes to part two of *The Waste Land*, in which 'St Mary Woolnoth kept the hours | With a dead sound on the final stroke of nine': Warner's poem may be located 'near' Eliot's Anglican church, but we are only 'near' *The Waste Land* in the sense of an intertextual 'departure' from the modernist text.[29] Warner replaces Eliot's 'Unreal city', a traumatised space with neurasthenic commuters after World War One (p. 53), with a postmodernist metropolis, in which the poet-narrator even doubts the authenticity of his arboreal interlocutor. Nor is this the utopian space of the modernist city imagined by Le Corbusier: Warner presents the reader instead with a postmodern city of expensively dressed City businessmen, who lord it over the London vista with their '*phallus*' ties as if they had escaped from the pages of Bret Easton Ellis' *American Psycho* (1991).[30] Deploying second-person narration in the same way as 'Métro', the poet-narrator invites the reader to assimilate his pastiche of the élitist, modernist poet who lords it over the city on a high balcony, the urban equivalent of Charles Baudelaire's symbolic albatross, that, like the proto-modernist poet, soars 'through space', 'rejoices in the tempest and mocks the archer down below'.[31] A neo-modernist overlord thus views a postmodernist London in which the city is merely a 'playground adventure', a myriad of playful 'loopholes', akin to John Ash's 'The Building', in which cities are 'no longer centres of government, military operation or bureaucracy', and 'exist solely to be enjoyed' as places for 'lawless amusements'.[32] However, the last line of the poem undercuts this vision: the narrator declares that to stare at a tree and doubt its authenticity is to 'miss the point entirely' (p. 41).

It would be too magniloquent to interpret the poem as symptomatic of the waning of postmodernism discussed by van den Akker, Gibbons and Vermeulen, but the closure certainly looks beyond the playful antics of the city and narrator in the first five stanzas. One potential reading of this line might be to accept it as an invitation to embrace and not reflect upon this postmodernist city. However, the 'point' here is ambiguous: the imperative 'Know' appears overly insistent, and can be resisted. Wondering whether a tree's bark has been 'planned' – with a pun on 'planed' – may be to 'miss the point' in terms of imaginatively constructing a postmodernist city that might be fundamentally flawed in its conception. This closure thus opens up a space for metamodernism in Gibbons, van den Akker and Vermeulen's understanding of the term: scathing, ironic and postmodern *ennui* gives way to an alternative landscape beyond the remit of the poem – and discussed further in Warner's *Hello. Your Promise has been Extracted* (2017) – which is not beholden to preconceptions of surface reality, and the disposable glitz outlined elsewhere in 'Near St Mary Woolnoth'.[33] In contrast, in *Hello. Your Promise has been Extracted* we are presented with a markedly different poet-narrator who is attentive to the historical atrocities underlying contemporary culture, and the permutations of Michael Rothberg's 'implicated' subject. No longer wallowing in élitist banter on a London balcony, the poet-narrator in Warner's third collection wonders what it means to be a 'global subject' in the contemporary world, where government taxes, elections, and economic disparities can no longer mean that his behaviour can be conceived as taking place in a postmodern city in which nothing matters, because nothing is 'true'.[34]

In contrast with the postmodernist environs of 'Near St Mary Woolnoth', in *Hello. Your Promise has been Extracted*, this metamodernist collection in Gibbons, van den Akker and Vermeulen's sense of the term engages with atrocious history, the implicated subject, prostitution and everyday violence. Echoing Keats's 'Ode to Melancholy' in the first line of the collection, the poet-narrator aligns one of Budapest's museums with Keats' 'Lethe': 'Today, you will not go to the House of Terror' (p. 10).[35] His refusal registers the potential pornography of violence in a name that intertwines the history of the Fascist and Communist regimes with the gothic. The photograph of an anonymous apartment building on page eleven bears a striking resemblance to the House of Terror, but without the latter's gaudy 'TERROR' banners draped from its roof. Warner's implication is that 'ordinary' violence commodified in the museum actually occurred in these European buildings, where 'gouls' of a 'bygone pogrom' line the pavements (p. 10). Thus the attendant photograph functions as the 'ghost' of the museum, and then registers the 'ghost' of the prostitute referred to – in parentheses – in the opposite lines. Prostitutes in Warner's work are always, partly, intertextual reworkings of Baudelaire and Voltaire's outsider figures. Nevertheless, Paul Batchelor criticises Warner for his representation of sex workers, which chimes, for this reviewer, with the collection's overall misogyny: 'the book's most striking characteristic is [its] blatancy [. . .] women are and suffer. Rape, murder and pimping prostitutes are typical activities for a man; whereas, when we finally see a woman doing something, she is likely to be serving the poet food, or giving him a blowjob'.[36] However, to depict instances of systemic violence towards and exploitation of women is not necessarily, of course, to endorse them. Here, the poet-narrator's desire registers his implication in this objectification of women, but he refuses to engage in a symbolic act of violence: he will not push his finger into a 'shrapnel-rent seam of render', an image that recalls Paul Muldoon's recourse to similar imagery in 'The Loaf', when the poet sticks his digit into 'the hole they've cut for a dimmer switch' (p. 10).[37] 'Render' forms a recurrent Surrealist image in Warner's collection: the 'rendering | around a point' in 'Nervometer' (p. 67) anticipates the cracked 'render' – a mixture of sand and cement – in the photographs in *Hello. Your Promise has been Extracted*, as well as the metaphorical 'rendering' in part one between commodified totalitarianism and sexual violence.[38] Rather than a blatant re-inscribing of misogyny that Batchelor detects in these tropes, there is certainly an aesthetic frisson in the refusal of 'render', in which the potentially prurient writing is formally complicit in the violence it deplores. Nevertheless, the poet-narrator is well aware of this potential for formal exploitation, as when, later on in the sequence, he notes that an artist in Lisbon received awards for pictures of emaciated prostitutes, 'whose bones jut like those of death-camp Jews' (p. 96).

In part one, the poet-narrator thus investigates his post-postmodernist implication in the pornography of history and the commodification of women. The implicated subject here acknowledges, is tempted by, but ultimately rejects the sex worker's swaying hips, and the temptation of commodified history. Yet he is still inextricably part of a post-postmodernist culture in which tourist museums, pimps and the 'prostitution' of history thrive, and a beneficiary of a system 'that generates dispersed and unequal experiences of trauma and well-being simultaneously'.[39] At the end of this section, the poet-narrator's response to this marketisation of history and systemic violence is to turn to the abjection that permeates *Hello. Your Promise has been Extracted*, with, for example, 'scum' (pp. 14, 22), 'piss' (p. 14), 'shit' (p. 18) and gloopy innards, as he implores the reader to beat their muscular tissue of the heart ('myocardium'), 'until it weeps' (p. 12). In an echo of Samuel Beckett's famous phrase from *The Unnameable* (1953) – registered in Warner's 'index' at the end of the collection (p. 123) – 'This is', the poet-narrator intones, 'the only way to go on' (p. 12). This assertion constitutes an attack on false sentimentality as a response to structural inequality, a theme that runs throughout *Hello. Your Promise has been Extracted*.

In the most extensive metamodernist exploration of the implicated subject in *Hello. Your Promise has been Extracted*, the poet-narrator describes a walk to a ballet with a female companion: this cultural excursion is undercut by an encounter with a drug addict that then spirals into ruminations on numerous incidents of violence and capitalist exploitation. The addict's 'desperate ecstasy' consists of a cheap mixture of crack cocaine, 'kerosene, rat poison [and] carbonic acid' (p. 74). (The use of laundry detergent, laxatives, caffeine or boric acid would be a more conventional way in which to 'cut' the drug [p. 74]). The oxymoron of 'desperate ecstasy' neatly summarises the contrast between the exclusive pleasures of the ballet – Poppy is 'dressed in a pretty dress' – and the addict's desperate 'hit': the link between drugs and bourgeois culture links with Brecht's conception of the 'culinary', and Harrison's depiction of heroin addicts outside the Frankfurt opera house in *The Gaze of the Gorgon* (1992). However, unlike in Brecht and Harrison's work, the emphasis in this section is on the contrast between the two parties: in a moment of Célinian harshness, the phrase to describe the unknown addict, 'Hag', is emphasised at the beginning of the line; the wizened woman is 'the same age' as Poppy, who is further infantilised since the poet-narrator has just helped her to bathe (p. 74). The characters' implication in a culture unable to cope with the suppression of drugs at the same time as high levels of addiction continue then spirals out into the subversion of the ballet excursion with various allusions to rape victims, orphans and 'everyday' trauma in Laura Berlant's sense of the term, such as the reference to the explosion in Tianjin on 12 August 2015 (pp. 74, 76).[40] As I recounted in Chapter 4, this incident was due, as the poet-narrator intimates, to the subterfuges of companies dominating the port, and traffic on the Hai river towards Beijing: with little external oversight, inter-family corruption and illegal hiring practices, the explosion was a direct result of unregulated capitalism, rather than merely an accident. Such passages in *Hello. Your Promise has been Extracted* have drawn the ire of critics such as Batchelor and Benjamin Myers: the former refers to Warner's litany of 'tortures and atrocities perpetrated on and by Johnny Foreigner'.[41] However, these critics miss the irony of the ambiguity of the final statement in this section, in which the second-person narrative throughout the collection is intensified to stress the reader's implication in the depicted violence: 'you're right, there's nothing you can do – there's nothing to be done' (p. 76).

A metamodernist approach to a world riven with everyday trauma and exploitation thus pervades *Hello. Your Promise has been Extracted*: the poet-narrator is implicated in a post-postmodernist world of 'simmering tensions [. . .] and—to be frank—frightening developments' that anticipate 'a clusterfuck of world-historical proportions'.[42] The poet-narrator confides that, looking back, postmodernism did not indicate the perpetuity of liberal democracy, as in Francis Fukuyama's *The End of History and the Last Man* (1992), but a hiatus between the post-*Wende* era in Europe, and the return of maximalist politics as an inversion of the centrist thinking of Tony Blair and Gerhard Schröder (pp. 12–13). '[H]istory is here again', the poet-narrator declares, just as for van den Akker, Gibbons and Vermeulen, we are moving towards an apocalyptic 'clusterfuck' (p. 17). The poet-narrator feels keenly that the 'distant pity' he felt as a child for young victims in Rwanda should now be seen as the 'historical luxury' of the implicated subject, as someone who, according to Rothberg, contributes to, inhabits or inherits 'regimes of domination but [does] not originate or control such regimes'.[43] However, the problem with the conception of history in this passage in *Hello. Your Promise has been Extracted* is that the focus on a postmodernist hiatus is undercut by its own examples: the massacre of the Tutsis who sheltered in the Pallothian mission church in

Gikondo, for instance, occurred on 9 April 1994. Similarly, the poet-narrator draws attention to the reader's implication in the systemic violence of racism through his overstatement that 'angry white cops shoot blacks repeatedly' in the US (p. 102), but when Rothberg discusses the murder of Trayvon Martin in 2012, he underscores the historical continuity of this violence from the era of lynching and the Jim Crow laws rather than outlining a lull in violence during the postmodern era.

Oscillate Wildly

My analysis above of Warner's 'Near St Mary Woolnoth' and *Hello. Your Promise has been Extracted* thus indicates the potential for analyses of contemporary poetry to respond to van den Akker, Gibbons and Vermeulen's account of metamodernism. Of course, this approach has been contested: compared to the certainty with which Vermeulen and van den Akker outline the historicity of metamodernism in their first article on the topic, for Peter Boxall, 'the historical language which is required to describe the passage past the far horizon of postmodernism is lacking, or unformulated'.[44] In relation to contemporary poetry, therefore, this version of metamodernism risks over-determinism, as with an intertextual approach overly reliant on the influence of modernist antecedents. Nevertheless, Linda Hutcheon still challenges us to find a 'new label [...] and name it for the twenty-first century'.[45] Outside of the 'knife fight in a phone booth' characteristic of contemporary British poetry, metamodernism certainly has the advantage of allowing for potentially more nuanced conceptualisations of post-postmodernism, whether in relation to a specific 'structure of feeling' in current historical developments, or a stratum of literary forms responding to early twentieth-century literature.[46] In other words, metamodernism risks over-determinism, but it also promises future nuances that Nealon's account of post-postmodernist poetry fails to achieve.

An objection to the term 'metamodernism' as discussed in this section so far might be that it merely joins a long list of equivalent critical terms such as 'neo-modernism', 'hypermodernism' and 'altermodernism'. Indeed, in 'Notes on Metamodernism', van den Akker and Vermeulen list Gilles Lipovetsky's 'hypermodern', Alan Kirby's 'digimodernism' and 'pseudo-modernism', Robert Samuels' 'automodernism' and Nicholas Bourriaud's 'altermodernism' as related, but not identical, terms (p. 3).[47] The first coinage in the list above, 'neo-modernism', echoes the neo-Victorian interest in novels such as Sarah Waters's *Affinity* (1999) to bring a postmodernist sensibility to bear on fiction set in a specific Victorian period. Tom McCarthy's *C* (2010), for example, is comparable in that it draws the reader's attention towards the birth of modernism in the technological advancements of the late nineteenth and early twentieth centuries. Yet the term metamodernism resonates beyond this concern with modernist origins and pastiche. Following a similar logic, but coming to a different conclusion, Motonori Sato has critiqued metamodernism as betraying its inextricability from postmodernism due to its reflexive prefix.[48] Far from registering a simple perpetuation of postmodernism – or constituting a critical anachronism – for Turner, van den Akker, Gibbons and Vermeulen, the term actually registers the legacy and continuing pertinence of postmodernism in Hutcheon's new, as yet unlabelled, period of history. For these critics, 'meta-', deriving from Plato's metaxis, allows – as Turner proposes – for 'an oscillation and simultaneity between and beyond the diametrically opposed poles' of modernism and postmodernism.[49]

What, however, does it mean if contemporary British poetry is conceived as 'oscillating', when it is already preoccupied with its own tensions between mainstream and 'innovative' poetry? Does the shuttling category of 'temperate' modernism, as it operates within these categories, merely oscillate wildly without formal distinction?[50] This 'meta-' in metamodernism is not unproblematic, since 'oscillation' (and 'shuttling') risks reifying opposing concepts, in which cultural critics can pick and choose between the two terms, rather than considering the particular historicities of modernism and postmodernism. As I argued in the Introduction, there is no instantiation of an uncontested postmodernist poetry, so how can contemporary poetry 'oscillate' with that which it does not and cannot recognise? Nevertheless, Plato's sense of metaxis, meaning 'in between', is pertinent to my engagement in this book with poetry that sits uneasily within rather than vacillates between the mainstream and the London and Cambridge Schools. In addition, 'meta-' denotes the self-reflexivity associated with postmodernism, yet the work of contemporary poets I have discussed in this book may be self-conscious about its deployment and transformation of the legacies of modernist writing, but it is not in itself a manifestation of postmodernism. The 'meta-' in metamodernism means 'with' and 'after' modernism: the prefix indicates that contemporary culture has not eluded the formal legacies of modernist literature, that are encapsulated in contemporary writers whose emphasis is on innovation, difficulty, generic and formal disruption, and 'hating' tradition properly through the revitalisation of modernist writing rather than playful negation.[51] 'Meta-' also evinces a necessary critical distance that resonates in terms of the modernist legacies discussed in this book: metamodernism in both intertextual and historicist understandings of the term does not, of course, indicate an uncritical endorsement of the Eurocentrism of early twentieth-century modernism, imperialism and the extreme right-wing politics of Pound and Wyndham Lewis. In Furlani's account of the concept, metamodernism denotes a 'derivation' and 'resemblance' to modernist literature, as well as 'succession' and 'change'.[52] As Furlani argues, metamodernists 'develop an aesthetic *after* yet *by means* of modernism. Where "post" suggests severance or repudiation, "meta-" denotes both change and the continuity apparent in metamodernists' efforts to engage with, and transform, modernist writing'.[53]

As I have argued throughout this book, the problem with this account of contemporary literature is that the 'transformation' of modernism can result in formal conservatism. In contrast, I have considered enigmatical poetics as a specific instance of contemporary writing that draws on modernist antecedents, but then transforms them into 'exasperating' poetics in collections as formally dissimilar as Hill's *Scenes from Comus* and Prynne's *Acrylic Tips* (2002). Adorno begins *Aesthetic Theory* with a claim that 'All efforts to restore' such elusive work 'by giving it a social function—of which art is itself uncertain and by which it expresses its own certainty—are doomed' (p. 1). Yet fifty years after Adorno's rumination, poetry is corralled into an equivalence with utilitarian texting or attenuated with instrumentalist attempts to make it representative of something other than the 'in-itself' of the poems themselves (p. 125). Only through the glorious uselessness of poetry that stubbornly resists all attempts to regulate it 'is the present domination of instrumental reason defied'.[54] The lyric poet thrives in '*désinvolture*', an artistic 'dispensation from the strictures of logic': any critic who attempts to apply 'extra-aesthetic' or 'causal' criteria to art 'blunders and trips in the twilight of the work'.[55] Instead, Adorno asserts in *Aesthetic Theory* that 'Great works wait' for their interpretation (p. 40). Due to the 'remainder' of Hill and Prynne's poetry that endures after the analysis of enigmatical poetics in this book, these 'Great works' are still waiting (p. 121).

Notes

Introduction

1. Rob Young and Irmin Schmidt, *All Gates Open: The Story of Can* (London: Faber and Faber, 2018), p. 458.
2. Geoffrey Hill, 'Poetry, Policing and Public Order (1)', www.english.ox.ac.uk/professor-sir-geoffrey-hill-lectures (accessed 12 July 2020). Hill refers to T. S. Eliot's phrase 'the exasperated spirit' in part two of 'Little Gidding' from *Four Quartets* (London: Faber and Faber, 1959 (1943)), p. 54.
3. Geoffrey Hill, 'How ill white hairs become a fool and jester', www .english.ox.ac.uk/professor-sir-geoffrey-hill-lectures (accessed 12 July 2020).
4. Lemn Sissay, 'Carol Ann Duffy and Geoffrey Hill: truly poetic heavyweights', www.theguardian.com/commentisfree/2012/jan/31/carol-ann-duffy-geoffrey-hill-punch-up (accessed 12 July 2020).
5. Hill, 'Poetry, Policing and Public Order (1)', www.english.ox.ac.uk/professor-sir-geoffrey-hill-lectures (accessed 12 July 2020). This book focuses on contemporary British poetry primarily because a monograph twice its size would have been required to engage with the multitude of enigmatical poetry across the globe. Future critical responses could investigate the term in relation to postcolonial, non-Anglophone and American poetry. Even within a British context, the author could have discussed, in addition, the work of numerous other poets, including Kelvin Corcoran, Michael Hofmann, Luke Kennard, Chris McCabe, Carrie Etter, Tom Jenks, Drew Milne, Peter Riley, Sam Riviere, Robert Sheppard, Zoë Skoulding, Scott Thurston, Matthew Welton and John Wilkinson. Moreover, as Andrew Thacker notes in relation to Jessica Berman's work on modernisms, the danger with transnational accounts of literature is that they are at risk of 'evacuating the geographical (and, I would add, historical and cultural) specificity of the writers and texts involved' (*Modernism, Space and the City* [Edinburgh: Edinburgh University Press, 2019], p. 15).
6. Young and Schmidt, *All Gates Open*, p. 458.

7. Hill, 'Poetry, Policing and Public Order (1)', www.english.ox.ac.uk/profes sor-sir-geoffrey-hill-lectures (accessed 12 July 2020).

8. Andre Furlani, *Guy Davenport: Postmodern and After* (Evanston, Illinois: Northwestern University Press, 2007), p. 150. Furlani is one of the first critics to discuss the concept of metamodernist poetry. However, his outline of metamodernism in the last chapter (pp. 150–6) then appears only sporadically in the subsequent analysis, as when he argues that Davenport's *The Jules Verne Steam Balloon* (1993) 'adheres to a metamodernism that proceeds beyond modernism as much as it repudiates postmodernism' (p. 159).

9. Timotheus Vermeulen and Robin van den Akker, 'Notes on Metamodernism', *Journal of Aesthetics and Culture*, 2 (2010), 2–14. These critics draw on Alexandra Dumitrescu's declaration in 2007 that metamodernism is 'a period term and a cultural phenomenon, partly concurring with (post)modernism, partly emerging from it and as a reaction to it' ('Interconnections in Blakean and metamodern space', www .doubledialogues.com/article/interconnections-in-blakean-and-metamodern -space (accessed 16 July 2020)).

10. Luke Turner, 'Metamodernist Manifesto', www.metamodernism.org (accessed 29 April 2020).

11. David James and Urmila Seshagiri, 'Metamodernism: Narratives of Continuity and Revolution', *PMLA*, 129(1) (2014), 87–98.

12. James – alongside Peter Boxall – has been one of the most active critics in drawing attention to the contemporary novel's self-conscious engagement with modernist writing in books such as *The Legacies of Modernism* (2011) and *Modernist Futures* (2012). Boxall's extensive work on modernist legacies in contemporary literature includes *Since Beckett: Contemporary Writing in the Wake of Modernism* (London: Continuum, 2009) and *Twenty-First-Century Fiction* (Cambridge: Cambridge University Press, 2013).

13. Robin van den Akker, Alison Gibbons and Timotheus Vermeulen, eds., *Metamodernism: Historicity, Affect and Depth After Postmodernism* (London/ New York: Rowman and Littlefield International, 2017); Nick Bentley, 'Trailing Postmodernism: David Mitchell's *Cloud Atlas*, Zadie Smith's *NW*, and the Metamodern', *English Studies*, 99(7–8) (November 2018), 723–43; Martin Eve, 'Thomas Pynchon, David Foster Wallace and the Problems of "Metamodernism"', *C21st Literature*, 1(1) (2012), 7–13, p. 8; Dennis Kersten and Usha Wilbers, eds., 'Metamodernism: A Special Issue', *English*, 99(7–8) (November 2018). Eve argues that metamodernism is not even a single strand of a new 'structure of feeling' and is 'insufficiently delineated from its antecedent'. He correctly points out their misreading of Kantian idealism and an overinvestment in neo-Romanticism (p. 11), but concedes that 'despite

its theoretical failings this new paradigm offers an interesting twist on postmodern discourse for literature' (p. 12). However, van den Akker, Vermeulen, James and Seshagiri all argue in different ways that the term does go beyond 'postmodern discourse', and that metamodernism points to the exhaustion of this discourse in a supposedly 'post-truth' age. In contrast, Eve contends that such a critical perspective is 'overly rooted in positivist historical thinking, seeking a parallel progression in its object of study' (p. 7). Nevertheless, to insist on postmodernism's undialectical continuation in the present in order to understand contemporary culture is a totalising discourse in the same way as stating that metamodernism performs the same function.

14. Peter Boxall used the phrase 'resurgent modes of realism' in relation to Ian McEwan's novel *The Children's Act* (2014) during his paper entitled 'Imagining the Future' at the AHRC research network symposium on metamodernism at Manchester Metropolitan University (31 January 2018).

15. Peter Barry, *Poetry Wars* (Cambridge: Salt, 2006), p.140.

16. Many members of the Cambridge School would argue that postmodernism never had any critical efficacy in relation to its poetics. I am aware that the term 'innovative' has been applied to the work of the London School and Language poets more often than the Cambridge School, which might prefer 'late modernist' or 'modernist-influenced'. However, there is no better alternative term that can be deployed in relation to these Schools, as opposed to mainstream writing.

17. Theodor W. Adorno, *Aesthetic Theory*, eds. Gretel Adorno and Rolf Tiedemann, trans. Robert Hullot-Kentor (London: The Athlone Press, 1997 [1970]), p. 335.

18. Joanna Moorhead, 'Carol Ann Duffy: "Poems are a form of texting"' (interview with Carol Ann Duffy), *The Guardian*, 5 September 2011 (www.theguardian.com/education/2011/sep/05/carol-ann-duffy-poetry-texting-competition (accessed 12 May 2020)).

19. R. P. Blackmur, *The Double Agent: Essays in Craft and Elucidation* (New York: Arrow Editions, 1935), p. 4.

20. James and Seshagiri, 'Metamodernism', pp. 90–1.

21. Fredric Jameson, *A Singular Modernity* (London/New York: Verso, 2012 [2002]), pp. 199, 150, 209. Rather than addressing the concerns of contemporary literature, Jameson's 'late' modernism ends abruptly with the work of Vladimir Nabokov and Samuel Beckett in the 1950s. In *Late Modernism: Art, Culture, and Politics in Cold War America* (Oxford/Philadelphia: University of Pennsylvania Press, 2010), Robert Genter expands on Jameson's conception of late modernism in the specific context of North American culture in the 1950s and 1960s. In contrast, Tyrus Miller locates late modernism in the 1920s and 1930s in *Late Modernism: Politics,*

Fiction, and the Arts Between Two World Wars (Berkeley/LA: University of California Press, 1999). Genter distinguishes between 'high' modernism, and the 'invigorated' late modernism of writers such as Kenneth Burke, Ralph Ellison and James Baldwin, and the 'romantic modernism' of, for example, the Beats (pp. 6, 8). Both Jameson and Genter concur in regarding late modernism as a teleological route to postmodernism. According to Jameson in *A Singular Modernity*, it is 'with this late modernism that postmodernism attempts radically to break' (p. 210). For Genter, the former provides the 'movement toward postmodernism' (*Late Modernism*, p. 10). In contrast, in *Late Modernist Poetics: from Pound to Prynne* (Manchester/New York: Manchester University Press, 2005), Anthony Mellors argues that 'postmodernism remains a nebulous category, constantly falling back onto the modernist tenets against which it is defined' (p. 3). Unlike Genter, Mellors extends late modernist poetics to 1975 in his study of 'the impact of the modernist occult on the "late modernism" of mid-century American poetry and the British poetry of the 1960s and 1970s' (p. 2).

22. Madelyn Detloff, *The Persistence of Modernism: Loss and Mourning in the Twentieth Century* (Cambridge: Cambridge University Press, 2009), p. 4. Raymond Williams's argument about the perpetuation of modernism in *The Politics of Modernism* (London/New York: Verso, 1989) is different to Detloff's 'patching' thesis. Williams focuses on the reified '"modern absolute"' of a 'high modernist aesthetic style that outlived its conditions of cultivation' in the 'imperial metropolis' (p. 38).

23. Detloff, *The Persistence of Modernism*, p. 4. Akin to van den Akker and Vermeulen, Detloff deploys Williams's 'structure of feeling' to describe the persistence of modernism. The modernist past 'is thus not an inert object to be studied in its alterity, but rather a "structure of feeling" [. . .] functioning in a "patched" present' (p. 10).

24. Geoffrey Hill, Michaelmas term lecture 2012 (untitled), http://media .podcasts.ox.ac.uk/engfac/poetry/2012-11-27-engfac-hill.mp3 (accessed 28 July 2020).

25. Fredric Jameson critiques the 'reminting' of the modern in *A Singular Modernity* (p. 7).

26. In *A Shrinking Island: Modernism and National Culture in England* (Princeton and Oxford: Princeton University Press, 2004), Jed Esty examines the 'recurrent tendency of commentators on the English scene to metaphorize literary change as national decline' in relation to conceptions of late modernism (p. 1). Esty's version of the latter is located in the mid-twentieth century, and 'the cultural transition between empire and the welfare state' (p. 3).

27. David James, *The Legacies of Modernism: Historicising Postwar and Contemporary Fiction* (Cambridge: Cambridge University Press, 2011), p. 1.
28. Hill, 'Poetry, Policing and Public Order (1)', www.english.ox.ac.uk/professor-sir-geoffrey-hill-lectures (accessed 12 July 2020).
29. Williams, *The Politics of Modernism*, p. 23; James, *The Legacies of Modernism*, p. 1. This focus on modernist legacies in both kinds of poetry distinguishes my work from Marjorie Perloff's focus on early twentieth-century antecedents in 'innovative' writing in *21st-Century Modernism: The "New" Poetics* (Malden/ Oxford: Blackwells, 2002). Perloff calls for the continuation of these categories when she surmises that 'what if, despite the predominance of a tepid and unambitious Establishment poetry, there were a powerful avant-garde that takes up, once again, the experimentation of the early twentieth-century?' (pp. 4–5). In Chapter 5, I analyse how Harrison's work – usually caricatured as anti-modernist – actually draws on the legacies of mythic 'double consciousness' in the work of Eliot and James Joyce. In that chapter, my analysis of Parmar's intricate reworkings of classical myth in relation to H. D.'s *Helen in Egypt* (1961) and Virginia Woolf's comments on the impersonality of the classics indicate that I have no wish in this book to totalise an overarching 'modernism'. Later in this Introduction, for example, I analyse the particular influence of Eliot's work on Hill's collection *Scenes from Comus*: as Williams notes, 'Although Modernism can be clearly identified as a distinctive movement [. . .] it is also strongly characterised by its internal diversity of methods and emphases [. . .] from the Futurist affirmation of the city to Eliot's pessimistic recoil' (p. 43).
30. Theodor W. Adorno, *Minima Moralia: Reflections from Damaged Life*, trans. E. F. N. Jephcott (London: Verso, 1978 [1951]), p. 52.
31. As I illustrate in Chapter 3, Hill uses these terms in his notebook drafts for *The Orchards of Syon* that are held in the Brotherton Library (Orchards of Syon workbooks, BC MS 20c Hill/2/1/52, p. 35).
32. Douglas Mao and Rebecca L. Walkowitz, eds., *Bad Modernisms* (Durham, North Carolina: Duke University Press, 2006), p. 3.
33. 'Enigmaticalness' is a necessarily awkward term in Robert Hullot-Kentor's translation of Adorno's *Ästhetische Theorie* (Frankfurt am Main: Suhrkamp Verlag, 2014 [1970]). There is no direct equivalent in English for the German phrase '*der Rätselcharakter*' (literally, 'puzzle-character' or 'puzzle-essence') (p. 183). I am grateful to Dr Angelica Michelis for our discussions about the translation of *Ästhetische Theorie*.
34. Adorno, *Ästhetische Theorie*, p. 184.
35. Charles Simic and Don Paterson, eds., *New British Poetry* (St Paul, Minnesota: Graywolf Press, 2004), p. xxx.

36. Hill, 'Poetry, Policing and Public Order (1)', www.english.ox.ac.uk/professor-sir-geoffrey-hill-lectures (accessed 12 July 2020).

37. Eleanor Cook, 'The Figure of Enigma: Rhetoric, History and Poetry', *Rhetorica: A Journal of the History of Rhetoric*, 19(4) (2001), 349–78, p. 352.

38. Earlier in *Aesthetic Theory*, Adorno ruminates on the 'enigmatic character of nature's language' (p. 73): natural beauty is indefinable, just as in music 'what is beautiful flashes up in nature only to disappear in the instant one tries to grasp it' (p. 72).

39. I refer here to the Great Sphinx at Giza, as opposed to the riddles of the sphinx in Greek mythology, or the *purushamriga* in South India.

40. Derek Attridge, *The Singularity of Literature* (London/New York: Routledge, 2004), p. 142. He writes that 'there can be no doubt that [Adorno's] *Aesthetic Theory* is among the most significant twentieth-century contributions to debates about artistic practice and response [...] Also influential has been Adorno's championing of modern art as resistant to, while at the same time arising out of it, the administrative and instrumental rationality that surrounds it.'

41. Attridge, *The Singularity of Literature*, p. 59.

42. Rare exceptions include Eleanor Cook's article and *Enigmas and Riddles in Literature* (Cambridge: Cambridge University Press, 2006), and Ian Balfour's 'Extreme Philology: Benjamin, Adorno, McCall and the Enigmas of Hölderlin', in *Tragedy, Translation and Theory: In Honor of the Work of Thomas J. McCall* (Baltimore: The University of Maryland Press, 2014) (no pp. no.). More often – but still rarely – Adorno's conception of the enigma is discussed in relation to art more widely, as in David S. Ferris's 'Politics and the Enigma of Art: The Meaning of Modernism for Adorno', *Modernist Cultures*, 1(2) (winter 2005), 192–208, and João Pedro's 'Truth and Enigma: Adorno and the Politics of Art', *New German Critique*, 45(3, 135) (November 2018), 73–95.

43. *OED*, 2nd edn; Curtis Gruenler, *Piers Plowman and the Poetics of Enigma: Riddles, Rhetoric and Theology* (Notre Dame, Indiana: University of Notre Dame Press, 2017); Shawn Normandin, '"Non Intelligent": the Enigmas of *The Clerk's Tale*', *Texas Studies in Literature and Language*, 58(2) (2016), 189–223.

44. *OED*, 2nd edn. In William Shakespeare's *Love's Labour's Lost* (1598), for example, the character Armado discourses on 'Some enigma, some riddle' with Moth and Costard (*Love's Labour Lost* (Leipzig: Bernhard Tauchnitz, 1868), p. 24).

45. Cook, 'The Figure of Enigma', pp. 350, 356.

46. *OED*, 2nd edn.

47. Cook, 'The Figure of Enigma', p. 362.

48. In contrast with these examples of modernist literature, Adorno's discussion of Edmund Mörike's rhyme about a mousetrap in this passage from *Aesthetic Theory* is initially surprising. Adorno's thesis is that interpretations cannot be tied to discursive content, thereby meaning that art cannot have a 'message' (p. 123). Mörike's 'Mousetrap Rhyme' describes a child circling a mousetrap whilst reciting a ditty about the animal's demise when it 'boldly [pays] us a visit tonight' (p. 123). If understood in terms of the 'discursive content' alone, the poem 'would amount to no more than sadistic identification with what civilized custom has done to an animal disdained as a parasite'. However, the implication of the rhyme's details suggests the opposite: even without an explicit, 'committed' message, 'abstaining from judgement', the poem operates as an indictment of a 'miserable, socially conditioned ritual' (p. 124). Adorno does not deploy 'Mousetrap Rhyme' as an example of enigmatic art, therefore, but as a means to continue his critique of supposedly *engagé* literature (p. 123).

49. Adorno, *Aesthetic Theory*, p. 118. My focus on enigmatical poetry differs from Marjorie Perloff's account of 'undetermined' poems in *The Poetics of Indeterminacy: Rimbaud to Cage* (Evanston, Illinois: Northwestern University Press, 1983 [1981]). Perloff splits modernist poetry into two strands, 'the Symbolist mode' and the '"anti-Symbolist" mode of indeterminacy or "undecidability," of literalness and free play, whose first real exemplar is the Rimbaud of the *Illuminations*' (p. vii). Eliot's *The Waste Land* (1922) thus connotes a 'very real fogbound London' (p. 11) within a 'perfectly coherent symbolic structure' (p. 13), whereas Rimbaud's work blocks 'all attempts to rationalize its imagery, to make it conform to a coherent pattern' (p. 10). In contrast, I would argue that the 'remainder' of enigmatical poetry exists in both 'interwoven strands' (p. vii), and arises from the visions of *Illuminations* (1886) as well as Eliot's transformation of central London. My version of the 'notion of the enigma' appertains to 'Symbolist'-influenced writers such as Eliot and Hill as well as 'innovative' poets, rather than explicitly to 'language construction' among 'avant-garde writers' (p. 66).

50. Tony Pinkney, 'Editor's Introduction: Modernism and Cultural Theory', in Williams, *The Politics of Modernism*, pp. 1–29, p. 5. As Pinkney notes, Williams's responses to modernist writing change over time: 'in his sixties, after his own realist "detour" in mid-career', he once again became 'as fascinated by the whole extraordinary Modernist project as a boy of eighteen at Cambridge' (p. 27); 'there is still much to learn', Williams claims in his article on 'The Politics of the Avant-Garde', 'from the complexities of its vigorous and dazzling development' (p. 62). Pinkney emphasises that there are two 'almost incompatible views of Modernism and the avant-garde' in Williams's essays: on the one hand, they are the

most advanced outposts of 'bourgeois dissidence' – which are then, according to Williams, nevertheless easily assimilated back into bourgeois and consumerist culture – but also 'on occasion the potential "warm current" in (Ernst Bloch's phrase) of an excessively scientific socialism' (p. 27). As with Williams's work, I maintain in this book a distinction between modernist writing and the avant-garde: in Prynne, Hill, Byrne and Parmar's work there may be a resistance to accommodation, but there is no attempt, as with Dada and Surrealism, to subvert the institutionalisation of literature and culture.

51. Moorhead, '"Poems are a form of texting"' www.theguardian.com/education/ 2011/sep/05/carol-ann-duffy-poetry-texting-competition (accessed 1 May 2020).

52. Hill, 'Poetry, Policing and Public Order (1)', www.english.ox.ac.uk/profes sor-sir-geoffrey-hill-lectures (accessed 12 July 2020).

53. James Byrne, *Blood/Sugar* (Todmorden: Arc, 2009), p. 71. As I note in Chapter 4, the inference here – that the diction cannot negate – is *not* that such poets produce writing of major importance.

54. Furlani, *Guy Davenport*, p. 150.

55. Hill, Orchards of Syon workbooks, BC MS 20c Hill/2/1/52, p. 35.

56. Geoffrey Hill, *Scenes from Comus* (London: Penguin, 2005), p. 66.

57. Geoffrey Hill, *The Orchards of Syon* (London/New York: Penguin, 2002), p. 14; Adorno, *Aesthetic Theory*, p. 121.

58. Ahren Warner, *Pretty* (Newcastle: Bloodaxe, 2013), p. 72.

59. Adorno, *Aesthetic Theory*, pp. 121, 125.

60. Geraldine Monk, *Ghost & Other Sonnets* (Cambridge: Salt, 2008), p. 33; Adorno, *Aesthetic Theory*, p. 121.

61. Marjorie Perloff discusses a different form of 'deaestheticized' writing in *Unoriginal Genius: Poetry by Other Means in the New Century* (Chicago and London: The University of Chicago Press, 2012 [2010]), noting 'the claim, now being made by conceptual poets from Kenneth Goldsmith to Leevi Lehto, Craig Dworkin to Caroline Bergvall, that it is possible to write "poetry" that is entirely "unoriginal" and nevertheless qualifies as poetry' (p. 12). Goldsmith, 'in a set of short manifesto statements for the blog of the venerable Poetry Foundation of America, announced his advocacy of conceptual or "uncreative" writing – a form of copying, recycling, or appropriation that "obstinately makes no claim on originality".'

62. Derek Attridge, 'Conjurers turn tricks on wizards' coat-tails', www .timeshighereducation.com/features/conjurers-turn-tricks-on-wizards-coat-tails/ 203931.article. Attridge developed this article from his inaugural lecture at the University of York (June 2006) (accessed 21 September 2020).

63. J. H. Prynne, 'A Letter to Steve McCaffery' (2 January 1989), *The Gig*, 7 (November 2000), 40–6.

64. J. H. Prynne, 'Acrylic Tips', in *Poems* (Tarset: Bloodaxe, 2005), pp. 533–48, p. 542.

65. Robert Sheppard, *The Poetry of Saying: British Poetry and its Discontents, 1950–2000* (Liverpool: Liverpool University Press, 2005), p. 2.

66. Charles Bernstein and Bruce Andrews, 'Repossessing the Word', in Charles Bernstein and Bruce Andrews, eds., *The Language Book* (Carbondale and Edwardsville: Southern Illinois University Press, 1984), pp. ix–xi, p. ix. The critical debates around metamodernism have often drawn on the novels of Tom McCarthy. McKenzie Wark is convincing when he asserts in the preface to *Remainder* (New York: Vintage, 2005) that McCarthy's novel is not postmodernist, but only in terms of its form rather than the book's concerns. It is by now a rather hackneyed comment that form cannot be divorced from content, yet this dialectical relationship in *Remainder* evidences a tension between the neo-realist prose – familiar to readers of contemporary British fiction, and exemplified by Ian McEwan's more recent novels – and McCarthy's concerns with the relationship between truth and fiction, iterative and linguistic play and the referent of trauma. The main character's obsession with the play of reconstruction formulates at the expense of the other characters' lives; at several points in the novel, he dismisses the workers who are integral to the reconstructions as just not mattering. In the early part of the novel, the protagonist sits in a café drinking too much corporate coffee, and presents the reader with a supposedly 'real' scene in which he engages in a conversation with a homeless man and invites him for a drink in a local café ostensibly to discuss his concerns. In a metafictional moment familiar to readers of postmodernist fictions such as Fowles's *The French Lieutenant's Woman* (1969) this passage is then revealed as fantasy: 'The truth is, I've been making all this up' (p. 54). Any engagement with the economics of homelessness (and the rights of workers) is suspended as the narrator begins to embark on his exploitative 'working through' via reconstructions. The author's satire on the Starbucks-like café and its loyalty scheme – at one point in the novel the protagonist buys nine small cappuccinos just in order to get a new loyalty card – establishes the book in a tradition of postmodernist satire familiar to readers of Ballard's novels or Will Self's fiction. It is hard not to make an equivalence between the cooking liver in the first reconstruction and Bloom's sizzling kidney in *Ulysses* (1922), but in this postmodernist novel verisimilitude is suspect in the sense that the 'spit and sizzle' (p. 58) is part of a performance; so much so that the air vents become clogged with fat after the multiple attempts to get rid of the smell of cordite. In many ways, the protagonist is the archetypal postmodernist subject lost in his amnesia: without friends or

romantic interest (such characters disappear from the text in the early part of the novel), parents, a job, children or economic dependants – he firmly rejects the possibility of donating some of his windfall to charities – he is left to piece himself together out of fragments, 'memories, imaginings, films' (p. 72). Hence the traumatic repetition leads to repetitions in the narrative: he forgets that he has already narrated an incident in Victoria Station when he parodies the homeless by wandering around asking for spare change even though 'I didn't need or want their change: I'd just received eight and half million pounds' (p. 216). The reader's distrust of this first-person narrator extends to his postmodernist interpretation of the bank robbery as an event of 'becoming' rather than a 'real' event in which an actor dies: 'it had never happened – and, this being not a real event but a staged one, albeit one staged in a real venue, it never would. It would always be to come, held in a future hovering just beyond our reach' (p. 251).

67. Hill, *Scenes from Comus*, p. 66.
68. David James, *Modernist Futures: Innovation and Inheritance in the Contemporary Novel* (Cambridge: Cambridge University Press, 2012), p. 5. In *True Friendship: Geoffrey Hill, Anthony Hecht, and Robert Lowell: Under the Sign of Eliot and Pound* (New Haven and London: Yale University Press, 2010), Christopher Ricks discusses the influence of the *Four Quartets* on different stanzas from *Scenes from Comus*. In relation to the opening and closing stanzas of 'The Argument of the Masque', Ricks argues perceptively that the 'beauty of this poem, most manifest in the sonorous exactitude of its weighting, owes something to the closing words of Eliot's closing poem' in the *Four Quartets*. Ricks pauses on the repeated phrase 'But the weight of the word, weight of the world, is' (twice in no. 20 and no. 1 of the 'Courtly Masquing Dances'), and points out that 'This particular exactitude would not have come to be, were it not for Eliot', and the line from 'Ash Wednesday', 'Still is the unspoken word, the Word unheard' (p. 4). Ricks leaves the syntactical echo standing, and does not ruminate further on the line's semantics. A poststructuralist reading of the line – that the world is synonymous with, and produced by, the word – does not sit easily with Hill's *oeuvre*. Instead, Hill conceives them as separate, but inextricable, and also not interchangeable. 'Word' and 'world' are engaged specifically in terms of 'weight', which links back to the 'weight' of consumerism in the previous section (no. 19), and the 'pondus' that Hill returns to throughout the collection (p. 12). '*[P]ondus*' in section 14 is defined as 'the pull of power' (p. 9); in no. 6 it means 'Moral corruption [...] inertia of malevolence' (p. 5). In section 14, Hill quotes Milton on the separation of poetry and the 'world' in *The Reason of Church Government Urged Against Prelatry* (1642). Milton leaves 'a calm and pleasing solitariness, fed

with cheerful and confident thoughts, to embark in a troubled sea of noises and hoarse disputes', separating the private sphere from the politics to come. In contrast, for Hill in *Scenes from Comus*, history, politics and the private sphere intertwine. Whereas section 14 dwells on the sinking of the Hood, the hanging 'is' at the end of 'weight of the word, weight of the world, is' recalls the emphasised 'is' in the most famous lines of post-Holocaust poetry: 'I have made | an elegy for myself it | is true' (*Collected Poems* (Oxford: Oxford University Press, 2015 [2013] p. 44). We are also 'weighted' with such history, tradition and erudition as readers from the outset of *Scenes from Comus*, rather than invited to create the poem entirely *through* our reading of the collection, or entertain a poststructuralist conception of language creating the world.

69. 'Scapes' can also mean 'escapes' (OED, 2nd edn).
70. Eliot, *Four Quartets*, p. 54.
71. Furlani, *Guy Davenport*, p. 150.
72. Ricks, *True Friendship*, p. 29.
73. Geoffrey Hill, *Collected Critical Writings* (Oxford: Oxford University Press, 2008), pp. 544, 540.
74. Hill's other, most prominent, modernist 'anxiety of influence' appertains, of course, to Pound. Reading Hill's *Collected Critical Writings*, it is striking how critical he is throughout the volume of Ezra Pound's politics. In the early essay 'Our Word is Our Bond', Pound 'is vulnerable to accusations that he naively and wilfully regarded his wartime broadcasts as being in some way traditionally privileged and protected by his status as a poet, "boasting of the sanctity of what [he] carried"; an attitude at best archaic and at worst arrogantly idiosyncratic' and 'complicitously egocentric' (pp. 146–7, p. 165). Whereas Hill quotes Pound approvingly at the beginning of 'The Enemy's Country' – in relation to the poet's need for reticence and restraint – in 'Language, Suffering, and Silence' the latter's claim to have confessed 'wrong without losing rightness' is 'grammatically self-serving [...] It sounds superficially right, but it is not right' (p. 400).
75. Furlani, *Guy Davenport*, p. 150.
76. Geoffrey Hill, 'Poetry Notebooks and Early Poems and Drafts (c. 1948–2005)', Notebook 58, BC MS 20c Hill/2, p. 36.
77. Franz Kafka, *The Blue Octavo Notebooks* (Cambridge, Massachusetts: Exact Change Books, 2016 [1948]), p. 26.
78. Hill, *Collected Critical Writings*, p. 171.
79. Miller, *Late Modernism*, p. 88.
80. Hill's response to *Comus* utilises Milton's poem as an intertextual touchstone for his own collection, rather than an extensive presence or remoulding of the Masque. As Peter McDonald argues, *Scenes from Comus* 'is neither

a commentary nor a rewriting, but rather a distanced and circumstantially ironic reflection on some of Milton's lines and motifs'; for example, 'the lady's praise of chastity, in the Masque, is set off against the vivid presence of a sensuality (in the figure of Comus) which she does not experience' ('Truly Apart' in *Times Literary Supplement*, 1 April 2005, p. 13). In section fourteen of 'The Argument of the Masque', for example, Hill notes that 'Milton's script | was briefly censored, bits of sex expunged | for the girl's sake' (p. 21): images of sensuality (Sabrina's 'trailing labiles' and 'lianas' in section three of 'Courtly Masquing Dances' [p. 16]) contrast with references to chastity (and impotence) throughout the sequence. In *Scenes from Comus*, Hill is much more concerned with Milton's work and biography as a whole, rather than *Comus* in particular: for example, section twenty-one of the middle sequence mentions Mary Powell, who married Milton in 1642; she left him soon afterwards, possibly due to the Royalist sympathies of her family.

81. John Milton, *The Reason of Church Government Urged Against Prelatry*, Book 2 (www.dartmouth.edu/~milton/reading_room/reason/book_2/text.shtml) (accessed 6 July 2020).

82. Hill, 'Poetry Notebooks and Early Poems and Drafts (c.1948–2005)', p. 23. The full version of the stanza is as follows:

That the lovely Eurasian woman
on the Euston to Wolverhampton express
knows her own mind as well as Lady Alice
and would fend for herself no less strictly
accosted on the Wye forest
picnic area by some club of bikes.

This unrestrainedly dull diction and grating enjambment can be found in a selection of poems taken at random from a *Poetry Book Society Bulletin*. A selection of poems at the end of the magazine include Maura Dooley's 'Habit' ('She used to say | *better to be at the pub* | *thinking of church* | *than at church* | *thinking of the pub*'), J. O. Morgan's 'Phonograph' ('I saw yellow smoke above a wood. | It lifted, stretched into long pale plumes') and the awkward enjambment in Judy Brown's 'The Corner Shop' ('Neighbours thought it was | gunfire, but inside the boys | were throwing bottles around') (*PBS Bulletin*, issue 248 [spring 1916], 27–8).

83. As McDonald notes in his review, 'Ever since *Canaan* (1996), it has been easy to deplore Hill's "difficulty", without seeing any difficulty in the term itself; but the poetry has been substantial, rather than "difficult", with the directness and candour of profound originality' (p. 13).

84. Hill's extract in Clare Brown and Don Paterson, eds., *Don't Ask Me What I Mean: Poets in Their Own Words* (Basingstoke/Oxford: Picador, 2003), p. 118.

85. Milton, *The Reason of Church Government Urged Against Prelatry*, Book 2, www.dartmouth.edu/~milton/reading_room/reason/book_2/text.shtml (accessed 6 July 2020).

86. Sean O'Brien, '*Scenes from Comus* by Geoffrey Hill', *The Independent*, 2 March 2005, www.independent.co.uk/arts-entertainment/books/reviews/scenes-from-comus-by-geoffrey-hill-6151493.html (accessed 30 September 2014).

87. Eric Ormsby, 'A Grand & Crabby Music', *The New York Sun*, 3 March 2005, www.nysun.com/arts/grand-crabby-music/10039/ (accessed 21 September 2016).

88. *Scenes from Comus* is dedicated to the composer Hugh Wood, and named after his work: the BBC premiered *Scenes from Comus* at the Proms in 1965. As Hill wryly remarks in section three, Wood's music 'would arouse Milton fór me, if he required | such service óf us. He doesn't, does he?' (p. 4).

89. A more recent version of the 'poetry wars' occurred in the form of Rebecca Watt's dismissal of Holly McNish's spoken-word poetry as amateurish and simplistic; Paterson came to the defence of the latter (performance) poet as her editor at Picador (www.theguardian.com/books/2018/jan/23/poetry-world-split-over-polemic-attacking-amateur-work-by-young-female-poets) (accessed 21 September 2020). Paterson responded to the attack on McNish at: www.theguardian.com/commentisfree/2018/jan/26/verses-spoken-word-row-poetry-young-female-poets (accessed 21 September 2020).

90. Hill, 'Poetry, Policing and Public Order (1)', media.podcasts.ox.ac.uk/kebl/general/2010-11-30-hill-poetry-keble.mp3 (accessed 12 July 2020).

91. Sheppard, *The Poetry of Saying*, p. 132.

92. Barry, *Poetry Wars*, pp. 179, xvi. Barry argues that the successful legacies of the poetry wars in the 1970s 'lies around us today—in the comparatively well-tempered acceptance that we live in a culture of poetries, not in one world dominated by an Establishment' (p. xii). Tolerated acknowledgement is not equivalent, of course, to creative and critical engagement. I would argue that Barry's contention that 'we are now in a "post-dualist" poetry world' remains idealist.

93. J. T. Welsh, *The Selling and Self-Regulation of Contemporary Poetry* (London: Anthem Press, 2020), pp. 21, 37, 32.

94. Roddy Lumsden, ed., *Identity Parade: New British and Irish Poets* (Newcastle: Bloodaxe, 2010), p. 103.

95. Adorno, *Aesthetic Theory*, p. 121.

96. David Kennedy, *New Relations: The Refashioning of British Poetry 1980–94* (Bridgend: Seren, 1996), p. 241; Adorno, *Aesthetic Theory*, p. 129.

97. John Redmond, *Poetry and Privacy: Questioning Public Interpretations of Contemporary British and Irish Poetry* (Bridgend: Seren, 2013), p. 10; 'Editorial', *PN Review*, 247 (May–June 2019), 2–3, p. 3; Hill, 'Poetry, Policing and Public Order (1)', www.english.ox.ac.uk/professor-sir-geoffrey-hill-lectures (accessed 12 July 2020); Alison Flood, 'Simon Armitage plans national "headquarters" for poetry in Leeds', *The Guardian*, 27 February 2020 (www.theguardian.com/books/2020/feb/27/simon-armitage-plans-national-headquarters-for-poetry-in-leeds-poet-laureate) (accessed 8 July 2020).

98. Hill, 'Poetry, Policing and Public Order (1)', www.english.ox.ac.uk/professor-sir-geoffrey-hill-lectures (accessed 12 July 2020).

99. Redmond, *Poetry and Privacy*, pp. 9–10.

100. Young and Schmidt, *All Gates Open*, p. 458. Of course, this 'secret' is potentially illusory, and the artwork would be 'solved' if it were uncovered. Instead, Schmidt's favoured artworks are so intriguing that he keeps returning to them, even if the fruitful task of searching for an isolated 'secret' may ultimately be fruitless. Nevertheless, there is an inherent danger too that hermeticism becomes confused with the sacred. As Genter argues, Marcel Duchamp's 'high' modernist imperative 'was to shield the artwork from any interpretive or cognitive distortion, guaranteeing in some sense its sacredness' (*Late Modernism*, p. 2).

101. Luke Turner, 'Metamodernism Manifesto' and 'Metamodernism: A Brief Introduction', www.metamodernism.org (accessed 29 April 2020). In contrast with Jeff Koons's 'vacuously overinflated ironic baubles', Turner praises the 'reengagement with materiality, affect and the sublime' in the work of, for example, Olafur Eliasson, Peter Doig and Guido van der Werve. Turner displays an awareness, however, that the clock cannot be turned back to a supposedly halcyon moment before the work of theorists such as Fredric Jameson and Jean-François Lyotard, so that contemporary writers and artists can ignore their critiques of 'grand narrative and universal truths'. Turner emphasises, quite simply, that we should not be 'forfeiting all that we've learnt from postmodernism'. Hence Vermeulen and van den Akker propose that metamodernist thinking must necessarily 'shuttle' between modernism and postmodernism, rather than asserting – as Hutcheon does in the second edition of *The Politics of Postmodernism* (2002) – that postmodernism is simply over. Vermeulen and van den Akker note that postmodernism is not, of course, a singular concept, and that Lyotard's description of the decline of metanarratives, for example, does not equate with Fredric Jameson's critiques of late capitalism. 'However', they continue, 'what these distinct phenomena share' is an opposition to the 'modern', any sense of utopia, to linear progress, grand narratives, Reason, functionalism and formal 'purism' ('Notes on Metamodernism', p. 3).

102. In *Style and Faith* (New York: Counterpoint, 2003), Hill berates Philip Larkin's dismissal of the modernist triumvirate of Pound, Picasso and Parker as 'postprandial' (p. 203). The Hull poet's reflex anti-modernism is a sign of 'narrow English possessiveness, with regard to "good sense" and "generous common humanity"' (p. 204). In turn, Basil Bunting attacked what he regarded as Hill's overly cautious and conservative poetics: 'He's got all the technique. He knows just how to do nothing wrong. Except

that there's nothing right. Just nothing there' (Richard Burton, *A Strong Song Tows Us: The Life of Basil Bunting* [Oxford: Infinite Ideas Ltd, 2013], p. 494).

103. Hill, Orchards of Syon workbooks, p. 35. It is not necessary to re-rehearse the post-war Marxist debates about modernist literature as an indulgent manifestation of bourgeois subjectivity, as in the infamous 1948 Soviet decree denouncing the formal decadence of modern music; or, as in György Lukács' *The Meaning of Contemporary Realism* (London: Merlin Press, 1979 [1963]), a crude Marxist conception of modernism as fascistic in its response to modern angst (pp. 36, 81).

104. Hill's extract in Clare Brown and Don Paterson, eds., *Don't Ask Me What I Mean: Poets in Their Own Words*, p. 118. Hill is quoting Theodor Hacker, and goes on to argue that 'legitimate difficulty (difficulty can of course be faked) is essentially democratic'.

105. Hill quotes this sentence from *The Double Agent: Essays in Craft and Elucidation* approvingly in 'Poetry, Policing and Public Order (1)', www.english.ox.ac.uk /professor-sir-geoffrey-hill-lectures (accessed 12 July 2020).

1 Contemporary British Poetry and Enigmaticalness

1. Theodor W. Adorno, *Aesthetic Theory*, eds. Gretel Adorno and Rolf Tiedemann, trans. Robert Hullot-Kentor (London: The Athlone Press, 1997 [1970]), p. 121; Theodor Adorno, *Ästhetische Theorie* (Frankfurt am Main: Suhrkamp Verlag, 2014 [1970]), p. 184.

2. Adorno, *Aesthetic Theory*, p. 118.

3. Roland Barthes, 'Death of the Author', in Dennis Walder, *Literature in the Modern World* (Oxford: Oxford University Press, 1990), pp. 228–32.

4. Adorno, *Aesthetic Theory*, p. 120.

5. Geoffrey Hill, 'Poetry, Policing and Public Order (1)' www.english.ox.ac.uk/ professor-sir-geoffrey-hill-lectures (accessed 12 July 2020).

6. T. S. Eliot, *The Use of Poetry and the Use of Criticism* (London: Faber and Faber, 1987 [1933]), pp. 17–18.

7. Hill, 'Poetry, Policing and Public Order (1)'.

8. It is rare to come across a critic as honest as David Wheatley who, in relation to Prynne's work, admits his frequent bafflement, since the poetry is 'lacking any pointers for the bewildered' (*Contemporary British Poetry* [London/New York: Palgrave, 2015], pp. 112–13). Subsequently, Wheatley quotes Peter Howarth's assertion that Prynne's readers 'could never really tell whether their own interpretations were precious finds or complete rubbish' (p. 115).

9. Derek Attridge, *The Singularity of Literature* (London/New York: Routledge, 2004), p. 142.

10. Peter Howarth, *The Cambridge Introduction to Modernist Poetry* (Cambridge: Cambridge University Press, 2012), p. 181.

11. Geoffrey Hill, *The Triumph of Love* (London/New York: Penguin, 1999 [1998]), p. 21; Howarth, *The Cambridge Introduction to Modernist Poetry*, p. 181.

12. Adorno, *Aesthetic Theory*, p. 16.

13. Adorno, *Ästhetische Theorie*, p. 185; *Aesthetic Theory*, p. 122.

14. Hill's untitled extract in Clare Brown and Don Paterson, eds., *Don't Ask Me What I Mean: Poets in Their Own Words* (Basingstoke/Oxford: Picador, 2003), p. 118. Hill is quoting Theodor Hacker, and goes on to argue that 'legitimate difficulty (difficulty can of course be faked) is essentially democratic' (p. 118). Despite this statement, Paterson still equates difficulty in this anthology solely with the 'postmoderns', who 'will gripe at the omission of their stars, but the PBS was always aimed at a general (i.e. non-academic and non-practising) readership, one which *ampersandeurs* neither possess nor actively seek' (p. xiv). This selection policy 'leaves that broad swathe in the middle, so often dismissed as the "mainstream", a word which nonetheless accurately designates those poets engaged with the English lyric tradition' (p. xiv). The problem with the latter comment is that writers from the London and Cambridge Schools, and Language poets, are equally engaged with this lyric tradition, but with divergent poetic results.

15. The 'literature of the absurd' usually refers to pan-European playwrights of the 1950s, including Beckett, Eugène Ionesco and Jean Genet. Martin Esslin coined the term in *The Theatre of the Absurd* (1961). Adorno returns to his earlier 'Commitment' essay in *Aesthetic Theory*, and argues that Brecht's politics are the least interesting aspect of his plays: what is most compelling is his reinvention of the formal aspects of drama. Given the ambiguities of the enigma, Adorno goes further and questions 'whether artworks can possibly be *engagé*' (p. 122). 'Today', he ruminates, '*engagement* inescapably becomes aesthetic concession' (p. 103).

16. *Ästhetische Theorie*, p. 183; *Aesthetic Theory*, p. 120.

17. Hill, 'Poetry, Policing and Public Order (1)'.

18. David James and Urmila Seshagiri, 'Metamodernism: Narratives of Continuity and Revolution', *PMLA*, 129: 1 (2014), 87–98.

19. My translation.

20. Of course, Adorno is writing about a different kind of 'deaestheticized' art in the later 1960s to the contemporary mainstream. 'Deaestheticization' refers forward here in *Aesthetic Theory* to the poetics of Bertolt Brecht that Adorno discusses three pages later: Brecht's poetry 'sabotages the poetic' (p. 123). This

subversion does not, however, converge with the 'reality principle': as soon as Brecht 'approximates an empirical report, the actual result [in poetry] is by no means such a report' (p. 123). In Brecht's 'polemical rejection of the exalted lyrical tone', 'the empirical sentences translated into the aesthetic monad acquire an altogether different quality. The antilyrical tone and the estrangement of the appropriated facts [as in Charles Reznikoff's *Holocaust* (1975)] are two sides of the same coin' (p. 123). Adorno then extrapolates on this process of defamiliarisation in relation to the concept of *engagé* literature that he first explores in his 1962 essay 'Commitment'. He questions whether any artwork (Brecht's work is still implicit four sentences later) can be *engagé* 'even when they emphasize their *engagement*', because artworks are not mere political statements, and are not restricted to their 'discursive content' (p. 123). Rather than return to the examples of Jean-Paul Sartre's plays and novels in 'Commitment', or Brecht's artworks, Adorno then deploys the curious example of Eduard Mörike's 'Mousetrap Rhyme', whose 'discursive content' might indicate that it amounts 'to no more than sadistic identification with what civilized custom has done to an animal distained as a parasite' (p. 123). In contrast, as I illustrated in the Introduction, Adorno argues that, by 'abstaining from judgment', Mörike's poem can be interpreted instead as 'the nonjudgmental reflex of language on a miserable, socially conditioned ritual' (p. 124).

21. If enigmatic works of art completely resisted interpretation, they would 'erase the demarcation between art and nonart' (p. 128). If this were so, then 'carpets, ornaments, all nonfigural things' might also 'longingly await interpretation' (p. 128).

22. In *Moving Words: Forms of English Poetry* (Oxford: Oxford University Press, 2013), Derek Attridge refers to the 'fitfulness with which sense gleams through the resistance to sense' in an untitled poem from Prynne's 1993 collection *Not-You* (p. 95).

23. Jacques Rancière, *The Politics of Literature*, trans. Julie Rose (Cambridge/ Malden: Polity Press, 2011), p. 6.

24. J. H. Prynne, 'A Letter to Steve McCaffery' (2 January 1989), *The Gig*, 7 (November 2000), 40–6.

25. J. H. Prynne, 'Acrylic Tips', in *Poems* (Tarset: Bloodaxe, 2005), pp. 533–48, p. 542. In 'Terra Nullius: Colonial Violence in Prynne's *Acrylic Tips*', Matthew Hall reads these lines as appertaining to substance abuse and halitosis (*Journal of British and Irish Innovative Poetry*, 8(1): 5 (2016), 1–30, p. 12).

26. *OED*, 2nd edn.

27. Prynne, p. 538; Adorno, *Aesthetic Theory*, p. 125. In *Moving Words*, Attridge takes issue with Prynne and Paterson's readings of sound in poetry. Attridge notes that 'there is no sign of a consensus on this issue among those who write

about poetry' (p. 77), and is unconvinced by Paterson and Prynne's complex and provocative theses. Paterson begins with a 'thoroughly Cratylist view of language' – in which some words are appropriate to the things they describe – 'dismissing the notion of the arbitrariness of the sign' (p. 79). Whereas Paterson detects 'strong' associations between sound and representation, however, Attridge, although not complying with Saussure's 'arbitrariness', can only see 'rather weak correspondence' (p. 80). Nevertheless, Attridge and Paterson agree that sound takes 'on meaning in poetry as a result of echoes and contrasts along the linear chain of language' (p. 80). Paterson insists further, though, that 'the task of the lyric poet is to create a verbal artefact in which [. . .] meaning – and with it emotion – is made to emerge from the sounds of words as much as from their sense' (p. 81). Hence Attridge and Paterson differ in the detailing of these 'echoes and contrasts': Paterson contends that effective lyricism will pair different vowel sounds with repetitive consonants, or 'repetitions from within one of the consonant groups'; Attridge retorts that rhyme is clearly 'based on *vowel* repetition combined with prior *consonant* variation: just the reverse of Paterson's fundamental principle' (p. 83). In Paterson's own poem 'Correctives', Attridge finds 'just what Paterson says we *shouldn't* find: striking patterns of [vowel] repetition and echo' (p. 92). In contrast, Prynne, in his 'characteristic dense and mannered style', asserts that the appropriate methodology to tackle sound in poetry is 'phonology not phonetics' (p. 87). Attridge concurs that an awareness of 'earlier meanings of words can, of course, play an important part in poetic understanding', but is unconvinced by Prynne's phonological reading of Wordsworth's 'Tintern Abbey', and concludes that 'awareness of earlier *pronunciation* is perhaps another matter' (p. 88).

28. Colin Winborn, '"Derangement from deep inside": J. H. Prynne's "Refuse Collection"', *PN Review* 175, 33: 5 (2007), 55–8, p. 55.

29. Aldous Huxley, *The Doors of Perception and Heaven and Hell* (London: Flamingo, 1994 [1977]), p. 40. In 'Terra Nullius: Colonial Violence in Prynne's *Acrylic Tips*', Hall reads the 'murderous head' as a spearhead, noting that the epigraph is taken from Donald Stuart's novel *Yandy* (1959) that describes the process of constructing spears (p. 7).

30. In contrast, Hall argues that these lines describe a broken relationship: 'digits here may indicate a phone call, or may link the line to 'his right arm | tied to creation', and the expression of care associated with a missing offspring' ('Terra Nullius: Colonial Violence in Prynne's *Acrylic Tips*', p. 15).

31. *OED*, 2nd edn. Amorous discourse cannot salvage the human here since the lover's hands are unfortunately 'like monkfish' (p. 544).

32. Jacques Derrida, 'No Apocalypse, Not Now (full speed ahead, seven missiles, seven missives)', *Diacritics*, 14: 2 (Summer 1984), 20–31, p. 20. In

Contemporary British Poetry, Wheatley notes that Michael Donaghy scoffs at 'innovative' poets' 'commitment' when he wonders 'how an experimental poem "composed from punctuation marks will help bring down the arms trade"' (p. 113). Wheatley rightly retorts that 'Donaghy's parody of the experimental poet drunk on self-delusion' depends on simplistic ideas of how poems *are* expected to interact with the arms trade: do the poems of Michael Donaghy or Sean O'Brien, he points out, '"help bring down the arms trade", but in a supposedly sensible and mainstream way?' (p. 113).

33. An example of 'engrish' from Tokyo posted on 2 March 2018 comprises the following: 'please give me a telephone call in an entrance hole. Moreover, I co-operation-wish-do-so that manners mode may set up beforehand at the time of an ON store' (www.engrish.com; accessed 22 September 2020).

34. As N. H. Reeve and Richard Kerridge argue in *Nearly Too Much: The Poetry of J.H. Prynne* (Liverpool: Liverpool University Press, 1995), lyricism in these poems does not establish 'self-sufficient or privileged moments, around which the world could be concentrically organized' but is 'already implicated in and mediated by a range of natural, social and economic processes' (p. 37).

35. Charles Simic and Don Paterson, eds., *New British Poetry* (St Paul, Minnesota: Graywolf Press, 2004), p. xxx.

36. David Caplan, *Questions of Possibility: Contemporary Poetry and Poetic Form* (Oxford: Oxford University Press, 2005), p. 9.

37. Theodor Adorno, *Minima Moralia: Reflections from Damaged Life*, trans. E. F .N. Jephcott (London: Verso, 1978 [1951]), p. 52.

38. Ezra Pound, *Make It New: Essays* (London: Faber and Faber, 1934).

39. The text of Gretel Adorno and Rolf Tiedemann's version of *Aesthetic Theory* is 'as it was in August 1969' when Adorno died, but, as they note, the structure inevitably differs from the version that Adorno would have published (p. 361).

40. Natalie Pollard responds more positively to the demotic when she interprets it in her edited collection as part of the 'unpredictable tonal features' of Paterson's work (*Don Paterson: Contemporary Critical Essays* [Edinburgh: Edinburgh University Press, 2014], p. 3). See, for example, the switch to '*I can't keep this bullshit up*' in the last part of 'Phantom' in *Rain* (London: Faber and Faber, 2009, p. 58).

41. Adorno, *Aesthetic Theory*, p. 120.

42. Don Paterson, *Landing Light* (London: Faber and Faber, 2003), p. 70.

43. In Bede's *Ecclesiastical History of the English People*, eds. Judith McClure and Roger Collins (Oxford/London: James Parker and Co., 1870), a noble opines that 'The present life of man on earth appears to me, O king, in comparison of that time which is unknown to us, such as if—when you are sitting at supper with your leaders and ministers, in the winter-time, a fire indeed having been lighted and

made to glow in the middle of the supper-room, but storms of wintry rain and snow raging everywhere without—a sparrow should come and fly very quickly through the house, entering by one door and going out afterwards by another' (book 2, chapter 13, p. 150).

44. Philip Larkin, *Collected Poems* (London: Faber and Faber, 1988), p. 196. At the closure of 'High Windows', 'the deep blue air, that shows | Nothing, and is nowhere, and is endless' (p. 165) is akin to the 'blanket absolution of the light' in Paterson's poem (*Landing Light*, p. 70). Critics such as Peter Robinson have commented on the similarities between Paterson's work and Larkin's verse, such as the switch between demotic and lyrical registers. Robinson notes that the 'elective affinity between vulgarly phrased directness and popular appeal goes back at least' to 'High Windows' (*Don Paterson: Contemporary Critical Essays*, pp. 131–44, p. 134).

45. Hill, 'Poetry, Policing and Public Order (1)', www.english.ox.ac.uk/professor-sir-geoffrey-hill-lectures (accessed 12 July 2020). Paterson may be deploying pastiche here, which would explain this hint of the 'poetry kit'.

46. Adorno, *Aesthetic Theory*, p. 120.

47. Peter Robinson, 'Punching Yourself in the Face: Don Paterson and His Readers', *Don Paterson: Contemporary Critical Essays*, pp. 131–44, p. 134.

48. I am referring here to Tim Kendall's essay that I discuss further in Chapter 2, 'Against "Contemporary Poetry"', *PN Review*, 179 (January–February 2008), 24–7, p. 26.

49. Carol Ann Duffy, *The Christmas Truce* (London: Picador, 2011), p. 11; *OED* 2nd edn. I discuss Hill's account of Duffy's poem further in Chapter 3.

50. Peter Howarth, *The Cambridge Introduction to Modernist Poetry*, p. 181; Adorno, *Aesthetic Theory*, p. 115.

51. Adorno, *Aesthetic Theory*, p. 16; Paterson, *Rain*, p. 58.

52. Adorno, *Aesthetic Theory*, pp. 126, 115. The lines scan as follows:

> **back home** *from* **the** *country of* **no songs**,
> *between* **the** **blue swell** *and the* **stony silence**
> **right down** *where the* **one thing meets** *the* **millions**
> *at the* **line** *of* **speech**, *the* **white** *assuaging* **tongues**. (p. 70)

These are not straightforward pentameters. Lines one, three and four deploy conventional metrical leeway at the beginning of the poetic line in different ways: lines one and three use a spondee, whereas line four begins with an anapaest. Metrical breaks also occur in line two, with 'swell', and in line three, with the three subsequent stresses in 'one thing meets'. The first line is also arguably catalectic, with a missing syllable at the end, unless 'songs' is read as having two syllables. Paterson's attentiveness to metre and punctuation can be adduced from his comments on the pentameter in Shakespeare's sonnets. In contrast with Helen Vendler, who detects trochaic and amphibrachic metre in the sonnets, Paterson argues that some critics overcomplicate the metrical analysis; sometimes, in order to avoid hypercatalectic metre. In relation to Vendler's comments, Paterson contends in *Reading Shakespeare's Sonnets* (London: Faber and Faber, 2012) that this 'is the sort of nonsense that can arise when you proceed with a great ear but only a partial understanding of how metre actually functions. There are no feet in English verse, only metrical patterns [. . . the poem] is in duple metre, like every other poem in the entire sequence [. . .] Can everyone please stop marking in the feet, and imagining caesurae where there's no punctuation to indicate a pause' (p. 377). Attridge quotes these sentences approvingly in *Don Paterson: Contemporary Critical Essays* (p. 33).

53. Paterson's depiction of England as a country with no songs in this stanza is unlikely to please experts in the history of English folk songs, such as Ben Harker and Peggy Seeger (see Harker's *Class Act: The Cultural and Political Life of Ewan MacColl* [London: Pluto Press, 2007]).

54. This redemptive ending might not appear to sit easily with Adorno's analysis of Beckett and Celan in *Aesthetic Theory*, yet Adorno argues that 'All artworks, even the affirmative, are *a priori* polemical. The idea of a conservative artwork is inherently absurd. By emphatically separating themselves from the empirical world, their other, they bear witness that that world should be other than it is; they are the unconscious schemata of that world's transformation' (p. 177). Paterson's affirmation of writing and communication at the end of the poem thus nevertheless indicates *a priori* that the depicted world of transience and forgetting 'should be other than it is'.

55. Similarly, but in relation to Paterson's *oeuvre* rather than an individual poem, Peter Howarth shrewdly points out that the battle between postmodernists, mainstream writers and performance poetry in the introduction to *New British Poetry* was actually about the contestation of these elements in Paterson's own work (*London Review of Books*, 35: 6 (21 March 2013), 31–3, p. 31).

56. In 'Terra Nullius: Colonial Violence in Prynne's *Acrylic Tips*', Hall reads this 'marked obduracy' differently, as a 'systematic incorporation of different discourses', resulting in not a resistance to, but an excess of, signification' (pp. 1–2). In contrast, in *Late Modernist Poetics: from Pound to Prynne* (Manchester/New York: Manchester University Press, 2005), Anthony Mellors argues that, in Prynne's work, 'The prospect of meaningfulness is always shadowed by the spectre of meaninglessness' (p. 167).

57. Geraldine Monk, *Ghost & Other Sonnets* (Cambridge: Salt, 2008), p. 3.

58. This collection shares more characteristics with mainstream writing than many other of Monk's books. Robert Sheppard argues that the 'haunting' sonnet form 'necessitates Monk subduing her characteristic textual and performative exuberance in deference to the frame; the internal pressure this causes results in 66 poems of concentrated power' (http://robertsheppard .blogspot.co.uk/2011/07/innovative-sonnet-sequence-eleven-of-14.html) (accessed 8 March 2018).

59. 'Lupine' here may mean (or also mean) 'lupine' in the sense of 'lupin', the tall flower and genus of the legume family, *Fabaceae*. Sheppard extrapolates on the 'ghostly' form in 'The Innovative Sonnet Sequence: Eleven of 14: Sonnets and Other Ghosts' (24 July 2011): 'Of course, the sonnet frame is a kind of ghost form and its subject matter haunts it as a kind of other of form, "Ghost of her ghosts" as one poem puts it.' (http://robertsheppard.blogspot.co.uk/2011/07/innovative-sonnet-sequence-eleven-of-14.html) (accessed 8 March 2018). I would take issue, however, with Sheppard's assertion that Monk eschews traditional metre entirely. Whether intentional or not, the two lines he deploys to indicate this eschewal actually comprise iambic tetrameter, with the usual metrical leeway at the beginning of the line (as in Paterson's poem quoted earlier): '**Strange ones** this **token is** for **you.**/ If you've **danced** with **me** you **must** be **true**'.

60. Hill, 'Poetry, Policing and Public Order (1)', www.english.ox.ac.uk/profes sor-sir-geoffrey-hill-lectures (accessed 12 July 2020).

61. *Aesthetic Theory*, p. 121. To deploy the 'reality principle' (p. 120), the overpowering scent may be the same 'Brut' aftershave that ends the second poem after the disturbing image of the 'Shady plankton mouth' (*Ghost & Other Sonnets*, p. 4). In this reading, the sonnet sequence unfurls its meanings as it proceeds, rather than necessarily in the individual poems. However, the critic of such enigmatic poetry has to concede that there may simply be no connection.

62. Hill, 'Poetry, Policing and Public Order (1)', www.english.ox.ac.uk/profes sor-sir-geoffrey-hill-lectures (accessed 12 July 2020).

63. Robert Sheppard, 'The Innovative Sonnet Sequence: Eleven of 14: Sonnets and Other Ghosts', http://robertsheppard.blogspot.co.uk/2011/07/innova tive-sonnet-sequence-eleven-of-14.html (accessed 22 September 2020).

64. Adorno, *Aesthetic Theory*, pp. 121, 120; Howarth, *The Cambridge Introduction to Modernist Poetry*, p. 181.

65. Sheppard, 'The Innovative Sonnet Sequence: Eleven of 14: Sonnets and Other Ghosts', http://robertsheppard.blogspot.co.uk/2011/07/innovative-sonnet-sequence-eleven-of-14.html (accessed 22 September 2020); Christine and David Kennedy, 'Poetry, Difficulty and Geraldine Monk's *Interregnum*' in Scott Thurston, ed., *The Salt Companion to Geraldine Monk* (Cambridge: Salt, 2007), pp. 11–27, p. 23.

66. Adorno, *Aesthetic Theory*, p. 120. As at the end of sonnet 25 ('One morning in Morecambe. Breakfast chairs | Shrouded. Room empty. Rolling news. No eggs' [p. 29]), the closure of sonnet 29 returns to the 'reality principle' with the 'Ruffle-down riot' of the 'Blinds I drew', the 'Burnt toast' and 'Spectaculars undreamt at | Breakfast' (p. 33).

67. Adorno, *Aesthetic Theory*, p. 120.

68. Adorno, *Aesthetic Theory*, p. 120.

69. *OED*, 2nd edn. *Aesthetic Theory*, p. 128.

70. Robert Sheppard, *The Poetry of Saying: British Poetry and its Discontents, 1950–2000* (Liverpool: Liverpool University Press, 2005), p. 2.

71. Adorno, *Aesthetic Theory*, p. 128; www.poetryfoundation.org/poetrymagazine/poems/17168/ars-poetica (accessed 13 March 2018).

72. *OED*, 2nd edn.

73. *OED*, 2nd edn.

74. Adorno, *Aesthetic Theory*, p. 116.

75. Hill, 'Poetry, Policing and Public Order (1)', www.english.ox.ac.uk/professor-sir-geoffrey-hill-lectures (accessed 22 September 2020).

76. Adorno ruminates on how artistic 'clownishness' 'recollects prehistory in the primordial world of animals' in *Aesthetic Theory* (p. 119). Apes perform 'what resembles clown routines', and humans 'have not succeeded in so thoroughly repressing their likeness to animals that they are unable in an instant to recapture it and be flooded with joy [. . .] In the similarity of clowns to animals the likeness of humans to apes flashes up'. The 'classicist' repression of the ridiculous thus simultaneously attempts to evade the echo of the 'primordial', and the enigmaticalness that is inextricable from the remainder.

77. Ken Edwards, 'The Two Poetries', *Angelaki*, 3(1) (April 2000), 25–36, p. 32.

78. I discuss Libeskind's 'Building with no Exit' in Rick Crownshaw, Jane Kilby and Antony Rowland, eds., *The Future of Memory* (London/New York: Berghahn, 2010), p. 57.

79. Adorno, *Aesthetic Theory*, p. 272.

80. Howarth, *The Cambridge Introduction to Modernist Poetry*, p. 215.

81. Ian Gregson, *Contemporary Poetry and Postmodernism: Dialogue and Estrangement* (Basingstoke: Macmillan, 1996), p. 11.

82. Lumsden uses this term in *Identity Parade: New British and Irish Poets* (Newcastle: Bloodaxe, 2010), p. 103.

83. This comment was posted as a response on Amazon to Paterson's *New British Poetry* (21 June 2004) (www.amazon.co.uk/New-British-Poetry-Don-Paterson/dp/1555973949) (accessed 22 September 2020). The reviewer notes that the 'UK poetry scene is smaller than its US counterpart, so the "poetry wars" there must be like a knife fight in a phone booth'; they also refer to Paterson's 'infuriating introduction'.

2 Continuing 'Poetry Wars' in Twenty-First-Century British Poetry

1. David James, *Modernist Futures: Innovation and Inheritance in the Contemporary Novel* (Cambridge: Cambridge University Press, 2012), p. 38.

2. David Caplan, *Questions of Possibility: Contemporary Poetry and Poetic Form* (Oxford: Oxford University Press, 2005), p. 9. As Barry writes in *Poetry Wars* (Cambridge: Salt, 2006), these skirmishes were 'a key moment in the history of contemporary British poetry, polarizing the rift between the "neo-modernists", who sought to continue the 1960s revival of the early twentieth-century's "modernist revolution", and the neo-conservatives, who sought to further the "anti-modernist counter-revolution" of the 1950s' (p. 1). In a Poetry Society meeting on 11 September 1975, the Chairman proposed a new manifesto: 'General and animated discussion followed', which included Barry MacSweeney's comment that 'We want no Kingsley - f . . . ing - Amis here' (p. 82).

3. Derek Attridge, *Moving Words: Forms of English Poetry* (Oxford: Oxford University Press, 2013), p. 78. The efficacy of Caplan's terms can be sensed most keenly when critics discuss the matters of production and literary institutionalisation. Attridge's comments on evaluating different kinds of poetry is eminently sensible, yet the distinct cultural histories of 'mainstream' and the London and Cambridge Schools indicate that 'good' poetry does not necessarily rise to critical recognition like cream in the whey vat of literary value.

4. www.amazon.co.uk/New-British-Poetry-Don-Paterson/dp/1555973949 (accessed 24 September 2020). The reviewer notes that the 'UK poetry scene is smaller than its US counterpart, so the "poetry wars" there must be like a knife fight in a phone booth'; as I recounted in Chapter 1, they also refer to Paterson's 'infuriating introduction' to *New British Poetry* (2004). The supposedly 'violent' exchanges between contemporary poets is a common theme: in a review of William Logan's *Guilty Knowledge, Guilty Pleasure: The Dirty Art of Poetry* (2014), for example, Duncan Wu comments that reviewers of poetry are 'prone [. . .] to revenge shootings in dark alleys' (*Times Higher Education*, no. 2, 156 (12–18 June 2014), 48–9, p. 48).

5. Charles Simic and Don Paterson, eds., *New British Poetry* (St Paul, Minnesota: Graywolf Press, 2004), pp. xxiv–xxv.

6. Geoffrey Hill, 'Poetry, Policing and Public Order (1)', www.english.ox.ac.uk /professor-sir-geoffrey-hill-lectures (accessed 12 July 2020).

7. Theodor Adorno, *Aesthetic Theory*, eds. Gretel Adorno and Rolf Tiedemann and trans. Robert Hullot-Kentor (London: The Athlone Press, 1997 [1970]), p. 121.

8. Caplan, *Questions of Possibility*, p. 9.

9. As I noted in the introduction, Hill quotes this sentence approvingly from *The Double Agent: Essays in Craft and Elucidation* (1935) in his first lecture as Oxford

Professor of Poetry (Geoffrey Hill, 'How ill white hairs become a fool and jester', www.english.ox.ac.uk/professor-sir-geoffrey-hill-lectures [accessed 12 July 2020]).

10. Natalie Pollard, ed., *Don Paterson: Contemporary Critical Essays* (Edinburgh: Edinburgh University Press, 2014), p. 7.

11. Charles Simic and Don Paterson, eds., *New British Poetry*, p. xxiii.

12. Don Paterson, *Landing Light* (London: Faber and Faber, 2003), p. 26. A lack of critical accuracy is evident elsewhere in *New British Poetry* when the commentary on John Burnside's work refers to 'that Burnside thing' which has 'almost added a new colour to the palette' (p. 26). Astonishingly, James Fenton's poems are 'like something built for man-powered flight' (p. 66).

13. As Peter Howarth argues in 'The Battle for the Centre Ground' (*PN Review*, 166 [December–March 2005]), Eliot was one of the originators of the poetry wars in his attacks on *Georgian Poetry* (1912), which was, according to Eliot, 'commercially successful and artistically bankrupt' because it 'pandered to "the General Reading Public", which knows no tradition, and loves staleness' (p. 43).

14. Don Paterson, 'The Dark Art of Poetry', www.poetrylibrary.org.uk/news/poetryscene/?id=20 (accessed 21 October 2015).

15. J. H. Prynne, 'A Letter to Steve McCaffery', 2 January 1989, *The Gig*, 7 (November 2000), 40–6. Prynne dismisses Language poets' attempts to create a readership for their work as 'every bit as restrictive in their ideological conformity as the most bourgeois texts written to satisfy the expectations of a predefined market' (p. 40). This interdependency is a 'radically-flawed' attempt to create the context in which the poetry is to be understood. Prynne also derides the persistent 'fetish' of '"humour"' in such poetry as 'uncontrolled, self-replicating triviality' (p. 46).

16. Paterson and Simic, eds., *New British Poetry*, p. xxxii.

17. Paterson and Simic, eds., *New British Poetry*, p. xxxii.

18. Adorno, *Aesthetic Theory*, p. 272.

19. Tristan Tzara, 'Dada Manifesto, 1918', in Rudolf Kuenzli, ed., *Dada* (London: Phaidon, 2006), p. 200.

20. T. S. Eliot, *Selected Essays* (London: Faber and Faber, 1951), p. 289.

21. Adorno, *Aesthetic Theory*, p. 165. Paterson's retort would be that it is naïve to think that poets can now circumvent the market economy. In an interview with Matthew Sperling, he argues that he would 'like to publish more experimental work, but there are huge sales issues, and we have no state subsidy. I've got accountants instead'. He adds that 'any editor should be proud of those difficult or unpopular poets they manage to keep in print' (*Don Paterson: Contemporary Critical Essays*, pp. 145–52, p. 147).

22. Geoffrey Hill, *Style and Faith* (New York: Counterpoint, 2003), p. 203. Howarth notes the similarities between Paterson's 'attacks on the

unreadability of postmodern poetry' and Larkin's scathing account of the 'academic institutionalisation' of modernism in *All What Jazz?* (1970) ('The Battle for the Centre Ground', p. 44).

23. Alan Golding, 'Language-Bashing Again', *Mid-American Review*, 8(2) (1988), 93–100, p. 93.

24. Pollard, ed., *Don Paterson: Contemporary Critical Essays*, pp. 32n, 2, 7. Paterson himself admits in *New British Poetry* that his introduction is unashamedly 'bad-tempered' (p. xxxiii). In contrast, the serenity of Attridge's criticism searches for the critical 'gems' amongst Paterson's angry polemics. An unlikely defence of Paterson's binary thinking can be found in Prynne's letter to Steve McCaffery: Prynne contends that in order 'to set out a possible zone of disagreement it is convenient to dramatise' (p. 44).

25. Paterson says that new poets are introduced to him by 'word of mouth. It's also by far the most reliable way; there's very little talent going round at any one time, and the jungle telephone's ringing off the hook when it shows up, meaning you'll often hear about folk from several sources at once [...] Ploughing through slush piles or reading hundreds of magazines has always been the most inefficient way of doing it' (*Don Paterson: Contemporary Critical Essays*, p. 145).

26. John Redmond, *Poetry and Privacy: Questioning Public Interpretations of Contemporary British and Irish Poetry* (Bridgend: Seren, 2013), p. 10. Robert Hampson and Peter Barry quote the critic Hugh Kenner approvingly (an expert on modernist literature) on the first page of *New British Poetries: the Scope of the Possible* (Manchester: Manchester University Press, 1993): Kenner writes that the current state of poetry (in 1988) is that of 'mediocrity, philistinism, and media-manipulation' (p. 1). In the context of American poetry, Christopher Beach notes in *Poetic Culture: Contemporary American Poetry Between Community and Institution* (Evanston, Illinois: Northwestern University Press, 1999) that even those poets such as 'Charles Olson, Robert Duncan, and Jack Spicer, who achieved the greatest importance within the alternative canon proposed by Donald Allen's 1960 anthology, have failed to make major inroads into the poetic mainstream either for themselves or for their successors, who have been largely excluded from consideration for public awards and prizes such as the Pulitzer, the National Book Award, the Guggenheim, and the NEA' (p. 8).

27. Pollard writes further that the poetry 'of those who employ long-standing historical forms, small variations in a largely regular field of language, recognisable modes of literary-historical allusion, and a familiar address to the readership tends to be judged more accessible, and marketable' (*Don Paterson: Contemporary Critical Essays*, p. 10). This is not to say that some 'innovative' writers did not also respond with aggressive behaviour: Paterson

contends that, during the 1990s and early twenty-first century, Sean O'Brien, Peter Porter, Billy Collins, Seamus Heaney and Michael Donaghy were the victims of internet 'trolls', but with his introduction to *New British Poetry* he had 'lowered [himself] to the level of the worst of their own trolls' (p. 149). '[T]heir' indicates that his response is only a partial redaction: before the reference to internet abuse he begins a sentence with 'As accurate as I think many of the statements in that essay were [. . .]' (p. 149).

28. Pollard, ed., *Don Paterson: Contemporary Critical Essays*, p. 149.
29. Quoted in *Don Paterson: Contemporary Critical Essays*, p. 139. The quotation comes from Ahren Warner's interview with Paterson in *Poetry London* (spring 2013), http://poems.com/special_features/prose/essay_warner_paterson.php (accessed 3 June 2020).
30. Pollard, ed., *Don Paterson: Contemporary Critical Essays*, p. 8.
31. Ken Edwards, 'The Two Poetries', *Angelaki*, 3(1) (April 2000), 25–36, p. 32.
32. Adorno, *Aesthetic Theory*, p. 121.
33. Hill, 'Poetry, Policing and Public Order (1)', www.english.ox.ac.uk/profes sor-sir-geoffrey-hill-lectures (accessed 12 July 2020).
34. Roddy Lumsden, ed., *Identity Parade: New British and Irish Poets* (Newcastle: Bloodaxe, 2010), p. 103.
35. Hill, *Scenes from Comus*, p. 54; Adorno, *Aesthetic Theory*, p. 165.
36. The first version of this stanza in the manuscripts for *Scenes from Comus* (held in the Brotherton Library) makes it clear that the first few lines describe a view from a plane:

> As the high-flying sun fades, the clouds become
> as black-barren as lava, wholly motionless,
> not an ashen wisp out of place. Are
> of the strangest landscapes – no, you fool, see
> the plane's <u>above</u> the clouds. I'm looking down
> on what [illeg.] basalt in its weight
> and how the fields are aglow with dark poppies
> and some authority's grand power briefly spread out
> old-gold imperial colours. Look back a shade,
> over your left shoulder | or mine absolute night
> comes | high-rearing after us

> ('Poetry Notebooks and Early Poems and Drafts (c. 1948– 2005)', Notebook 58, BC MS 20c Hill/2, p. 29).

37. Örnólfur Thorsson, ed., *The Sagas of Icelanders* (London/New York: Penguin, 2000 [1997]), p. xxxiii.
38. Orchards of Syon workbooks, BC MS 20c Hill/2/1/52, p. 35. Gudrid first appears towards the end of the manuscript version of *Scenes from Comus*,

below a list of pills (notebook 58, n.p.n.). Gudrid 'was the wife of Thorfinn Karlsefni and the mother of Snorri, the first person of European ancestry to be born in America [...] After a pilgrimage to Rome, she lived out her life as an anchoress in Iceland, and from her were descended several of the early bishops of Iceland' (*The Sagas of Icelanders*, p. xxxiii). In 'Eirik the Red's Saga', she is described as 'the most attractive of women and one to be reckoned with in all her dealings' (p. 655). Hill may have been reminded of her character by a 'flight attendant' who appears in the manuscripts for *Scenes from Comus* as 'That six | footer blond straight out of the sagas' (notebook 58, p. 36).

39. Hill quotes Ezra Pound's aphorism from 'Envoi (1919)' in *The Enemy's Country: Words, Contexture, and other Circumstances of Language* (Oxford: Clarendon Press, 1991), pp. 83–102, pp. 93, 102.

40. Geoffrey Hill, 'Poetry, Policing and Public Order (1)', www.english.ox.ac.uk/professor-sir-geoffrey-hill-lectures (accessed 12 July 2020). The second quotation is from *New British Poetry* (p. xxx).

41. Adorno, *Aesthetic Theory*, p. 165.

42. Sheppard writes disparagingly of 'an empirical lyricism of discrete moments of experience' (*The Poetry of Saying*, p. 2). Lot's wife is turned into a pillar of salt when she looks back at Sodom (*Genesis*, book 19). Orpheus tried to bring his wife Eurydice back from the dead with his enchanting music. She had to walk behind him before she reached the upper world; however, when Orpheus glanced at her, she was sent back to the underworld.

43. Hill, 'Poetry, Policing and Public Order (1)', www.english.ox.ac.uk/professor-sir-geoffrey-hill-lectures (accessed 12 July 2020).

44. Discrepancies within Paterson's opposition are also borne out in Hampson and Barry's *New British Poetries*. In the chapter 'The British Poetry Revival, 1960–75' (pp. 15–50), Eric Mottram praises John Matthias' *Twenty-Three Modern British Poets*, in which the 'mainstream' poet Ted Hughes appears. (As Jonathan Bate notes in *Ted Hughes: the Unauthorised Life* (London: HarperCollins, 2015), Mottram tutored Hughes in his second year at Pembroke College (p. 73).) In the introduction to *New British Poetries*, however, Hughes – despite his provocative imagery and the obduracy of collections such as *Cave Birds: An Alchemical Cave Drama* (1978) – remains a key poet for the maligned 'general reader', who wishes only for 'surface difficulty' (p. 4). Mottram also attacks Donald Davie as a 'mainstream' writer akin to Larkin or Amis (p. 21), whereas Hampson and Barry applaud his attack on the Movement in *Under Briggflatts* (p. 1).

45. Hill, 'Poetry, Policing and Public Order (1)', www.english.ox.ac.uk/professor-sir-geoffrey-hill-lectures (accessed 12 July 2020).

46. Adorno, *Aesthetic Theory*, p. 165.

47. Joanna Moorhead, 'Carol Ann Duffy: "Poems are a form of texting"' (interview with Carol Ann Duffy), *The Guardian*, 5 September 2011 (www .theguardian.com/education/2011/sep/05/carol-ann-duffy-poetry-texting-competition) (accessed 12 May 2020).

48. David Crystal, *Txtng: The Gr8 Db8* (Oxford: Oxford University Press, 2009), *passim*.

49. Hill, 'Poetry, Policing and Public Order (1)', www.english.ox.ac.uk/profes sor-sir-geoffrey-hill-lectures (accessed 12 July 2020).

50. Jeffrey T. Nealon, *Post-Postmodernism or, the Cultural Logic of Just-in-Time Capitalism* (Stanford: Stanford University Press, 2012), p. 167.

51. Hill, 'Poetry, Policing and Public Order (1)', www.english.ox.ac.uk/profes sor-sir-geoffrey-hill-lectures (accessed 12 July 2020).

52. Hill, 'Poetry, Policing and Public Order (1)', www.english.ox.ac.uk/profes sor-sir-geoffrey-hill-lectures (accessed 12 July 2020). As I outlined in the Introduction, Hill rails against the supposed 'vitality' of the contemporary poetry scene in the UK, with its burgeoning prizes and presses, and outlines instead a decline in the quality of poetry since Pound's work in the 1950s. In the context of American poetry, Beach argues similarly in *Poetic Culture* that, despite the 'publishing volume of poetry' exceeding that of 1965 by 'a magnitude of ten to one', 'the sheer volume of mediocre verse that reaches print makes it difficult for the most challenging or innovative poetry to find its way to a wider public venue' (p. 45). Hill and Beach echo Joseph Epstein's point in 'Who Killed Poetry?' that there has been a qualitative decline in US poetry since the modernist generation of Pound and Eliot (*Commentary*, 86: 2 [1988], 13–20).

53. Moorhead, '"Poems are a form of texting"' (interview with Carol Ann Duffy), *The Guardian*, 5 September 2011 (www.theguardian.com/education/2011/sep/ 05/carol-ann-duffy-poetry-texting-competition) (accessed 12 May 2020).

54. Geoffrey Hill, 'Poetry, Policing and Public Order (1)', www.english.ox.ac.uk /professor-sir-geoffrey-hill-lectures (accessed 12 July 2020).

55. Beach, *Poetic Culture*, p. 65. In *Poetic License: Essays on Modernist and Postmodernist Lyric* (Evanston: Northwestern University Press, 1990), Marjorie Perloff echoes A. Alvarez's description of the archetypal Movement poet in *The New Poetry*, and typifies the US mainstream poet as 'the poet as boy or girl next door, cheerfully noneccentric, indeed, wilfully ignorant of such things as philosophy or literary criticism' (p. 60).

56. Lemn Sissay, 'Carol Ann Duffy and Geoffrey Hill: truly poetic heavyweights', www.theguardian.com/commentisfree/2012/jan/31/carol-ann-duffy-geoffrey-hill-punch-up (accessed 12 July 2020). As Sissay puts it, 'Geoffrey Hill, the Oxford professor of poetry, in the blue corner, throws a slug at Carol Ann Duffy, the poet laureate, in the red corner: at a lecture in Oxford, Hill likened

Duffy to a Mills & Boon writer'. As I pointed out in the Introduction, Duffy's response to Hill's criticism was a dignified silence. Her account of Hill after his death on 1 July 2016 was laudatory: 'he was, in poetry, a saint and a warrior who never gave an inch in his crusade to reach poetic truth [. . .] he could suddenly illuminate, like lightning over a landscape' (www.theguardian.com /books/2016/jul/01/geoffrey-hill-one-of-the-greatest-english-poets-dies-aged-84) (accessed 24 September 2020).

57. Moorhead, '"Poems are a form of texting"' (interview with Carol Ann Duffy), *The Guardian*, 5 September 2011 (www.theguardian.com/education/2011/sep/05/ carol-ann-duffy-poetry-texting-competition) (accessed 12 May 2020). 'Death of a Teacher' is available at https://poetryshark.wordpress.com/2016/02/22/poetic-transformations-in-death-of-a-teacher-by-carol-ann-duffy-poem-analysis/ (accessed 24 September 2020).

58. In *New British Poetries*, Robert Hampson and Peter Barry critique 'democratic' poetry in the form of the 'general poetry reader' who will 'tolerate a degree of surface difficulty, but only so long as the subject matter remains essentially familiar, domestic and re-assuring' (p. 4).

59. The quotation is from Che Guevara's speech 'On Growth and Imperialism' at the Ministerial Meeting of the Inter-American Economic and Social Council (CIES) in August 1961. Guevara is quoting from the Declaration of Havana.

60. *OED*, 2nd edn (my italics).

61. Martin Gilens and Benjamin I. Page, 'Testing Theories of American Politics: Elites, Interest Groups, and Average Citizens', in *American Political Science Association*, 12(3) (September 2014), 564–81. These drawbacks of democracy are not new: Greek *dēmokratia* was always, of course, élitist in that women, slaves and non-landowners were denied a vote.

62. Herbert Read, *The Politics of the Unpolitical* (New York: Routledge, 1943), p. 6. In *The Intellectuals and the Masses: Pride and Prejudice among the Literary Intelligentsia, 1880–1939* (London: Faber and Faber, 1992), John Carey reads the modernist response to José Oretga y Gasset's 'triumph of "hyperdemocracy"' (p. 3) as an attempt to exclude 'newly educated (or "semi-educated") readers, and so preserve the intellectual's seclusion from the "mass"' (p. vii).

63. Jeffrey A. Winters, 'Oligarchy and Democracy', *The American Interest*, 7(2) (2011), www.the-american-interest.com/2011/09/28/oligarchy-and-democracy (accessed 4 August 2020).

64. Hill, 'Poetry, Policing and Public Order (1)', www.english.ox.ac.uk/professor-sir-geoffrey-hill-lectures (accessed 12 July 2020).

65. Robin van den Akker, Alison Gibbons and Timotheus Vermeulen, eds., *Metamodernism: Historicity, Affect and Death after Postmodernism* (London/ New York: Rowman and Littlefield International, 2017), p. 16. Vermeulen

and van den Akker outline the metamodernist period as the '2000s', which they define as running between 1999 and 2011 (p. 22). As the Greek protests against austerity indicate, one of the essential features of this period incorporates the rise of anti-centrist politics in the form of leftist anti-globalisation movements and right-wing popular movements, reacting against the 'politics that came to dominate the postmodern years, culminating in the "thirdway" of, say, Bill Clinton, Tony Blair and Gerhard Schröder' (pp. 12–13).

66. Don Paterson, *Landing Light* (London: Faber and Faber, 2003), p. 26.

67. Hampson and Barry, *New British Poetries*, p. 4.

68. Tim Kendall, 'Against "Contemporary Poetry"', *PN Review*, 179 (January–February 2008), 24–7, p. 26.

69. Beach indicates that the same is true of Ashbery and Robert Creeley in the US: they would not be considered to be mainstream writers, and yet (in 1999) they were 'two of the best-selling and most widely taught poets in America' (*Poetic Culture*, p. 17).

70. Hill, 'Poetry, Policing and Public Order (1)', www.english.ox.ac.uk/professor-sir-geoffrey-hill-lectures (accessed 12 July 2020).

71. According to Mottram, an 'innovative' poet touting their first collection will not be published by Faber and Faber, Chatto & Windus, Picador or Cape – the largest publishing houses for twenty-first-century poetry in Britain. Contemporary poetry publishing has achieved a paradox whereby publication on a 'leading' poetry list does not mean that the author is capable of achieving singularity in the sense defined by Derek Attridge in *The Singularity of Literature* (2004): poems that are rich enough in their linguistic complexity to be read in different ways at different times. To assert this paradox in a different way, much of contemporary poetry is produced for readers who do not like to read poetry.

72. Hampson and Barry, *New British Poetries*, pp. 29–30; Hill, 'Poetry, Policing and Public Order (1)', www.english.ox.ac.uk/professor-sir-geoffrey-hill-lectures (accessed 12 July 2020).

73. Hill, 'Poetry, Policing and Public Order (1)', www.english.ox.ac.uk/professor-sir-geoffrey-hill-lectures (accessed 12 July 2020).

74. Peter Howarth, *The Cambridge Introduction to Modernist Poetry* (Cambridge: Cambridge University Press, 2012), p. 171.

75. Anonymous, 'Introduction', *Angel Exhaust 9: Tyranny and Mutation: New Radical Poets* (summer 1993), 4–5, p. 5. The editors write instead of 'our staple audience of hardened modernists' (p. 5).

76. Alison Flood, 'Carol Ann Duffy is "wrong" about poetry, says Geoffrey Hill', *The Guardian*, 31 September 2012, www.theguardian.com/books/2012/jan/31/carol-ann-duffy-oxford-professory-poetry (accessed 3 August 2020).

77. Hill, 'Poetry, Policing and Public Order (1)', www.english.ox.ac.uk/profes sor-sir-geoffrey-hill-lectures (accessed 12 July 2020).
78. Carol Ann Duffy, *The Christmas Truce* (London: Picador, 2011), p. 11.
79. In 'Burnt Norton', Eliot refers to a pool surface that 'glittered out of heart of light' (*Four Quartets* [London: Faber and Faber, 1949 (1941)], p. 14). Given Hill's antipathy towards the *Four Quartets* – that I noted in my introduction in relation to *Scenes from Comus* – it is not unlikely that he would extend this criticism to Eliot's diction.
80. Hill, 'Poetry, Policing and Public Order (1)', www.english.ox.ac.uk/professor-sir-geoffrey-hill-lectures (accessed 12 July 2020); Michael Symmons Roberts, *Mancunia* (London: Cape, 2017), p. 23.
81. Hill, 'Poetry, Policing and Public Order (1)', www.english.ox.ac.uk/profes sor-sir-geoffrey-hill-lectures (accessed 12 July 2020).
82. Instead of 'glittering rime', Hill refers to the 'gleam' of rime in Ludlow castle (p. 29).
83. Hill, 'Poetry, Policing and Public Order (1)', www.english.ox.ac.uk/professor-sir-geoffrey-hill-lectures (accessed 12 July 2020).
84. Carol Ann Duffy, *The Bees* (London: Picador, 2012), p. 3.
85. Hill, 'Poetry, Policing and Public Order (1)', www.english.ox.ac.uk/profes sor-sir-geoffrey-hill-lectures (accessed 12 July 2020).
86. Throughout *The Bees*, Duffy is not afraid of the obvious full rhyme, as in 'Last Post' ('warm French bread | and all those thousands dead' [p. 4]), or the moon's 'poetry kit', in which the face from 'Echo' is 'like the moon in a well' (p. 6). However, these examples contrast with the effective switch in register and sound in 'Ariel', where Shakespeare's *The Tempest* (1611) confronts contemporary dangers ('Where the bee sucks, | neonicotinoid insecticides') (p. 11), the singular deployment of the moon image in 'Mrs Schofield's GCSE', where 'poetry | pursues the human like the smitten moon' (p. 15), or the 'hovering' verb that completes the first line of 'Cold': 'the snowball which wept in my hands' (p. 58).
87. Kenneth Hopkins, *The Poets Laureate* (Wakefield: EP Publishing Limited, 1973), pp. 25–6. Hopkins notes that Dryden was the first official Laureate after a patent from 1670 confirmed his role, and simultaneous appointment as Historiographer Royal (p. 15). In 1616, Ben Jonson was issued a 'pension of 100 marks, and this pension was clearly in recognition of his services as a poet', but he was not an official Poet Laureate (p. 17).
88. Hopkins, *The Poets Laureate*, p. 75. Hopkins notes that even Cibber ridiculed himself in a set of verses in the *Whitehall Evening Post*, 'which he kept anonymous until *An Apology for the Life of Colley Cibber* came out in 1740' (p. 75).
89. Ted Hughes, *Collected Poems*, ed. Paul Keegan (London: Faber and Faber, 2003), pp. 803, 806, 807.

90. Hopkins, p. 211. Hopkins adds that Laureates such as C. Day Lewis have also generously 'given the prestige of their office to literary causes and movements calculated to enlarge, enhance and preserve our literature' (p. 214). Duffy has worked extensively with children: her initiatives include the 'Mother Tongue Other Tongue' competition, which celebrates multilingual poetry in schools. Like C. Day Lewis, she has 'brought poetry to the young, and there could hardly be a more valuable service in a Laureate' (p. 214).

91. Before Dryden's official role as Poet Laureate, Charles I gave Jonson 'one Terse of Canary Spanish wyne yearely' (Hopkins, *The Poets Laureate*, p. 17). Betjeman actually reinvented the annual perk in the form of 720 bottles of sherry.

92. Charlotte Dobson, 'Carol Ann Duffy pens a new ode to the . . . gas meter', www.manchestereveningnews.co.uk/news/greater-manchester-news/carol-ann-duffy-pens-new-11207172 (accessed 3 August 2020).

93. Wendy Elliott, the shop manager of Duffy's local Oxfam shop in Didsbury in 2010, notes that the Poet Laureate wrote 'Oxfam' for the charity's first Bookfest in 2009: the festival is 'meant to highlight the good work that Oxfam does' (www.manchestereveningnews.co.uk/news/greater-manchester-news/poet-laureate-attend-oxfam-festival-890163) (accessed 3 August 2020).

94. Adorno, *Aesthetic Theory*, p. 165.

95. Geoffrey Hill, 'Simple, Sensuous, and Passionate', *Poetry Book Society Bulletin*, 191 (winter 2001), p.5.

96. I am quoting here partly from the manuscript version of this stanza held in the Brotherton Library:

> men of seventy have nuisance value.
> I snorkel into contrived sleep, I wake,
> I address the mirror: *spare me my own*
> *rancour and ugliness*. It too is naked (p. 36)

appears as the following lines in notebook 57:

> My sleep
> finds its expression these days through a mask
> not of perversion – perversion's a fine thing –
> neither of Comus, child of Ludlow's Circe
> but of new-senile practical ugliness (p. 12)

97. Hill, 'Simple, Sensuous, and Passionate', p. 5.

98. Adorno, *Aesthetic Theory*, p. 121.

99. Hill, *Scenes from Comus*, p. 41.

100. Adorno, *Aesthetic Theory*, p. 17.

3 Committed and Autonomous Art

1. Geoffrey Hill, *The Orchards of Syon* (London/New York: Penguin, 2002), pp. 65, 14.

2. Eleanor Cook, 'The Figure of Enigma: Rhetoric, History and Poetry', *Rhetorica: A Journal of the History of Rhetoric*, 19(4) (2001), 349–78, p. 352.

3. Theodor W. Adorno, *Aesthetic Theory*, eds. Gretel Adorno and Rolf Tiedemann, trans. Robert Hullot-Kentor (London: The Athlone Press, 1997 [1970]), p. 121; Geoffrey Hill, 'Poetry, Policing and Public Order (1)', www.english.ox.ac.uk/pro fessor-sir-geoffrey-hill-lectures (accessed 12 July 2020).

4. Adorno, *Aesthetic Theory*, p. 121.

5. In *The Selling and Self-Regulation of Contemporary Poetry* (London: Anthem Press, 2020), J. T. Welsh critiques the term 'autonomous', at the same time as he attacks neoliberal versions of creativity that equate the latter with the entrepreneurial. In contrast to Adorno 'treating art and commerce as separate spheres', Welsh deploys Pierre Bordieu's concept of 'symbolic' capital, and argues that poetry's 'relatively low economic value becomes part of its heightened cultural value' (p. 9). In *Aesthetic Theory*, Adorno actually writes of the impossibility of art and socio-economic pressures existing as 'separate spheres': '[a]rt holds true to the shudder' not by rejecting these encroachments, but by enfolding them into the artworks (p. 118). Hence autonomous art should not be regarded as escaping the market economy, but it nevertheless responds to the latter through recalcitrant rhetoric.

6. Theodor Adorno, *Ästhetische Theorie* (Frankfurt am Main: Suhrkamp Verlag, 2014 [1970]), p. 184.

7. Andre Furlani, *Guy Davenport: Postmodern and After* (Evanston, Illinois: Northwestern University Press), 2007, p. 150; David James and Urmila Seshagiri, 'Metamodernism: Narratives of Continuity and Revolution', *PMLA*, 129(1) (2014), 87–98.

8. Andre Furlani, *Guy Davenport*, p. 150. As Irene Morra argues throughout *Verse Drama in England, 1900–2015: Art, Modernity and the National Stage* (London/New York: Bloomsbury, 2016), such verse plays are a neglected aspect of modern and contemporary poetry. Morra notes that the common perception of verse drama is that it is 'slowly woven from pastel shades of twee' (p. 1). Harrison's attempts to revitalise the form intend to subvert the 'odour of sanctity', as he regards it, surrounding T. S. Eliot's verse plays (p. 121).

9. Raymond Williams, *The Politics of Modernism*, ed. Tony Pinkney (London/New York: Verso, 1989), p. 90; Tony Harrison, *Plays Three* (London: Faber and Faber, 1996). As the performance notes for *The Labourers of Herakles* explain – when it was staged at the University of Leeds (11 November 2017) – the play was 'an entry at the Eighth International Meeting on Ancient Greek Drama at Delphi, Greece. It was a co-production of the European Cultural Centre of

Delphi and the National Theatre Studio, and was staged on 23rd August 1995 in a specially (half-) constructed venue: the building site that was designated as the new theatre for the European Cultural Centre of Delphi. The production was sponsored, appropriately, by the Herakles General Cement Company of Greece, which was involved in the building project, and whose silo, cement mixers and bags played an important part in the performance'.

10. In an article held in the Brotherton archive, Armitage focuses on the aspects of Harrison's poems that can make 'cry-babies out of the blokes in the boozer': the dominant version of Harrison's relationship with modernism tells a story in which the poet undergoes a 'Eureka' moment akin to Philip Larkin's repudiation of W. B. Yeats when the Leeds poet begins to write *The School of Eloquence* sequence in the mid-1970s (BC MS 20c ARMITAGE/8). Switching to the example of Thomas Hardy, Larkin no longer wished, he contested, to 'jack himself up' into poetry, just as Harrison desires to be the poet his father might read in his family sonnets (*Required Writing: Miscellaneous Pieces 1955–1982* [London: Faber and Faber, 1983], p. 175). Harrison's work has been read as simply complying with John Carey's attack on modernism's insidious snobberies in *The Intellectuals and the Masses* (1992): for Carey, modernism – as he describes it in his recent autobiography – has an inherent 'anti-democratic animus', that 'cultivates obscurity and depends on learned allusions, comprehensible only to the highly educated' (*The Unexpected Professor: an Oxford Life in Books* [London: Faber and Faber, 2014], pp. 330, 327). In this book, I challenge this critical orthodoxy: firstly, in the context of Harrison's engagement with Brecht's work in this chapter, and later in Chapter 5 in relation to his fictionalisation of myth in contemporary settings, a narratological tactic that Joyce, Eliot and other modernist writers were the first to exploit extensively. Modernist references and influences abound in Harrison's collection *The Loiners* (1970), such as the rewritings of Joseph Conrad's work in the poems 'The Heart of Darkness', 'The White Queen' and the two 'PWD Man' poems; even the beard of Conrad appears in 'Doodlebugs'. In the contemporaneous poem 'The Bonebard Ballads', we encounter the disarming élitism of Harrison asking the reader to go and see Goya's painting 'A Dog Buried in the Sand' in the Prado gallery in Madrid, if the reader wants to understand the last two lines of his poem (*Selected Poems* [London: Faber and Faber, 1987 (1984)], p. 103). Alert to what he perceived as an 'anti-democratic animus' in these lines, Larkin bluntly commented 'Why the fucking hell should I?' (Philip Larkin, 'Under a Common Flag', *The Observer*, 14 November 1982, p. 23; Carey, *The Unexpected Professor*, p. 330). Harrison's refusal to translate the Latin epigraph to 'Newcastle is Peru' – that

originates from Seneca's *Medea* (50 BCE) – is reminiscent of Eliot and Pound's similar refusals in *The Waste Land* (before the footnotes) and the *Cantos* (1925), or John Fowles's infamous completion of *The Magus* (1965) with the opening and untranslated lines from an anonymous Latin lyric entitled 'The Vigil of Venus'. At the end of *The Loiners*, an untranslated epigraph from Rimbaud's *Oeuvres Complètes* (1966) introduces 'Ghosts: Some Words Before Breakfast': '*C'est mon unique soutien au monde, à present!*' (*Selected Poems*, p. 72). In the culture/barbarism dialectic that runs throughout Harrison's work, he tends not to underscore such erudition, as in the film-poem *Metamorpheus* (2000) that I discuss in Chapter 5.

11. Theodor Adorno, 'Commitment', in *Aesthetics and Politics*, eds. Perry Anderson, Rodney Livingstone and Francis Mulhern (London: Verso, 2007 [1977]), pp. 177–95, p. 177.

12. Harrison's interview comment – quoted by Morra – that 'if people can't understand you lose them very quickly' can only be regarded as ironic in this context (p. 209). Brecht would no doubt not have approved of these untranslated openings to Harrison's plays, and would have regarded them as unnecessarily élitist.

13. Adorno, 'Commitment', p. 177. The term 'committed and autonomous art' is necessary because it differentiates between 'art for art's sake' – that Adorno argues is a false version of autonomous art – and the work of Kafka, Beckett and Hill, that may superficially appear disengaged, but which is actually intent on embodying the structural inequalities of, and historical iniquities caused by, heteronomy.

14. Adorno, 'Commitment', p. 177. I discuss Mörike's work 'On Lyric and Society' and Hill's collection *The Triumph of Love* in *Holocaust Poetry* (Edinburgh: Edinburgh University Press, 2005), p. 75.

15. In 'On Experimental Theatre', Brecht writes about the 'culinary' as 'spiritual dope traffic', and calls for art that can turn 'from a home of illusions to a home of experience' (John Willett, ed., *Brecht on Theatre* (London: Methuen, 1964 [1957]), pp. 130–5 [p. 135]). As I noted in Chapter 1, Michael Donaghy scoffs at 'innovative' poets' detachment from the 'general poetry reader', and wonders how a 'committed' experimental poem "composed from punctuation marks will help bring down the arms trade"' (David Wheatley, *Contemporary British Poetry* [London/New York: Palgrave, 2015], p. 113). However, a mainstream poem has never aided either in the abolishment of the international arms trade.

16. Theodor Adorno, 'Engagement' in *Noten zur Literatur* I (Frankfurt: Suhrkamp Verlag, 1974), pp. 409–30, p. 409; Adorno, 'Commitment', p. 177.

17. Adorno, 'Commitment', p. 177.

18. Fredric Jameson argues that Adorno's conclusions are not 'satisfactory' because they present a 'Lukács-type "reflection theory" of aesthetics, under

the spell of a political and historical despair that [. . .] finds praxis henceforth unimaginable', in an 'anti-political revival of the ideology of modernism' ('Reflections in Conclusion' in *Aesthetics and Politics*, p. 209). However, 'Commitment' does not present committed and autonomous art as a simple 'reflection' of 'political and historical despair' but – as the original title for the German publication suggests – a form of deflected 'engagement'. Nor is direct 'praxis' the primary concern of Adorno's essay when faced with the 'deluge': as I point out later in this section, Adorno nevertheless argues that Kafka's prose 'compels the change of attitude which committed works merely demand' (p. 97).

19. Through committed literature, Sartre wishes to emphasise readers' capacity to 'awaken' their 'free choice' to change reality, whereas Adorno stresses that the 'very possibility of choosing depends on what can be chosen' (p. 180). In an Adornoian moment in Brecht's *The Resistible Rise of Arturo Ui* (London: Methuen, 1976 [1958]), the character Givola announces that 'Each man | Is free to do exactly as he pleases' (p. 94): hesitantly, the Ciceronian goes out, two bodyguards follow him, and '*a shot is heard*'. Giri then proclaims, 'All right, friends, Let's have your free decision!', and '*All raise both hands*' (p. 94). Adorno's critical approach to Sartre's notion of free choice does not entirely preclude the notion of choice, whereas the editors of *Aesthetics and Politics* contend that 'Sartre's belief in the efficacy of individual engagement seems much less questionable than a theory in which the production of "autonomous" works of art is little less than magical' (p. 147).

20. 'Commitment', p. 184. In *Marxism and Modernism: an Historical Study of Lukács, Brecht, Benjamin, and Adorno*, Eugene Lunn argues that Brecht's position adheres to a 'common vulgar Marxist identification' of fascism with capitalism (London: Verso, 1985 [1982], p.138). However, Adorno's account of fascism as 'a conspiracy of the wealthy and powerful' is just as reductive as Brecht's presentation of Nazis as gangsters, and does not take account of a myriad of historical factors contributing to Hitler's electoral victory, such as the overwhelming support of lower-middle-class Germans.

21. However, the criticisms that Adorno directs towards other 'committed' Brecht plays are less surefooted. The philosopher objects to *Mother Courage and Her Children* (1941) because it attempts to reconstruct mid-twentieth-century capitalism in the context of the 'old lawless days' of the seventeenth century (p. 186), and is thereby a 'false social model' (p. 187). This claim takes a blinkered approach to the rise of the mercantile classes in Europe – including characters akin to Mother Courage – from the fourteenth century onwards, and the intensification of capital interests in the sixteenth and seventeenth centuries. Moreover, Adorno argues implausibly that the children's deaths in *Mother Courage and Her Children* are not a direct result

of the Thirty Years' War, or the mother's attempts at profiteering: the fact that she 'has to be absent to earn some money' when they are killed 'remains completely generic to the action' (p. 186). Francis McDonagh's translation of '*ganz allemein*' ('generally') from 'Engagement' (p. 420) into 'generic' is confusing here: Mother Courage's absence to earn money – particularly after her botched attempt to bargain for the life of her second son, Swiss Cheese – is central to the play's interpretation, as she 'shrinks' into an 'agent of social processes', a process that Adorno praises only three pages before his attack on *Mother Courage and Her Children* (p. 183). Brecht thus attempts to stress her misplaced guile rather than praise, as many audiences do, her stubbornness and 'humanity'. This particular 'false social model' is actually the construct of misguided literary criticism, and Adorno's attempt to shore up his argument that *Mother Courage and Her Children* undergoes a process of '*ästhetische Reduktionsprozeß*' ('aesthetic reduction') ('Commitment', p. 92; 'Engagement', p. 416). Despite his focus on enigmatical art as an intensely political form, Adorno underemphasises the 'doubleness' required in Brecht's allegory, as the latter presents the action of the Thirty Years' War as analogous to but not coterminous with 'the functional capitalist society of modern times' (p. 186). As Adorno concedes in his qualified praise for Brecht's innovations in dramatic form, if autonomous art can also be committed, then committed art can also, at times, encompass the autonomous. This thinking is central to my analysis in this chapter of Harrison's verse plays: I stress their 'committed' formal successes, particularly in their reimagining of Brecht's alienation effects that pervade the poetry's engagement with Herakles.

22. In *Bertolt Brecht: a Literary Life* (London: Bloomsbury, 2014), Stephen Parker notes the problem in translating '*Verfremdungseffekte*': 'the term is generally known in English as the "Alienation Effect" or "A-effect". We [and I] will adopt that usage, even though the sense is better rendered by "estrangement" or "defamiliarization"' (p. 352). Peter Brooker makes the same point in Peter Thompson and Glendyr Sacks' *The Cambridge Companion to Brecht* (Cambridge: Cambridge University Press, 2006 [1994]), p. 217. As Brooker argues, 'A-effects' do not originate *only* in Brecht's theatre, but also in the texts that mostly influenced Brecht, such as 'the political theatre of Erwin Piscator and German agitprop; the cabaret of Frank Wedekind and the work of the music hall comedian Karl Valentin; Charlie Chaplin and American silent film; Asian and revolutionary Soviet theatre; as well as Shakespeare and Elizabethan chronicle plays' (p. 211).

23. Adorno, 'Engagement', p. 425.

24. Adorno, 'Commitment', p. 182.

25. The Jocelyn Herbert archive (part of the National Theatre archive), 'Carnuntum' notebook, JH/1/21, n.p.n. In another postcard dated August 1995, Harrison writes that their collaborative experiences are 'truly amazing. I've never felt more fulfilled or happy, and I will treasure our days together as long as I live. You have given me so much and I am deeply grateful for everything' (JH/1/21).

26. JH/3/54, n.p.n. (entries dated 20 May 1995 and 21 July 1995).

27. Tony Harrison archive, the Brotherton Library, 'Carnuntum 2' notebook, BC MS 20C Harrison/03/KAI, pp. 328–9.

28. Herbert, 'Carnuntum' notebook, JH/1/21, n.p.n.

29. As Oliver Taplin concludes in 'The Chorus of Mams', *The Labourers of Herakles* 'is not likely to go down as Harrison's greatest theatre work. Both text and performance betray signs of being put together under pressure' (Sandie Byrne, ed., *Tony Harrison: Loiner* [Oxford: Clarendon Press, 1997], pp. 171–84 [p. 180]). Taplin witnessed the first performance, and admits that the audience response was '"mixed"', due perhaps to the play's didacticism, or failed 'commitment' to plain speaking: 'they may well have also found the didactic message of Phrynichus [. . .] too overt [. . .] Arguably, even, Harrison failed to fulfil his own admirable maxim: that the play should be self-sufficiently accessible, without requiring any homework or footnotes' (p. 182).

30. Herbert, 'Carnuntum' notebook, JH/1/21, n.p.n.

31. Philip Glahn, *Bertolt Brecht* (London: Reaktion Books, 2014), p. 102.

32. Tony Harrison, *Plays Three*, pp. 65, 81.

33. Herbert, 'Carnuntum', JH/2/8, n.p.n.

34. In the pasted-in article in workbook one, 'From Roman legionary to Robocop', Oliver Gillie remarks that 'we think the "thumbs up" signal meant that the gladiator should live, but we have nothing to prove this' (p. 15).

35. Parker, *Bertolt Brecht: A Life*, p. 269. The reason for Bollux's name is indicated in workbook one: Harrison includes sections from Thomas Wiedemann's *Emperors & Gladiators* (1992), one of which mentions that Commodus 'kept among his minions certain men named after the private parts of both sexes' (p. 275).

36. Lunn argues that Adorno's 'treatment of Brecht was narrow and one-sided. He never seriously engaged the question of the potentiality of Brecht's montage and distancing methods except as they were manifested within the playwright's particular political framework. That they were capable of being used more fruitfully by Brecht than in Adorno's damning examples, or that they might provide a key for other less politically blinded artists, was missing from his account' (p. 276). Lunn's summary of Adorno's critical blind-spots in relation to Brecht's work is a fair analysis, and Harrison forms an example of a 'less politically blinded artist', in contrast with the impact of Brecht's

communist sympathies on the first version of *The Measures Taken* (1930). Ironically, as Lunn points out, some Russian communists found this play treasonable in its apportioning of blame to communist characters rather than solely to the aristocracy, that 'won Brecht Moscow's embarrassed strictures' (p. 132). As Parker notes, 'Most were disinclined to take lessons in party discipline from a figure who was not even a KPD member' (p. 280).

37. Lunn, *Marxism and Modernism*, p. 54. As Oliver Double and Michael Wilson note in their chapter on Brecht and cabaret, he wished to 'stir' the audience at one point by 'hiring two clowns to pretend to be spectators, bandying opinions about other audience members, making comments about the play and placing bets on its outcome' (Thompson and Sacks, p. 58). The influence of Frank Wedekind on Brecht, and, by proxy, Harrison, is instructive in this context: Wedekind's cabaret-style theatre 'never loses sight of the present moment and the particular venue in which it takes place'; Wedekind also wrote about popular theatre and the importance of the circus in the 1880s (pp. 56, 59).

38. Andre Furlani, *Guy Davenport*, p. 150.

39. Herbert, 'Carnuntum 2', BC/MS/20c/Harrison/03/KAI, p. 247.

40. An article pasted into the third notebook also records Hercules defending the empire, but 'there are so many of these faults and meannesses recorded of Hercules by the ancients, that when one considers them, one is apt almost to lose sight of his great character: and to wonder how they could ever have given him the very foremost place in this distinguishing class of heroes; of those very few, who by their virtue obtained a place among the chief of all the celestial deities, in the highest heaven' (p. 591).

41. Herbert, 'Carnuntum 2', BC/MS/20c/Harrison/03/KAI, p. 249.

42. Harrison pastes a section of Pierre Grimal's *The Civilisation of Rome* (1963) into the back of the second workbook, in which Grimal points out that any reference to 'Roman cruelty' is simplistic: 'this inclination to realism led to an effort to represent legendary episodes, in all their horror, as truthfully as possible [...] We need not attribute these barbarous extravagances to a perversity or cruelty peculiar to the Roman plebs. There is no lack of evidence for similar cruelties and perversions in other parts of the empire, even, if we are to believe Apuleius, in Greece itself' (p. 436).

43. The potential distortions of 'committed' art are evident in other attempts at multidirectional memory in *The Kaisers of Carnuntum*. In the second notebook, Harrison writes 'Hitler/Mussolini!' next to a reference to Commodus' shaved head (p. 271), and pens 'Caesar, Caesar, Caesar' alongside 'Zieg Heil' (p. 357). Subsequent attempts to allegorize Fascism in terms of an emperor in ancient Rome arise in the text when, for example, Commodus refers to the 'Roman Reich' (p. 70). Didacticism is sometimes at

the expense of metaphorical efficacy, as when Harrison compares the slaughtered beasts to 'Jews' (p. 517). A more successful multidirectional link is established in the workbooks between the historical dictatorships and antisemitism in Austria in the 1990s: the first workbook contains an article on Jörg Haider, and his political programme demanding '"Austria for the Austrians"' (p. 96), as well as a piece by Ian Trayhor on how 'One in five Austrians believe that the rights of Jews in Austria should be restricted' (p. 44).

44. JH/3/15, n.p.n.
45. Herbert, 'Carnuntum' notebook, JH/1/21. Kustow's review also notes that at one point, 'Two performing bears broke loose backstage. As stagehands scurried after them (one getting clawed in the chase), Barry Rutter was stranded centre stage with three caged lions and a tiger, and no fellow actor in sight.' Brecht refers to the breaking of 'illusion' through alienation effects in 'From the Mother Courage Model' (*Brecht on Theatre*, pp. 215–22, p. 217).
46. 'On Experimental Theatre' in *Brecht on Theatre* (p. 136).
47. Frederick Baker review of *The Kaisers of Carnuntum*, 'Roman arena comes full circle' in the Herbert archive, 'Carnuntum' notebook, JH/1/21, n.p.n.
48. Harrison, 'Carnuntum 2', BC/MS/20c/Harrison/03/KAI, p. 322.
49. Tony Harrison, *Plays Three*, p. 89.
50. Carol Chillington Rutter, 'Harrison, Herakles, and Wailing Women "Labourers" at Delphi', *New Theatre Quarterly*, 13(50) (May 1997), 133–43, p. 140.
51. Adorno, 'Commitment', p. 189.
52. Herbert, 'Carnuntum' notebook, JH/1/21, n.p.n.
53. *The Norton Shakespeare*, 3rd edition (London/New York: W. W. Norton, 2015), p. 3165.
54. Herbert, 'Carnuntum' notebook, JH/1/21, n.p.n.
55. Adorno, 'Commitment', p. 190.
56. Workbook one presents the possibility of the ostriches symbolising Marcus Aurelius: 'Every ostrich that I slew | reminded me of pater, you'; 'I represent all you ignored [. . .] You are the fucking ostrich' (p. 204).
57. Harrison, 'Carnuntum 2', BC/MS/20c/Harrison/03/KAI, p. 238.
58. Harrison, *Plays Three*, p. 100. As Marianne McDonald argues, 'Harrison simplifies history to make his contrast. Marcus Aurelias was in fact a great warrior, who could only write in moments snatched from keeping his empire in order' ('Marcus Aurelias: the Kaiser of Carnuntum', www.didaskalia.net/issues/vol2no3/harrison.html [accessed 28 September 2019]).
59. My italics.
60. The date of the *Historia Augusta* is contested, but it most likely first appeared in the fourth century AD.

61. In 'Observing the Juggler: an actor's view', Rutter refers to the 'Castle car park in Carnuntum', which 'was proof positive that given the square yards and the Bleacher seats, plus a few cubic metres of sand, we can do *Trackers* anywhere' (Neil Astley, ed., *Bloodaxe Critical Anthologies 1: Tony Harrison* [Newcastle: Bloodaxe, 1991], p. 416).

62. Herbert, 'Carnuntum' notebook, JH/1/21, n.p.n.

63. In Rome's Conservatori museum, the *Imperial Clemency* (176–180 AD) relief displays Aurelias' alleged mercy, with an outstretched hand, to 'barbarian' prisoners of war. However, his retracted middle fingers betray a distaste towards the kneeling figures. Similarly, Commodus, trapped underneath Aurelias' tower in Herbert's stage set, potentially courts empathy as the verse play's equivalent of the relief's barbarians.

64. JH/3/54, n.p.n. (entry dated 21 July 1995).

65. As the notes to the Leeds performance explain, 'Miletos, an Athenian colony in Asia Minor (modern Turkey), was sacked by the Persians suppressing the Ionian revolt (499–493 B.C.) by Greek cities of Asia Minor. They slaughtered almost the entire male population, and enslaved the women and children. The Athenian tragedian Phrynichos wrote *The Capture of Miletus* in 494 B.C.: it is referred to in Harrison's play with its Greek title *Halosis Miletou*. If the historian Herodotus is to be believed, the play was too distressing for the Athenian audience, moving them to tears, and causing them to fine him for reminding them of their misfortune and to ban future performances.'

66. Harrison, *Plays Three*, p. 133.

67. Harrison, *Selected Poems*, pp. 179, 180.

68. Bertolt Brecht, *Poems 1913–1956*, eds. John Willett and Ralph Manheim (London: Methuen, 1987 [1976]), pp. 252–3.

69. Neil Astley, ed., *Bloodaxe Critical Anthologies 1: Tony Harrison*, p. 67.

70. Geoffrey Hill, *The Triumph of Love* (London/New York: Penguin, 1999 [1998]), p.82.

71. Hill deploys this term approvingly in his seventh lecture as Oxford Professor of Poetry in 2012 (http://media.podcasts.ox.ac.uk/engfac/poetry/2012-11-27-engfac-hill.mp3) (accessed 28 July 2020).

72. Theodor Adorno, 'Commitment', p. 191; Geoffrey Hill, *The Orchards of Syon* (London: Penguin, 2002), p. 1. 'Now' could be glossed as an emphatic, avuncular 'so'; or, more likely, as denoting that 'now', at this time, there is no due season.

73. T. S. Eliot, *Selected Poems* (London: Faber and Faber, 1954), p. 51.

74. Geoffrey Hill, The Orchards of Syon workbooks, BC MS 20c Hill/2/1/52, p. 9.

75. Hill, notebook 52, pp. 13, 19.

76. Hill, notebook 52, p. 14. 'Hippo' simultaneously connotes the hippocampus, which Hill associates with the Hippodrome the next time the theatre is mentioned in notebook fifty-three (pp. 84, 85).

77. T. S. Eliot, *Four Quartets* (London: Faber and Faber, 1959 [1941]), p. 26; Hill, notebook 52, p. 35. The 'shadows' in the draft for the first stanza soon encompass life's 'exits', and María Casares, who plays the princess 'who is Death' in Jean Cocteau's film *Orphée* (1950) (p. 9). Thinking 'ahead' in section III to the point when his dates will be 'crammed in' after his name (p. 3), the narrator is exasperated that there is no 'solution' to the fact that 'We are [. . .] near death' (p. 4). In notebook fifty-three, Hill is 'Newly into ageing' (53, p. 96), which finally becomes the struggle indicated in the bunched stresses at the beginning of section XLII: '**Up against age**ing and **dying**' (p. 42); this opening represents the 'Beautiful though grim' 'stamina' and stoicism required two sections earlier in XL (p. 40). In the notebook, Hill then begins – due to this ageing process – to 'fancy'

> the labour of flight: a low geared-heron
> returning to its pool; the way that gulls
> beat and tack; the man-o-war bird (53, p. 96)

'[O]ld dying' remains intertwined with the lyrical: the heron is 'retiring to its pool' in the next notebook (notebook 54, p. 13).

78. Hill, notebook 52, p. 35; Hill, *The Orchards of Syon*, p. 1.

79. Theodor Adorno, *Ästhetische Theorie* (Frankfurt am Main: Suhrkamp Verlag, 2014 [1970]), p. 184; *Aesthetic Theory*, p. 121.

80. 'Eboracum' originates from the Celtic 'Eburacon'. The 'Ebor Handicap' held at York is for horses three years and older. The cathedral has been beset in recent times by expensive repairs: extensive damage was caused by a fire in 1984; the renovation of the Great East Window (2007–18) cost an estimated twenty-three million pounds.

81. Derek Attridge discusses close readings that are too 'powerful' in his article 'Conjurers turn tricks on wizards' coat-tails', www.timeshighereducation.co.uk/story.asp?sectioncode=26&s (accessed 28 September 2019).

82. Adorno, *Aesthetic Theory*, p. 121.

83. I co-organised Hill's reading at the University of Salford with Jeffrey Wainwright on 1 July 2000.

84. Adorno, 'Commitment', p. 191.

85. *The Cantos of Ezra Pound* (New York: New Directions, 1996), p. 816.

86. Jeffrey Wainwright, *Acceptable Words: Essays on the Poetry of Geoffrey Hill* (Manchester: Manchester University Press, 2005), p. 120.

87. 'Stanley Edgar is Dead; Critic, Author and Teacher, 51', www.nytimes.com /1970/07/31/archives/stanley-edgar-hyman-is-dead-critic-author-and-teacher-51-bennington.html (accessed 28 September 2020).

88. The workbooks indicate Hill's struggle to achieve this majestic end to the third section: 'the maples torch the swamp', 'the swamp/maples put themselves to the torch', 'the swamp-maples torch the sun' and then (less convincingly) the 'swamp-maples torch the foxy wilderness' (notebook 52, p. 21).

89. Robert Macfarlane, 'Gravity and Grace in Geoffrey Hill', *Essays in Criticism*, 58(3) (2007), 237–56, p. 247.

90. Robert Macfarlane, 'Gravity and Grace in Geoffrey Hill', p. 251.

91. My italics.

92. T. S. Eliot, *Selected Poems*, p. 31.

93. Matthew Arnold, 'Dover Beach', in Kenneth Allott, ed., *Arnold: Poems* (London: Penguin, 1985 [1954]), pp. 181–2.

94. As Thomas Day notes, *The Orchards of Syon* is 'self-confessedly less angry, more forgiving, than its predecessor, *Speech! Speech!*' ('French Connections in Geoffrey Hill's *The Orchards of Syon*', *Essays in Criticism*, 6(1) (January 2010), 26–50, p. 26).

95. Theodor Adorno, 'Commitment', p. 177.

96. Ted Hughes, *Collected Poems* (London: Faber and Faber, 2003), p. 36.

97. Hill, Michaelmas term lecture 2012 (untitled), http://media.podcasts.ox.ac.uk/engfac/poetry/2012-11-27-engfac-hill.mp3 (accessed 28 September 2020).

98. See my discussion of this passage in *Holocaust Poetry*, pp. 76–7. I note that 'the reference to Daniel (3: 6) evokes specifically Jewish suffering (and triumph): when Nebuchadnezzar demanded that whoever did not worship his golden image be cast into the midst of a "burning fiery furnace" [. . .] By transforming the furnace into an image of the Holocaust [in *The Triumph of Love*], Hill simultaneously drains the narrative of any sense of triumph' (p. 76).

99. Paul Celan, *Breathturn into Timestead: the Collected Later Poetry*, trans. Pierre Joris (New York: Farrar Straus Giroux, 2014), p. 461.

100. John Felstiner, *Paul Celan: Poet, Survivor, Jew* (London: Yale University Press, 1995), p. 30.

101. John Lyon, 'Geoffrey Hill's Eye Troubles' in John Lyon and Peter McDonald, eds., *Geoffrey Hill: Essays on His Later Work* (Oxford: Oxford University Press, 2012), pp. 112–26, p. 118; Wainwright, *Acceptable Words*, p. 108. Lyon writes that 'this is a louder poetry, more unseemly and improperly behaved, more extremely self-disrupting in respect of both register and subject matter' (p. 118).

102. Jeremy Noel-Tod, 'Awkward Bow' (review of *The Orchards of Syon*), *London Review of Books*, 25(5) (6 March 2003), 27–8, p. 27.

103. Celan, *Breathturn into Timestead*, p. xl; Furlani, *Guy Davenport*, p. 150.

104. Celan, *Breathturn into Timestead*, p. xlvii.

105. Rowland, *Holocaust Poetry*, p. 62.

106. Felstiner, *Paul Celan*, pp. 165, 167.

107. Theodor Adorno, *Minima Moralia*, trans. E. F. N. Jephcott (London: Verso, 1978 [1951]), p. 25.

108. Brecht, *Poems 1913–1956*, pp. 330–1, p. 331. The 'house-painter' is, of course, Hitler. In 'To Those Born Later' (1938), Brecht similarly asks what 'kind of times are they, when | A talk about trees is almost a crime | Because it implies silence about so many horrors' (pp. 318–9, p. 318).

109. Felstiner, *Paul Celan*, p. 92.

110. April Warman, 'Language and Grace', *The Oxonian Review*, 3(1) (15 December 2003) (www.oxonianreview.org/wp/geoffrey-hill-the-orchards-of-syon) accessed 28 September 2020); Adorno, 'Commitment', p. 177. In 'Geoffrey Hill: The Corpus of Absolution', Ernest Hilbert notes that the title also refers to 'a translation of St. Catherine of Siena's *Dialogo*, a series of meditations on the division between God and the human soul' (www.cprw.com/Hibert/hill.htm) (accessed 4 June 2019).

111. Lunn, *Marxism and Modernism*, p. 155.

112. Stanley Mitchell, 'Introduction', in Walter Benjamin, *Understanding Brecht*, trans. Anna Bostock (London: New Left Books, 1973 [1966]), pp. vii–xix, p. ix.

113. Furlani, *Guy Davenport*, p. 150; Tom Kuhn and Steve Giles, eds., *Brecht on Art and Politics* (London: Methuen, 2003), p. 25.

114. Cook, 'The Figure of Enigma: Rhetoric, History and Poetry', p. 352; *Brecht on Art and Politics*, p. 47; Adorno, 'Commitment', pp. 177, 188.

115. I am referring back here to Adorno's phrase 'uncompromising radicalism' in 'Commitment', p. 188.

4 Iconoclasm and Enigmatical Commitment

1. Eleanor Cook, 'The Figure of Enigma: Rhetoric, History and Poetry', *Rhetorica: A Journal of the History of Rhetoric*, 19(4) (2001), 349–78, p. 352.

2. Kayo Chingonyi, '"It has to appear like a gift": An Interview with Ahren Warner', 16 June 2013, https://kayochingonyi.com/2013/06/16/it-has-to-appear-like-a-gift-an-interview-with-ahren-warner/ (accessed 5 June 2020).

3. Franz Kafka, *The Blue Octavo Notebooks* (Cambridge, Massachusetts: Exact Change Books, 2016 [1948]), p. 26; Theodor W. Adorno, *Aesthetic Theory*, eds.

Gretel Adorno and Rolf Tiedemann, trans. Robert Hullot-Kentor (London: The Athlone Press, 1997 [1970]), p. 165.

4. David James, *The Legacies of Modernism: Historicising Postwar and Contemporary Fiction* (Cambridge: Cambridge University Press, 2011), p. 2; Douglas Mao and Rebecca L. Walkowitz, eds., *Bad Modernisms* (Durham, North Carolina: Duke University Press, 2006), p. 3.

5. Ahren Warner, *Pretty* (Newcastle: Bloodaxe, 2013), p. 79; *Confer* (Newcastle: Bloodaxe, 2011), p. 41.

6. James, *The Legacies of Modernism*, p. 3.

7. Tony Williams, 'You ask for a song' (review of *Confer*), *Magma*, 52 (March 2012), 57–8, p. 58; Michael Woods, review of *Pretty*, *Iota*, 93 (2013), 131–2, p. 132.

8. Chingonyi, '"It has to appear like a gift": An Interview with Ahren Warner', 16 June 2013, https://kayochingonyi.com/2013/06/16/it-has-to-appear-like-a-gift-an-interview-with-ahren-warner/ (accessed 5 June 2020).

9. As I noted in the Introduction, Hill makes these comments about Pound and Eliot in his November 2011 lecture as Oxford Professor of Poetry, www.english.ox.ac.uk/professor-sir-geoffrey-hill-lectures (accessed 29 September 2020).

10. Charles Simic and Don Paterson, eds., *New British Poetry* (St Paul, Minnesota: Graywolf Press, 2004), p. xxiii; Theodor W. Adorno, *Aesthetic Theory*, p. 125.

11. In her review of *Confer*, Carol Rumens notes that 'Having positioned itself against difficulty, Bloodaxe has made a sensible revision in adding Ahren Warner to its list' ('Medium, Conjurer, Flâneur' [*Poetry Review*, 101(4) (winter 2011), 95–8, p. 97]). Nevertheless, as I discuss later in this chapter, Bloodaxe has also published the work of, for example, J. H. Prynne, B. S. Johnson and Basil Bunting.

12. Don Paterson, *Rain* (London: Faber and Faber, 2009), p. 58.

13. Roddy Lumsden, ed., *Identity Parade: New British and Irish Poets* (Newcastle: Bloodaxe, 2010), p. 103.

14. James Byrne, *Blood/Sugar* (Todmorden: Arc, 2009), p. 71.

15. Richard Burton, *A Strong Song Tows Us: the Life of Basil Bunting* (Oxford: Infinite Ideas Ltd, 2013), p. 206.

16. Burton, *A Strong Song Tows Us*, p. 105.

17. As with David James's incisive and expansive exploration of form in *Discrepant Solace* (Cambridge: Cambridge University Press, 2019), I invoke the word to indicate 'stylistic tenor and texture, idioms of diction, syntactical and rhythmic connotations, as well as the overarching organization of a given narrative' (p. 6).

18. Peter Howarth, *The Cambridge Introduction to Modernist Poetry* (Cambridge: Cambridge University Press, 2012), p. 215.
19. Adorno, *Aesthetic Theory*, pp. 34, 35.
20. Andre Furlani, *Guy Davenport: Postmodern and After* (Evanston, Illinois: Northwestern University Press, 2007), p. 150; James, *The Legacies of Modernism*, p. 3.
21. Outsiders are vulnerable as well as distinctive, as when Bardamu registers his outlandish cowardice as a World War One solider, at the same time as he remains, like his comrades, 'meat' for the enemy (Louis-Ferdinand Céline, *Journey to the End of the Night*, trans. Ralph Manheim [Richmond: Alma, 2012 (1932)], p. 15). The description of the colonel as 'tangled meat' connects with the portrayal, three pages later, of the regiment's rations as 'pounds and pounds of gut, chunks of white and yellow fat, disembowelled sheep with their organs every which way, oozing little rivulets into the grass' (p. 18).
22. James, *The Legacies of Modernism*, p. 2.
23. Francis Scarfe, ed., *Baudelaire: The Complete Verse* (London: Anvil, 1986), p. 203.
24. Michael Rothberg, *The Implicated Subject: Beyond Victims and Perpetrators* (Stanford: Stanford University Press, 2019), p. 1.
25. Ahren Warner, *Hello. Your Promise has been Extracted* (Newcastle: Bloodaxe, 2017), p. 76.
26. James Byrne, '*I am a Rohingya:* Poetry from the World's Largest Refugee Camp and Beyond', *Kenyan Review* (https://kenyonreview.org/kr-online-issue/literary-activism/selections/james-byrne-763879) (accessed 9 June 2020).
27. Adorno, *Aesthetic Theory*, p. 125.
28. James, *Legacies of Modernism*, p. 3.
29. In Artaud's essay 'Coleridge the Traitor', the Romantic poet is dismissed as 'a weakling' (*Anthology*, trans. Jack Hirschman [San Francisco: City Lights, 1965], pp. 128–34, pp. 134). In his 'Letter against the Kabbala' (4 June 1947) (pp. 113–23) he states that he 'abhors' the 'old kike spirit' in Kafka's work. Despite Artaud's assertion to Madame Toulouse in October 1924 that there was 'nothing doing' with Surrealism, by 10 November, his photograph appeared in the first issue of *La Révolution surrealiste*, co-edited by Pierre Naville and Benjamin Péret, that also contained work by Breton and Pierre Riverdy (Ronald Hayman, *Artaud and After* [Oxford: Oxford University Press, 1977], pp. 54–5). He broke with Surrealism in summer 1926, after he tried 'to act as mediator between Breton and Jean Paulhan, who had been appointed editor of the *N.R.F.* when Rivière died in 1925' (p. 63). In November 1925, Artaud was officially expelled from the group after a meeting at Café de la Prophète, and referred to in the minutes as

a 'decaying carcass' (p. 64). Artaud's 'outsider' status thus does not equate with that of the Surrealists in general: whilst 'the iconoclasm of the other Surrealists was charged with *joe de vivre*', Artaud, as Breton put it, '"carried around with him the landscape of a Gothic novel, torn by flashes of lightning"' (p. 63).

30. Hayman, *Artaud and After*, p. 55.
31. Antonin Artaud, *Collected Works*, volume I, trans. Victor Corti (London: Caldar and Boyars, 1968), p. 76. In 'Van Gogh: The Man Suicided by Society', Artaud contends that 'a sick society invented psychiatry to defend itself against the investigation of certain visionaries whose faculties of divination disturbed it' (*Anthology*, p. 135).
32. Warner, *Pretty*, p. 64; Artaud, *Anthology*, p. 34.
33. Artaud, *Anthology*, p. 35; Antonin Artaud, *Oeuvres Complètes*, volume I (Pais: Gallimard, 1956), p. 89.
34. Warner, *Pretty*, pp. 66, 70; Adorno, *Aesthetic Theory*, p. 120.
35. Warner, *Pretty*, p. 64; Adorno, *Aesthetic Theory*, p. 118.
36. Warner, *Pretty*, pp. 68, 67; Geoffrey Hill, 'Poetry, Policing and Public Order (1)', www.english.ox.ac.uk/professor-sir-geoffrey-hill-lectures (accessed 12 July 2020).
37. Warner, *Pretty*, p. 64.
38. Artaud, *Collected Works*, p. 76.
39. Artaud, *Oeuvres Complètes*, p. 87; Warner, *Pretty*, p. 63; Artaud, *Anthology*, p. 38.
40. Philip Larkin, *Letters to Monica*, ed. Anthony Thwaite (London: Faber and Faber, 2010), p. 319.
41. Artaud, *Oeuvres Complètes*, p. 76.
42. Artaud, *Oeuvres Complètes*, p. 87; Artaud, *Anthology*, p. 26.
43. Artaud, *Anthology*, p. 38.
44. Adorno, *Aesthetic Theory*, p. 118; Artaud, *Anthology*, p. 38.
45. Artaud, *Oeuvres Complètes*, p. 95; Warner, *Pretty*, p. 72; Artaud, *Anthology*, p. 38; Artaud, *Collected Works*, p. 75.
46. James, *The Legacies of Modernism*, p. 3.
47. Artaud, *Oeuvres Complètes*, p. 95; Warner, *Pretty*, p. 72.
48. Artaud, *Collected Works*, p. 76.
49. Artaud's dismissal in this passage of the intellectual as 'pigshit' (*Anthology*, p. 38) works its way into the texture of Warner's collection as whole. 'Metousiosis' in *Pretty*, for example, contains a strikingly Artaudian declaration:

> So many nights I wake to find myself like this,
> tracing the contours of my self – near catatonic – [. . .]
> where, beneath the glaze of *cogitans*, touch
> can trigger surety – flesh and bone assurance —
> beyond this party trick of intellect (p. 45)

'[C]ontours', 'catatonic', 'nerves', 'touch', 'flesh', 'bone', 'intellect': the lexical field of 'Nervometer' infiltrates this passage from 'Metousiosis'. Moreover, 'this party trick of intellect' recalls the 'all writing is pigshit' section from *Le Pèse-Nerfs* (*Anthology*, p. 38), and the line from part one of 'Nervometer', 'You must not admit too much literature' (*Pretty*, p. 63). Warner begins the last line of his translated sequence with a word absent from the original French, 'Uncovered' (p. 75), that emphasises a state beyond speech: similarly, 'Metousiosis' contrasts the 'surety' of the naked, and blemished, body with the 'party trick of intellect' (p. 45). The 'party trick' of 'Metousiosis', with its references to Rainer Maria Rilke's 'Second Elegy', Paul Cezanne, Egon Schiele and Aeschylus, would no doubt have incurred Artaud's scathing tone: artistic references are entirely absent from *Le Pèse-Nerfs*. If the momentarily iconoclastic dismissal of intellect constitutes Furlani's metamodernist 'continuity' from *Le Pèse-Nerfs*, then the 'departure' lies in Warner's focus in this passage on the poet-narrator's bodily minutiae, such as the alienated hand that becomes a 'puppet', to the extent that 'flesh and bone' provides succour to the poet's nocturnal angst. In contrast, Artaud's corporeal '*minutiae*' – apart from the machinations of the 'skull' (p. 67) – are almost entirely absent from *Le Pèse-Nerfs*: there is no sense that the somatic can provide a reassuring alternative to the insubstantial 'mental substance' of 'res cogitans'.

50. Eliot, *Selected Poems*, p. 11.

51. James, *Discrepant Solace*, p. 7.

52. Paul McDonald, 'From Paris to Emerging Poets', *Envoi*, 169 (February 2015), 72–6, p. 73 (my italics). Michael Woods similarly refers to an 'attractive edginess to this sequence that engages with a destabilising Artaudian impulse' (p. 132).

53. T. S. Eliot, ed., *Literary Chapters of Ezra Pound* (London: Faber and Faber, 1960), p. 12. Pound is writing specifically about neo-Georgian poetry.

54. Hayman, *Artaud and After*, p. 37.

55. *OED*, 2nd edn.

56. Warner, *Pretty*, p. 72.

57. Warner, *Confer*, p. 64.

58. Artaud, *Anthology*, pp. 322–7.

59. The French poet's radical theory of the 'theatre of cruelty' is alluded to here in relation to film: Warner compares Artaud's conception of theatre as an unsettling space in which an audience needs to confront and exorcise its worst fears to the cathartic propensities of contemporary thrillers. Artaud detected in early film an artistic form in which his 'theatre of cruelty' might thrive, but he grew to deplore the 'star'-based system of Hollywood, despite his brief career as an actor in the 1920s: Warner alludes to his largest film role,

in *Napoléon* (1927), directed by 'Monsieur [Abel] Gance' (*Pretty*, p. 15). At the poem's closure, Warner refers to Artaud's grimace, in a suitably Surrealist fashion, as a 'Messerschmidt', which, in turn, gestures towards the French poet's internment during World War Two. This 'grimace' is finally described in a register and diction that anticipates *Le Pèse-Nerfs*: the 'Messerschmidt' is 'galvanic' (p. 15), an adjective that denotes a sudden production of an electric current; the phrase also subtly evokes Artaud's shock treatment for mental illness in Rodez.

60. F. Scott Fitzgerald, *The Great Gatsby* (London: Penguin, 1950 [1926]), p. 59.

61. Ezra Pound, '*Dans un Omnibus de Londres*', *Collected Shorter Poems* (London: Faber and Faber, 1968), p. 160.

62. Andrew Thacker, *Modernism, Space and the City* (Edinburgh: Edinburgh University Press, 2019), pp. 172, 179.

63. Albert Bermel, *Artaud's Theatre of Cruelty* (London/New York: Methuen, 2001 [1977]), p. 28; Thacker, p. 179.

64. Richard Aldington, 'In the Tube', *The Egoist*, 2(5) (1 May 2015), 74. In 'A Fresh look at Arthur Rimbaud's "Métropolitain"', Michael Spencer outlines the French poet's appreciation of the London underground in 1872 during his peregrinations with Paul Verlaine (*Modern Language Review* 63[4] [October 1968], 849–53). The abstract, 'vivid and unexpected colours' in Rimbaud's poem contrast with Aldington and Warner's focus on the passengers, rather than disturbing scenery that gives way to the respite of the pastoral (p. 851).

65. Warner, *Confer*, p. 30.

66. Artaud, *Anthology*, p. 158.

67. Peter Jones, ed., *Imagist Poetry* (Harmondsworth: Penguin, 2001 [1972]), p. x.

68. Bermel, *Artaud's Theatre of Cruelty*, p. 28.

69. Warner, *Confer*, p. 30; Aldington, 'In the Tube', p. 74. Similarly, F. S. Flint looks 'in vain for a sign, | For a light' in the eyes of the 'mass' in his poem 'Tube' (*Otherworld Cadences* [London: Poetry Bookshop, 1920], p. 36). However, Flint's poem differs from Aldington's (and Warner's) in that the 'mass' is not beyond coercion: poets can 'leaven' it until the crowd 'changes', and attains an artistic 'spirit that moves'.

70. Artaud, *Anthology*, p. 158; Jones, ed., *Imagist Poetry*, p. x; Warner, *Confer*, p. 30.

71. *OED*, 2nd edn; Ezra Pound, 'Hugh Selwyn Mauberley', in *Ezra Pound: Selected Poems 1908–1959* (London: Faber and Faber, 1975), pp. 98–112, p. 101.

72. Aldington, 'In the Tube', p. 74.

73. Deborah L. Parsons, *Streetwalking the Metropolis: Women, the City and Modernity* (Oxford: Oxford University Press, 2000), p. 25.

74. Hill, 'Poetry, Policing and Public Order (1)', www.english.ox.ac.uk/professor-sir-geoffrey-hill-lectures (accessed 12 July 2020).

75. Parsons, *Streetwalking the Metropolis*, p. 3; Warner, *Confer*, p. 30.

76. Céline, *Journey to the End of the Night*, p. 18.

77. Thacker, *Modernism, Space and the City*, p. 180.

78. Warner, *Confer*, p. 30.

79. Warner refers to Apollinaire in section XIV in relation to his alleged stealing of the *Mona Lisa* (*Pretty*, p. 26). Due to his foreign background, and radical views, Apollinaire was considered to be a prime suspect, and was arrested on 22 August 1911, but released after five days. Two years later, Vincenzo Perggia, an ex-employee of the Louvre, was arrested when he attempted to sell the painting to an art dealer.

80. This incident occurred on 25 August 1944: there are at least three different versions of the story; in the least plausible one, Hemingway offers Picasso a scrap of an SS uniform, and claims he killed the soldier who owned it. It is unclear how Warner intends the reader to interpret this story. The pun on grenadine/grenade, in addition to the phrases that describe Picasso's activity before the incident – he 'would wander' past the Gestapo, and 'natter' over a coffee – perhaps imply opprobrium of the painter's civilian status during the war, as opposed to Hemingway's inclusion in the liberating US army (*Pretty*, p. 19).

81. Peter Buse, Ken Hirschkop, Scott McCracken and Bertrand Taithe, *Benjamin's Arcades: An unguided tour* (Manchester: Manchester University Press, 2005), p. 4.

82. Furlani, *Guy Davenport*, p. 150.

83. Francis Scarfe, ed., *Baudelaire*, p. 179.

84. Buse et al, *Benjamin's Arcades*, p. 53.

85. James, *The Legacies of Modernism*, p. 3.

86. Warner's interest in the word '*désinvolte*' links to Adorno's reference to '*désinvolture*' in *Aesthetic Theory* that encapsulates the lyric poet's 'dispensation from the strictures of logic' (p. 55).

87. Artaud, *Anthology*, p. 38.

88. Philip Larkin, *Collected Poems* (London: Faber and Faber, 1988), p. 102.

89. Francis Scarfe, ed., *Baudelaire*, p. 16. The '*putain*' also forms a specific intertextual link: 'Paquette' refers to a prostitute in Voltaire's *Candide* (1759), who infects Pangloss with syphilis and later squanders the protagonist's money. The full passage from *Les Fleurs du Mal* is as follows:

> *Aimi qu'un débauché pauvre qui baise et mange*
> *Le sein martyrisé d'une antique catin,*
> *Nous volons au passage un plaisir clandestin*
> *Que nous pressons bien fort comme une vieille orange*

Scarfe translates this as: 'Like any poverty-stricken lecher who kisses and nibbles an old whore's martyred breasts, we steal more furtive pleasure on the way down and squeeze it to the last drop like a wizened orange' (p. 53).

90. Hayman, *Artaud and After*, p. 6.

91. Baudelaire rails against prostitution as an 'ant-heap', weaving 'its furtive passage everywhere, like an enemy planning a surprise attack; it burrows through the city's filth like a worm filching away men's food' (*Baudelaire*, p. 189). The translator detects sarcasm in Baudelaire's '*Les femmes de plaisir*' in 'Morning Twilight', and translates the phrase as 'The women of "pleasure"', with the added 'rubber gloves' of quotation marks (p. 203). As in the passage about the 'ant-heap', Baudelaire's moral stance is clear: these women have '*la paupière livide,* | *Bouche ouverte, dormaient de leur sommeil stupide*' ('with bleary eyelids and gaping mouths, [they] were sleeping their stupid sleep') (p. 203).

92. The stark differences between these two playwrights have often been remarked: Artaud's emphasis on popular theatre as a form of catharsis, 'a facing of the worst that could happen', for example, contrasts with Brecht's sense of socialist education through his *Lehrstücke*, which I discussed in Chapter 3. However, they do concur that theatre is not a space for the 'culinary' but a 'social necessity' – even if some form of vicarious pleasure might inevitably be involved (Bermel, *Artaud's Theatre of Cruelty*, pp. 14, 11).

93. It could be argued that Warner's satire forms a specifically postmodernist, rather than modernist-influenced, diatribe against the 'culinary', since postmodernist writers such as Bret Easton Ellis and J. G. Ballard similarly critique rampant commodification in their novels. However, the difference lies in Ballard and Ellis's simultaneous fascination with the subject matter from popular culture that they criticise in novels such as *American Psycho* (1991), *The Atrocity Exhibition* (1970) and *Crash* (1973).

94. Parsons, *Streetwalking the Metropolis*, p. 10.

95. Adorno, *Aesthetic Theory*, pp. 225–6; Warner, *Hello. Your Promise has been Extracted*, p. 92.

96. Adorno, *Aesthetic Theory*, p. 226; Warner, *Pretty*, pp. 18, 13.

97. This incident was due, as the poet-narrator intimates, to the corrupt activities of the companies dominating the port, and traffic on the Hai river towards Beijing: with little external oversight, inter-family corruption and illegal hiring practices, the explosion was a direct result of unregulated capitalism, rather than merely an accident.

98. Rothberg, *The Implicated Subject*, p. 1.

99. Jade Cuttle, 'The talented poets living in the world's largest refugee camp', *The Daily Telegraph*, 26 July 2019, 25–6, p. 25.

100. James Byrne and Shehzar Doja, eds., *I am a Rohingya: Poetry from the Camps and Beyond* (Todmorden: Arc, 2019).

101. James Byrne, *Places You Leave* (Todmorden: Arc, 2021), p. 7.

102. Adorno, *Aesthetic Theory*, p. 120; Byrne, *Places You Leave*, p. 7.

103. Byrne, '*I am a Rohingya:* Poetry from the World's Largest Refugee Camp and Beyond', https://kenyonreview.org/kr-online-issue/literary-activism/se lections/james-byrne-763879 (accessed 10 June 2020).

104. Byrne and Doja, eds., *I am a Rohingya*, p. 32.

105. *The Cantos of Ezra Pound* (New York: New Directions, 1996), p. 816.

106. James, *Discrepant Solace*, p. 24.

107. Adorno, *Aesthetic Theory*, p. 125.

108. Adorno, *Aesthetic Theory*, p. 125; T. S. Eliot, 'Tradition and the Individual Talent', *Selected Essays* (London: Faber and Faber, 1951 [1932]), pp. 13–22, p. 21.

109. Adorno, *Aesthetic Theory*, p. 120; James, *Discrepant Solace*, p. 27.

110. James, *Discrepant Solace*, p. 27.

111. W. B. Yeats, *Selected Poetry*, ed. A. Norman Jeffares (London: Pan, 1974 [1962]), p. 99.

112. James Byrne, *The Caprices* (Todmorden: Arc, 2020), pp. 64, 51.

113. Victor I. Stoichita and Anna Maria Coderch draw attention to ambiguity within the image too, but only in terms of its 'sexual undertones', rather than visual identification: 'it will probably always be impossible to determine with any certainty whether the satire of avarice also contains sexual undertones, as the two purses featured in the foreground and certain ambiguous gestures in the middle distance might lead us to believe' (*Goya: The Last Carnival* [London: Reaktion Books, 1999], p. 203).

114. There is a comparable ambiguity in the '*Tantalus*' image. Tantalus' wringing of hands may denote his impotency in the face of the young woman draped across his stomach. The sturdy blocks in the image contrast, in this reading, with the frailties of human desire; nature, and natural desires, are squashed into the side of the frame. However, Byrne's last line, 'the shadow weight of sky across a tomb', hints at another possibility, in which the thwarted desire is at the expense of the dead woman; the diagonal line in the top right-hand corner of the frame mirrors the slanted line of the raised tomb later in the sequence, in '*And still they don't go!*' (p. 80). Just as Tantalus' son Pelops in Greek myth was offered as a sacrifice to the gods, Tantalus pleads with the gods in the poem for his son's reincarnation (Hermes gave life again to Pelops in the original myth). This possibility is even clearer in Byrne's first version of the poem in *Everything Broken Up Dances* (North Adams: Tupelo Press, 2015), in which Tantalus is 'ghosting Hades', and 'crush[es] [his] love under a tombstone' (p. 38).

115. Adorno, *Aesthetic Theory*, p. 129.

116. The original poem has 'Blake's', but I presume this possessive is a misprint. I have decided to correct the original, rather than insert an obtrusive '[*sic*]' or '[Blakes]' within the line's parentheses.

117. Ben Jacobs and Oliver Laughland, 'Charlottesville: Trump reverts to blaming both sides including "violent alt-left"', www.theguardian.com/us-news/2017/aug/15/donald-trump-press-conference-far-right-defends-charlottesville (accessed 20 April 2020).

118. *Poems of Mr John Milton* (London: Humphrey Moseley, 1645), p. 104.

119. Percy Bysshe Shelley, *The Major Works*, eds. Zachary Leader and Michael O'Neill (Oxford: Oxford University Press, 2003), pp. 400–11, p. 404.

120. James Byrne, *Withdrawals* (Newton-le-Willows: Knives Forks and Spoons Press, 2019), p. 21

121. *Poems of John Milton* (London/New York: Thomas Nelson and Sons Ltd, n.p.d), p. 9.

122. Adorno, *Aesthetic Theory*, p. 225.

123. Adorno, *Aesthetic Theory*, p. 126; James Byrne, *White Coins* (Todmorden: Arc, 2015), p. 14.

124. *OED*, 2nd edn.

125. James, *Discrepant Solace*, p. 27; Byrne, *White Coins*, p. 11.

126. James, *Discrepant Solace*, p. 27.

127. Adorno, *Aesthetic Theory*, pp. 121, 126.

128. Geoffrey Hill, The Orchards of Syon workbooks, notebook 52, BC MS 20c Hill/2/1/52, p. 35.

129. Hill, notebook 52, p. 35.

130. Paul Stubbs, review of *Blood/Sugar*, *The Black Herald*, 1 (January 2011), 34–6, p. 36.

131. Byrne, *Blood/Sugar*, pp. 72, 75; Ted Hughes, *Collected Poems* (London: Faber and Faber, 2003), pp. 33–4, p. 34.

132. Helen Carr, *The Verse Revolutionaries: Ezra Pound, H.D. and the Imagists* (Harmondsworth: Penguin, 2013), p. 462.

133. www.bloodaxebooks.com/about (accessed 10 April 2020).

134. Adorno, *Aesthetic Theory*, pp. 115–16.

135. Eliot, 'Tradition and the Individual Talent', p. 17.

136. James, *Modernist Futures*, p. 89.

137. Julian Barnes, *The Sense of an Ending* (London: Vintage, 2012 [2011]), p. 22. The 'wrangle for the ring' here echoes Larkin's poem 'Wild Oats', and 'Dockery and Son' is referred to twice on page 104. Webster's prayer for the ordinary also recalls Larkin's 'Born Yesterday' that praises 'Nothing uncustomary' (Philip Larkin, *Collected Poems* [London: Faber and Faber, 1988], p. 84). This poem was penned for the christening of Kingsley Amis's daughter, Sally. As with Larkin's positive appraisal of

Hull's ordinariness throughout his later life, Webster contends that he is 'not odd enough not to have done the things I've ended up doing with my life' (p. 64).

138. Zadie Smith, *NW* (London: Penguin, 2013 [2012]), pp. 28, 29.
139. Adorno, *Aesthetic Theory*, pp. 124, 122, 121.

5 The Double Consciousness of Modernism

1. Roddy Lumsden, ed., *Identity Parade: New British and Irish Poets* (Newcastle: Bloodaxe, 2010), p. 103.
2. Sandeep Parmar, 'Not a British Subject: Poetry and Race in the UK', https://lareviewofbooks.org/article/not-a-british-subject-race-and-poetry-in-the-uk (accessed 19 May 2019).
3. Michael Bell, *Literature, Modernism and Myth: Belief and Responsibility in the Twentieth Century* (Cambridge: Cambridge University Press, 1997), p. 78.
4. Edith Hall mentions this text in *The Return of Ulysses: A Cultural History of Homer's Odyssey* (Baltimore: The Johns Hopkins University Press, 2008), pp. 133–4. There are relatively few pre-modernist examples of the fictionalisation of myth in Hall's wide-ranging book, such as Pavel Katenin's *The Old Soldier Gorev* (1835), which transfers the *Odyssey* to 'a real, Russian contemporary community' set during the Napoleonic Wars (p. 25).
5. Bell, *Literature, Modernism and Myth*, p. 34.
6. Andre Furlani, *Guy Davenport: Postmodern and After* (Evanston, Illinois: Northwestern University Press, 2007); David James and Urmila Seshagiri, 'Metamodernism: Narratives of Continuity and Revolution', *PMLA*, 129(1) (2014), 87–98.
7. Theodor W. Adorno, *Aesthetic Theory*, eds. Gretel Adorno and Rolf Tiedemann, trans. Robert Hullot-Kentor (London: The Athlone Press, 1997 [1970]), p. 126.
8. Hall, *The Return of Ulysses*, p. 52.
9. I am grateful to my colleague Dr David Miller for our discussions about myth, Romanticism and fictionality.
10. Alfred Tennyson, *Poetical Works* (London/New York: Oxford University Press, 1959 [1953]), p. 51.
11. T. S. Eliot, 'The Waste Land', in *The Norton Anthology of English Literature*, Volume 2 (New York/London: W. W. Norton, 2006), p. 2302.
12. Michael McKeon, *The Origins of the English Novel, 1600–1740* (Baltimore, Maryland: Johns Hopkins University Press, 2002 [1987]).
13. Ezra Pound, *The Cantos of Ezra Pound* (New York: New Directions, 1993 [1973]), p. 3; Theodor W. Adorno and Max Horkheimer, *Dialectic of*

Enlightenment, trans. John Cummins (London: Verso, 1986 [1944]), p. 46. As Hall notes, Pound's project 'is more than a Modernist plunge into the abyss of myth: he is creating his own version of the poet's traditional homage to the *Odyssey* as the very text that he rightly believed constitutes the source of the Western poetic subject' (*The Return of Ulysses*, p. 25). Working with the original texts was essential to Pound's philosophy: 'Better mendacities', as he puts it in 'Hugh Selwyn Mauberley', than 'the classics in paraphrase!' (*Selected Poems 1908–1959* [London: Faber and Faber, 1975], p. 99).

14. Bell, *Literature, Modernism and Myth*, p. 78; Adorno and Horkheimer, *Dialectic of Enlightenment*, p. 46.

15. This counterpointing is central to many other of Harrison's dramatic works, such as *Akin Mata* (1966) and *The Common Chorus* (1992), as a 'combination of fixed form and fleeting content' (Tony Harrison, *Collected Film Poetry* [London: Faber and Faber, 2007], p. xi). I am grateful to Dr Rachel Bower from the University of Leeds for pointing out this quotation, and for our discussions about *Akin Mata*.

16. Antony Rowland, *Holocaust Poetry* (Edinburgh: Edinburgh University Press, 2005), p. 101.

17. Michael Rothberg, *Multidirectional Memories: Remembering the Holocaust in the Age of Decolonisation* (Stanford: Stanford University Press, 2009), p. 3.

18. Hall tracks the multitudinous reimaginings of *The Odyssey* in the work of, for example, Pound and Joyce. It is telling that Prometheus rather than Odysseus is more predominant in Harrison's work. There is certainly an Odyssesian sensibility behind *V* (1985) that tracks the poet's journey from his Beeston youth to exile in the geographical specificities of north Leeds, and in which the skinhead appears as a kind of ghost in a libation that ironically invokes the spirit of the living poet. Yet it is Harrison's reconstruction of the atrocities of the twentieth century via Prometheus that predominates in his later work. Harrison may well have been reacting to what Adorno and Horkheimer evaluate as Odysseus' bourgeois propensities. In a wonderfully tongue-in-cheek passage in *Dialectic of Enlightenment*, they undercut Odysseus' attempt to prove his identity to Penelope through his detailed account of his construction of their marriage bed: Odysseus is 'the proto-typical bourgeois – the with-it hobbyist [imitating] the actual labor [*sic*] of a craftsman' (p. 74). In the archive of Harrison's correspondence in the Brotherton Library, Harrison also documents his struggle to find a modern idiom for Homeric Greek (BC MS 20c Harrison OS/FAD-RBL Correspondence). Harrison has been asked to consider a radio drama adaptation of *The Odyssey* for the BBC, and responds as follows: 'I've immersed myself again in the Greek text with a lot of excitement though I couldn't, for all my attempts, find a modern way into it that would have

made my own style take off [. . .] after a lot of soul-searching I have to give priority to my original work. The piece I am working on is a large scale theatre work and it would be hard to alternate the work with translating and dramatizing *The Odyssey* (letter to Janet Whitaker, 11 June 2002, p. 1).

19. Sandeep Parmar, *Eidolon* (Bristol: Shearsman Books, 2015), p. 65. Parmar argues that Woolf's point is that 'we essentially cannot *know* the Greeks because we are so culturally different and their age was not one of aesthetic "schools" or development phases but one that was somehow locked crystalline into a monolithic antiquity' (p. 64). However, Woolf's essay 'On Not Knowing Greek' in *The Common Reader* (London/Toronto: The Hogarth Press, 1975 [1925]) is actually more about 'knowing' Greek: she suggests, for example, that we 'know' Electra through her dialogue (p. 43). Readers are also impressed by 'heroism itself' (p. 44) in *Electra* (414–420 BCE) and *Antigone* (441 BCE). Allegedly, we appreciate Antigone, Ajax and Electra as the 'originals' of the human character, as opposed to Chaucer's mere 'varieties of the human species' in the *Canterbury Tales* (1387–1400) (p. 44). Nevertheless, Woolf stresses that there are geographical, historical and linguistic reasons for this seemingly 'impersonal' literature, so that 'they admit to us a vision of the earth unravaged, the sea unpolluted, the maturity, tried but unbroken, of mankind' (pp. 54–5). Contemporary readers do not know 'how the words sounded, or where precisely we ought to laugh, or how the actors acted' (p. 39).

20. Simon Armitage, 'On Tony Harrison', *Stand*, no. 215, Vol. 15 (3), 2017, 7–11, p. 8.

21. This proto-modernist influence arises in one of the most quoted stanzas from *V*: 'You piss-artist skinhead cunt, you wouldn't know | and it doesn't fucking matter if you do, | the skin and poet united fucking Rimbaud | but the *autre* that *je est* is fucking you' (*Selected Poems*, p. 242). In an effort to both widen and close the distance between the poet and skinhead, Harrison reverts to 'T.W.' in order to distinguish his learning from the skinhead, at the same time as the demotic language draws the poet into his interlocutor's linguistic ambit. Of all the examples in literature that Harrison could have drawn from in his specific case of othering, it is telling that he deploys a proto-modernist influence from over twenty years earlier. The French writer is a sign of the poet's cultural supremacy over the skinhead, but Rimbaud is also integrated in this stanza's vision of someone who can encapsulate, like the French author, the 'skin and poet'. Yet there is also something odd about the meaning of these lines, and the way Rimbaud is deployed, that goes beyond the hidden inference of Harrison 'hating' the skinhead through the aural pun on '*je est*', which sounds the same as '*je hais*' ('I hate'). Harrison's quotation from Rimbaud's work comes from *Lettres du Voyant* (1871), and Rimbaud's

letters to Charles Izambard and Paul Demeny. '*Je* est autre' comes from a passage which (in Marjorie Perloff's translation) reads: 'It is wrong to say: I think. One ought to say: I am being thought | I is another. If brass wakes up a trumpet, it is not its fault' (*The Poetics of Indeterminacy: Rimbaud to Cage* [Evanston, Illinois: Northwestern University Press, 1983 (1981)], p. 60). Trumpeting his erudition, the poet nevertheless acknowledges his origins in the 'brass' of working-class culture that encompasses the skinhead. Perloff understands these lines from Rimbaud's letter to mean that 'the "schizoid" poet stands back and inspects his "moi" as if it belonged to somebody else' (p. 61). Harrison's deployment of Rimbaud thus induces a selective reading of his letters and poetry, since Harrison does not wish to create a 'verbal field where the identity of the "I" is dissolved' (p. 62). This impacts on a reading of the quoted stanza, since Harrison as poet-figure insists oddly that it 'doesn't matter' if the skinhead knows Rimbaud's work, or understands what 'the *autre* that je est' means (*Selected Poems*, p. 242). The Rimbaud beloved of poststructuralist poets and critics who creates an elusive 'verbal field' is no use to a poet-figure who wants to stress the difference between the author and skinhead, even if the latter were au fait with French and symbolist poetry (*The Poetics of Indeterminacy*, p. 62). It would 'fucking matter' in that if the skinhead knew Rimbaud he might well *be* the poet: in a sense, *V* ultimately suggests that he is, since the skinhead is figured as a classical 'shade', and an alternative vision of the poet himself (*Selected Poems*, p. 242). This strange case of it 'not mattering' if the skinhead can draw on proto-modernist literature also draws attention to the odd use of 'but' in this stanza. The poet-figure presents Rimbaud as akin to the author: someone who can 'unite' the 'skin and poet', so that there would be no need for the '*je*' to be '*autre*'. The conjunction between the third and fourth line distinguishes between the examples of the poet and Rimbaud, in the sense of 'but' as meaning 'otherwise', 'on the contrary' or 'on the other hand' rather than 'only' or 'except'. But surely 'and' would be more appropriate here, since the two examples show the same process: to paraphrase, the skinhead and poet are united in Rimbaud just as they are in the poet-figure, not in contrast to Rimbaud. 'But' is here not an innocuous conjunction, but an example of what Adorno terms a weak 'coordinating particle' in his essay 'On Epic Naiveté' (*Notes to Literature*, vol. 1, trans. S. W. Nicholson [New York and Chichester: Columbia University Press, 1991], pp. 24–9, pp. 27–8). It reveals an uneasiness in the metaphorical chain of the skinhead/Rimbaud/Harrison/poet that runs throughout this stanza, and *V* as a whole. It also indicates disquiet about the proto-modernist intertext here, as if the literary connection between Rimbaud and Harrison is as equally fraught as the link between the two poets and the skinhead.

22. Armitage, 'On Tony Harrison', p. 11. In 'Summoned by Bells', Harrison's entanglement in issues of democracy draws more openly on a modernist intertext: he pastiches the form of the first section of Pound's 'Hugh Selwyn Mauberley', with its trimeters and tetrameters. Rather than John Betjeman's verse autobiography, the title alludes to Pound's apparent despising of church bells: in *Ezra Pound's Kensington* (1965), Patricia Hutchins comments on the 'unkind' bells of St Mary Abbotts, which – according to James Campbell – 'aggravated his incipient derangement' ('Home from Home', *The Guardian*, 17 May 2008, www.theguardian.com/books/2008/may/17/poetry3 [accessed 17 May 2017]). As Adrian Barlow recounts in his article 'Ring Out, Wild Bells!', it 'appeared to [Pound] impossible that any clean form of teaching cd. lead a man, or group, to cause that damnable and hideous noise and inflict it on helpless humanity' ('Ring Out, Wild Bells', 5 June 2015, http://adrianbarlowsblog.blogspot.co.uk /2015/06/ring-out-wild-bells.html [accessed 17 May 2017]). Harrison begins the poem with an imagined quotation from Pound: '*O Zeppelins! O Zeppelins!* | prayed poet E.P. | *any Boche gets 60 pence* | *to bust this campanolatry!*' (*The Gaze of the Gorgon* [Newcastle: Bloodaxe, 1992], p. 24). 'Summoned by Bells' reveals that Harrison's equivalent of Pound's 'Doubles, triples' and 'caters' – usually rung on ten-bells and other higher odd-bell stages – is the sound of house alarms. Securicor alarms interfere with Harrison's rhythm and concentration: it is not surprising that the fourth stanza contains a metrical break precisely on the word 'bells'. These 'new bells of John Bull' are, for Harrison, entwined with his vision of nationalistic mass culture, complete with its jingoistic nationalism, deadening popular culture (encapsulated in video consumption) and religious genuflection. Harrison caricatures himself here as the modernist 'outcast', who is about to leave his house for, presumably, a poetry reading, his 'bag there ready packed' with books. As with the poet in 'Hugh Selwyn Mauberley', Harrison depicts himself as out of key with his time, striving through such readings to 'resuscitate the dead art | Of poetry' (*Ezra Pound: Selected Poems 1908–1959*, p. 98). According to Harrison's poem, this 'dead art' can only be revitalised in a democracy obsessed with the temporalities of popular trash. Harrison paradoxically rails against the consumerist masses in the most accessible of Pound's forms – the quatrains at the beginning of 'Hugh Selwyn Mauberley' – before the poem begins to fragment in part IV. As Sandie Byrne notes in *H, v & o: The Poetry of Tony Harrison* (Manchester: Manchester University Press, 1998), 'Summoned by Bells' ends on a distinctly bourgeois vision of the illiterate thief who steals the 'curosity''s books (p. 108). The poem's stance on popular culture, and modern Britain as the 'half savage country' of 'Hugh Selwyn Mauberley', is symptomatic of the 'second modernist ideology' of

a resistance to popular culture (Raymond Williams, *The Politics of Modernism*, ed. Tony Pinkney [London/New York: Verso, 1989], p. 5).

23. David James, *The Legacies of Modernism: Historicising Postwar and Contemporary Fiction* (Cambridge: Cambridge University Press, 2011), p. 2.
24. Adorno, *Aesthetic Theory*, p. 120.
25. Bell, *Literature, Modernism and Myth*, p. 78.
26. Harrison, 'ΟΡϕΕΑΣ' ('Orpheus') notebook (c. 1998), BC MS 20c Harrison/03/ORP, pp. 15, 17. The last two quotations are pasted in from Ivan M. Linforth's *The Arts of Orpheus* (Berkeley and Los Angeles: University of California Press, 1941). Harrison then moves on to the first mention of the Thracian women cutting off Orpheus' head and fastening it to a lyre, and subsequently throwing it into the river or sea (*The Arts of Orpheus*, pp. 128–9; workbook, p. 28). Virgil's *Georgics* (29 BCE) then follow, and the first reference to the head singing after Orpheus' death (p. 28).
27. Harrison, 'ΟΡϕΕΑΣ' ('Orpheus') notebook, p. 257.
28. The amount of material on Sappho in the workbook suggests that she had a more extensive presence in the original conception of the film. There are references, for example, to Yopie Prins's *Victorian Sappho* (Princeton, New Jersey: Princeton University Press, 1999), and a leaflet for a tourist shop in Skala Eressou (Harrison, 'ΟΡϕΕΑΣ' ['Orpheus'] notebook', p. 191). On a postcard to Harrison held in the Brotherton archive (14 September 1999), the cameraman Alistair Cameron notes that shots of Harrison's plastic head 'went brilliantly' in 'Eresos (Dyke City) again!' (Harrison, 'Correspondence', BCMS 20c Harrison OS/FAD-RBL). Harrison's continued interest in Eressou is indicated in an article included at the end of the Orpheus workbook (not long before the screening of the film-poem) by Stephanie Theobald and Michael Howard, entitled 'Lesbians go mad in Lesbos' (*The Guardian*, 14 September 2000), discussing the town's reaction to a proposed 'Wet Pussy Pool Party' (pp. 294–5).
29. The article 'Book tells it straight about sex lives of ancient Greeks', published in *The Guardian* (16 August 1999), discusses Nikos Vrissimtzis' *Love, Sex and Marriage in Ancient Greece: A Guide to the Private Life of the Ancient Greeks* (1999) (Harrison, 'ΟΡϕΕΑΣ' ['Orpheus'] notebook, pp. 167–8).
30. Harrison, 'ΟΡϕΕΑΣ' ('Orpheus') notebook, p. 150.
31. Jonathan West, letter to Mrs Holland, 17 August 1999, p. 1 (Harrison, 'ΟΡϕΕΑΣ' ['Orpheus'] notebook, p. 150).
32. Harrison, 'ΟΡϕΕΑΣ' ('Orpheus') notebook, pp. 7–8. The pasted-in quotation about the pit originates from an article by Professor Toucho Zhecher.

33. Angela Carter, 'Notes from the Front Line', in Michelene Wandor, ed., *On Gender and Writing* (Boston/London: Pandora Press, 1983), pp. 69–77, p. 69; Tony Harrison, *Collected Film Poetry*, p. 386.

34. Bell, *Literature, Modernism and Myth*, p. 34.

35. Harrison, *Collected Film Poetry*, p. 398.

36. Theodor Adorno, 'Commitment', in Perry Anderson, Rodney Livingstone and Francis Mulhern, eds., *Aesthetics and Politics* (London: Verso, 2007 [1977]), pp. 177–95, p. 177.

37. Adorno, *Aesthetic Theory*, p. 121.

38. Harrison, 'OPφEAΣ' ('Orpheus') notebook, pp. 17, 22, 33.

39. Harrison must have been unaware of the demands of what was named the Research Assessment Exercise in 2000. The 'Codgers' line in the workbook is replaced with the two lines: 'I think it needs that ancient scream | to pierce the skulls of Academe' (Harrison, 'OPφEAΣ' ['Orpheus'] notebook, p. 234).

40. Oliver Taplin, 'Contemporary Poetry and Classics', in *Classics in Progress: Essays on Ancient Greece and Rome* (Oxford: The British Academy [Oxford University Press], 2002), pp. 1–20, p. 11.

41. Harrison, *Collected Film Poetry*, p. 385.

42. Theodor Adorno, *Negative Dialectics*, trans. E. B. Ashton (New York: Seabury Press, 1973 [1967]), p. 367.

43. Adorno, *Aesthetic Theory*, p. 126.

44. Nabina Das, review of *Eidolon, Mascara Literary Review*, 23 August 2016, http://mascarareview.com/nabina-das-reviews-eidolon-by-sandeep-paramar (accessed 14 July 2017).

45. Adorno, *Aesthetic Theory*, pp. 126, 121.

46. Robert Sheppard, *The Poetry of Saying: British Poetry and its Discontents, 1950–2000* (Liverpool: Liverpool University Press, 2005); Parmar, 'Not a British Subject', https://lareviewofbooks.org/article/not-a-british-subject-race-and-poetry-in-the-uk (accessed 19 May 2019).

47. Harrison, *Collected Film Poetry*, p. 398; Euripides, *The Trojan Women – Helen, The Bacchae*, trans. Neil Curry (London/Cambridge: Cambridge University Press, 1981), p. 7. Harrison's celebration of humanist carpe diem grates against Bell's sense of the modernist self as 'consciously ungroundable', just as Eliot's later retreat into Catholicism does not fit into Bell's sense of an identity with 'no essential centre' which 'lies at the heart of modernism' (p. 36). In contrast to postmodernist writers in whose work identity is 'ungroundable' in its multiplicity, and in a constant state of becoming, Harrison's modernist sensibility intuits 'unity within incommensurable differences' (p. 80). Akin to writers such as Eliot – but with very different ideological results – Harrison is 'obliged' in poems such as 'The Grilling' from *Under the Clock* to meditate closely 'on what it meant to have a conviction, since, in the cultural

fragmentation of modernity, any belief inevitably became more arbitrary, relative, and self-conscious' (p. 3). In this poem, Harrison follows that archetypal modernist philosopher, Nietzsche, in his affirmation of life 'on the model of art' (p. 27). Reacting against Schopenhauer's philosophy, in which the aesthetic forms an opposition to everyday life and its woes, Nietzsche interpreted mythic narratives not as ideals divorced from human existence, but as a way of living (p. 27). Similarly in 'The Grilling', Harrison interweaves the satyrs and his Bacchic celebration of choice morsels and imbibing with the shadow of Vesuvius. Harrison also adheres to the mythic 'double consciousness' of Joyce in his counterpointing through impiety, that Bell underplays in *Literature, Modernism and Myth*. Bloom's ablutions become part of a reimagined *Odyssey* just as the satyrs with their refulgent appendages arise out of the fiery detritus of Vesuvius and twentieth-century history in 'The Grilling' (p. 39). Bell writes of the post-war turn in Europe against myth, largely – unlike Mann's work – in response to fascism (p. 5): he singles out Adorno and Horkheimer's *Dialectic of Enlightenment* (1944) as having been particularly persuasive in its criticism of the 'pre-civilised' world of mythic powers, crystallised in the section of the *Odyssey* in which the bound Odysseus struggles against the irrational charms of the Sirens' song (pp. 132–3). However, like Bell – and unlike Adorno and Horkheimer – Harrison does not regard myth as coterminous with atavistic nostalgia. Ultimately, 'The Grilling' is engaged in the urgent problem of 'what it might now mean to live a conviction, what it is to inhabit a belief' (p. 3).

48. Bettany Hughes, *Helen of Troy: Goddess, Princess, Whore* (London: Pimlico, 2006 [2005]), p. xxxv.

49. H. D., *Helen in Egypt* (Manchester: Carcanet, 1985 [1961]), pp. vii, 129.

50. Hughes explains that *eidolon* is a Greek word meaning a 'ghost, an image or idea' (p. 11). Later in *Helen of Troy* she is 'an *eidolon* that burns with projected emotion' (p. 116). Hughes notes Stesichorus' second version of the Helen myth (pp. 160–1), but the latter covers only two pages of her wide-ranging book.

51. Adorno, *Aesthetic Theory*, p. 126.

52. Walt Whitman, 'Eidolons', www.infoplease.com/primary-sources/poetry/walt-whitman/walt-whitman-eidolons (accessed 17 June 2020).

53. Eleanor Cook, 'The Figure of Enigma: Rhetoric, History and Poetry', *Rhetorica: A Journal of the History of Rhetoric*, 19(4) (2001), 349–78, p. 352.

54. Whitman, 'Eidolons', www.infoplease.com/primary-sources/poetry/walt-whitman/walt-whitman-eidolons (accessed 17 June 2020); Parmar, *Eidolon*, pp. 65, 67.

55. Robert Hullot-Kentor, 'Translator's Introduction', *Aesthetic Theory*, pp. i–xxi, p. xvi.

56. Parmar, *Eidolon*, p. 26; H. D., *Helen in Egypt*, p. 12.

57. Hughes, *Helen of Troy*, p. 66; Parmar, *Eidolon*, p. 26.

58. Lawrence Durrell, *Collected Poems* (London: Faber and Faber, 1968), p. 273; *OED*, 2nd edn.

59. Parmar, *Eidolon*, p. 56; Durrell, *Collected Poems*, p. 273.

60. Anna Reading, 'Memobilia: The Mobile Phone and the Emergence of Wearable Memories', in *Save As . . . Digital Memories* (New York/ Basingstoke: Palgrave, 2009), pp. 81–95, p. 81.

61. Instead of the 'butchery' of her eyes, in *Helen in Egypt* Achilles is transfixed by Helen's eyes, 'shimmering as light on the changeable sea' (p. 54).

62. Durrell, *Collected Poems*, p. 273. In *Virginia Woolf's Greek Tragedy* (London/ New York: Bloomsbury, 2020 [2019]), Nancy Worman engages with Woolf's ambivalent approach to imperialism. The novelist's 'Greek metonymies' frequently serve to 'critique the brutalities of empire', but they also 'shape her passionate pursuit of modernist aesthetics that tends to view Greece with a fondly proprietary eye' (p. 80). Woolf's exoticisation of Greece and the classics 'has uncomfortable political underpinnings, since it colludes with imperialist and colonialist perspectives' at the same time as the novels appear to critique the values of the latter (p. 16). She does not simply endorse Euripides' impersonality: any consideration of 'Woolf's use of Greek and Greece must take into account the figuring of the female as outsider and colonized, in relation to which "Greece" both shares this status and stands in opposition to it' (p. 4).

63. Durrell, *Collected Poems*, p. 273; Parmar, *Eidolon*, p. 31.

64. Hughes, *Helen of Troy*, p. 218.

65. Theodor Adorno, 'Commitment', in R. Livingstone, P. Anderson and F. Mulhern, eds., *Aesthetics and Politics*, trans. F. MacDonagh (London: New Left Books, 1977), pp. 177–95, p. 189.

66. Tony Harrison, *Under the Clock* (London/New York: Penguin, 2005), p. 40; Das, review of *Eidolon*, http://mascarareview.com/nabina-das-reviews-eidolon-by-sandeep-paramar (accessed 14 July 2017).

67. Harrison, *Under the Clock*, p. 39; Parmar, *Eidolon*, pp. 68, 36.

68. Armitage, 'On Tony Harrison', p. 8.

Conclusion

1. Geoffrey Hill, 'Poetry, Policing and Public Order (1)', www.english.ox.ac.uk /professor-sir-geoffrey-hill-lectures (accessed 12 July 2020). Hill refers to T. S. Eliot's phrase 'the exasperated spirit' from part two of 'Little Gidding' in *Four Quartets* (London: Faber and Faber, 1959), p. 54.

2. Geoffrey Hill, 'Monumentality and Bidding', www.english.ox.ac.uk/professor-sir-geoffrey-hill-lectures (accessed 16 July 2020).

3. Hill, 'Poetry, Policing and Public Order', www.english.ox.ac.uk/professor-sir -geoffrey-hill-lectures (accessed 12 July 2020).

4. Geoffrey Hill, Michaelmas Term lecture (27 November 2012), www .english.ox.ac.uk/professor-sir-geoffrey-hill-lectures (accessed 16 July 2020).

5. Geoffrey Hill, 'Legal Fiction and Legal "Fiction"', www.english.ox.ac.uk/pro fessor-sir-geoffrey-hill-lectures (accessed 16 July 2020); David James, *The Legacies of Modernism: Historicising Postwar and Contemporary Fiction* (Cambridge: Cambridge University Press, 2011), p. 2.

6. David James and Urmila Seshagiri, 'Metamodernism: Narratives of Continuity and Revolution', *PMLA*, 129(1) (2014), 87–98.

7. Hill, 'Legal Fiction and Legal "Fiction"', www.english.ox.ac.uk/professor-sir-geoffrey-hill-lectures (accessed 16 July 2020).

8. David James and Urmila Seshagiri, 'Metamodernism: Narratives of Continuity and Revolution', *PMLA*, 129(1) (2014), 87–98, p. 87.

9. Timotheus Vermeulen and Robin van den Akker, 'Notes on Metamodernism', *Journal of Aesthetics and Culture*, 2 (2010), 2–14; Robin van den Akker, Alison Gibbons and Timotheus Vermeulen, eds, *Metamodernism: Historicity, Affect and Depth After Postmodernism* (London: New York: Rowman and Littlefield International, 2017); Andre Furlani, *Guy Davenport: Postmodern and After* (Evanston, Illinois: Northwestern University Press, 2007); Luke Turner, 'Metamodernism Manifesto' and 'Metamodernism: A Brief Introduction', www.metamodernism.org (accessed 29 April 2021); Nick Bentley, 'Trailing Postmodernism: David Mitchell's *Cloud Atlas*, Zadie Smith's *NW*, and the Metamodern', *English Studies*, 99: 7–8 (November 2018), 723–43; Dennis Kersten and Usha Wilbers, eds., 'Metamodernism: A Special Issue', *English*, 99: 7–8 (November 2018).

10. Theodor W. Adorno, *Aesthetic Theory*, eds. Gretel Adorno and Rolf Tiedemann, trans. Robert Hullot-Kentor (London: The Athlone Press, 1997 [1970]), p. 121.

11. James and Seshagiri, 'Metamodernism', p. 97.

12. A secret is different to an enigma, of course: the former suggests a single entity that can be discovered; the latter connotes a conundrum that may never be solved.

13. Hill, 'Legal Fiction and Legal "Fiction"', www.english.ox.ac.uk/professor-sir-geoffrey-hill-lectures (accessed 16 July 2020).

14. Jeffrey T. Nealon, *Post-Postmodernism or, the Cultural Logic of Just-in-Time Capitalism* (Stanford: Stanford University Press, 2012), p. 153.

15. Metamodernist poetry's resistance to commodification registers a point of overlap between the two different versions of metamodernism. In the third AHRC symposium on metamodernism at the University of Oslo

(21 September 2018), Tim Vermeulen referred to these poetics of resistance as akin to a 'pinching of the map', in which overriding consumerism remains intact, but can be challenged by metamodernist art.

16. Tony Harrison, *The Inky Digit of Defiance: Selected Prose 1966–2016* (London: Faber and Faber, 2017), p. 288.

17. Adorno, *Aesthetic Theory*, p. 120.

18. Hill, Michaelmas Term lecture, 27 November 2012, www.english.ox.ac.uk/professor-sir-geoffrey-hill-lectures (accessed 16 July 2020).

19. Hill, 'Legal Fiction and Legal "Fiction"', www.english.ox.ac.uk/professor-sir-geoffrey-hill-lectures (accessed 16 July 2020).

20. Hill, Michaelmas Term lecture, 27 November 2012, www.english.ox.ac.uk/professor-sir-geoffrey-hill-lectures (accessed 16 July 2020); Hill, 'Legal Fiction and Legal "Fiction"', www.english.ox.ac.uk/professor-sir-geoffrey-hill-lectures (accessed 16 July 2020).

21. Hill, Michaelmas Term lecture, 27 November 2012, www.english.ox.ac.uk/professor-sir-geoffrey-hill-lectures (accessed 16 July 2020).

22. Hill, Michaelmas Term lecture, 27 November 2012, www.english.ox.ac.uk/professor-sir-geoffrey-hill-lectures (accessed 16 July 2020); Peter Barry, *Poetry Wars* (Cambridge: Salt, 2006), p. 137.

23. For some poetry critics such as Marjorie Perloff, tracking the legacies of modernism signals a return to neglected aspects of early twentieth-century literature in order to circumvent the 'tired dichotomy' between modernism and postmodernism, whereas for others (including the critic Ken Edwards) 'innovative' poetry is symptomatic of a 'parallel tradition' that has flourished throughout the postmodern era (*21ˢᵗ-Century Modernism: The "New" Poetics* [Malden/Oxford: Blackwells, 2002], p. 1; Ken Edwards, 'The Two Poetries', *Angelaki*, 3/1 [April 2000], 25–36, p. 32).

24. These critics are drawing, of course, on Raymond Williams's use of the phrase 'structure of feeling' as a way of characterising a delicate, elusive and yet tangible aspect of our cultural activities. Williams wishes to describe the common characteristics of any particular historical moment, but without any idealist sense of the 'spirit' of an epoch. Rather than a definable zeitgeist, Vermeulen and Akker refer to a 'new generation' of artists who are increasingly abandoning 'the aesthetic precepts of deconstruction, parataxis, and pastiche' in favour of 'reconstruction, myth, and metaxis' ('Notes on Metamodernism', p. 2).

25. Adrian Searle, 'Altermodern Review: "The Richest and Most Generous Tate Triennial Yet"', www.theguardian.com/artanddesign/2009/feb/02/altermodern-tate-triennial (accessed 16 July 2020).

26. As both a symptom and a means of resistance, metamodernism is necessarily 'shot through with productive contradictions, simmering tensions,

ideological formations and – to be frank – frightening developments (our incapacity to effectively combat xenophobic populism comes to mind)' (*Metamodernism*, pp. 5–6). Centrist politics is now giving way to leftist anti-globalisation and right-wing popular movements, and yet the 'neoliberal path' still dominates, 'leading to a clusterfuck of world-historical proportions' (p. 17). In the same volume, Josh Toth notes that 'the very rhetorical strategies' (such as critiques of the concepts of 'truth' and 'authenticity') that 'we typically associate with postmodernism are now being deployed by the political right' ('Toni Morrison's *Beloved* and the Rise of Historioplastic Metafiction', pp. 41–53, p. 42).

27. James MacDowell, 'The Metamodern, the Quirky and Film Criticism', in *Metamodernism*, pp. 25–40, p. 28. MacDowell proposes the 'quirky' as 'a useful lens through which to view strands of contemporary culture' (p. 26), and endorses post-ironic films that are self-conscious but also contain 'metamodern' moments such as the 'quirky' turn from the main narrative in *The Fantastic Mr Fox* (2009) in which the eponymous creature sheds a tear at the plight of the feared wolf.

28. Ahren Warner, *Pretty* (Newcastle: Bloodaxe, 2013), p. 72.

29. David James, *The Legacies of Modernism: Historicising Postwar and Contemporary Fiction* (Cambridge: Cambridge University Press, 2011), p. 3; T. S. Eliot, *Selected Poems* (London: Faber and Faber, 1954), p. 53.

30. Ahren Warner, *Confer* (Newcastle: Bloodaxe, 2011), p. 41.

31. Francis Scarfe, ed., *Baudelaire: The Complete Verse* (London: Anvil, 1986), p. 59.

32. David Kennedy, *New Relations: The Refashioning of British Poetry 1980–94* (Bridgend: Seren, 1996), p. 18.

33. These authors trace the 'waning', for example, of disaffection, irony and the spectacular in contemporary European culture (*Metamodernism*, p. 2).

34. As Rotherg writes in *The Implicated Subject: Beyond Victims and Perpetrators* (Stanford: Stanford University Press, 2019), as taxpayers, 'we are indeed all implicated in the actions of our government, whatever our ideological opposition to or affective disengagement from particular policies' (p. 19).

35. John Keats, 'Ode on Melancholy', *The Norton Anthology of Poetry*, ed. Margaret Ferguson, Mary Jo Salter and Jon Stallworthy, 5th edition (New York/London: W. W. Norton, 2005), p. 937.

36. Paul Batchelor, review of *Hello. Your Promise has been Extracted*, www .newstatesman.com/culture/poetry/2018/01/poets-nuar-alsadir-and-ahren-warner-reveal-intriguing-habits-perception (accessed 10 January 2020).

37. Paul Muldoon, 'The Loaf', *Moy Sand and Gravel* (London: Faber and Faber, 2002), p. 47.

38. Warner, *Pretty*, p. 67. Curiously, 'rendering' occurs in *Aesthetic Theory* too, as a trope for the critical process as it attempts to understand works of art (p. 186). Walter Benjamin's attention in 'Surrealism' to the minutiae of urban ephemera includes a focus on 'roof tops, lightning conductors, gutters, verandas [...] stucco work' (*One Way Street and Other Writings*, trans. Edmund Jephcott and Kingsley Shorter [London: Verso, 1992], pp. 225–39, p. 228). These details all feature in Warner's photographs in *Hello. Your Promise has been Extracted*.

39. Rothberg, *The Implicated Subject*, p. 12.

40. Lauren Berlant, 'The subject of True Feeling: Pain, Privacy, and Politics', in Sara Ahmed, Jane Kilby, Celia Lury, Maureen McNeil and Beverley Skeggs, eds., *Transformations: Thinking Through Feminism* (London: Routledge, 2000), pp. 33–47.

41. Batchelor, review of *Hello. Your Promise has been Extracted* (21 January 2018), www.newstatesman.com/culture/poetry/2018/01/poets-nuar-alsadir-and-ahren-warner-reveal-intriguing-habits-perception (accessed 10 January 2020). Benjamin Myers is similarly offended by the 'sensationalism' of such historical evocations (www.worldliteraturetoday.org/2018/july/hello-your-promise-has-been-extracted-ahren-warner) (accessed 25 January 2020). Myers concludes that 'this is not how Celan does it'.

42. Gibbons, van den Akker and Vermeulen, *Metamodernism*, pp. 5, 17.

43. Rothberg, *The Implicated Subject*, p. 1.

44. Peter Boxall, *Twenty-First-Century Fiction* (Cambridge: Cambridge University Press, 2013), p. 59. In his paper 'Imaging the Future' at the first AHRC research network symposium on metamodernism at Manchester Metropolitan University (31 January 2018), Boxall referred instead to the 'reanimation of formal histories' and 'resurgent modes of realism' in Ian McEwan's *The Children's Act* (2014).

45. Linda Hutcheon, *The Politics of Postmodernism* (London: Routledge, 2002 [1989]), p. 181.

46. www.amazon.co.uk/New-British-Poetry-Don-Paterson/dp/1555973949 (accessed 30 September 2020). As I noted in the Introduction and Chapter 1, the reviewer avers that the 'UK poetry scene is smaller than its US counterpart, so the "poetry wars" there must be like a knife fight in a phone booth'.

47. In Lipovetsky's *Hypermodern Times* (Cambridge/Malden: Polity Press, 2005), the hypermodern defines 'a new social and cultural climate', that each day moves 'a little further away from the relaxed, carefree attitudes of the postmodern years' (p. 45). Individual freedom begets personal regulation, combined with 'anxiety about a future fraught with risk and uncertainty'

(p. 6). However, hypermodernity – akin to Vermeulen and van den Akker's 'oscillations' – 'is the reign neither of absolute happiness, nor of total nihilism' (p. 25): the 'astonishing' fact is that 'the society of mass consumption, emotional and individualistic as it is, allows an adaptable spirit of responsibility to coexist with a spirit of irresponsibility' (p. 26). Chiming with Gibbons, van den Akker and Vermeulen's sense of the return of affect and empathy, 'the frenzy of "always more" does not kill off the qualitative logic of "not more, but better" and the importance of feelings: it gives them, on the contrary, a greater social visibility, a new mass legitimacy' (p. 55).

48. Sato's comments were made during a symposium on metamodernism at Radboud University (Nijmegen) (29 October 2015).

49. Turner, 'Metamodernism: A Brief Introduction', www.metamodernism.org (accessed 29 April 2020).

50. Adorno, *Aesthetic Theory*, p. 34.

51. Theodor W. Adorno, *Minima Moralia: Reflections from Damaged Life*, trans. E. F. N. Jephcott (London: Verso, 1978 [1951]), p. 52.

52. Furlani, *Guy Davenport*, p. 150.

53. Furlani, *Guy Davenport*, p. 149.

54. Martin Jay, *Adorno* (Cambridge, Massachusetts: Harvard University Press, 1984), p. 159.

55. Adorno, *Aesthetic Theory*, p. 55.

Bibliography

Adorno, Theodor W., *Aesthetic Theory*, eds., Gretel Adorno and Rolf Tiedemann, trans. Robert Hullot-Kentor (London: The Athlone Press, 1997 [1970]).

Ästhetische Theorie (Frankfurt am Main: Suhrkamp Verlag, 2014 [1970]).

'Commitment', in Perry Anderson, Rodney Livingstone and Francis Mulhern (eds.), *Aesthetics and Politics* (London: Verso, 2007 [1977]), pp. 177–95.

'Engagement' in *Noten zur Literatur* I (Frankfurt: Suhrkamp Verlag, 1974), pp. 409–30, p. 409.

Minima Moralia: Reflections from Damaged Life, trans. E. F. N. Jephcott (London: Verso, 1978 [1951]).

Negative Dialectics, trans. E. B. Ashton (New York: Seabury Press, 1973 [1967]), p. 367.

'On Epic Naiveté' (*Notes to Literature*, vol. 1, trans. S. W. Nicholson (New York and Chichester: Columbia University Press, 1991), pp. 24–9.

Adorno, Theodor W. and Max Horkheimer, *Dialectic of Enlightenment*, trans. John Cummins (London: Verso, 1986 [1944]).

van den Akker, Robin, Alison Gibbons and Timotheus Vermeulen, eds., *Metamodernism: Historicity, Affect and Depth after Postmodernism* (London: New York: Rowen and Littlefield International, 2017).

Aldington, Richard, 'In the Tube', *The Egoist*, 2(5) (2015), 74.

Anonymous, 'Introduction', *Angel Exhaust 9: Tyranny and Mutation: New Radical Poets* (Summer 1993), 4–5.

Armitage, Simon, 'On Tony Harrison', *Stand*, no. 215, 15(3) (2017), 7–11.

Arnold, Matthew, 'Dover Beach', in Kenneth Allott, ed., *Arnold: Poems*, (London: Penguin, 1985 [1954]), pp. 181–2.

Astley, Neil, ed., *Bloodaxe Critical Anthologies 1: Tony Harrison* (Newcastle: Bloodaxe, 1991).

Attridge, Derek, 'Conjurers turn tricks on wizards' coat-tails', www .timeshighereducation.co.uk/story.asp?sectioncode=26&s (accessed 27 July 2020).

Moving Words: Forms of English Poetry (Oxford: Oxford University Press, 2013)

The Singularity of Literature (London/New York: Routledge, 2004).

Balfour, Ian 'Extreme Philology: Benjamin, Adorno, McCall and the Enigmas of Hölderlin', in *Tragedy, Translation and Theory: In Honor of the Work of Thomas J. McCall* (Baltimore: The University of Maryland Press, 2014), https://romantic-circles.org/praxis/mccall/praxis.2014.mccall.balfour.html (accessed 19 May 2021).

Barry, Peter, *Poetry Wars* (Cambridge: Salt, 2006).

Barry, Peter and Robert Hampson, eds., *New British Poetries: The Scope of the Possible* (Manchester: Manchester University Press, 1993).

Barthes, Roland, 'Death of the Author', in Dennis Walder, ed., *Literature in the Modern World* (Oxford: Oxford University Press, 1990), pp. 228–32.

Batchelor, Paul, Review of *Hello. Your Promise Has Been Extracted* (21 January 2018), www.newstatesman.com/culture/poetry/2018/01/poets-nuar-alsadir-and-ahren-warner-reveal-intriguing-habits-perception (accessed 10 January 2020).

Beach, Christopher, *Poetic Culture: Contemporary American Poetry Between Community and Institution* (Evanston, IL: Northwestern University Press, 1999).

Bede, *Ecclesiastical History of the English People*, eds. Judith McClure and Roger Collins (Oxford/London: James Parker and Co., 1870).

Bell, Michael, *Literature, Modernism and Myth: Belief and Responsibility in the Twentieth Century* (Cambridge: Cambridge University Press, 1997).

Benjamin, Walter, 'Surrealism', in *One Way Street and Other Writings* (London: Verso, 1992), trans. Edmund Jephcott and Kingsley Shorter, pp. 225–39.

Bentley, Nick, 'Trailing Postmodernism: David Mitchell's *Cloud Atlas*, Zadie Smith's *NW*, and the Metamodern', *English Studies*, 99(7–8) (2018), 723–43.

Berlant, Lauren, 'The Subject of True Feeling: Pain, Privacy, and Politics', in Sara Ahmed, Jane Kilby, Celia Lury, Maureen McNeil and Beverley Skeggs, eds., *Transformations: Thinking Through Feminism* (London: Routledge, 2000), pp. 33–47.

Bermel, Albert, *Artaud's Theatre of Cruelty* (London/New York: Methuen, 2001 [1977]).

Bernstein, Charles and Bruce Andrews, 'Repossessing the Word', in Charles Bernstein and Bruce Andrews, eds., *The Language Book* (Carbondale and Edwardsville, IL: Southern Illinois University Press, 1984), pp. ix–xi.

Blackmur, R. P., *The Double Agent: Essays in Craft and Elucidation* (New York: Arrow Editions, 1935).

Boxall, Peter, *Since Beckett: Contemporary Writing in the Wake of Modernism* (London: Continuum, 2009).

Twenty-First-Century Fiction (Cambridge: Cambridge University Press, 2013).

Brecht, Bertolt, *Poems 1913–1956*, eds. John Willett and Ralph Manheim (London: Methuen, 1987 [1976]).

The Resistible Rise of Arturo Ui (London: Methuen, 1976 [1958]).

Brown, Clare and Don Paterson, eds., *Don't Ask Me What I Mean: Poets in Their Own Words* (Basingstoke/Oxford: Picador, 2003).

Burton, Richard, *A Strong Song Tows Us: The Life of Basil Bunting* (Oxford: Infinite Ideas Ltd, 2013).

Buse, Peter, Ken Hirschkop, Scott McCracken and Bertrand Taithe, *Benjamin's Arcades: An Unguided Tour* (Manchester: Manchester University Press, 2005).

Byrne, James, *Blood/Sugar* (Todmorden: Arc, 2009).

    The Caprices (Todmorden: Arc, 2020).

    Everything Broken Up Dances (North Adams: Tupelo Press, 2015).

    '*I Am a Rohingya: Poetry from the World's Largest Refugee Camp and Beyond*', *Kenyan Review* (https://kenyonreview.org/kr-online-issue/literary-activism/s elections/james-byrne-763879) (accessed 9 June 2020).

    Places You Leave (Todmorden: Arc, 2021).

    White Coins (Todmorden: Arc, 2015).

    Withdrawals (Newton-le-Willows: Knives Forks and Spoons Press, 2019).

Byrne, James and Shehzar Doja, eds., *I Am a Rohingya: Poetry from the Camps and Beyond* (Todmorden: Arc, 2019).

Byrne, Sandie, *H, v & o: The Poetry of Tony Harrison* (Manchester: Manchester University Press, 1998).

    ed., *Tony Harrison: Loiner* (Oxford: Clarendon Press, 1997).

Caplan, David, *Questions of Possibility: Contemporary Poetry and Poetic Form* (Oxford: Oxford University Press, 2005).

Carey, John, *The Intellectuals and the Masses: Pride and Prejudice among the Literary Intelligentsia, 1880-1939* (London: Faber and Faber, 1992).

    The Unexpected Professor: An Oxford Life in Books (London: Faber and Faber, 2014).

Carter, Angela, 'Notes from the Front Line', in Michelene Wandor, ed., *On Gender and Writing* (Boston/London: Pandora Press, 1983), pp. 69–77.

Celan, Paul, *Breathturn into Timestead: The Collected Later Poetry*, trans. Pierre Joris (New York: Farrar Straus Giroux, 2014).

Céline, Louis-Ferdinand, *Journey to the End of the Night*, trans. Ralph Manheim (Richmond: Alma, 2012 [1932]).

Chingonyi, Kayo, '"It has to appear like a gift": An Interview with Ahren Warner', 16 June 2013, https://kayochingonyi.com/2013/06/16/it-has-to-appear-like-a-gift-an-interview-with-ahren-warner (accessed 5 June 2020).

Cook, Eleanor, 'The Figure of Enigma: Rhetoric, History and Poetry', *Rhetorica: A Journal of the History of Rhetoric*, 19(4) (2001), 349–78.

    Enigmas and Riddles in Literature (Cambridge: Cambridge University Press, 2006).

Crownshaw, Rick, Jane Kilby and Antony Rowland, eds., *The Future of Memory* (London/New York: Berghahn, 2010).

Crystal, David, *Txtng: The Gr8 Db8* (Oxford: Oxford University Press, 2009).

Cuttle, Jade, 'The talented poets living in the world's largest refugee camp', *The Daily Telegraph*, 26 July 2019, 25–6.

Das, Nabina, review of *Eidolon*, *Mascara Literary Review*, 23 August 2016 (ht tp://mascarareview.com/nabina-das-reviews-eidolon-by-sandeep-para mar) (accessed 14 July 2017).

Day, Thomas, 'French Connections in Geoffrey Hill's *The Orchards of Syon*', *Essays in Criticism*, 6(1) (January 2010), 26–50.

Derrida, Jacques, 'No Apocalypse, Not Now (full speed ahead, seven missiles, seven missives)', *Diacritics*, 14(2) (Summer 1984), 20–31.

Detloff, Madelyn, *The Persistence of Modernism: Loss and Mourning in the Twentieth Century* (Cambridge: Cambridge University Press, 2009).

H. D., *Helen in Egypt* (Manchester: Carcanet, 1985 [1961]).

Duffy, Carol Ann, *The Bees* (London: Picador, 2012).

The Christmas Truce (London: Picador, 2011).

Dumitrescu, Alexandra, 'Interconnections in Blakean and metamodern space', www .doubledialogues.com/article/interconnections-in-blakean-and-metamodern-space (accessed 16 July 2020).

Durrell, Lawrence, *Collected Poems* (London: Faber and Faber, 1968).

Edwards, Ken, 'The Two Poetries', *Angelaki*, 3(1) (April 2000), 25–36.

Eliot, T. S., *Four Quartets* (London: Faber and Faber, 1949 [1941]).

Literary Chapters of Ezra Pound (London: Faber and Faber, 1960).

Selected Essays (London: Faber and Faber, 1951).

Selected Poems (London: Faber and Faber, 1954).

The Use of Poetry and the Use of Criticism (London: Faber and Faber, 1987 [1933]).

Epstein, Joseph, 'Who Killed Poetry?', *Commentary*, 86(2) (1988), 13–20.

Euripides, *The Trojan Women – Helen, The Bacchae*, trans. Neil Curry (London/ Cambridge: Cambridge University Press, 1981).

Eve, Martin, 'Thomas Pynchon, David Foster Wallace and the Problems of "Metamodernism"', *C21st Literature*, 1(1) (2012), 7–13.

Felstiner, John, *Paul Celan: Poet, Survivor, Jew* (London: Yale University Press, 1995).

Ferris, David S., 'Politics and the Enigma of Art: The Meaning of Modernism for Adorno', *Modernist Cultures*, 1(2) (winter 2005), 192–208.

Fitzgerald, F. Scott, *The Great Gatsby* (London: Penguin, 1950 [1926]).

Flood, Alison, 'Simon Armitage plans national "headquarters" for poetry in Leeds', *The Guardian*, 27 February 2020 (www.theguardian.com/books/20 20/feb/27/simon-armitage-plans-national-headquarters-for-poetry-in-leeds-poet-laureate) (accessed 8 July 2020).

Furlani, Andre, *Guy Davenport: Postmodern and After* (Evanston, IL: Northwestern University Press, 2007).

Genter, Robert, *Late Modernism: Art, Culture, and Politics in Cold War America* (Oxford/Philadelphia: University of Pennsylvania Press, 2010).

Gilens, Martin and Benjamin I. Page, 'Testing Theories of American Politics: Elites, Interest Groups, and Average Citizens', *American Political Science Association*, 12(3) (September 2014), 564–81.

Glahn, Philip, *Bertolt Brecht* (London: Reaktion Books, 2014).

Golding, Alan, 'Language-Bashing Again', *Mid-American Review*, 8(2) (1988), 93–100.

Gregson, Ian, *Contemporary Poetry and Postmodernism: Dialogue and Estrangement* (Basingstoke: Macmillan, 1996).

Gruenler, Curtis, *Piers Plowman and the Poetics of Enigma: Riddles, Rhetoric and Theology* (Notre Dame, Indiana: University of Notre Dame Press, 2017).

Hall, Edith, *The Return of Ulysses: A Cultural History of Homer's Odyssey* (Baltimore: The Johns Hopkins University Press, 2008).

Hall, Matthew, 'Terra Nullius: Colonial Violence in Prynne's Acrylic Tips', *Journal of British and Irish Innovative Poetry*, 8(1) (2016), 5, 1–30.

Harrison, Tony, 'Carnuntum 2' notebook, the Tony Harrison archive, the Brotherton Library, BC MS 20c Harrison/03/KAI.

BC MS 20c Harrison OS/FAD-RBL Correspondence.

BC MS 20c Harrison/03/ORP 'ΟΡφΕΑΕ' ('Orpheus') notebook (c.1998).

The Gaze of the Gorgon (Newcastle: Bloodaxe, 1992).

The Inky Digit of Defiance: Selected Prose 1966–2016 (London: Faber and Faber, 2017).

Plays Three (London: Faber and Faber, 1996).

Selected Poems (London: Faber and Faber, 1987 [1984]).

Under the Clock (London/New York: Penguin, 2005).

Hayman, Ronald, *Artaud and After* (Oxford: Oxford University Press, 1977).

Herbert, Jocelyn, Archive (part of the National Theatre archive), 'Carnuntum' notebook, JH/1/21.

Hill, Geoffrey, *Collected Critical Writings* (Oxford: Oxford University Press, 2008).

Collected Poems (Oxford: Oxford University Press, 2015 [2013]).

The Enemy's Country: Words, Contexture, and other Circumstances of Language (Oxford: Clarendon Press, 1991).

'How ill white hairs become a fool and jester', www.english.ox.ac.uk/professor-sir-geoffrey-hill-lectures (accessed 12 July 2020).

'Legal Fiction and Legal "Fiction"', www.english.ox.ac.uk/professor-sir-geoffrey-hill-lectures (accessed 16 July 2020).

Michaelmas term lecture 2012 (untitled), http://media.podcasts.ox.ac.uk/engf ac/poetry/2012-11-27-engfac-hill.mp3 (accessed 28 July 2020).

'Monumentality and Bidding', www.english.ox.ac.uk/professor-sir-geoffrey-hill-lectures (accessed 16 July 2020).

The Orchards of Syon (London/New York: Penguin, 2002).

The Orchards of Syon workbooks, The Brotherton Library, BC MS 20 c Hill/2/1/52.

'Poetry Notebooks and Early Poems and Drafts (c.1948–2005)', Notebook 58, BC MS 20c Hill/2.

'Poetry, Policing and Public Order (1)', www.english.ox.ac.uk/professor-sir-geoffrey-hill-lectures (accessed 12 July 2020).

Scenes from Comus (London: Penguin, 2005).

'Simple, Sensuous, and Passionate', *Poetry Book Society Bulletin*, 191 (winter 2001), 5.

Style and Faith (New York: Counterpoint, 2003).

The Triumph of Love (London/New York: Penguin, 1999 [1998]).

Hopkins, Kenneth, *The Poets Laureate* (Wakefield: EP Publishing Limited, 1973).

Howarth, Peter, *The Cambridge Introduction to Modernist Poetry* (Cambridge: Cambridge University Press, 2012).

Hughes, Bettany, *Helen of Troy: Goddess, Princess, Whore* (London: Pimlico, 2006 [2005]).

Hughes, Ted, *Collected Poems* (London: Faber and Faber, 2003).

Hutcheon, Linda, *The Politics of Postmodernism* (London: Routledge, 2002 [1989]).

Huxley, Aldous, *The Doors of Perception and Heaven and Hell* (London: Flamingo, 1994 [1977])

James, David, *Discrepant Solace* (Cambridge: Cambridge University Press, 2019).

   The Legacies of Modernism: Historicising Postwar and Contemporary Fiction (Cambridge: Cambridge University Press, 2011).

   Modernist Futures: Innovation and Inheritance in the Contemporary Novel (Cambridge: Cambridge University Press, 2012).

Jameson, Frederic, *A Singular Modernity* (London: Verso, 2012 [2002]).

Jay, Martin, *Adorno* (Cambridge, Massachusetts: Harvard University Press, 1984).

Kafka, Franz, *The Blue Octavo Notebooks* (Cambridge, Massachusetts: Exact Change Books, 2016 [1948]).

Kendall, Tim, 'Against "Contemporary Poetry"', *PN Review*, 179 (January–February 2008), 24–7.

Kennedy, Christine and David Kennedy, 'Poetry, Difficulty and Geraldine Monk's *Interregnum*' in Scott Thurston, ed., *The Salt Companion to Geraldine Monk* (Cambridge: Salt, 2007), pp. 11–27.

Kennedy, David, *New Relations: The Refashioning of British Poetry 1980–94* (Bridgend: Seren, 1996).

Kersten, Dennis and Usha Wilbers, eds., 'Metamodernism: A Special Issue', *English*, 99(7) (November 2018), 719–722.

Kuhn, Tom and Steve Giles, eds., *Brecht on Art and Politics* (London: Methuen, 2003).

James, David and Urmila Seshagiri, 'Metamodernism: Narratives of Continuity and Revolution', *PMLA*, 129(1) (2014), 87–98.

Kuenzli, Rudolf, ed., *Dada* (London: Phaidon, 2006).

Larkin, Philip, *Collected Poems* (London: Faber and Faber, 1988).

   Letters to Monica, ed., Anthony Thwaite (London: Faber and Faber, 2010).

   Required Writing: Miscellaneous Pieces 1955–1982 (London: Faber and Faber, 1983).

   'Under a Common Flag', *The Observer*, 14 November 1982, p. 23.

Lipovetsky, Gilles, *Hypermodern Times* (Cambridge/Malden: Polity Press, 2005).

Lukács, György, *The Meaning of Contemporary Realism* (London: Merlin Press, 1979 [1963]).

Lumsden, Roddy, ed., *Identity Parade: New British and Irish Poets* (Newcastle: Bloodaxe, 2010).

Lunn, Eugene, *Marxism and Modernism: An Historical Study of Lukács, Brecht, Benjamin, and Adorno* (London: Verso, 1985 [1982]).

Lyon, John, 'Geoffrey Hill's Eye Troubles' in John Lyon and Peter McDonald, eds., *Geoffrey Hill: Essays on his Later Work* (Oxford: Oxford University Press, 2012), pp. 112–26.

MacDowell, James, 'The Metamodern, the Quirky and Film Criticism', in *Metamodernism: Historicity, Affect and Depth After Postmodernism* (London: New York: Rowman and Littlefield International, 2017), pp. 25–40.

Macfarlane, Robert, 'Gravity and Grace in Geoffrey Hill', *Essays in Criticism*, 58(3) (2007), 237–56.

Mao, Douglas and Rebecca L. Walkowitz, eds., *Bad Modernisms* (Durham, North Carolina: Duke University Press, 2006).

McCarthy, Tom, *Remainder* (New York: Vintage, 2005).

McDonald, Paul, 'From Paris to Emerging Poets', *Envoi*, 169 (February 2015), 72–6

　'Truly Apart', *Times Literary Supplement*, 1 April 2005, www.the-tls.co.uk/tls/re views/literature_and_poetry/article708873 (accessed 30 September 2015).

McKeon, Michael, *The Origins of the English Novel, 1600–1740* (Baltimore, Maryland: Johns Hopkins University Press, 2002).

Mellors, Anthony, *Late Modernist Poetics from Pound to Prynne* (Manchester/ New York: Manchester University Press, 2005), p. 67.

Miller, Tyrus, *Late Modernism: Politics, Fiction, and Arts Between the World Wars* (Berkeley/LA: University of California Press, 1999).

Milton, John, *Poems of Mr John Milton* (London: Humphrey Moseley, 1645).

　The Reason of Church Government Urged Against Prelatry, Book 2, www .dartmouth.edu/~milton/reading_room/reason/book_2/text.shtml (accessed 6 July 2020).

Mitchell, Stanley, 'Introduction', in Walter Benjamin, ed., *Understanding Brecht*, trans. Anna Bostock (London: New Left Books, 1973 [1966]), pp. vii–xix.

Monk, Geraldine, *Ghost & Other Sonnets* (Cambridge: Salt, 2008).

Moorhead, Joanna, 'Poems are a form of texting' (interview with Carol Ann Duffy), *The Guardian*, 5 September 2011 (www.theguardian.com/educa tion/2011/sep/05/carol-ann-duffy-poetry-texting-competition) (accessed 12 May 2020).

Morra, Irene, *Verse Drama in England, 1900–2015: Art, Modernity and the National Stage* (London/New York: Bloomsbury, 2016).

Nealon, Jeffrey T., *Post-Postmodernism or, the Cultural Logic of Just-in-Time Capitalism* (Stanford: Stanford University Press, 2012).

Noel-Tod, Jeremy, 'Awkward Bow' (review of *The Orchards of Syon*), *London Review of Books*, 25(5) (6 March 2003), 27–8.

Normandin, Shawn, '"Non Intellegent": the Enigmas of *The Clerk's Tale*', *Texas Studies in Literature and Language*, 58(2) (2016), 189–223.

O'Brien, Sean, '*Scenes from Comus* by Geoffrey Hill', *The Independent*, 2 March 2005, www.independent.co.uk/arts-entertainment/books/reviews/ scenes-from-comus-by-geoffrey-hill-6151493.html (accessed 30 September 2014).

Ormsby, Eric, 'A Grand & Crabby Music', *The New York Sun*, 3 (March 2005), www .nysun.com/arts/grand-crabby-music/10039.com (accessed 9 June 2016).

PBS Bulletin, issue 248 (spring 1916), pp. 27, 28.

Parker, Stephen, *Bertolt Brecht: a Literary Life* (London: Bloomsbury, 2014).

Parmar, Sandeep, *Eidolon* (Bristol: Shearsman Books, 2015).

Parsons, Deborah L., *Streetwalking the Metropolis: Women, the City and Modernity* (Oxford: Oxford University Press, 2000).

Paterson, Don, 'The Dark Art of Poetry', www.poetrylibrary.org.uk/news/poetrys cene/?id=20 (accessed 21 October 2015).

Landing Light (London: Faber and Faber, 2003).

Rain (London: Faber and Faber, 2009).

Reading Shakespeare's Sonnets (London: Faber and Faber, 2012).

Pedro, João, 'Truth and Enigma: Adorno and the Politics of Art', *New German Critique*, 45(3), 135 (November 2018), 73–95.

Pinkney, Marjorie, *21st-Century Modernism* (Malden/Oxford: Blackwells, 2002).

Poetic License: Essays on Modernist and Postmodernist Lyric (Evanston, IL: Northwestern University Press, 1990).

The Poetics of Indeterminacy: Rimbaud to Cage (Evanston, IL: Northwestern University Press, 1983 [1981]).

Unoriginal Genius: Poetry by Other Means in the New Century (Chicago and London: The University of Chicago Press, 2012 [2010]).

Pinkney, Tony, 'Editor's Introduction: Modernism and Cultural Theory', in Williams, *The Politics of Modernism*, pp. 1–29.

Pollard, Natalie, ed., *Don Paterson: Contemporary Critical Essays* (Edinburgh: Edinburgh University Press, 2014).

Pound, Ezra, *The Cantos of Ezra Pound* (New York: New Directions, 1996).

'*Dans un Omnibus de Londres*' (www.bartleby.com/300/777.html) (accessed 17 April 2020).

Ezra Pound: Selected Poems 1908–1959 (London: Faber and Faber, 1975).

Make It New: Essays (London: Faber and Faber, 1934).

Prynne, J. H., 'Acrylic Tips', in *Poems* (Tarset: Bloodaxe, 2005), pp. 533–48.

'A Letter to Steve McCaffery' (2 January 1989), *The Gig*, 7 (November 2000), 40–46.

Rancière, Jacques, *The Politics of Literature*, trans. Julie Rose (Cambridge/Malden: Polity Press, 2011).

Read, Herbert, *The Politics of the Unpolitical* (New York: Routledge, 1943).

Reading, Anna, 'Memobilia: The Mobile Phone and the Emergence of Wearable Memories', in *Save As … Digital Memories* (New York/Basingstoke: Palgrave, 2009), pp. 81–95.

Redmond, John, *Poetry and Privacy: Questioning Public Interpretations of Contemporary British and Irish Poetry* (Bridgend: Seren, 2013).

Reeve, N. H. and Richard Kerridge, *Nearly Too Much: The Poetry of J.H. Prynne* (Liverpool: Liverpool University Press, 1995).

Ricks, Christopher, *True Friendship: Geoffrey Hill, Anthony Hecht, and Robert Lowell: Under the Sign of Eliot and Pound* (New Haven and London: Yale University Press, 2010).

Rothberg, Michael, *The Implicated Subject: Beyond Victims and Perpetrators* (Stanford: Stanford University Press, 2019).

Multidirectional Memories: Remembering the Holocaust in the Age of Decolonisation (Stanford: Stanford University Press, 2009),

Rowland, Antony, *Holocaust Poetry* (Edinburgh: Edinburgh University Press, 2005).

Rumens, Carol, 'Medium, Conjurer, Flâneur', *Poetry Review*, 101(4) (winter 2011), 95–98.

Rutter, Carol Chillington, 'Harrison, Herakles, and Wailing Women "Labourers" at Delphi', *New Theatre Quarterly*, 13(50) (May 1997), 133–43.

Sampson, Fiona, *Beyond the Lyric: A Map of Contemporary British Poetry* (London: Chatto and Windus, 2012).

Scarfe, Francis, ed., *Baudelaire: The Complete Verse* (London: Anvil, 1986).

Searle, Adrian, 'Altermodern Review: "The Richest and Most Generous Tate Triennial Yet"', www.theguardian.com/artanddesign/2009/feb/02/altermo dern-tate-triennial (accessed 16 July 2020).

Shakespeare, William, *Love's Labour's Lost* (Leipzig: Bernhard Tauchnitz, 1868 [1598]).

Sheppard, Robert, *The Poetry of Saying: British Poetry and its Discontents, 1950–2000* (Liverpool: Liverpool University Press, 2005).

Simic, Charles and Don Paterson, eds., *New British Poetry* (St Paul, Minnesota: Graywolf Press, 2004).

Sissay, Lemn, 'Carol Ann Duffy and Geoffrey Hill: Truly Poetic Heavyweights', www.theguardian.com/commentisfree/2012/jan/31/carol-ann-duffy-geoffrey -hill-punch-up (accessed 12 July 2020).

Spencer, Michael, 'A Fresh look at Arthur Rimbaud's "Métropolitain"', *Modern Language Review*, 63(4) (October 1968), 849–53.

Stoichita, Victor I. and Anna Maria Coderch, *Goya: The Last Carnival* (London: Reaktion Books, 1999).

Taplin, Oliver, 'Contemporary Poetry and Classics', in *Classics in Progress: Essays on Ancient Greece and Rome* (Oxford: The British Academy [Oxford University Press], 2002), pp. 1–20.

Tennyson, Alfred, *Poetical Works* (London/New York: Oxford University Press, 1959 [1953]).

Thacker, Andrew, *Modernism, Space and the City* (Edinburgh: Edinburgh University Press, 2019).

Thompson, Peter and Glendyr Sacks, *The Cambridge Companion to Brecht* (Cambridge: Cambridge University Press, 2006 [1994]).

Thorsson, Örnólfur, ed., *The Sagas of Icelanders* (London/New York: Penguin, 2000 [1997]).

Turner, Luke, 'Metamodernism: A Brief Introduction', www.metamodernism.org (accessed 29 April 2020).

'Metamodernist Manifesto', www.metamodernism.org (accessed 29 April 2020).

Vermeulen, Timotheus and Robin van den Akker, 'Notes on Metamodernism', *Journal of Aesthetics and Culture*, 2 (2010), 2–14.

Wainwright, Jeffrey, *Acceptable Words: Essays on the poetry of Geoffrey Hill* (Manchester: Manchester University Press, 2005).

Warman, April, 'Language and Grace', *The Oxonian Review*, 3(1) (15 December 2003), www.oxonianreview.org/wp/geoffrey-hill-the-orchards-of-syon (accessed 5 May 2019).

Warner, Ahren, *Confer* (Newcastle: Bloodaxe, 2011).

Hello. Your Promise has been Extracted (Newcastle: Bloodaxe, 2017).

Pretty (Newcastle: Bloodaxe, 2013).

Welsh, J. T., *The Selling and Self-Regulation of Contemporary Poetry* (London: Anthem Press, 2020).

Wheatley, David, *Contemporary British Poetry* (London/New York: Palgrave, 2015).

Williams, Raymond, *The Politics of Modernism*, ed. Tony Pinkney (London/New York: Verso, 1989).

Williams, Tony, 'You ask for a song' (review of *Confer*), *Magma*, 52 (March 2012), 57–8, p. 58.

Willet, John, ed. and trans., *Brecht on Theatre* (London: Methuen, 1964 [1957]).

Winborn, Colin, '"Derangement from Deep Inside": J. H. Prynne's "Refuse Collection"', *PN Review* 175, 33(5) (May–June 2007), 55–58.

Winters, Jeffrey A., 'Oligarchy and Democracy', *The American Interest*, 7(2) (2011), www.the-american-interest.com/2011/09/28/oligarchy-and-democracy (accessed 3 August 2020).

Wylie, Alex, *Geoffrey Hill's Later Work: Radiance of Apprehension* (Manchester: Manchester University Press, 2019).

Yeats, W. B., *Selected Poetry*, ed. A. Norman Jeffares (London: Pan, 1974 [1962]).

Young, Rob and Irmin Schmidt, *All Gates Open: The Story of Can* (London: Faber and Faber, 2018).

Index

Printed in the United States
by Baker & Taylor Publisher Services

Printed in the United States
by Baker & Taylor Publisher Services